CONFEDERATE GENERAL
WILLIAM DORSEY PENDER

CONFLICTING WORLDS
NEW DIMENSIONS OF THE AMERICAN CIVIL WAR
T. Michael Parrish, Series Editor

CONFEDERATE GENERAL
WILLIAM DORSEY PENDER

THE HOPE OF GLORY

BRIAN STEEL WILLS

LOUISIANA STATE UNIVERSITY PRESS
BATON ROUGE

Published with the assistance of the V. Ray Cardozier Fund.

Published by Louisiana State University Press
lsupress.org

Copyright © 2013 by Louisiana State University Press
All rights reserved. Except in the case of brief quotations used in articles or reviews, no part of this publication may be reproduced or transmitted in any format or by any means without written permission of Louisiana State University Press.

Louisiana Paperback Edition, 2025

DESIGNER: Michelle A. Neustrom
TYPEFACE: Chaparral Pro

COVER IMAGE: Library of Congress.

LIBRARY OF CONGRESS CATALOGING-IN-PUBLICATION DATA

Wills, Brian Steel, 1959–
   Confederate General William Dorsey Pender : the hope of glory / Brian Steel Wills.
     pages cm. — (Conflicting worlds: new dimensions of the American Civil War)
   Includes bibliographical references and index.
   ISBN 978-0-8071-5299-7 (cloth : alk. paper) — ISBN 978-0-8071-5300-0 (pdf) — ISBN 978-0-8071-5301-7 (epub) — ISBN 978-0-8071-8494-3 (paperback) 1. Pender, William Dorsey, 1834–1863. 2. Generals—Confederate States of America—Biography. 3. Confederate States of America. Army—Biography. 4. United States—History—Civil War, 1861–1865—Campaigns. I. Title.
   E467.1.P367W55 2014
   355.0092—dc23
   [B]

2013017770

To my mentor and friend,
Emory M. Thomas

LIST OF ILLUSTRATIONS *ix*

PREFACE *xi*

INTRODUCTION: Lee's Fighting Carolinian *1*
1. Young Pender (1834–54) *7*
2. First Blood (1854–58) *20*
3. "Unexplored Country" (1858–61) *39*
4. A "Lion" Roars (March–June 1861) *54*
5. "My Dancing Days Are Over" (July 1861–February 1862) *82*
6. A Presidential Salute (February–June 1862) *111*
7. "Mrs. W. D. Pender's Husband" (June–July 1862) *132*
8. "I Know You Will Hate to Hear This" (July–September 1862) *151*
9. "Drive Those Scoundrels Out" (September–December 1862) *168*
10. "You Must Hold Your Ground, Sir!" (January–May 1863) *190*
11. "I Am Tired of Invasions" (May–July 1863) *216*

EPILOGUE: A "Good Fight" Finished and Remembered *239*

NOTES *247*

BIBLIOGRAPHY *281*

INDEX *295*

ILLUSTRATIONS

Map 1 West/Northwest Territory *27*
Map 2 Wright Expedition, 1858 *32*
Map 3 Seven Pines (Fair Oaks) *127*
Map 4 Mechanicsville (Beaver Dam Creek) *140*
Map 5 Second Manassas (Second Bull Run) *161*
Map 6 Fredericksburg *183*
Map 7 Chancellorsville *206*
Map 8 Gettysburg *230*

Figures follow page 110

Figure 1 Pender's Writing Implement
Figure 2 Pender's Saber and Scabbard
Figure 3 Pender's Prayer Book
Figure 4 Ambrose Powell Hill
Figure 5 Thomas J. "Stonewall" Jackson
Figure 6 Second Manassas (Second Bull Run)
Figure 7 Pender's Uniform Coat
Figure 8 Pender's Uniform Pants after Gettysburg
Figure 9 Bas-Relief Detail on Pender Monument

PREFACE

William Dorsey Pender has fascinated me in my journey through the American Civil War because he was such a complex and interesting individual, reflected in the substantial amount of personal correspondence he had with his wife that survived the war. Pender established a reputation within the Army of Northern Virginia as one of Robert E. Lee's ablest young battlefield generals, willingly thrusting himself into harm's way and experiencing numerous wartime injuries before sustaining a fatal one as a result of the fighting at Gettysburg. What he might have thought as the war turned from that "high tide" to the eventual ebb of Appomattox, Bennett Place, et cetera could only be speculated, but while living he remained devoted to the Confederate cause and always mindful of North Carolina's place in the contest.

Studying Pender's voluminous correspondence was at once daunting and revealing. William W. Hassler's excellent published collection contained most of these letters, coupled with basic editorial material that the editor freely explained he had designed so as to let Pender speak largely for himself. Anyone interested in the North Carolinian's story has owed a debt to Professor Hassler. The existence of the originals at the Southern Historical Collection in Chapel Hill offered the researcher the opportunity to compare and contrast these sources. Such a comparison here requires a brief explanation concerning their use and citation.

In the end notes the reader will see two forms of citation for many of the Pender letters. Most initial references will be to the original letters, followed where possible by the Hassler editions to provide readers with easy access to that published material for further study. The exceptions will be the material Hassler left out of his work, for reasons that are usually, but not always, clear. Thankfully very rare, anomalies or discrepancies occurred where a letter Hassler included in his collection could not be found in the original files, and thus the published version is the only source cited. In the interest of full disclosure, this writer took a copy of the Hassler text for comparison, especially for the purpose of determining material that had not been included in that edition and to verify, in a general but systematic manner, the accuracy of Hassler's transcriptions. It is a credit to that scholar's efforts that these proved consistently faithful to the originals.

Such a study of the life of an individual has also required assistance from many other sources. Numerous persons at various libraries and archives have been generous with their time and expertise. A few of these deserve particular mention. The staff of the Southern Historical Collection at the University of North Carolina in Chapel Hill has been enormously helpful, not only in supplying my requests for research materials but also by providing copies of these materials when needed. In addition, individuals at the North Carolina Department of Archives and History offered similar support, as did archivists and students at various major university repositories and the National Archives. John and Ruth Ann Coski provided information or sent copies of material from the Museum of the Confederacy in Richmond. Richard Somers, Art Bergeron, and their colleagues at the U.S. Army History Institute in Carlisle, Pennsylvania, lent their considerable talents and expertise at tracking down Pender-related material there. John Bass, of Spring Hope, North Carolina, shared his interest in Pender and valuable information, particularly items concerning the general's religious experiences, as well as some of the outstanding pork produced by Bass Farms, Inc.

Members of the Department of History and Philosophy at the University of Virginia's College at Wise were helpful and the institution supported this project by providing the means required for research and writing, including a semester leave. The Kenneth Asbury Chair of History, now held by my dear friend and esteemed colleague Mark Clark, made time available in the summer and funding for travel. Special appreciation goes to Provost and Senior Vice Chancellors David Smith and Gil Blackburn as well as to Darlene Moore. Robin Benke and his excellent staff at the John Cook Wyllie Library assisted with interlibrary loans and access to sources. Rhonda Bentley helped in various and important ways in the process.

The same has been true since assuming the directorship of the Center for the Study of the Civil War Era at Kennesaw State University in Georgia. Assistance with sources through the Horace W. Sturgis Library has been superb, as has the support from Dean Richard Vengroff and the Dean's Office personnel in addition to Megan MacDonald and Gayle Wheeler in the Department of History and Philosophy. Michael Shaffer has been instrumental in helping me to keep the juggling balls aloft during the process of completing the book.

I am also particularly appreciative of the interest Mike Parrish and Rand Dotson demonstrated in this project for inclusion in the series, Conflicting Worlds: New Dimensions of the American Civil War. I am grateful to all of the individuals associated with Louisiana State University Press who helped make publication possible, particularly Kevin Brock for his expert copyediting. Thanks go to Heather Harvey for producing the maps for the volume.

To my wife and our family in Wise, Virginia, and Peachtree City, Georgia, I owe the greatest appreciation. Elizabeth patiently read all of the material I placed before her and offered her suggestions. Over that time, she has heard a great deal about Dorsey and Fanny Pender. It goes without saying that this book is better for her many contributions.

Finally, I have chosen to dedicate this work to Emory M. Thomas, who as my major professor at the University of Georgia guided me through the labyrinth of graduate school with deftness and wisdom. I have tried to express my appreciation to him in other ways as well, but I hope that this serves to reaffirm my gratitude in a tangible form. Thank you, E.T.

CONFEDERATE GENERAL
WILLIAM DORSEY PENDER

Introduction

LEE'S FIGHTING CAROLINIAN

———•———

I am gradually losing my best men, Jackson, Pender, Hood.
—ROBERT E. LEE, SEPTEMBER 1863

Patriot by nature, soldier by training, Christian by faith.
—EPITAPH ON WILLIAM DORSEY PENDER'S GRAVESTONE

———•———

Robert E. Lee had every reason to be distressed in the summer of 1863 as he tallied the butcher's bill of the three-day battlefield ordeal of Gettysburg, particularly with regard to the toll it had taken on his command structure. In the past others had stepped forward to fill the void left by those who had fallen, but in terms of numbers and talent, many of the latter would be difficult to replace now. In September 1863, with those losses still present so painfully in his mind, the Southern field commander quietly revealed his emotions to the Confederacy's chief executive. "I am gradually losing my best men," Lee wrote plaintively to Jefferson Davis, "Jackson, Pender, Hood."[1]

Students of the American Civil War might not be surprised that Lee mentioned the names of Thomas Jonathan "Stonewall" Jackson and John Bell Hood among the "best" subordinates who served under him in the first half of the conflict. But what of the name that the general inserted between the two more well known of his Army of Northern Virginia lieutenants? Who was Pender that the Confederate chieftain made a special point of lamenting his loss?

Even while the conflict raged, and certainly since it concluded, contemporaries and students alike have chided General Lee for at least appearing to favor Virginians over subordinates from other Southern states. Yet two of the three names chosen for inclusion in this unique listing were not Virginians. Only Jackson hailed from that vaunted Commonwealth. Hood was a Kentuckian by birth and a Texan by adoption. William Dorsey Pender was a North Carolinian. What all three of these officers had in common, aside from the ultimate sacrifice Lee thought that each had made to the cause of the Confederate States of America—the general fearing the worst from Hood's severe wounding at Chickamauga—was that each had demonstrated himself to be a fighting general upon whom he could rely in the thickest of the action and under the direst of circumstances. Each had served conspicuously on the major battlefields of the Civil War in the eastern theater. Each had suffered lesser wounds before being struck down for a fateful, final time (as Lee mistakenly assumed in the case of Hood). The Confederate commander considered Jackson his "right arm" and trusted him implicitly to carry out orders often couched in wide discretion. Hood led some of the army's finest shock troops for much of the early part of the war. Pender became Lee's fighting North Carolinian, ever present in the heaviest combat and frequently wounded as a result of his exposure to enemy fire.

Ironically, one of the strongest proponents of Virginia's paramountcy in the Civil War also produced one of the grandest expressions of praise for North Carolina's soldiers, including Pender. Jubal Early, the crusty ex-Confederate, observed after the war, "I can say in all sincerity, that there were no better troops from any state in all that grand army than the North Carolina soldiers, and of all that bright galaxy of heroes who yielded their lives for their country's cause while serving with that army, the names of Anderson, Branch, Pender, Daniel, Ramseur, and Gordon of the cavalry, will stand among the foremost."[2]

There were a number of talented young officers who rose through the ranks of both sides during the war. These men projected enormous promise, and some few managed to survive long enough to demonstrate that promise to one degree or another. Even so, it seemed that too many were unable to escape the terrible crucible of battle. Historians Grady McWhiney and Perry Jamieson may have placed more responsibility on the cultural heritage of the South than could be supported, but they were correct in noting that Southern officers were prone to risk themselves in combat in ways that led to an inordinate amount of self-sacrifice. "Confederate generals not only led their forces into battle," McWhiney and Jamieson explained, "they died with them." Indeed, the authors determined that the numbers were disproportionately high for this type of behavior and the seemingly inevitable outcome it engendered. "Twenty-one of the seventy-seven Confederate generals who were killed or mortally wounded in battle had been shot at least once before they received their fatal injuries."³ Dorsey Pender was one of these, wounded three times before his death at age twenty-nine. Stephen D. Ramseur, William R. J. Pegram, and James Dearing were among the other bright and capable young Confederate officers who did not live to see the outcome of the struggle. Ramseur suffered wounds at Malvern Hill, Chancellorsville, and Spotsylvania before receiving his mortal wound at Cedar Creek. Pegram, the bespectacled artillerist whose devotion to the Confederacy was without peer, received a mortal wound while directing his pieces in the chaotic fighting at Five Forks. Dearing, whom all described in the highest terms, died after trying to defend High Bridge on Lee's road to Appomattox.⁴

Each of these men and others like them embodied the traits of a generation in transition. They sought to remind themselves of what had gone before them, particularly with regard to their Revolutionary Era ancestors and the success achieved (in their eyes) by the intervening generations of fellow white Southerners, while confronting and embracing a changing and frequently bewildering world. Writing of Pegram, historian Peter Carmichael captured much of the essence of Dorsey Pender as well when he observed that the Virginian "shared his age group's conviction that ambition, if properly channeled through faith and courage, fueled action and created the possibility of greatness."⁵ It was the melding of these factors in the heat of war that the North Carolinian sought for himself. It was the desire to establish himself as worthy that drove him so earnestly to attempt to secure a place in both earthly and heavenly spheres.

Like these other young men, Pender rose in the ranks through merit and determination in a career marked by an ambition to serve effectively and a thorough devotion to the cause of Southern independence. His courage matched his character. Indeed, the greatest vulnerability in Pender's military personality was the risk he subjected himself to through the manner in which he led his troops in battle. Because he felt that example was essential to inspiring the best effort from those who followed him, Pender never shied from locating himself at or near the front and frequently felt the sting of battle as a result. It was the final wounding he sustained during the second day at Gettysburg that offered his former commander the opportunity for an assessment of the consequences of that stroke of misfortune. In a rare moment of retrospective candor after the war, General Lee observed that Pender's wounding had deprived the army of the chance for victory in that important engagement.⁶

Later generations of historians also assessed William Dorsey Pender's role and his loss to a debilitating wound on July 2 as significant to the fighting at Gettysburg. Glenn Tucker offered his injury as one of the reasons for "victory and defeat" in the great battle.[7] Pulitzer Prize–winning author Douglas Southall Freeman, who followed Pender closely in his study of leadership in the Army of Northern Virginia, noted simply of the general's absence at Gettysburg, "They miss[ed] him on the 3rd of July, 1863."[8] Finally, popular writer Shelby Foote maintained that in addition to other factors in that pivotal engagement in Pennsylvania, "In a sense, it all went back to the fall of Pender."[9]

Such speculation aside, there was no doubt that by 1863, William Dorsey Pender had reached a status as one of the premier fighting generals in the Army of Northern Virginia. Buttressed by a West Point education and service at various prewar posts that included some valuable experience in combat in the Pacific Northwest, Pender nevertheless stood ready at the creation of the Southern Confederacy to resign his commission in the Old Army to join the fledgling nation. As a proud native of the Old North State, he exhibited the highest expectations of his troops and demanded the best that his state could offer in support of the struggle for Southern independence. Above all he required the greatest performance from himself. He wanted to be the best soldier he could be and win the accolades that this stature would bring. Yet careful to balance his ambition with thoughtful introspection, Pender desired to treat others fairly and constantly sought progress and improvement over the imperfections he recognized in his own character and personality.

At the same time as the young man struggled to understand himself better in the roles of soldier and officer, he strove to define himself as a husband and a father. Pender was a novice in both matrimony and parenthood, learning the expectations of others and determining the manner in which he could perform to his own demanding standards. He was seldom content with the place he occupied and drove himself constantly to improve what he deemed to be significant, if often troubling, elements of his persona.

Pender grappled with his religious beliefs, becoming a Christian soldier in every sense and thereby establishing a stronger bond with his God while forging an indelible one with his troops in battle. He warred with the impulses that drove him and that he felt, deeply and sincerely, marked him as a human being: vanity, devotion, loyalty, and perfectionism. In the voluminous correspondence that began with his service on the western frontier to his final letter from Pennsylvania in 1863, Pender represented the notion advanced by

Michael Barton in his study *Goodmen* that "Southern officers were likely to evaluate character anytime they wrote anything."[10]

Pender composed powerful and candid confidential letters to his wife, Fanny, often expressing his views more openly and honestly than was prudent and always revealing the inner turmoil he felt at being torn between duty to his profession and devotion to his family. Yet he was never one to give himself over to half measures for convenience or safety's sake. He spent his life preparing himself should the cause for which he served demand his life and separate him through death on the battlefield from everyone he held most dear.

Ironically, given the trove of writing he left behind, Pender was renowned for being a man of few words when in the company of others. There was no doubt that he had a young man's exuberance for life. Yet if he expressed regret occasionally for letting his emotions get the better of him, he was capable of understanding the social boundaries that marked his world. As his faith grew deeper, perhaps mirroring the dangers that seemed to intensify simultaneously, he developed an acceptance of divine direction that allowed him to face any situation with a sense of calmness and equanimity that others must have envied. He came to embrace the notion most firmly that whatever earthly fate awaited him, the outcome was under the control of a higher presence, and in the end, a better one would follow.

General Lee must have recognized some of these traits as he watched the youthful soldier develop into assignments of higher command and authority. By age twenty-nine, Pender was the youngest major general in the Confederate service. Yet before he turned thirty he was gone, a casualty of the war for which he had left Fanny and their boys, Turner, Dorsey, and Stephen (born after the general's death), to undertake.

For Pender, the life and character of the Apostle Paul, whom according to one source Dorsey "greatly admired," became a model for his own. During the difficult days following Gettysburg, he engaged in studying and contemplating the scriptures. On the Sunday before his untimely death, Pender was so moved by the example the religious figure had set that he enthusiastically observed to a visitor, "What a splendid character!"[11]

Indeed, the words found in Paul's epistle to the Colossians, "Christ in you, the hope of glory" (Colossians 1:27), came to symbolize the essence of Dorsey Pender's life. The North Carolinian spent much of his earthly journey as an adult searching for "glory" in multiple aspects of that term. At the end, the most public of expressions—the words selected for the tombstone that would rest permanently before him in the quiet graveyard of Calvary Episcopal Church in Tarboro, North Carolina—summarized the essence of his mortal existence: "Patriot by nature, soldier by training, Christian by faith."[12] William Dorsey Pender would have asked for no greater legacy for himself than those final sentiments entailed.

1

YOUNG PENDER

(1834–54)

•——•

Don't be facetious, Mr. Pender.
—WEST POINT MATHEMATICS PROFESSOR GUY PECK

Swinging arms marching from M[ess] H[all] at dinner.
—ONE OF CADET WILLIAM DORSEY PENDER'S WEST POINT INFRACTIONS

•——•

William Dorsey Pender remained a proud North Carolinian for all of his brief twenty-nine years. Although his antecedents hailed from Virginia, his parents, James and Sarah Routh Pender, were longtime residents of the area near the small community of Tarboro, in Edgecombe County, North Carolina. James engaged in farming as his principle occupation and owned a substantial amount of property along Town Creek. He and Sarah also raised a family, adding a son to it on February 6, 1834. Dorsey, as he was known in family circles, was the youngest of three boys and a girl. The eldest was Robert, born in 1820, already into his teenaged years when his brother came into the world. Their sister, Patience, was next in age, born in 1828. The third child, David, preceded the last sibling by three years (1831).[1] The two youngest boys were closest in age and appeared to have created a special bond between them. In writing to his wife years later, Dorsey described David as "my most beloved relative."[2]

James Pender established himself as a successful planter on land that had passed down from the earliest settlement of the Penders in colonial America. By 1850 his holdings included over five hundred acres and twenty-one slaves.[3] This level of property ownership placed the family in the upper echelons of Edgecombe citizenry. The population levels a decade later set the number of slaves higher than whites in the county, with a modest listing of free blacks and persons of foreign birth.⁴ Although Dorsey would be well established in a life outside the region of his birth and youth, he remained in close contact with family members and held emotional ties to the Tarboro area in particular for the remainder of his years.

Growing up on the family's extended acreage in rural eastern North Carolina, Pender had the world as his playground and two older brothers with whom he could share experiences and from whom he could learn life's lessons. Dorsey's son Samuel Turner later recorded that his father spent his youthful years "in the labors of the farm and the usual sports of country life—riding, hunting, fishing, etc."⁵ It had to have been an idyllic world filled with youthful adventure. Dorsey's subsequent life offered glimpses of the development his personality and character underwent in those formative years. He would later refer to Town Creek with nostalgic affection, though at the same time with the realization that he had reasons for leaving that life behind him when he did. "I am very anxious to know how you will stand the exceeding quiet and dullness at Town Creek," he commented to his wife in late 1861. "I know I could not stand it and how you will I cannot imagine."⁶

Doting parents who wanted the best for their youngest child characterized his world at that time in his life as well. Dorsey revealed this bond between himself and his parents to his wife as she contemplated living with them for a time during the war. "They are fond parents," he explained to Fanny, "both fond and proud of me. I am the pride of Papa's life. You will be surprised to see how proud of me he is, although he says but little at home about me."⁷ Perhaps the father's inability to communicate openly such feelings with his son pushed the boy, and later the young man, to even greater achievements. Certainly, Pender never lost a sense of insecurity about himself, which he exposed occasionally in his public actions and frequently in his private expressions. Throughout his life, that same gnawing factor provided a springboard for the ambition that propelled him forward.

Although spiritual faith would help define his adult life, Dorsey left no indication from his childhood that either of his parents practiced any form of religious faith. Historian William Hassler observed that James and Sarah "provided absolutely no religious climate for the Pender children." He added, "Consequently, Dorsey grew to manhood a non-Christian, who was ignorant of the Bible."⁸ As Pender became increasingly attuned to his own religious development, under the powerful influence of his wife, he sought opportunities to open a similar path for his parents to follow. "Read the Bible to them and try to interest them in it," he advised Fanny in the fall of 1861. "My father's condition troubles me, for I know he has been a great sinner, and it is time for him to repent." Realizing her impact on his own life, Dorsey explained, "You know not what influence you will be able to have on them," and expressed the hope that in such matters they "only want instruction."[9]

Yet if he missed a religious foundation that could sustain him in his life's journey, as the youngest of several children, Pender received plenty of personal attention. Despite the playful antagonisms of sibling rivalry and the usual familial frictions, Dorsey ultimately came to appreciate his brothers, especially his oldest, Robert. During the Civil War, he felt obliged to encourage Fanny to return "some little the great many kindnesses brother Robert and his wife have done for me." Then he added hastily, "You have no idea how much he and David have done for me."[10] Family meant a great deal to Dorsey, and the legacy of brotherly assistance and affection traced back to his earliest years.

Robert had created a successful mercantile concern in Tarboro and, with the benefit and perspective of age and experience, took a proprietary interest in his younger brother's welfare and prospects. Undoubtedly, when he offered the lad a job in his establishment, the elder brother hoped to provide stability and opportunity for the youth as well as lessons on maturity and discipline in addition to employment.

Robert Pender would always represent something of an authority figure for Dorsey, and the distance in their ages and the elder brother's focus on his livelihood created a separation that continued through their lives. In a wartime letter to his wife, Dorsey revealed what must have been a longstanding, if usually simmering, bit of resentment. "I approve [of] your sending the bill to brother Robert," he remarked in April 1863. "It will either make him ashamed of himself, which it ought to, or it will furnish him with [the] information that he desires." Dorsey hoped the exercise would accomplish even more: "It may teach him a little lesson, namely to forget sometimes that he is a business man, bringing every transaction down to cents. If he is my brother I must say it was a very small thing to him." Still, if Robert could not help being who he was, "a purely business man," Dorsey had to accept that his assistance over the years had been invaluable. Even so, the younger Pender could not resist a final, almost reflexive, jab. "He has been generous in his way to me."[11]

The complex relationship the brothers shared was also marked by genuine affection. When scarlet fever wracked Robert Pender's household, taking with it one child and his wife, Emeralda James Pender, Dorsey reacted with sorrow and sympathy. "The same day I received your letter," he explained to Fanny on June 25, 1862, "I received one from David giving me the intelligence of the death of poor little Julie & the almost certainty that Sister James could remain in this world but a few hours." Her doctors had offered no hope of recovery. "What a terrible blow it will be to brother Robert, for she has been to him a noble wife and to her children an irreparable mother." Dorsey lamented the loss and then observed, "I wish you were there . . . to help him, but it is too late now," although he was certain that under the circumstances his sister, Patience, had "done all" that anyone could do for their anguished sibling.[12]

Dorsey Pender was barely a teenager when he tried his hand as a clerk in the store Pender & Bridgers. One biographer has noted that through this period the young fellow "prized nothing so much as the ability to maintain composure and decorum in any situation," although it is uncertain just what incident or set of incidents prompted such a conclusion.[13] Certainly, Dorsey must have demonstrated early on in his life the quiet and carefully considered assessments he constantly made regarding the world around him and his place in it. But this experience chiefly illustrated the unwillingness of a bright and capable youth merely to accept whatever lot life seemed destined to assign to him. He wanted to control his own destiny, not leave it to others to dictate or determine the course he would follow, even if such a force was a well-meaning relative.

Despite his brotherly affections, Pender chafed at his association with Robert's firm. In notes for a sketch that appeared in *South Atlantic Magazine* in 1877, one of Dorsey's sons depicted his father's opinion of the position. "Mercantile business was very irksome to the future soldier," Samuel Turner observed, noting that his father remained "dissatisfied" with his employment in this rather sedentary vocation.[14] Besides whatever monetary security or moral enrichment he might derive from his employment, the work did not appeal to his sense of adventure or offer him sufficient personal fulfillment for him to want to remain in it indefinitely. Clearly, Pender longed to make something of himself on his own accord and saw little hope for personal fulfillment and advancement if he remained in the shadow of his older brother.

As he contemplated his course in life, Dorsey Pender would not have had reason to feel he had much in common with his future West Point classmate Oliver Otis Howard. But the young man from Maine appeared to have embraced the same concerns about the track of his early life that his counterpart in North Carolina held for himself as he pondered an appointment to the U.S.

Military Academy at West Point, New York. Howard wrote that he found himself "coming to the quick conclusion to be 'something or nothing,' to sacrifice ease to ambition," and made the decision "to accept the appointment."[15] Facing the prospects of clerking in a small-town store that might have provided him with a measure of comfort and security and, of no small importance, a means of support, Dorsey nevertheless chose to trade any sense of this form of "ease" for the excitement and challenge that would come through the rigors of a military education and a career in the army.

In 1850 Pender got that opportunity when he obtained a nomination for admission to the U.S. Military Academy.[16] Secretary of War George W. Crawford made the appointment at the behest of Congressman John R. J. Daniel, and Pender accepted it formally on May 6. The acceptance came with a statement from his father noting his approval of Dorsey's "conditional appointment as Cadet." Additionally, James Pender asserted, "he has my full permission to sign articles by which he will bind himself to serve the United States eight years unless sooner discharged."[17]

Pender was just over sixteen years old when he secured his appointment to the military academy.[18] Among his classmates were James Ewell Brown Stuart, George Washington Custis Lee, Stephen Dill Lee, John Pegram, and fellow North Carolinian Samuel Turner Shepperd, with whom Dorsey became particularly close.[19] The opportunity to obtain an education at the nation's expense seemed less a motivation than the chance to establish a career that would take him beyond the limits of farming and retail sales in North Carolina.

Dorsey Pender possessed an adequate level of educational preparation for entry into West Point, but he also enjoyed political connections that would prove useful in getting him through its doors. The brother of Robert Pender's business partner, and a Pender cousin, Robert R. Bridgers, was influential in the process. Thus, Pender embarked upon a new phase in his life. Historian James L. Morrison Jr. has noted that these cadets, called "plebes" in their first year, began as "the lowest of the low in the West Point social order," with their right to admission verified, their personal cash confiscated, their assignments made, and their equipment and sparse furniture issued.[20]

All of this indoctrination in the early phases of the West Point education was to be part of the overall process of "weaning" the initiate from civilian life and "breaking in" the young man to his new military one.[21] Author Stephen Ambrose concluded, "West Point made life hard for the cadets in order to turn out finished soldiers."[22] Naturally, any person who could not adapt himself or cope with the rigors of the new environment would be finished in another sense, but Pender had no special difficulty in this regard. After the war a writer noted simply, "As [a] cadet he was modest and unassuming in his intercourse with his fellows, respectful to his instructors and tractable to the discipline of the institution."[23]

One of the common experiences for the new arrivals was to have a nickname bestowed on them. In the world of West Point, cadets obtained colorful labels that usually projected messages about the individual's physical character or personality. Often the names were meant as humorous jabs. Thus, a beardless Jeb Stuart, not yet the well-groomed and plumed cavalier that he would become during the Civil War, was "Beauty" or "Beaut" as ironic homage to his appearance at the time.

Pender acquired the name "Poll."[24] A biographer, Kenrick N. Simpson, noted that Pender's cadet peers applied the term "for some obscure reason."[25] Another speculated that the name emanated from Pender's reluctance to express himself, the opposite of a talkative bird.[26] A contemporary chronicler suggested that such a notion was well grounded. "His words were not many, but exceedingly comprehensive and to the point. Like all great soldiers, he was not a man of words but of action."[27] Pender did not divulge a reason for the epithet, if he knew one, but added further evidence supporting it when he observed in an aside to his wife in April 1862: "You always say I do not talk to you. I talk but little to anyone."[28]

Classmate Oliver O. Howard remembered Dorsey a little differently, though fondly. "He was rather small in stature, full of quiet humor when a cadet, and quite popular." If Pender said relatively little in comparison to others, people seemed to be drawn to his more engaging social qualities. According to Howard, "Our mathematical professor at West Point, Guy Peck," himself a second lieutenant and instructor while Pender settled in at the academy, "used to say to him, in his inimitable style, as he would ask some queer question during recitation: 'Don't be facetious, Mr. Pender.'"[29] Such a mischievous streak would explain how Dorsey Pender and the rambunctious Samuel Shepperd became such close friends.

Another cadet who attended the academy at the same time was probably closer to the truth when he admitted later, "it is beyond my ken to tell why . . . William D. Pender, of North Carolina, was dubbed 'Poll,' but he was." Still, Wharton Green probably revealed a great deal when he added a retrospective note. "On the fields of glory, with which his name became historic, he was wont to make his legions do his talking for him."[30]

Even so, Pender had no difficulty expressing himself on paper, although the West Point years represented a surprising and unfortunate dearth of such correspondence. He may not have been content to make his opinions known at that point in his life, or the letters simply did not survive. In any case, he was wise to concentrate on comprehending his new environment rather than exerting himself before others for the sake of attention. By getting to know the lay of the land, as it were, he could make better decisions concerning his place in it.

Whatever the case in relation to Dorsey Pender, the application of nicknames, like the hazing of the plebes, served two purposes. First, these behaviors established the superiority of the veteran cadets over the newcomers. Second, they helped forge a bond between the plebes and the institution, as well as with each other. The alteration of individuality in favor of collective identity allowed the development of the class as a whole in addition to helping transform the young men into soldiers.

According to one historian, the goal of the faculty was "to turn out not just Christian gentlemen but Christian soldiers, so the virtues of duty, loyalty, honor, and courage were emphasized more at West Point than anywhere else."[31] This tendency to meld the martial with the religious became increasingly true for Dorsey Pender long after he had left the academy, but it could not have helped being rooted in this early experience.

The impression of the institution and its geographical setting would have been a significant one for the young man from eastern North Carolina, but any early impressions soon changed as the business of educating and developing the "plebes" unfolded. Initially assigned to the general encampment established for all cadets on the plain at West Point, Pender experienced his first taste of the academy while learning basic infantry drills designed to acclimate the civilian to military life and discipline. It was in this unique environment that cadets received practical lessons. This instruction varied for the members of each class but emphasized a great deal of physical activity to supplement the theoretical learning they were expected to absorb.

Camp Gaines, named for an impulsive veteran of the Second Seminole and Mexican-American Wars, Major General Edmund P. Gaines, became Pender's transitional residence for those first months.[32] These summer exercises affirmed for the young men the order and discipline of the military, with its prescribed times for rising, policing the grounds, drills, inspection, parade, meals, and going to bed.[33] The activities also were meant to be impressive visually, with vast rows of tents and well-ordered company streets stretching across the broad plain. The ceremonies that occurred when the cadets struck the tents and returned to the barracks for the colder seasons were particularly memorable to those who witnessed or participated in them.[34]

Celebrations made the whole experience more palatable. The Fourth of July prompted an entire day of festivities, while a ball marked the close of the summer season at the end of August. Despite the nearly constant drilling and instruction, there was time for other activities as well, and there were always the visitors who stopped to watch the pageantry.[35] The quiet lad from North Carolina must have been caught up in the whirlwind of activity and attention that had thrust him so suddenly into such a vibrant and dynamic world.

Pender, Stuart, Shepperd, and their colleagues soon settled into the classroom and drill routine so important to that development. "We came into [the] barracks on the first of September," Cadet Stuart observed to a cousin, "and since that time 'hard study' has been our constant watchword." The first critical academic event for which they were preparing themselves was the "semi-annual Examination" in January, with a second round of examinations in June. Those who could not succeed would be "found deficient and sent home," as twenty-two of his and Pender's colleagues learned when they stood for examination the first time.[36]

Pender found that he had more than sufficient skills to allow for his academic success. But if he was prepared to apply himself in that regard, the educational regimen at the military academy proved a robust challenge, with its daily recitations meant to guarantee that the student was engaged properly in his studies. Class ranking ultimately depended upon the examinations in January and June, but the demands were quite heavy from day to day. As one historian explained, "All told, the boys spent between nine and ten hours daily in class or studying, approximately three hours in military exercises, two hours in recreation, and two hours at meals."[37]

The young North Carolinian struggled for a time in his study of the foreign language of choice for the military service of the day, ranking a paltry thirty-ninth in French.[38] Still, by the end of his first year at the academy (termed the Fourth Class), Pender stood a respectable seventeenth of seventy-one listed cadets, largely on the strength of a ranking of twelfth in math and for having only twenty-eight demerits to blemish his record.

Pender's ranking in mathematics was especially crucial for his success given the importance of the subject at the institution. O. O. Howard and Custis Lee led the class as a whole at one and two respectively, with Jeb Stuart at eighth, but Stephen D. Lee at twenty-eighth and Sam Shepperd at twenty-ninth lagged behind the North Carolinian.[39]

In his Third Class year, Pender slipped to nineteenth of sixty members overall, dropped in mathematics to the same rank, and recorded an even lower score in drawing. He continued to struggle mightily with French, posting a dismal thirty-six ranking in that subject. Likewise, the trend was negative with regard to demerits. Pender left even the exuberant Stuart in the dust with eighty-four (to Stuart's forty-nine), but his lapses could not compete with his new compatriot Shepperd, who managed to put 147 black marks by his name.[40]

Perhaps Pender was feeling the need to assert himself, or he simply may have suffered from his association with his more carefree colleague. He certainly maintained an enduring affection for Sheppard and may have admired his friend's ability to test the staid limits of West Point's order and discipline. Having the infractions publicized at evening parade seemed not to have deterred a young man who so often later expressed a concern about his reputation in the eyes of others.[41] But these may have been the means by which he demonstrated to his comrades that he was one of them. If he was quiet to the point of aloofness, a mischievous expression now and then would ensure that he was not trying to act in a superior manner that would put at risk his associations with his peers.

Like all of the survivors of their first two years at West Point, Pender could look forward to the rare experience of a furlough during the third summer. Rather than go into the summer encampment with everyone else, he and his classmates had the opportunity to enjoy the only leave of absence they would be granted until graduation. When he returned to the barracks and the routine of the academy, Cadet Pender prepared for the final phases of his West Point experience. By his Second Class year (1853), he could finally put French behind him. His overall ranking remained virtually the same at twenty (of fifty-four total members of his class), and his demerits remained high, at 88, while his classroom performance was showing some sign of improvement. Pender scored seventeenth in philosophy and twelfth in drawing, but chemistry replaced language as his lowest course, with a score of twenty-nine. His friend Sam Shepperd, holding the thirty-fifth spot overall, continued to have his problems, putting another triple-digit number of demerits on the books (145) and resting in the lower tier of all of his courses.[42]

Pender may have strayed briefly from the serious course he had initially set for himself at the academy, but the demands for him to continue were compelling, lest he be forced to return to his brother's store and the dullness of that routine in Tarboro. To his credit, Pender responded to the challenge. His final year was academically his best. He secured the highest score of his West Point career in cavalry tactics by placing fifth in the class and was twelfth in English. But in each of the other four courses, he remained in the middle of the pack, including a ranking of twenty-one in artillery, the branch of the service to which he was destined to be assigned after graduation.

Interestingly, for a young man who would be so absorbed with issues of honor and integrity throughout his life, Pender managed only a ranking of twenty-five in ethics, which was well behind Jeb Stuart's position at nine. As might be expected given previous performances, Sam Shepperd lagged behind at thirty-eight and put seventy-two more demerits on his account.[43]

For his part, Pender's demerit infractions were hardly indicative of the reputation he achieved later as a rigid, even autocratic, officer who emphasized and expected strict order and discipline from his men. The North Carolinian's "delinquencies" in 1853 included having his tent "out of order at Evening parade" (three demerits on June 21) and "Swinging arms marching from M[ess] H[all] at dinner" (one demerit on July 10). His dress cap was occasionally "out of place," his camp stool or shoes inappropriately stowed or improperly prepared for inspection, and his uniform coat left unbuttoned.

Pender's worst period for demerits came in the summer months of 1853, when he amassed no less than thirty-eight from the end of June to the end of August. His most uncharacteristic infractions were his absence or lateness at roll call and the four demerits he received on November 22 for "allowing bread to be thrown on the floor of M.H. from his table at dinner."[44] It is not known what the circumstances were with regard to this last incident. Perhaps it was retaliation against the actions of another, for it is doubtful that he was simply careless enough to drop his bread accidentally.

Dorsey Pender was certainly no Robert E. Lee, who had gone through his entire academy career unscathed, nor a Custis Lee, who had no demerits in his Fourth Year and only thirteen in his First. But he was no Sam Shepperd either, who was repeatedly gigged for being inattentive, "Laughing at drill," or "Talking in ranks." Shepperd must have had a particularly good time when the cadets participated in pontoon drills on the morning of August 18, 1853, for he garnered six black marks for "Highly disorderly conduct while going from pontoon drill to camp a.m." The young man must have made a delightful friend and boon companion, but this behavior caused Sheppard to be late frequently, and his constant clowning around could not have put him, or anyone associated with him, in a positive light when it came to the assessment of superiors. His poor ranking in artillery, at thirty-three, was probably less due to his aptitude than his attitude, as best explained by the four demerits he received when "Not prepared on his lesson on Arty on the 11th [of July 1853]."[45]

Yet the West Point environment had more than discipline and classroom education to offer the cadets. It contained many positive role models for them to emulate if they chose. The biographer of one of Pender's instructors, Cadmus Wilcox, suggested that impressionable young men like the "tough, dark-eyed, olive-skinned North Carolinian" would have responded eagerly to such figures. Although young himself, Wilcox had packed a great deal of experience in a short army career that included service in Mexico.[46]

Pender had other sources of inspiration as well. Throughout his career at the academy, he remained an avid reader, at least in terms of the books he checked out. His interests ranged from classic novels and poems to history and biography. Both he and Shepperd had similar tastes, and occasionally one followed the other in reading a book the first had returned. History dominated the list in 1850 and 1851. Dorsey read works on Napoleon, George Washington, and Oliver Cromwell, interspersed with the tales of conquering Mexico or Peru. Undoubtedly with thoughts of home during that first winter at West Point, he also settled beneath his reading lamp with a two-volume history of North Carolina. By 1853 his literary interests had expanded considerably. Dorsey was soon thoroughly immersed in literature, which must have contributed to his success in English.[47]

Of course, matters other than academics and class rankings, demerits and books, intruded in the lives of those who studied at West Point. O. O. Howard of Maine recalled "that unpleasant feuds existed in the corps of cadets, and as a rule, the subject of slavery was at the bottom of the controversy."[48] While the New Englander suffered for a period of time from ostracism by some classmates, particularly among the Southerners, Jeb Stuart from Virginia maintained that there was not "as marked antipathy as the times would suggest were we 'cits,' but there seems to be a sentiment of mutual forebearance."[49] In any case, the commitment to study and the drill field left little time for anything else. The subordination of the individual to the good of the military service and discipline helped limit sectionalist expressions as well. Melding persons of varying political and geographical backgrounds and viewpoints into a larger whole was an essential part of the experience.

Likewise, West Pointers could usually place larger political issues in context. "President making, and politics in general are things which Cadets allow to trouble them very little," Stuart explained to a relative in April 1853. "We have a few of the chivalry as well as some rank abolitionists but they take very good care to keep quiet," he concluded."[50] Howard harbored such antislavery feelings yet reflected a similar view of the place of politics at the academy, observing to his mother, "No political excitement ever gets within this secluded prison."[51] On such matters, and probably not surprising given his reticence at this stage in his life, Pender made no impression one way or the other on his peers regarding the heated issues of the day. Whatever he felt concerning sectional questions such as slavery, tariffs, or the like, Pender kept his views to himself while he remained at the academy.

It is difficult to say how much other distractions of a more social nature complicated his progress at West Point. He received five demerits for "visiting" on the morning of December 27, although it is unclear what the exact nature was of the offensive social call.[52] Dorsey Pender was not one to indulge in the temptations that lay just outside of West Point's strictly guarded world. The extremes of the weather during the winter of 1853–54 particularly could not have been conducive to much extracurricular activity, even if the cadet from North Carolina had been so inclined.[53]

Once the harsh conditions subsided, the pace of events picked up considerably. Edward Hartz, a contemporary of Pender's but behind him a year at West Point, noted the intense period "from the 15th of March to the commencement of the June Examinations" in a letter to his father. He followed the outline of progress for each class and explained that the "1st or graduating class," of which the North Carolinian was a part, was busy in "the practice of Military Engineering, consisting of 'staking' out fortifications (permanent), redoubts, Entrenchments, and other offensive and defensive works which make up the scientific part of our trade."[54] Pender was learning his craft, whatever his military duties might require once he left these studies behind.

The future soldier's most serious challenge at this phase in his training occurred when he jeopardized his cadet rank by his failure to submit a report while acting as officer of the day. Pender had risen from corporal and sergeant to lieutenant by this time, but the lapse caused the loss of rank and a heavy dose of demerits. The six strikes he received constituted the single-largest blow to his conduct record. It was not clear why the breach occurred, but contrary to the assertion by one biographer that Pender had learned the "consequences" of abiding by "military regulations," his subsequent behavior did not indicate as much.[55] The following March Pender failed to affix his signature to a guard report as required and accumulated another five black marks on his account.[56] He would one day be a stickler for paperwork and protocol, but the lesson had apparently yet to take fully.

Pender survived the regimen to approach graduation on July 1, 1854. Of the forty-six members who comprised the graduating class with him, Pender held the nineteenth place, Custis Lee the first, Jeb Stuart the thirteenth, Stephen Lee the seventeenth, and his good friend Sam Shepperd the thirty-sixth.

How much William Dorsey Pender actually gained from his West Point education might not be so easily measured. To be sure, he learned military order and discipline, and he excelled at cavalry tactics, the importance of which would be driven home to him in his future service on the frontier. But as one student of the Regular Army asserted, West Point was not the best place to obtain preparation for confronting the Native Americans or their specialized tactics. The academy, Robert Utley observed of its graduates, "sent them forth to learn Indian fighting by hard experience."[57] Nor, as another student of West Point noted, was the focus intended to be as much on the practical as on the theoretical side of martial matters. "The men who controlled the institution," historian James Morrison asserted, "viewed its mission as being the production of engineers who could also function as soldiers rather than the reverse."[58] Even so, the sense of confidence Pender gained in himself and his abilities was an aspect of his education that could not be easily dismissed or diminished.

Like other graduates, Dorsey Pender's class standing determined his branch of service in the army, with the coveted engineering positions going to those with the highest rankings. Pender was set to enter the U.S. Army as a brevet second lieutenant, with an initial assignment to the artillery. He would now have the means to establish himself in his avocation and in the process prove to himself and the world that he belonged there.

2

FIRST BLOOD
(1854–58)

•────•

Is Miss Fanny Shepperd married yet?
—JEB STUART TO HIS WIFE, FLORA

He grappled the Indian and hurled him from his horse.
—LAWRENCE KIP ON WILLIAM DORSEY PENDER AT SPOKANE PLAINS

•────•

So much of the world lay before William Dorsey Pender as he celebrated his matriculation from the U.S. Military Academy at West Point. He had challenged himself successfully, and his reward was a commission in the nation's armed forces. In the service of his country, he was about to be required to travel great distances, to be introduced to adventures of which he had at best only read or dreamed. The young man had to be both excited and anxious about what lay ahead, while also understanding that, given his profession, the world before him would be fraught with dangers as well as opportunities. Nevertheless, he could draw upon his personal reserves of training and coolness to answer whatever challenges might arise.

With these basic elements in place, Dorsey Pender accepted his role as a newly minted second lieutenant.[1] His commission, signed by President Franklin Pierce and Secretary of War Jefferson Davis on January 10, 1855, announced Pender's appointment as "Second Lieutenant in the Second Regiment of Artillery," to date from August 16, 1854.[2] He proudly wrote of the receipt of his commission from Fort Myers, Florida, in February 1855.[3]

But before Lieutenant Pender took up his assignment, he had the benefit of a furlough granted to all graduates from the military academy upon the completion of their curriculum requirements. He used this opportunity to return to his home on Town Creek in North Carolina before embarking on his tour of duty. Pender also planned to spend a portion of this last unobligated time visiting Good Spring, the home of Congressman Augustine Shepperd and his good friend Samuel, located near Salem in the western portion of the state. Dorsey remembered this time in his life fondly, always looking back at his brief visits to the Shepperd home simultaneously as something of an oasis and an ideal.

By the time Pender arrived at his friend's house, the Shepperd family was already undergoing a transition. Three of the siblings, Frank, Hamilton, and William Henry, had already reached adulthood. Mary Frances, or "Fanny," was next in age to Sam, while younger brother Jacob, or "Jake," and their sister Pamela were still in their preteen years.[4] The presence of these family members meant that youth pervaded the household and enhanced the energy and liveliness of a home already girded to embrace and salute its returning West Point graduate and his associates before they traveled to their respective postings.[5]

Undoubtedly, during this interlude Dorsey enjoyed the company of Sam, but a large measure of the Shepperd home's allure also came from one of its charming hostesses, fourteen-year-old Fanny. She was the older of the congressman's two daughters, born to Augustine and Mary Sheppard on March 9, 1840. Historian William Hassler described her at this time as a "petite, light-complected belle, who possessed talents as a pianist."[6] Fanny was also said to have exhibited a lovely singing voice, all charms calculated to have an appeal to potential suitors like her brother's friend.

Pender's companions in this period of respite before assuming his official duties included Jeb Stuart as well Shepperd. For the time being, these three were fast friends. "I sometimes think that the taste of classmates for each other's society particularly West Pointers is unequalled by the strongest attachment," the Virginian observed from Salem, "and what is more remarkable it becomes more and more intense as time continues."[7] Basking in the glow of their graduation in the summer of 1854, any days of difficulties in the future remained obscured. The most immediate concern for the trio was the termination of their furloughs.

By October 19, 1854, Pender had made his way to the country's distant southern frontier at Fort Myers, Florida, below Tampa. Detailed as part of a squad trailblazing a direct route between Fort Myers and Fort Thompson inland from the coast, the North Carolinian had his first experience with that tropical environment. When Pender returned from this assignment, he held the responsibilities of post adjutant for a brief time. Then he was once more "in the field" in the early spring on "detached service."[8]

These excursions prevented the young officer from suffering too greatly from the malady of boredom that plagued many of the soldiers spread across the vast geographical distances of the continent. Tedium and routine were the most common companions for these men. Pender had not yet been in the profession long enough to experience the feelings of one comrade, who lamented in his diary, "It is melancholy to think how I am spending my best days, in this out the way place."[9]

Whatever he may have felt in anticipation of greater adventures—and perhaps martial glory—Lieutenant Pender quickly found that his place with the 2nd U.S. Artillery was not exactly what he had had in mind. He began to contemplate a change to a branch of the service he felt would be better suited to his tastes and training.

On April 14, 1855, Pender raised the subject with the secretary of the army, J. C. Dobbin, based upon vacancies created in the 2nd U.S. Dragoons by the transfer of other officers from that regiment. The young officer was also not above using any influence and connections he had to his advantage. As part of his arsenal of persuasion, Pender included a letter of introduction from Judge Thomas Ruffin and offered Dobbin the assurance, "I should not encroach upon your time, if I were not from North Carolina, and that many of my relatives and friends are personally acquainted with you."[10] By May he felt sufficiently confident to apply directly to the adjutant general, Colonel Samuel Cooper, for transfer to the 2nd Dragoons.[11]

Within a matter of days, notification left the War Department that effective from the third of March, Pender was being transferred to the 1st U.S. Dragoons. Although not to the 2nd as he had requested, the assignment carried the rank of second lieutenant.[12] Upon his acceptance of his new duties, Pender received notification from Secretary of War Jefferson Davis to "repair without delay to Fort Leavenworth, Kansas Territory, where you will proceed with the first detachment of recruits to the Head Quarters of your regiment in New Mexico, and report to your Colonel, who will assign you to a company."[13] Apparently, the news traveled slowly, for it was not until a month later, on June 21, that Pender acknowledged these orders.[14] Jaded by mundane activities such as road building, Pender could not know that his transfer was taking him out of Florida just prior to the outbreak of a third Seminole war.[15]

As he made his way westward to take up his new duties, Pender had the opportunity for a brief reunion with Sam Shepperd at Fort Leavenworth. But circumstances for his friend took a tragic turn when "a malarial disease" struck the former classmate. It was certainly likely that given the time period provided for Pender to report to New Mexico that he was able to remain by his ailing friend's side, but any comfort he could provide was of no avail. Samuel Sheppard worsened and died from the effects of cholera on June 27, 1855.[16]

The death of his close friend had a profound effect on Pender. The loss devastated him. Yet there was one bright element to the darkness that had so suddenly enveloped him. Pender was already deeply in love with Sam's sister Fanny, and the tragedy brought the pair closer together in their grief. There must have been some solace in their mutual circumstance, and it likely only strengthened their developing relationship.

Nevertheless, Pender had to subordinate his grief to his duty, as required of any good soldier, and seemed to have done so. The post returns for Fort Leavenworth showed him as having left on September 23, 1855, under orders to report to Jefferson Barracks in Missouri.[17] He did not remain in Missouri long before going to Fort Thorn, in New Mexico Territory.[18] The monthly report of February 1856 listed the lieutenant as having arrived on the twenty-first and in command of a company of the First Dragoons since January 26.[19]

This station would certainly not appear to be an attractive one aesthetically for the men assigned there. Established in 1853 along the Rio Grande to protect a trail leading to California, Fort Thorn "occupied an unhealthful site on the edge of an extensive marsh," according to one historian, and was abandoned as a permanent post six years later.[20] The young lieutenant's state of mind surely could not have aided him in accepting such adverse conditions. Yet despite the gloom associated with the unexpected death of his friend and the difficult natural environment in which he now found himself, Pender appeared to have acclimated to life there satisfactorily enough.

Another West Point classmate, Jeb Stuart, noted his friend's state of mind with regard to his new posting. "I received a long letter from Mr. Pender by the Santa Fe mail of April," he wrote his niece Lizzie Peirce from Kansas in June. "He is very much pleased with New Mexico and is stationed at Camp Thorn, N.M." Stuart had his own hands full in "Bleeding Kansas," as the area was rapidly and popularly becoming known, noting his concern, "we will have hot work here in Kansas, [where] murders are committed on both sides every day, and a soldier was shot from his horse while riding along the other day." Yet for the warrior who enjoyed adventure as much as attention, Stuart may not have envied Pender's quieter lot, despite his admission that at Fort Leavenworth, at least in the summer of 1856, "Every one goes armed."[21]

New Mexico Territory was not brewing with the same level of intensity as Kansas, but soldiers there had to be ready for action as well. Pender was barely settled in his routine when he and his command had orders to confront hostile Indians in March. The young officer may have regretted that his West Point training had not prepared him for the kind of warfare he was about to undertake, but his first engagement with an enemy would provide him with field experience.

The principal culprits in this instance were Mogollon Apaches, who had enjoyed some previous immunity from interactions with whites by the remoteness of their mountain refuges but increasingly staged raids that army policymakers thought required a response.[22] To that end, two columns of mixed troops, infantry and dragoons, including Lieutenant Pender, left Forts Craig and Thorn to pursue and suppress these hostile activities. As historian Robert Utley has explained, these forces "penetrated the Mogollon Mountains" and "smashed a Mogollon rancheria, killed or wounded several Indians, and recovered 250 stolen sheep."[23]

Because of the nature of the record keeping, Pender's exact role during this period has remained unclear. According to George Cullum's authoritative biographical compendium of West Pointers, the North Carolinian was with the command when it engaged the enemy in the Sierra Almagre in 1856. The Fort Thorn post report for the month of March seemed to corroborate this timing initially, with a notation that Pender was on detached service "on an expedition to the Mogollon Mountains," but a subsequent reference indicated his having "left Company and Post March 6, 1856." Cullum recorded Pender as, "Scouting, 1856, being engaged against the Apache Indians in a Skirmish at Almagre Mountain, N.M., Mar. 20, 1856." Certainly by April, the lieutenant was otherwise engaged: "Two officers Lieut. William D. Pender & 10 men left Post April 25, 1856 on Indian Scout."[24]

Pender's time in this part of New Mexico proved to be as truncated as his short stint in Florida. By May he had transferred to Fort Union and left for that posting on the twentieth of the month.[25] That installation, established on July 26, 1851, largely to protect individuals moving along the Santa Fe Trail, was located well north of Fort Thorn and northeast of Santa Fe.[26] Departmental headquarters promptly cut orders for Lieutenant Pender "as escort to [a] Government surveying party," a duty that put him back on detached service as of June 16, 1856, lasting until August.[27]

The transient nature of his military service since leaving West Point continued as Pender prepared to depart New Mexico for the California coast and the tiny outpost of Fort Tejon. This post had only been established a short time earlier, in the summer of 1854, to provide a military presence near the Tejon Indian reservation.[28] Fortunately, for the much traveled junior officer, he did not have to learn an entirely new system as this transfer involved elements of the 1st Dragoons.[29]

Pender's time in California would prove eventful, though not for the reasons he might have suspected. He had been on duty there for less than a month when the region experienced a severe earthquake.[30] A report included a description of the effect of the natural phenomenon in understated tones. "The Post was visited by several severe shocks of an earthquake on the 9th inst. which have continued at intervals of a few hours up to the present time, damaging the buildings more or less."[31] Fort Tejon's commander did not indicate if the damage was "more" or "less," although accounts suggested the destruction was quite extensive, fortunately with few resulting casualties.

A newspaper from the area recorded that at the time of "the shock," a couple of companies of dragoons, "who had just arrived from New Mexico, were having their horses herded in [the] Kern river valley." The report indicated that for these unsuspecting troopers, the effect was significant. "It very unceremoniously tipped over their coffee pots, their camp kettles, and themselves also." Even more impressive was the shift in the flow of the river, now found to be "running up stream." In addition to a number of uprooted trees, "large quantities of fish were thrown upon [the] banks [of nearby Tulare Lake]."[32] Despite what must have been an unsettling set of circumstances for a person who had lived much of his life outside areas prone to such natural phenomena, Pender left no personal assessment of these events.

At any rate, the young lieutenant had little opportunity to contemplate such occurrences, for that same month his superior ordered him to proceed, with another junior officer and "a detachment of forty-two enlisted men of the 1st Dragoons," to the area of Los Angeles "to protect the citizens of that place from the depredations of a Band of outlaws."[33] Pender reached the town early in the company of departing Lieutenant Colonel B. L. Beall and in time to enjoy a serenade from a brass band arranged for the popular commander.[34] A week later a local newspaper recorded the arrival of the troops themselves.[35] Pender remained on this "detached service" until mid-February.[36]

The expedition must have met with success, for the *Los Angeles Star* congratulated the efforts of the soldiers "who marched here on the request of the citizens" and since had done "good service for the people." Pender's contingent of ten men took responsibility for watching the San Fernando Pass, while other troops guarded another point to secure the area. Local residents seemed to have welcomed this mission to protect them and their interests.[37]

With this duty accomplished, Pender returned to Fort Tejon, where he was present on the rolls as another spring began.[38] Yet once more his sojourn at the post was short, although this time Pender and his comrades in the 1st Dragoons traveled northward rather than returning to Texas or the East Coast. Their first destination was Fort Reading, which had been founded in northern California in 1852 to provide protection for the miners who had poured into the area and soon served as the headquarters for the Northern District of California.[39] Subsequently, Pender transferred to other points in the northwest, including Forts Vancouver and Walla Walla in Washington Territory and Fort Dalles in nearby Oregon.[40]

The new assignments offered the possibility for action, and this time not against small bands of outlaws as had been the case in California. The Hudson's Bay Company had established Fort Vancouver originally in the mid-1820s. It later became part of the chain of U.S. outposts in the region, receiving its official designation as a fort in July 1853.[41] Soldiers of the 9th U.S. Infantry, under Major Edward J. Steptoe, created a post at Walla Walla in the fall of 1856 as a means of asserting military control over that area.[42] Fort Dalles, located at "The Dalles," a long narrows of the Columbia River that marked the end of the Oregon Trail, was established earlier in May 1850, designated as a fort three years later, and significantly improved in 1856.[43] Each of these outposts would play a role in this phase of Dorsey Pender's Old Army career, but first the East and a budding romance beckoned the young warrior to return home.

Pender secured a furlough early in 1857 to enable him to "attend to important business." The authorization allowed him a week but granted him permission to obtain an extension of twenty days if he required it.[44] By that summer, his friend Jeb Stuart, now at Fort Riley in Kansas Territory, observed: "Lieut. Pender is now I hear on leave of absence. I also learned that he had been to Mr. Shepperd's—did you see or hear of him?" The dashing future cavalier of the Confederacy, who would become famous for his ability to gather intelligence for General Robert E. Lee, was groping for news here of the friend he termed "a fine fellow" and whom he hoped "to meet . . . somewhere in my wandering

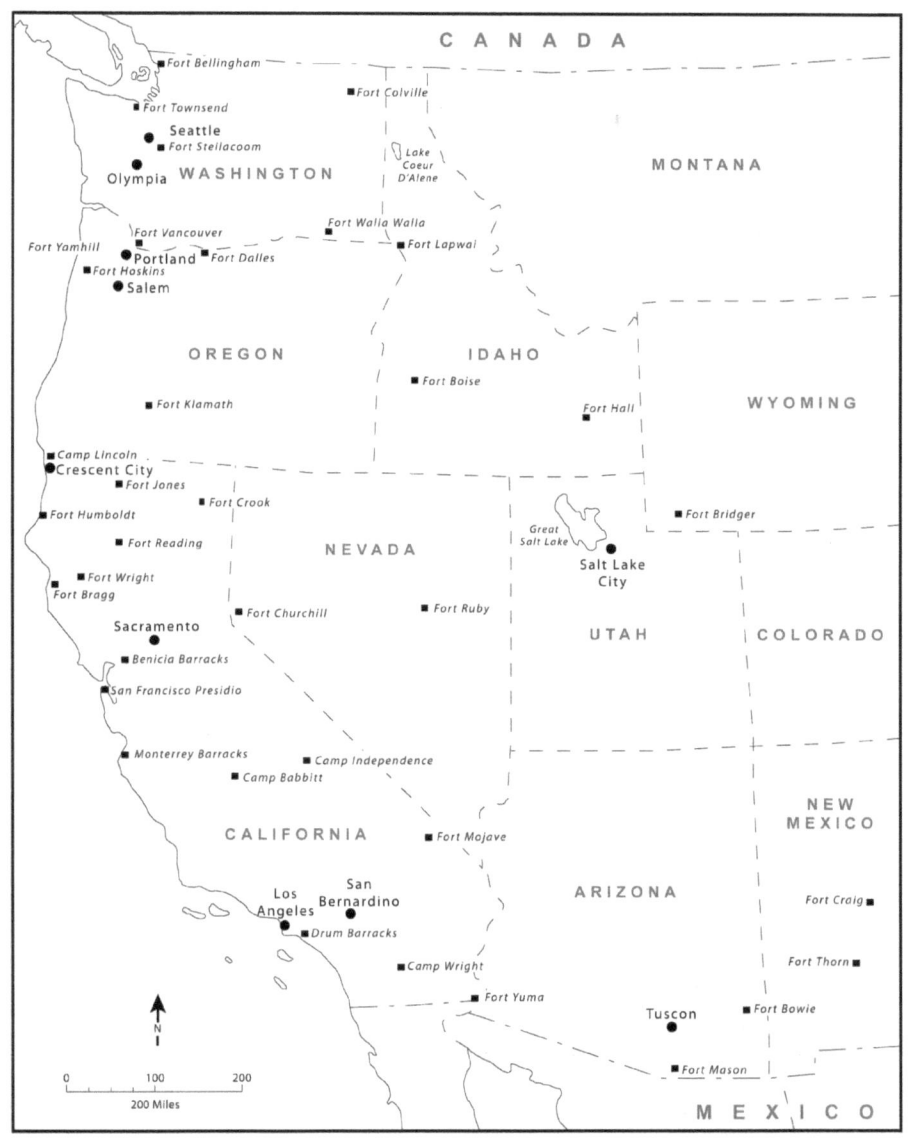

Map 1. The West/Northwest Territory in which Pender served in the Regular Army and saw his earliest major military action. Map by Heather Harvey.

next summer." Intriguingly, Stuart wanted his niece to learn, "Is Miss Fanny Shepperd married yet?"[45]

It is difficult to know precisely what Stuart had in mind with his final query. He had himself become engaged and married to Flora Cooke in a matter of months two years previously. Although he did not say so directly, Stuart surely would have connected his friend Dorsey with the sister of their West Point classmate and anticipated that their marriage was a matter of time. Certainly, he was on the right track with regard to the personal nature of Pender's leave of absence.

Under the circumstances, Pender must have felt that he had to travel around the globe to get home from California. It was a long and tiring journey that required virtually every form of transportation imaginable. As always happened on such occasions, when he finally reached his destination, there was precious little time left for him to enjoy the comforts of home or to share with Fanny.

Since leaving West Point, Pender had experienced life at military posts on the fringes of Florida, New Mexico, California, Oregon, and Washington. He would soon return to active service in the far northwest, following his all-too-brief furlough. Given how difficult he found it later to spend only a short time with Fanny before being separated from her, Dorsey must have experienced a struggle with this departure too. Not knowing what the future would hold, perhaps he pondered during his long return trip across the country that marriage to Fanny was the only solution to his misery. In any event, his return to the northwest kept him employed busily enough to allow him to put his mind elsewhere.

Dorsey Pender had at least one positive professional development as he anticipated reporting for duty. Although formal notification did not leave the War Department until the end of September, as of May 17, 1858, Pender held the rank of first lieutenant in the 1st Regiment of Dragoons. He was still out in the field when the notice of his promotion, signed by Secretary of War John B. Floyd, reached Fort Walla Walla in Washington Territory.[46] The paperwork apparently lagged, for the post report for the month of May continued to list Pender as a second lieutenant, although he had been given responsibility for Company E since May 22 as a result of the death of its commander, William Gaston.[47] The wheels of promotion ground slowly for everyone in those days, but Pender would always grasp at such indicators to validate his worthiness and illustrate his personal and professional standing.

Even so, all was not smooth as he traveled westward. Pender bristled at one of his first assignments as he made his way back to the Washington and Oregon Territories. The active service of the dragoons was hard on officers and men alike, causing not an inconsiderable amount of disaffection. The extreme solution was either resignation or desertion, and thus the need for recruits and replacements remained high. This was the task that Pender was now called upon to undertake. He found it distasteful. Demonstrating a tendency that would not ingratiate him much with some of his superiors, Pender voiced his displeasure in writing. In this case, he was convinced that either one of two available infantry officers would suffice to carry out the duty of shepherding recruits, a task he felt was "unjust" for taking him away from what he considered to be more-important duties. As it was, under these orders his detachment of dragoons at Fort Dalles from Companies I and C would be forced to forego his services as an officer while he was thus occupied. Fortunately for the headstrong lieutenant, there were no negative ramifications for his unorthodox official complaint.

As a junior officer, Pender continued to endure the routine duties that fell to him, including generating the appropriate amount of paperwork. In the summer months of 1858, he dutifully forwarded information regarding two deserters from the company to his superior, Major W. W. Mackall, in San Francisco.[48] Fort Walla Walla must have seemed like a sieve to the young lieutenant and undoubtedly influenced his future attitudes concerning less-than-faithful service among the men under his command. Fortunately, from his perspective at least, the lieutenant's yearning for more-active service was about to be fulfilled.

In the summer of 1858, Pender became part of a campaign sent out against "the Northern Indians" in retaliation for an earlier attack that had led to a humiliating setback for the U.S. military. In May Major Steptoe had taken a force of 164 troopers and two light mountain howitzers deep into Indian territory after several killings had unsettled the region. Despite the firepower his command represented, it proved no match for as many as 1,000 Native American assailants in an engagement that transpired on May 17. In that fighting Captain Oliver Hazard Perry Taylor of Company C, 1st Dragoons fell with a fatal wound to the neck while his counterpart in Company E, Lieutenant William Gaston, also suffered a mortal wound.[49] Several privates died in the fighting, with the number of wounded mounting alarmingly as the day wore on and the combat continued.

The men had managed to secure high ground and erect some makeshift barricades, from which they waged a defense. Yet not only had the beleaguered command found itself surrounded, it also began to run critically low on ammunition. The troops collected spare rounds and passed them to the men on the outer ring so they could continue an effective resistance, but the situation appeared increasingly desperate.

Following an impromptu council of the remaining officers, Steptoe determined that the best course for the survival of his men lay in lightening the command and making a dash for safety. His Nez Perce scouts discovered a path that would take them past their opponents once darkness had descended, and the soldiers hastily made preparations to move, including strapping the badly wounded to their horses and burying the two howitzer tubes. Finally, when all was in readiness, the survivors slipped off into the night while a sergeant and a picked detail stayed behind longer and fanned the camp fires to provide the illusion of the command's continued presence. In less than a month after the column had left Fort Walla Walla, it staggered back with a dozen wounded and everyone haggard and worn by the ordeal.[50]

The response was almost instantaneous by army standards as reinforcements and supplies poured into the region to support a punitive expedition. The new commander of the Department of the Pacific since June 1857, Brigadier General Newman S. Clark, relocated to Fort Vancouver and immediately consulted with the commander of the failed expedition, Major Steptoe, and the officer who would lead the next campaign, Colonel George Wright. For the men themselves, there was incessant drilling that now took on a new sense of urgency and significance. Lieutenant Lawrence Kip of the 3rd Artillery recorded the intensified training that everyone now willingly endured: "At nine in the morning, we have dress parade; at half-past nine, we drill for an hour . . . at twelve, the men are practiced at firing at a mark and estimating distances; at five in the evening, we have drill; and at half-past six, guard mounting. Drilling, too, is a very different matter from what it is at post in time of peace. Then, it is a sort of *pro forma* business, in which neither officers nor men take much interest. Now, it is invested with a reality, since all are conscious that our success in the field depends perhaps upon the state of discipline."[51]

Of this new regimen another officer recalled, "From the 25th of June till the 7th of July I lost no time in preparing my force to fight Indians." Erasmus D. Keyes, whose artillerists would serve as infantrymen on this occasion, put into place rigorous training for them. "I had numerous targets the height of a man set up at various distances on even and uneven ground, and for several hours every day, Sundays not excepted, I caused the soldiers, individually and collectively, to fire at those targets," he explained. "In every case they were required to estimate the distance, which was afterwards told, and required to adjust their aim accordingly." Keyes felt strongly that such preparations could mean the difference between life and death on the battlefield. "The effect of that drilling was wonderful," he concluded, noting an additional benefit: "I estimated it as giving a quadruple value to my numbers."[52] Certainly, the fire discipline being created would come in handy once the expedition was underway.

Lieutenant Pender left no account of the effect such efforts made upon him or his men. But as a young and impressionable junior officer, he was bound to have been affected by witnessing the preparations for warfare going on around him. This was a long way from the days on the plains of West Point when he had exhibited a tendency to take such matters more lightly, especially in the company of his carefree companion Sam Shepperd.

By August, Colonel Wright, a veteran of more than thirty-five years, determined that the troops were ready to set out. His orders were simple and explicit: "You will attack all hostile Indians with vigor; make their punishment severe, and persevere until the submission of all is complete." Supporting the 9th Infantry's colonel, who commanded the expedition, were Major William N. Grier of the 1st Dragoons and Captain Keyes of the 3rd Artillery. Grier's subordinates in the saddle were Lieutenants Henry B. Davidson (Company E), David McM. Gregg (Company H), and Pender (Company C).[53] The North Carolinian had received an earlier assignment to replace Lieutenant Gaston, now he was successor to Captain Taylor, both of whom had perished on the Steptoe expedition. Certainly for him and for the command as a whole, motivation for the upcoming campaign was not going to be difficult to attain. The dragoons were veterans of the May excursion, with the memory of that setback and the desire to avenge their defeat and losses still fresh in their minds.[54] The rank and file experienced these desires even more intensely when word arrived that the victorious Indians were sporting trophies from the fight and threatening to annihilate any column that dared to venture across the Snake River.

The expedition began as the column left Fort Walla Walla on August 15, 1858.[55] The number of personnel engaged in the operation ranged from 700 to 900 regulars, civilian employees, and Nez Perce scouts. Within a few days the force reached the Snake River at a point where it was wide but fordable. A fortification named for the fallen Captain Taylor was already underway on

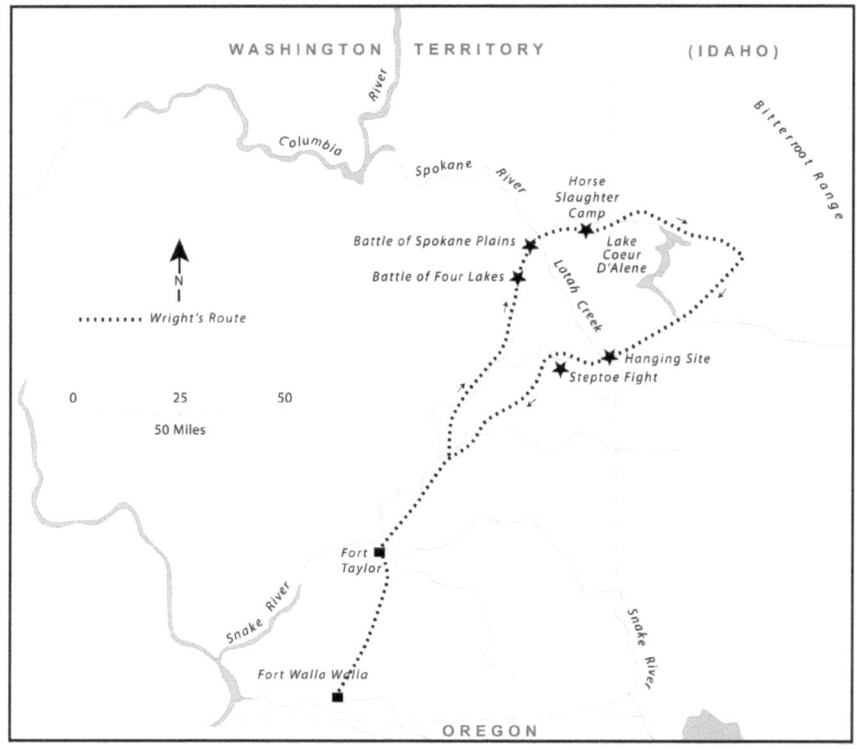

Map 2. The path of the Wright Expedition of 1858, sent to avenge the Steptoe Disaster of the previous spring. Map by Heather Harvey.

ground overlooking the river, at which a company of artillery would remain to secure the crossing against any threat that materialized. The quartermaster of the expedition also supervised the construction of a flatboat that would aid the men in crossing the Snake when the time came. In the meantime, the command remained in the vicinity for about a week while the men transferred supplies and equipment to packs, the wagons being too unwieldy to move in the terrain once they had crossed the river. Inauspiciously to the superstitiously minded, a storm briefly delayed the river crossing.[56]

Finally, in the early hours of August 25, the lead elements of the column passed over the Snake. It would be into the following day before the entire force was on the opposite side of the river.[57] By the end of the month, the command was well along its route, moving northeastward in its search for hostile forces. Despite the fact that two artillerists had died from "eating poisonous roots" and the annoying efforts of the Native Americans to burn the grassland in an attempt to deny the army's animals sufficient sustenance, little occurred militarily except for an exchange of a few shots over long distance. Generally, the warriors the troopers encountered demonstrated the discretion of remaining out of effective range, and the soldiers refused to be lured into chasing small parties into canyons and depressions in which ambushes could be carried out easily. The pace proved slow, and the command adhered to a meticulous order of march, remaining under strict rules that regulated their behavior in hostile territory. Even so, the men continued to expect a fight and would not have to wait long for the relatively peaceful interlude to subside.

On August 31, Nez Perce scouts reported the presence of hostile forces. After a period of baiting the troopers from a relatively safe distance, these warriors tried to set fire to the tall grasses and use the smoke to generate confusion and to serve as a screen for closing with their opponents. Although the tactic failed, the antagonists must have recognized that a fight was eminent.

The next morning, September 1, Wright's command stirred from a fitful sleep to see their adversaries assembled on a hill that blocked their path. Remembering Steptoe's fate, Wright detailed a portion of his force to defend his train and sent others forward to clear the hill. Major Grier and his dragoons, with the assistance of the infantry and dismounted artillerymen, accomplished the immediate task easily, but the high ground revealed a large body of combatants just beyond that was prepared to resist them. One participant later recorded the sensation as he stared down on a plain that featured four lakes and dotted by pines, ravines, and gullies: "On the plain below us we saw the enemy. Every spot seemed alive with the wild warriors we had come so far to meet. . . . They seemed to cover the country for some two miles."[58]

The sight must have been impressive indeed, but if the troopers were intimidated, they did not show it. Wright deployed the men on foot to move forward and drive their adversaries onto the open ground, where the dragoons could be unleashed against them with better expectation of success. As the range closed, the fire grew heavier and steadier, and the rounds began to find their marks. Several warriors fell, but others scooped them up hurriedly and carried them off.[59]

One eyewitness recorded that Wright held his dragoons in check while the rest moved forward on foot. The riders awaited the call to mount and when it came "were launched at the enemy, through the intervals in the ranks of the infantry."[60] In the chaos of battle, the dragoons at last had their opportunity. "Charge the rascals!" Grier called out over the din of battle, and the pounding of horses' hooves increased as the mounted troopers advanced.[61]

One account reflected the ferocious character of the charge as the "horse-soldiers with their reins in their teeth, their knives [sabers] in their right hands and their revolvers in their left, gallop[ed] madly toward their opponents."[62] The fighting was fierce as the dragoons slashed with their sabers in both directions at anyone who came within their reach. "It was a race for life," a junior officer recalled, noting that the jaded dragoon mounts could not keep up with the more rested Indian ponies.[63] Even so, at least one officer was able to come to mortal blows with an opponent before that individual could escape. Captain Erasmus Keyes recalled, "Lieutenant Gregg, who was a splendid *sabreur*, overtook one of the flying rascals, and with a blow of his blade split his skull in two."[64] Infantry fire and a howitzer round punctuated the command's success. Exhaustion from the extended fighting caused the advance to be halted, but the men were not too tired from their exertions to give their commander a hearty celebratory cheer in honor of his leadership.[65]

The effect of the running battle on the army column was clear, as Lieutenant Lawrence Kip later recorded. "A number of our men had never before been under fire," he observed, "but begrimed and weary as they were, we could see in their faces how much they enjoyed the excitement of the fight."[66] Experiencing the contradictory sensations of combat for the first time, Dorsey Pender no doubt shared the anxiety and exhilaration with his men. He found that he did not relish taking the lives of others but that he would do his full duty and could remain calm and clear headed even amid the turmoil of warfare.

Even so, it was unclear precisely how much Pender participated in the affair. By one account, his horse "took a ball in the neck," but since the qualification "not too badly" followed that description, the nature of the injury may not have been sufficient to cause the lieutenant to drop out of the fight.[67] In an after-action report, Colonel Wright recorded on September 2, Pender could take pleasure in knowing that his was among the names mentioned: "The major commends particularly the coolness and gallantry of Lts. Davidson, Pender & Gregg, each in command of a troop, for the handsome and skillful manner in which they brought their men into and conducted them through the fight."[68]

The participants could also look back on the Battle of the Four Lakes, as the engagement became known, with the comforting awareness that none of the officers or their men had died or suffered severe wounds. Local newspaper headlines trumpeted their martial exploits. "The Hostiles Completely Routed," Olympia's *Pioneer and Democrat* proclaimed, with the garish addendum, "10 Savages Killed!!!"[69]

The command took the next several days for badly needed rest. As much as anything, the mounts needed a chance to recover, for if another fight were to take place, the dragoons would undoubtedly be called upon again. The march resumed early on September 5. Setting off across the Spokane Plain, the troops encountered another party of warriors about five miles from the previous encampment. Once more these adversaries tried the expedient of lighting the prairie grass on fire, this time with slightly more success (although the sustained gunfire of the troopers drove them off).[70]

Lieutenant Kip provided a perspective to the scenes he witnessed. "An open prairie here intervening, Major Grier passed the skirmishers with his own and Lt. Pender's troops and charged the Indians, killing two and wounding three." Kip then recorded what for his North Carolina colleague was the most dramatic event that had yet occurred in his military career. "Among the incidents of the fight was one which happened to Lieutenant Pender. Firing his pistol as he charged, just as he dashed up to the side of an Indian he discovered that his revolver had caught on the lock and was useless." Pender remained composed despite the distressing turn of events. "He had not time to draw his saber, and was obliged, therefore, to close with his enemy," the chronicler explained. "He grappled the Indian and hurled him from his horse, when a soldier behind dispatched him."[71] It must have been particularly gratifying for Pender to read the specific mention he received in the official reports for the expedition. "The Major speaks in the highest terms of the gallantry of Lt. Pender commanding Company 'C.'"[72] Indeed, he would later refer to these notices by his superior as evidence of his merit for obtaining higher rank.

Pender also received special mention from a newspaper correspondent who was traveling with the expedition. Styling himself "Coeur D'Alene," the writer forwarded detailed letters from the field describing the action as he saw it. In the fighting at Spokane Plains, Pender was part of the dragoon force that stood ready for "a favorable moment" to "charge down with their commands which had already dealt such deadly blows in the battle of the Four Lakes." At the appropriate time the "anxious men and horses" moved "like lightning" to "overtake, cut down, and leave on the field" a number of their adversaries.

"We killed two chiefs and many other Indians, wounded a large number," the writer noted and, just as effectively in trying to limit their opponents' mobility, "killed and captured many horses." Among the items salvaged from the debris on the ground was "the pistol worn by Lieut. Gaston in Steptoe's battle, his horse, [and] saddle." The correspondent offered widespread praise for the operation but noted particularly that "Lieut. Pender acted during the fight with marked gallantry" as he valiantly "dispatched" a warrior in close-hand fighting.[73]

For the time being, the column settled into camp for the night "to let men and animals rest," as one participant explained.[74] Artillerist Keyes remembered that in the aftermath of the fighting, he "dismounted, took a glass of wine, gave orders not to disturb me, and lay down on my back to rest." He added, "For half an hour I did not move a muscle, and felt the whole time that if I did move one I should die." The recuperative effect of the tactic worked, and in short order Keyes reappeared refreshed. "Never before, or since," he concluded, "was I so nearly finished by the toil of war."[75] What Dorsey Pender must have felt as he thought back on the events that had so dramatically unfolded can only be surmised, but he was surely as exhausted by his experience as his colleague had been.

As welcome as the rest might be for men and animals, it was of necessity short lived. Wright and his officers had no way to know at the time that they had broken the Indian resistance decisively. There remained the reasonable expectation that more campaigning, and hard fighting, lay ahead of them. Early on September 7 the troops set out to continue their pursuit of such warriors who maintained their defiance.[76]

Whatever the soldiers thought about their opponents' intentions, at least some of the Native American leaders wanted only to signal their desire for peace. One of the Spokane Indian chiefs, educated by missionaries so that he spoke English "tolerably well," requested a meeting with Colonel Wright. Shortly afterward, he rode into Wright's camp but found that the army veteran was as blunt as his victories allowed him to be. "I have met you in two battles; you have been badly whipped; you have had several chiefs and many warriors killed or wounded; I have not lost a man or animal," Wright informed him. He then reminded the chief that he had come to fight and that the end of their resistance was inevitable, in one manner or another. Following the exchange, the colonel sent his adversary away to gather his people and spread the word that peace must be had or "war will be made on you this year and next, and until your nation shall be exterminated."[77]

At the same time, the command sought to reduce the abilities of their opponents to sustain any defiance. These efforts took the aspects of a scorched-earth policy that resulted in the confiscation or destruction of herds of Indian animals and a rich harvest of stacked wheat. One witness recorded that the soldiers took what they could use for their own purposes and burned the remainder, "so that desolation marked our tracks."[78] The commander of the expedition reported simply, "For the last eighty miles our route has been marked by slaughter and devastation; 800 horses and a large number of cattle have been killed or appropriated for our use." In addition, he illustrated the effect on food stockpiles by noting the destruction of "large quantities of wheat and oats."[79]

Over the next few weeks, the colonel met with the leaders of each of the warring tribes to compel them to come to terms. The first of the resultant agreements came at the Coeur d'Alene mission on September 17, 1858. Among the numerous witnesses and signatories to the agreement, entitled "Preliminary Articles of a Treaty of Peace and Friendship Between the United States and the Coeur D'Alene Indians," was 2nd Lieutenant W. D. Pender of the 1st Dragoons.[80]

About this time, Wright ordered and had carried out the executions of several individuals deemed to be the worst offenders during the hostilities. Keyes later recalled that he termed the location "the Camp of Death."[81] Lieutenant Pender was not present when the Yakima warrior Qualchin rode into camp on September 24 and suffered the swift and grisly fate of being hanged.[82]

Pender's absence came as a result of his involvement as a member of a detachment detailed for the difficult duty of returning to the scene of the Steptoe fighting. Lawrence Kip noted, "The party will be gone about two days, and consists of three companies of dragoons—Major Grier's, Lieutenants Gregg's and Pender's—together with Lieutenant White, with the howitzer mules to bring in the guns." The principal scribe of the expedition recorded that at about noon on September 25, the men returned to the main camp, their special and solemn mission completed. "They reached there [the Steptoe Battlefield] twelve o'clock the day before," Kip explained, finding no remaining warriors but gathering the soldiers' remains and the buried howitzers. The ground over which the fighting had taken place must have presented an eerie aspect that the men shared with their compatriots when they returned to the main camp. Kip described the "whole battle field" as "a scene of desolation," with the sun-bleached bones of the soldiers who could not be retrieved at the time of the fight "scattered around."[83]

The troopers located their fallen comrades and retrieved the buried artillery tubes. A participant noted the solemnity with which the men went about their tasks and the quiet that prevailed as they worked. He recalled that some of them secured "a pair of shafts of one of the guns" and "fashioned and framed it into a rude cross and erected it upon the ground." With this duty performed, the command "left the spot in mournful silence."[84]

On September 25 Colonel Wright reported the reunion of the recovery party with the main body, bringing with them "the remains of Capt. Taylor and Lt. Gaston who fell in the battle, and also the two howitzers abandoned by the Troops when they retreated," before proceeding to Fort Walla Walla.[85] The column reached that post on October 5, participated in a congratulatory review, and accepted the honors of a campaign, which historian Robert Utley maintained, "would feed the fond reminiscences of its participants for the rest of their lives."[86]

Only the solemn duty remained of burying the dead, as one witness explained, "with military honors, the ceremony being invested with all the pageantry which was possible, to show respect to the memory of our gallant comrades." Kip noted, "All the officers, thirty nine in number, and the troops at the post, amounting to 800 (reinforcements having arrived since our departure), were present and took part in the ceremonies." Pender would have watched the somber procession of riderless horses "draped in black, having on them the officers' swords and boots," being escorted "behind the coffins" and listened to the volleys fired over the graves in martial tribute.[87]

These final salutes were only the last tangible indications of what had been a whirlwind campaign that had thrust Dorsey Pender into the most significant combat he had yet experienced. The chance for assessment would come in the quieter days that lay ahead, but the young officer could note with satisfaction that he had performed his duties satisfactorily. He had led his men into battle and received special notice from his superiors for his efforts. He learned that he could face a dangerous opponent and remain calm and collected, even when confronted with unexpected and unwelcome developments. Prone to introspection, Pender often questioned himself but sought measures of his merit in the eyes of others. There was much from this recent service of which he could be proud, but it had also caused enormous anxiety for one who was waiting anxiously in North Carolina for word from him and was only interested in his safe return.

3

"UNEXPLORED COUNTRY"
(1858–61)

⸺•⸺

Fighting is supposed to be my profession, and my wife must get used to the idea.
—DORSEY PENDER TO FANNY

I know if any gallantries are performed, you would want
to hear of your husband getting a share of them.
—DORSEY PENDER TO FANNY

⸺•⸺

Lieutenant Pender had emerged from his trial by combat unscathed. He would shortly undertake new assignments and describe moving through an "unexplored country" to Fanny in terms that reflected the exhilaration and sense of adventure he felt as a soldier and that served, unwittingly to him perhaps, as a metaphor for his life.[1] But the challenges and dangers associated with his career were not his alone to bear. Pender may not have realized it, unless Fanny expressed herself to him in any correspondence between them that has not survived, but this active period of campaigning apparently remained etched in her mind due to the concerns she felt over his safety and the effects her fears had on her own sense of well-being.

Later Fanny's older brother Hamilton observed to Pender that her "nervousness" in "worrying" about him had first affected her health while he was engaged in Wright's punitive expedition against the Indians in 1858. The situation arose initially because, as Dorsey explained to Fanny, "you loved me and allowed it to get the better of you." He expressed his appreciation of this feature in his young bride, in retrospect, and concluded sincerely, "If ever [a] man loved and worshipped a wife, I do you."[2] Fanny would never stop worrying about him, regardless of any assurances he might offer her.

Before September was out, a flurry of requests poured into departmental headquarters by officers who wished to obtain furloughs following this period of intense action in the field. Pender sent in his paperwork alongside several others, but timing, as well as rank and seniority, did not favor his cause. One historian noted, "Lieutenant Pender requested a two-month leave for urgent business in the East and for visiting; [Captain Andrew Jackson] Smith had submitted an application previous to his, so Pender's had to wait."[3] Patience was never a strong point with the North Carolinian, but a relationship with his superior that would grow increasingly testy was not likely to have eased the sense of aggravation he experienced either. For now, he had no choice but to bide his time.

Even so, by November 1858 the toils and dangers of the Wright expedition in the Pacific Northwest must have seemed a distant memory as Pender focused on Fanny and his desire to start a life with her. At the end of the month, he wrote hurriedly to Colonel Samuel Cooper from New York to report that his "address for the next thirty days will be Tarboro, N.C."[4] In his excitement Pender must have reevaluated his timetable. He forwarded a second message the next day, adding a request for "an extension of the same until the 1st of May next."[5] He would need the extra time away from his formal duties because he was about to embark upon another journey into a different unknown. William Dorsey Pender was returning to North Carolina to wed the woman who he had loved from the time he first saw her.

Service in the distant northwestern territories had kept them apart, and further delays plagued the lovelorn officer before he could finally reach North Carolina. But clearly, Dorsey had determined that whatever the obstacles he might have to surmount, such a separation should not continue indefinitely. On February 1 he informed his superiors that he would be located at Tarboro for the month.[6] Two weeks later he also acknowledged receipt of his commission as first lieutenant.[7] His life and career were rapidly falling into place in a way he could have hardly envisioned just a few short years earlier at West Point. Indeed, the preparations for the most important event in his life outside his military career were now rapidly reaching a climax.

On March 3, 1859, Mary Frances "Fanny" Shepperd, the sister of deceased West Point classmate Samuel Turner, became William Dorsey Pender's wife following an exchange of vows at her home, Good Spring, taken before the Reverend A. H. Houghton.[8] Fanny brought to the marriage a strong personality that may have been hidden to initial acquaintances behind the social conventions of the day and a "slight" frame. But as William W. Hassler observed, she was a "firm-willed" woman. She apparently had little compunction about sharing her views with her husband, particularly on the spiritual matters that she felt were crucial to his eternal fate. Hassler noted that with this burden on her heart, Fanny "undertook to convert her irreligious husband to the Episcopal faith in which she had been raised."[9]

The bride and groom spent their first days as a married couple in Tarboro, surrounded by friends and family. Many years later an associate recalled their first meeting, "soon after his marriage at his wedding reception at his brother's residence, Robert Pender, in Tarboro." William Gaston Lewis remembered being "impressed with his very pleasant manners, and his fine military bearing." He did not record the beauty or character of the bride, but writing as he was after the war at the request of an individual who wanted to know his thoughts concerning Pender, Lewis's focus in this instance remained understandably on the groom.[10]

Another companion visited with Pender in his camp near Richmond in 1862 and recalled those happy times at Good Spring. Dorsey wrote Fanny at the time about their nostalgic reminiscences. "We talked about when I was married and he said he was sorry when the affair was over as he was enjoying himself very much." The friend remembered a woman he had met at the gathering and now told Dorsey how he continued to think about her. "It felt like old times," Pender explained somewhat wistfully, "for [his friend] Almond [Heart] was always a great favorite of mine."[11]

The Penders' honeymoon was destined to be brief, however, before the new husband's military obligations once more intruded. This time Fanny would be with him, at least as much as circumstances permitted. In any case, she would be much closer and see him more often than her presence in North Carolina had allowed. In addition to Fanny, Pender planned to bring with them a personal servant, Laura Smith, apparently for the purpose of assisting his wife.[12]

Dorsey Pender's relationship with individual slaves and the institution of slavery seemed to have been more of a casual and practical one than his relatives in North Carolina experienced. His transient military existence prevented him from settling down in such a way as to require intimate contact with slaves. Laura was a case in point. Until his marriage, Pender's life as a bachelor junior officer on the frontier was of necessity spartan. He had no need of slaves or personal body servants and was making an insufficient income to allow for the purchase or maintenance of such labor in any case. Initially, in his letter seeking an extension of his furlough in March 1859, he referred to Laura as a "servant" and then clarified her status more accurately to that of "a slave."[13] Yet if he was imprecise concerning her status, he was growing increasingly comfortable in his own as a master. In one of his first wartime letters to Fanny in April 1861, he applauded her decision to punish Laura by whipping her and assured his wife paternalistically, "you may tell her for me that if she does not mind she will get a good one from me when I get there."[14] Yet there was no malice evident in this case or afterward toward Laura specifically or slaves in general. Pender appeared to have looked upon such persons as the time period and contemporary attitudes called for him to do and considered them to be childlike and in need of his guidance. If this meant being reminded of and encouraged to submit to authority, then that would have to be done without remorse or regret. This was the social context in which he operated and that colored his views of the world around him.

By mid-March the entourage was in the nation's capital, but Pender learned to his chagrin that the outbound transportation for New Orleans had "sailed two days sooner than I supposed." If he was perturbed at himself for miscalculating the steamer's departure or at having to make another request for an additional two weeks to straighten out the situation, he still hoped to be back at duty only "about ten days after my present leave will have expired."[15]

The wayfarers finally left Washington, D.C., on April 5, 1859, bound for the distant territory to which Pender had been stationed now for the better part of three years. They would soon have another addition to the family with the birth of Samuel Turner Pender on November 28, 1859, named in honor of Fanny's deceased brother and Dorsey's West Point colleague and close friend.[16]

By June 25 the extended leave of absence that had embraced what surely must have seemed an excessively brief honeymoon ended as Lieutenant Pender reported for duty at Fort Walla Walla. Over the next several months, he would be absent from the post while on detached duty and in September became so ill as to cause him to relinquish his command for a time. Pender recovered from the sickness, but in early October he transferred to Fort Vancouver.[17]

When the year 1860 opened, Pender was at Vancouver as part of the installation's regular garrison. His status as first lieutenant continued until late March, when the post commander, Andrew Jackson Smith, had to travel to Fort Dalles to sit on a court of inquiry. Pender accepted temporary command of the company in Smith's absence, but by April 14 the captain was back and the lieutenant returned to his regular duties. Within another month, Pender would leave the post under special orders from the Department of Oregon for another active assignment in the field.[18]

Through this whirlwind of activities and momentous personal milestones for Dorsey Pender, there were also significant changes in the complexion of the military department to which he was attached. The newly created Department of Oregon came under the command of William S. Harney, an Indian fighter noted for aggressiveness and ruthlessness.[19] The general had reached Fort Vancouver on October 24, 1858, just after Pender hastened to North Carolina and his marriage to Fanny. Harney soon found himself as much at odds with his own lieutenants, the Hudson's Bay Company, and the British, as with hostile Native Americans.

Pender's focus was fortunately on more pleasant pursuits while his department became embroiled in a controversy over disputed territory with Great Britain. The San Juan Island crisis threatened the cordial relations between the countries that had developed slowly after the War of 1812. Harney and his principal subordinate, Captain George Pickett, were determined to enforce their claim of the disputed region as solely American, even to the point of arms. Although cooler heads managed to prevail, the situation remained volatile, and Harney's recalcitrant attitude prompted his dismissal from the department.[20]

Pender had been absent through much of Harney's controversial tenure and on detached service at the end of it. Even so, in the small world that was the Regular Army in those days, a commander's reputation was bound to be well known by all. In addition, with threats of Indian troubles continuing, the necessity of a military response remained high. In late June 1860 Pender observed in a letter to Fanny, "I hope Gen. Harney will have left for the states before this [letter] gets in, and then I think Col. Wright would do up this affair quickly and effectually."[21]

The lieutenant's wish for a change in command was realized shortly afterward when his old superior, George Wright, assumed authority of the department on July 5. The veteran commander entered into a volatile situation brought about when disgruntled Snake River Indians caused sufficient difficulties to warrant military attention. Wright was prepared to oblige as he had done earlier in 1858, and Pender could once again expect to take a part in the expedition.[22]

The circumstances were very different for Pender as he engaged in this new Indian campaign in the Oregon Territory. As a bachelor he had looked at combat as a part of his duties without much thought on the potential ramifications for others. Now as a husband and new father, he must have faced this duty with both a sense of exhilaration and concern, for his fate affected the lives of his wife and child directly. In the course of his detached service, Dorsey sent letters back to Fanny as often as he could as a means of staying connected with her. In each instance he tried to make them informative yet reassuring to the wife who waited so anxiously for his return. On the one hand, he wanted her to know the kind of warrior that he was, brave in the face of danger and true to his men and mission, a worthy and worthwhile choice for a husband. On the other, he did not want her to worry unduly as to what might happen to him as he rode into skirmishes or across the vast country in which innumerable dangers might lie in wait for him. It was the delicate kind of balancing act that he would follow for the rest of his life when his obligations carried him onto hostile fields.

In this campaign the command mostly followed trails already blazed, but the young officer seemed particularly pleased by the notion that a portion of the expedition allowed him to trailblaze new paths. "We have been over fifty miles of unexplored country just now," Pender explained to Fanny on June 19. "Emigrants were through this country in 45," he added, contradicting the ideal he had just established for his wife, "and I suppose after trying all the routs [sic] have come to the conclusion that the usual route by Snake river is the best. They were guided in former times by old trappers & if there had been such merits in this route they would undoubtedly have chosen it." Still, for the purposes of this expedition, the choice seemed to be a sound one. "The grass & water so far has been very good, and our animals look as well, the mules better, than when we started."[23]

Dorsey knew better than to express too much open satisfaction at being apart from his new bride. He was quick to assure her that for all of the adventure, the commander of the expedition "is as anxious to get back to [Fort] Vancouver as I am." But the relationship that troubled him most was not between himself and Fanny, it was with his superior, Captain A. J. Smith. Lieutenant Pender seemed to have anticipated at least the possibility of a conflict from the outset. In his first letter from the field to his wife, he noted that the captain would "be out tonight," apparently joining the operation already in progress. "Do not fear any trouble between us," he tried to assure her. "I shall try to have as little to say & do [with him] on this trip as possible."[24]

But in a month's time, undoubtedly under the stresses and strains of the extended tour of duty, an eruption between the officers occurred. "The Captain pitched into me the other day," Dorsey reported to Fanny, "but I gave him as good as he sent & since we have been on the best of terms." The deterioration of relations between the men had been coming. "Previous [to] that time he had slighted my position—which I told him some time ago—never seeming to be pleased [and] never letting me know what he was going to do, never consulting me, or any other recognition of my position," Pender explained. "I told him he had treated me injustly [sic]." Fortunately for the junior officer, this confrontation ended with a positive result. Pender was able to add, "But now he is like his old self agreeable, tells me his plans, etc."[25]

Still, if relations between some of the officers were becoming more "agreeable," the distance Dorsey felt from Fanny was excruciating. "I know you must feel lonely for I do even when stirring around with company," he confessed.[26] To lessen the pain of the separation somewhat, he carried a photographic image of her with him. "Oh! darling you know not what a pleasure looking at your likeness gives me. It is almost like looking at your self." Of course, reality offered less solace. "If I could see that self," the trooper ventured wistfully, "but we must make the best of it." At any rate, he was convinced that their reunion would be all the sweeter. "We will love each other, enjoy the company of each other so much the more when we meet." Indeed, even the "dear boy" Turner would "have to stand in the back ground for a good long time."[27]

The loneliness had not subsided two days later when Pender wrote from his camp on the Columbia River. He waxed eloquently about his love for Fanny and her "superior" qualities of "goodness . . . intelligence youth & beauty." He could ask for nothing else in a spouse and promised to keep his letters coming, "for whenever I get particularly lonely I shall keep company with my little girl by means of writing." Such solicitation was undoubtedly the mark of a young marriage, but Dorsey also was concerned that even so short a time after the birth of Turner, Fanny might be with child once more. He offered a thinly veiled reference to an earlier "query as to your probable condition" but said nothing more revealing about the subject for the moment.[28] Subsequently, he continued that line of inquiry in the same oblique fashion, asking Fanny to write him often and tell him "all about yourself, how strong you are, whether you have grown any further, what you do, etc."[29]

Even with these concerns, after a month on duty away from her, Pender was finally beginning to enjoy a sense of personal equilibrium. "I took our seperation to [sic] much to heart," he admitted in June, "for we must get to bear it patiently, for it will come, and in the state of mind that I have been in

I could not do my duty propperly [sic], and neither of us want the dear wife to interfere with that."

The example of the infidelity of one officer's wife rankled Pender particularly. "She ought to be burnt & quartered," he exclaimed harshly through a mix of colorful punishment metaphors, "for after every thing else to have abused the confidence of a brother officer." The indiscretion was all the worse for the wedge that it threatened to drive into a small cadre of officers. "We of all others ought to protect each other's wives, having to place confidence in each other," he observed. "It seems to me, if I were in [that officer's] place, I should go crazy, after first commiting [sic] murder."

Whatever marital difficulties others might experience, Dorsey knew that Fanny worried most about his health and well-being. He took especial pains to let her know that although his "fair" was "a little different from what my dear wife use[d] to fix for me," he was reasonably well situated in that regard. Even in the remote territory through which they marched, there was sufficient food for the men. "A good appetite for eating, smoking, & sleeping, what more?" he asked rhetorically. Of course, there remained some appetites for which gratification would have to continue to be delayed. "Oh! at night how I would like to have you, even between my rough blankets & hug you to my heart."[30]

By the end of June, Pender had news of a different nature to convey to Fanny, still waiting anxiously for him at Fort Vancouver. The command had experienced combat, albeit a small and inconsequential skirmish. Dorsey explained that "on the 23rd just as we were getting into Camp about one hundred & fifty [warriors came] down upon us with whoops & yells. About sixty were mounted & the rest on foot." For all of the attendant chaos, there were few casualties in the fight and none among the troopers themselves. "We killed one of them certain & we think three, several wounded, captured six horses & killed one," he cataloged. "Our men were all very enthusiastic," he related, but with responsibility "to defend our train," Pender had to exert his greatest energies at restraining the men "from following the Indians too far."

The fight had been of short duration, but Pender's verve in telling the story indicated that he viewed the action as a significant milestone in his military career. Nevertheless, he also recognized the anxiety that the tale would engender in Fanny's mind. "Do not be alarmed, for we are in no danger," he wrote her about his confrontation with the Indian warriors, "for even if they choose to fight any more, they have but few poor guns & we have arms that will kill five hundred yards away." Pender added quickly, "I forgot to say we got their guns, arrows, powder, balls, etc." Still, he could not exactly contain himself. "We have as brave an[d] gallant set of men as ever fought Indians," he observed, brimming at the memory of the engagement. "You ought to have heard the shouts when an Indian would be hit or turn & run." Even the lieutenant's bodyservant had gotten into the fray. "Jim was as cool as possible going around with a carbine [and] making them scatter."

Yet Dorsey knew that Fanny would be "alarmed" at the potential for danger. This prompted him to remind her: "While in the army one had better do his own duty whatever it may be, and he will have the approval at least of his own conscience. I know my wife too well to think that she would like to see me shirking hardship or even danger when it becomes necessary to encounter them." He closed his observations on this matter with a mild rebuke at any such reticence on her part for him. "Darling do not trouble yourself about the Indians. Fighting is supposed to be my profession, and my wife must get used to the idea."[31]

The duality expressed in this letter remained a hallmark of the correspondence Dorsey carried out with Fanny throughout their lives together. He preferred to recount whatever was on his mind, sometimes with excruciating honesty and insight, yet also sought to mitigate her concerns and fears. For him, combat was a test; for her, it was the potential for his death or injury. "Don't fear darling that I shall not take good care of myself, for besides the happiness of my precious wife, selfish motives would make me do so, I have too much happiness ahead to willingly give it up. I only fear it may make me to [sic] anxious, for I know if any gallantries are to be performed, you would want to hear of your husband getting a share of them."[32] Of course, had she the opportunity to exert her will on the situation, she would assuredly pass on his honor as a soldier to have him safely back in her arms.

Pender was certainly concerned about his own conduct and how others would perceive it. Nevertheless, his desire to see his wife, even for a short duration, prompted him to ask for a leave, "to go in, so I might see you," but his nemesis Captain Smith denied the request on the grounds that "he wants my services here." On second thought, Dorsey explained, he regretted making the request, concluding that his superior "was right in refusing" and adding that in any case, "I dislike the idea of giving him the chance to refuse me." Pender's common sense also dictated that a journey of "six hundred miles through Indian Country" would be unwise. Again he counseled patience, as much to himself as to her, and assured Fanny of his "loving devotion."[33]

Pender thought he could predict the end of an active campaigning season approaching. "Cheer up my darling wife," he wrote at the beginning of August, "and try to stand the remaining two months." There was always still the possibility of danger, but he hoped that his own sense of confidence would bolster hers. "Do not be alarmed about my safety," he reminded her once more. "If for no other reason my wife would be sufficient to prevent my rashly running into danger, but that is not my nature." Then Dorsey noted, without an apparent understanding of any contradiction, "If I may be allowed to claim any one merit it is prudence & coolness in an emergency." In a resigned sense of consolation, he concluded, "We are strong, too strong I fear to meet the Indians for they will never meet soldiers unless they think they are superior."[34]

While he waited to engage any adversaries he might encounter, Pender continued to try to regulate the affairs of his wife and family from a distance. He was a paternalist who could not help worrying about Fanny's ability to function without him. But she was clearly learning to conduct matters in his absence and simultaneously demonstrating an aptitude for such matters that Dorsey alternately admired and rejected. "Darling accept my apology for not giving you as much credit as you deserve as a financier," he noted on August 1. This was just another of her "superior qualities," he added, "for in good course you have managed the money affairs better than I could have done."[35]

The lieutenant was forwarding his pay vouchers to his wife. Even so, he still could not quite reconcile himself to this new order of things, dictated by his absence in the field. "But do not trouble yourself about any of these matters," he explained two days later, "for I do not want my wife to be a business woman."[36]

Pender remained vitally concerned about his reputation and saw Fanny as a reflection upon himself, as her husband, more than anything else. "Honey I am glad you do not dance the fancy dances with any one but myself putting his arm around your waist." His attitude was less a matter of social convention than an indication of his own insecurity. "I do not think the less of other ladies doing these things, but prefer your not doing so," he stated firmly. "One thing [is] certain Capt. Smith must never do it again. That I am determined upon." Pender would always be a man of contradictions, as his later behavior in a similar setting would reveal, but he placed Fanny on a pedestal that he often felt put her out of his reach and simultaneously sought to exercise control over her as much as circumstances would allow. His aspiration to be worthy of her drove him, but he could not think of himself in a framework that sacrificed the position he saw as the dominant figure in the home.

When Fanny's younger sister, Pamela, was confirmed in the church, the act created an internal discourse for Dorsey that was as problematic as it was promising. As he did so frequently, he shared this feeling with Fanny. "I only wish I were fit to [do] the same," he told her. "Darling I try very hard to be good. I want to be a comfort and assistance to you instead of a draw back." For him, Fanny was also a religious ideal. "A Christian woman," he explained, "is the most Heavenly of earthly creatures."[37] But he could not shake his vices entirely, as when he noted that he wished for Fanny to express his appreciation "for the tobacco" that a colleague had sent him.[38]

Still, Pender found himself occupied fully with his duties while in the field, and these consumed much of his time and attention. He allowed Fanny to intrude into that space, though usually for the purpose of confirming his status for her. Although the year featured a presidential election that would prove enormously important in his life and for the nation, Pender's focus remained confined to a narrower sphere. His prewar letters contained no angry diatribes against the rising Republican Party, the abolitionists, or anyone else involved in the growing sectional rift. There was no talk of what he would do if the nation came apart in some manner. Only once did he offer a political remark, and that proved to be quite cryptic. On that occasion, Pender and a recently arrived officer "spent a very pleasant day chatting on every imaginable subject." He offered nothing of substance to illustrate these discussions except to say that they had involved "[p]rincipally politics."[39] It may have been simply that Dorsey did not wish to bother Fanny with political details or his opinions on them. Certainly, despite the remoteness of the region in which he served from affairs happening east of the Mississippi River, politics in the northwest proved as volatile and energetically embraced there as elsewhere during this turbulent period.[40]

To be sure, Pender tried to remain connected to matters outside his sphere of immediate operations. In addition to addressing other needs, he requested of Fanny, "if you have a late Harper's Monthly or a novel put them up [to me] also." He thought another returning colleague could "bring out plenty" of newspapers, and these should be sufficient to satiate his appetite for current events.[41] She must have been able to respond satisfactorily, for in the next letter, he expressed his appreciation to her for sending him a "bundle" and "how thankful I felt for the Harpers."[42] Before long, he asked her to discontinue the practice, "for I shall have no chance to read them," and as an afterthought that had not occurred to him before, "it was subscribed to for you."[43]

Fortunately for the newlyweds, two elements were conspiring to shorten the amount of time they would remain away from each other. The first of these concerned the state of the command as Pender assessed it, particularly with regard to supplies. The second related to the inability of the troops to engage an elusive enemy. Both meant that a sustained campaigning effort would prove difficult and unproductive.

"We leave here [on] the 21st for another scout," Lieutenant Pender explained to his wife on August 18, quickly adding for her peace of mind, "but as it is homeward feel impatient to start." Even with orders to remain in the field, practical considerations were going to dictate a short duration for the campaign. "Our provisions are out on the 20th Sept. so you see we can not stay out longer," Pender observed optimistically. The condition of the men was also deteriorating, and this would not be an element that could be ignored indefinitely. "Great many of our men are barefooted & ragged, in a general state of dilapidation," he observed with an eye to the effects of such developments on the state of their combat effectiveness.

Hostile warriors also appeared to have vanished. "We have not been able to find the Indians, & do not expect to do so," Pender explained. "They seem to have seperated [sic] into families living in the bushes & rocks." Even the cordial relations he had cultivated with his superior were experiencing renewed tension. "Capt. Smith goes in command of this scout, very much to our disgust. He is looked upon by every one as exceedingly weak, but as we old sort expect to find the Indians he will do as well as any one else, and probably better." Still, he assured Fanny, "I get on quietly enough," and added a sense of the success of his newly developed interpersonal skills. "I have not had a cross word with the Captain in over a month so you see I am practicing phylosophy [sic]."[44]

Pender was anxious to please his spouse and inquired about her and their son regularly, though always in a manner that returned the focus on him. Regularly, he couched his comments in personal terms. "I spoke of the sickness of the men, do not let it trouble you so far as I am concerned for I was never better in my life."[45] Dorsey Pender's universe remained largely centered wherever he happened to be and on matters that concerned him most directly.

Finally in late August, the roving soldier returned to Fort Vancouver and his family. On September 18 they relocated to Fort Walla Walla.[46] A month later the lieutenant received an assignment that must have made his wife's mind even easier. The post returns for October placed Pender's name under the heading "Transferred" and listed him as "Appointed Adj. of the Regt. accepted and left post Oct. 23rd 60 to join Hd. Qrs. at Fort Tejon, Cal."[47] Even this stopover at his old station was brief, for on November 8, when he assumed the role as the chief administrative officer of the 1st Dragoons, he relocated to San Francisco.[48]

One of the responsibilities for which Pender now rode a desk rather than a horse was recruiting for the unit. On November 27 he requested the sum of four hundred dollars for that purpose, which he thought would carry him through the remainder of the year.[49] Although his effectiveness in fulfilling his duties in a volatile national environment would be difficult to assess, he remembered some of his associates from these brief days in California with a mixture of both pleasure and thinly veiled contempt.

The election of 1860 served as a context for Pender as he continued his recruitment efforts and paperwork. Four candidates competed for the country's highest office, but a split between Democrats supporting Stephen Douglas and John C. Breckinridge, in addition to moderates who embraced Constitutional Unionist John Bell, assured that they would not garner enough support to win. The elevation of the Republican presidential candidate, Abraham Lincoln, threatened to render moot any plans Pender might have for himself in the nation's service. But it was another of the Carolinas—South Carolina—that pushed the crisis to a head when the leading lights of a state convention passed an ordinance of secession on December 20, 1860, in response to the election results. Within a month, five more states in the Deep South had joined the Palmetto State in departing from the Union, and others seemed likely to follow, although the fate of North Carolina was much less certain.

At the end of January 1861, Pender once more found himself compelled to move.[50] This time the transfer was supposed to take him back across the Mississippi to the famed Carlisle Barracks in Pennsylvania. There he would be involved in cavalry instruction, in which, no doubt, his West Point training—he had done well in cavalry tactics after all—and his subsequent combat experience would be expected to come in handy in polishing and shaping the recruits assembled there.

But Dorsey Pender was not due to carry out instruction to recruits, at least in Pennsylvania, for national events were rapidly reconfiguring the career he had built for himself. Eloquent and quietly forceful, President Lincoln's inaugural address struck a chord with many white Southerners, though not the one he had intended. With references that rejected the notion that any individual state could decide "upon its own mere motion, [that it] can lawfully go out of the Union," he dismissed the instruments of *"resolves* and *ordinances"* as "legally void" and labeled as "insurrectionary or revolutionary" any associated "acts of violence." For Lincoln, "the momentous issue of civil war" passed to the "dissatisfied countrymen" of the seceded states.[51]

Although Pender seemed not to have made a habit of expressing himself extensively in any public forum on current political events, he recognized the difficulties of fulfilling the obligations of his military duty to the nation while remaining true to North Carolina and the South. Son Samuel Turner insisted that his father did not choose his side in the growing sectional rift "until, on a visit to his father-in-law, he read President Lincoln's proclamation [the inaugural address]" and thereby resolved his own course of action.[52] But a letter that posted from High Point, North Carolina, on March 4, the same date Lincoln offered his inaugural comments, contained an apology for being "hurried off so unceremoniously" as Pender headed toward Montgomery, Alabama. There the representatives of the new Southern republics were gathering to determine a combined course of action and encourage other states to join them in their historic enterprise.[53]

It was not until March 9, 1861, that Pender informed Colonel Lorenzo Thomas that he would not be reporting for duty in compliance with his orders from the national government. "I have the honor to say in justice to myself that when I asked and obtained permission to delay reporting in person at Carlisle, Pa., I fully intended to report," he explained to Thomas. Political developments had altered the situation, however, and challenged his ability to conform to his initial intentions. For Pender, "the course the President has indicated he shall pursue renders it impossible for me to serve in any position that may at any time bring me into deadly conflict with that section of the Country to which I belong." Yet the ever-sensitive Pender was less concerned that his superior chide him for leaving the Regular Army, potentially to engage in a rebellion against it, than to be clear that the colonel understand, "I did not obtain a leave from you under false pretenses."[54] Thus, he cast his own die with the Confederacy. Even earlier than others who faced the same dilemma of remaining in the Old Army or resigning from it in the aftermath of the firing on Fort Sumter, William Dorsey Pender had made his decision.

Neither indecision nor doubt plagued Pender at this critical moment. From North Carolina, on the same day he wrote Colonel Thomas, the lieutenant dashed off a hasty note to serve as official notice of his intentions to Secretary of War Simon Cameron. "I have the honor hereby to tender the resignation of my Commission in the United States Army," he wrote the secretary of war, jettisoning any of the promise his career had held in that service.[55] The North Carolinian was anxious to carve out a place for himself in the unfolding drama.

Even as he embodied a high level of enthusiasm, Pender knew well that he was engaged in a risky enterprise. To his wife and confidant, he noted: "I shall never regret resigning, whatever may turn up. I felt now as I felt then, that I could not serve the U.S.A."[56] Pender may have experienced "a pang of regret at the severance of many dear and tender ties" to his Old Army friends and compatriots, as Samuel Turner Pender later insisted of his father, but the soldier followed the dictates of his choice without any real hesitation.[57] The post reports for Carlisle Barracks substantiate the timeline that Pender had followed, listing him under "absent" on the March 1861 report but noting: "W. D. Pender, 1st Lieut., 1st Dgns. Since March 14, 1861, without leave."[58] As he had earlier observed in closing his communication to the commander at Carlisle, he was now, "W. D. Pender, late [of the] U.S.A."[59]

4

A "LION" ROARS
(March–June 1861)

•———•

Dined to day with the most beautiful girl in Suffolk—
and it has [a] great many very pretty ones.
—COLONEL WILLIAM DORSEY PENDER

The Colonel is quite a lion.
—WILLIAM DORSEY PENDER ABOUT HIMSELF

•———•

In the spring of 1861, Dorsey Pender found himself in danger of languishing in the backwater of any conflict that might emerge despite the bold action he had taken in resigning his commission before his state had left the Union. He tried to remedy this situation by first traveling to Raleigh to see Governor John W. Ellis in the hopes of obtaining a field command. He then left for the capital of the newly developing Confederate nation at Montgomery, Alabama, to offer his services to Secretary of War Leroy Pope Walker. For a time it looked as if Pender would be a captain of infantry, a promise he seemed to have received orally, at least. The commission would be worth $1,350 annually, and he assured Fanny, "I shall be pretty well up the list of captains."

But the infantry held little allure for Pender, nor surprisingly did the cavalry, given his prewar service in the dragoons. Perhaps because of the years he had spent in the saddle on the frontier, Pender claimed in a letter to his wife, "I applied for the Artillery, not wanting to go in the mounted service any more, preferring to be more stationary." He undoubtedly forgot how much he had once longed to obtain a transfer from the "stationary" artillery posting he had held at Fort Myers, Florida, fresh out of West Point. But he certainly recognized the benefits of his education at the academy and the status that education brought. "They are giving all graduates the first places," he explained to Fanny. He was deeply worried that he might be left behind, for practical reasons as much as for political ones, telling his wife, "I began to think of where bread was to come from." But then Pender rallied and was "once more himself" when friends gave him assurances that all would come right in the end. "They say I got here in the nick of time," he observed, "as they are very busy making out appointments to day."[1]

Pender remained busy himself, while North Carolina remained in the Union. As one historian has noted of the Old North State during this transitional period, "North Carolinians were disturbed about national events, although they had no clear vision of what action they should take."[2] Pender's "vision" was much clearer, and this was in part because he saw his prospects as better under the Confederate banner than that of the Union. This was not to say that he calculated everything in terms of self-interest, but that element was a critical factor in his thought processes and decision making.

A biographer of the general noted that another historian's insistence that Pender demonstrated himself through his statements to be "an eager secessionist and ardent Confederate" could not be "farther from the truth."[3] Yet Pender exhibited tremendous passions and often shifted his arguments from the one pole of enthusiasm to the opposite one of depression on subjects that ranged from the South as a whole to North Carolina in particular and, of course, to himself.

Another scholar described Pender's "articulation of nationalism and allegiance to the Confederacy" as reflective of "sentiments and reactions shared by other Southern soldiers."[4] Of course, Pender could have been a "nationalist" or "ardent secessionist" who saw the threat to the Confederate nation or the South as paramount and sought to defend it. He could also have been a "state's rights advocate" who preferred to focus on North Carolina above all else. Pender surely did not "want to see his country ripped apart by war" and desired "to defend his native state," as Edward Longacre has maintained, but he just as clearly did not see his state's fortunes, or his own, outside of the context of the Confederate States of America, which had so recently come into being and toward which he now so eagerly sought to attach his fortunes.[5]

If family connections could shed any light on sentiment, a tricky proposition during this conflict especially, descriptions of Dorsey's older brother David suggested that strong feelings for Southern rights were not out of the question. Letters composed by at least two advocates of David Pender's efforts to secure a position were unequivocal in their establishment of his pro-

Southern credentials. Dorsey's elder brother and sometime patron, David apparently held strong views with regard to the South and state's rights. In late 1861 one individual termed him as "an original Southern rights man and not a latter day convert."[6] Another characterized the elder brother as "an original member of the Southern rights party."[7] It should be noted that such comments came from individuals promoting David's services to Confederate officials and thus ought to be viewed appropriately. Certainly, such expressions of one brother would not confirm automatically that another held the same positions with similar intensity. Nevertheless, the elder Pender had a continuing influence and role in his younger brother's life, and a similarity in viewpoints ought not be dismissed entirely.

Nothing in Dorsey Pender's makeup or subsequent actions suggested that he held a contrary position. Indeed, within a month he seemed absolutely sure concerning his stance on Southern patriotism. "Enclosed I send you the Flag of the Confederate States," he wrote Fanny on April 3. "That is our Flag, for it is yours as much as mine and by it you must stick." Pender expected indications from his wife of political solidarity too. "Own to me Darling," he implored, "that you are a Democrat." Should she make this assurance, he promised, "You have no idea what satisfaction it would be to have you say [so]."[8]

Unlike the time on the northwestern frontier when Dorsey Pender had been occupied with trying to establish himself in his career and create a life with Fanny, larger political issues now began to take on greater significance. As would be the case throughout the secession crisis and the war, Pender placed his focus on such events largely through the prism of his native state. "I am delighted to hear that N.C. has gone for a convention to give the state [a] chance, if nothing else," he observed to Fanny in March.[9] In this instance his knowledge was limited and out of date, for although the state legislature put forward a referendum on the question of a secession convention in January, the voters defeated it in a close outcome in late February.[10] In the same balloting, unionist delegates to the proposed convention outpolled secessionists, seventy-eight to forty-two.[11] North Carolina's "chance" would have to wait.

Regardless of what North Carolina might do or to which branch of the service or specific unit the Confederate military authorities assigned him, Pender assured his wife that he would be alright. In the case of an unacceptable choice, he could always resign from any unit if he felt compelled to do so, although "I hope & believe that will not take place, for the few days that I have been a civilian have rather put a damper on my notion of civil life." Whatever prospects he faced as a soldier, they were bound to exceed any he could expect as a private citizen. "The idea of no money & no way to make any is not very pleasant," he concluded logically enough. At any rate, he promised not to "regret" what he had done to this point.[12]

With his mind set firmly, Pender notified Secretary Walker of his availability. "I have the honor to state that I have recently resigned my Commission as 1st Lieut. in the U.S. Army," he explained, "and to apply for an appointment in the army (Artillery Corps preferred) of the C.S.A." In the event that the secretary had not been able to peruse the Old Army files, he informed Walker that his service had not been without distinction. "I beg leave to state that I have been mentioned three times for conduct in Indian engagements." Furthermore, if the brave commission of one's duties in the face of the enemy were not enough, there was the fact that he had not waited for his home state to leave the Union. "I would also state that I am from North Carolina and resigned my Commission March 9th 61, and graduated at West Point in 1854."[13]

Pender's focus was understandably on the choice he had made. A bit more perspective might have reminded him that he was actually one of a number of similarly positioned individuals now seeking a new line of work. A student of North Carolinian West Pointers noted that "sixteen resigned their commissions in the United States Army when war became imminent to cast their lots with the state to which they were accredited."[14] In more ways than one, Pender was among friends, though he also had significant competition for whatever positions might be available for such men.

Pender had additional support in trying to obtain a place for himself in the Confederate forces from other key figures, including his father-in-law, Congressman Shepperd, and family friend Robert R. Bridgers. Indeed, Bridgers knew Pender well. The Tarboro native could speak extensively concerning the young man's qualities and did so in a letter to Thomas Ruffin at about the same time. He reported Pender's desire "for an office in the army of the Southern Confederation" and verified the North Carolinian's qualifications, "if he should apply." Bridgers noted the officer's resignation and "past service" as indicators of his willingness to adhere himself to the new nation. "He has been in the army U.S. about eight years has been in active service on the Pacific the most of the time and has some good fighting in some of the Indian Campaigns." Calling him "the youngest officer in the recruiting service [at the time of his resignation]," Bridgers added that Pender "has a very good mind, and excellent habits and more than an ordinary reputation for drilling new recruits.[15] This last characterization was bound to be appreciated by anyone who recognized the skills needed by the Confederate States in creating its armed forces. Citizens could not become good soldiers unless they received adequate training and preparation.

North Carolina governor John Ellis also threw his weight into the question of an assignment for the young officer. In a letter to President Jefferson Davis, the governor stated: "It affords me pleasure to bear testimony to the high character of Lt. P. as a gentleman and an officer. He is a product of West Point and has served since that time, with credit to himself in the U.S. Army."[16] All in all, Pender could not have asked for, nor genuinely expected, better support for his entry into Confederate service.

As Pender had surmised, the timing was propitious, for he received a letter from the Confederate War Department that bestowed upon him a commission as captain of artillery to take effect on March 16, 1861. The appointment represented a significant elevation in rank from his previous standing that nevertheless propelled him back to the branch of service he had left behind so hastily at the advent of his U.S. Army career. Still, he was enthusiastic about his new assignment. As stipulated, he immediately notified Adjutant General Samuel Cooper of his acceptance, proudly signing the letter with the new rank beneath his name.[17]

Pender was satisfied to have the waiting over and the promise of a salaried position providing him with even more income than he would have received as a captain of infantry. The new artillery captain expected to leave for Pensacola, Florida, momentarily, a development he professed to welcome when compared to remaining in the chaotic hubbub of Montgomery. He promised to forward some money to his wife in Salem, North Carolina, as soon as he received his pay and assured her that his income "in these hard times" would be better than what he might have done in "commencing on a small scale raising stock."

For Dorsey Pender, soldiering was preferable to ranching, farming, or working in a store, however much he might grumble. There were also the tangential benefits that came with all of the excitement he claimed to disdain and the attention he reveled in receiving. "I have been treated with great politeness by every one," he told Fanny sincerely, reflecting a concern he would continue to have regarding the opinion of others toward him.

For the moment, at least, Pender's status seemed to be assured and provided him with a sufficient indication of his worth to the new nation. In addition to his training and former service, he attributed the attention he was receiving to the zeal with which he had embraced the Southern cause. "I rather put a feather in my cap by resigning so promptly. They have at least given me a good position."[18]

Fanny remained worried that hostilities might occur that would once more put her husband in danger. Dorsey tried to assuage her fears. "In the first place we have no war as yet," he explained accurately enough, "and if we do I should have been in it whether I had come here or not." His proximity to Montgomery was not the issue, he was trying to tell her. "Bred to the profession I could not have had the courage to have stood by without taking a hand," he observed, in much the way he had once described himself and their relationship when he served in Washington Territory just after they were married.[19]

Whatever his new station might be, Pender remained a paternalist, feeling a strong sense of responsibility for his wife and son. He chafed at having to attempt to fulfill that duty from afar but felt bound to exert such control over domestic affairs as he believed society dictated. Fanny was at her family's home in Salem, but he felt that she still needed his guiding hand, even in matters over which she had the best perspective. This was especially true when it came to servants. "Do not let Laura get the upper hand of you," he instructed, "recollect [that] she comes of a hard headed race."[20] Without Fanny's original letter, it is difficult to know what sparked this advice, but clearly Dorsey felt the need to express it as he did. In this he did not differ significantly from the planter who sought a tractable and docile workforce.

As it turned out, the stationary life of a seacoast artillerist was not how Pender was destined to serve the fledgling Confederate States of America. On the same day that he speculated about his transfer, he received word that the secretary of war had changed his mind and wanted the North Carolinian to "remain" in Montgomery "for the present." He took the time that evening to compose a short note to Fanny, letting her know about the change, and prepared to await further developments.[21]

Yet any disappointment he may have felt about not moving from the isolated Southern capital proved minimal. Only a few days later, he received an assignment that must have struck him as both intriguing and perplexing: the Confederate government planned to send him to Baltimore, Maryland, on a surreptitious mission to inspect and forward recruits for the Southern forces.

Deemed by one modern historian as "the strangest, and most successful," of the Confederate recruiting efforts in the Upper South, the Baltimore initiative sprang from the imaginative mind of a U.S. senator from Texas, Louis T.

Wigfall.²² Pender became the ranking military figure on the scene, receiving his orders on March 21 from Adjutant General Cooper. "You will proceed with as little delay as practicable to Baltimore, Md., on duties connected with the military service," Cooper instructed. The adjutant general reminded the captain that he was to be "governed by the verbal instructions already communicated to you by the Secretary of War."²³ With Maryland's own fate in the Union remaining an open question, the assignment would have to be carried out with the utmost delicacy.

Cooper and the War Department were prepared to render such assistance as they could to the North Carolinian on his covert mission. On the same day Cooper cut Pender's orders, Secretary of War Walker requested that Senator Wigfall remain in the Washington, D.C., area for the time being rather than hasten to Montgomery. "Although it would be most agreeable to have you here," the war secretary explained to the politician, "it occurs to me that you could render more efficient service by remaining in Baltimore until our recruiting depot is fully and successfully established as an institution." For that purpose, he informed the Texan that he was dispatching a young and energetic officer. "Captain Pender, the officer to be sent from here to inspect and superintend the shipment of the men, is directed to place himself under your orders, and will remain in Baltimore for some weeks." Wigfall was to be responsible for the logistics of the operation, including providing any funds Pender "may require within the scope of his business."²⁴

Adjutant General Cooper passed word of Walker's plans to Brigadier General Pierre Gustave Toutant Beauregard in Charleston on the same day. "I am instructed by the Secretary of War to inform you that Capt. William D. Pender, of the Corps of Artillery, has been sent to Baltimore, Md., to direct the recruiting service in that city, whose duty it will be to have every recruit examined and passed by a medical officer previously to his being accepted [into Confederate service.]" In addition, Pender was responsible for transferring acceptable prospects "from time to time as they accumulate" to Charleston, where they were to be "enlisted into the Army of the Confederate States" and brought in to augment the forces already gathered there.²⁵

By March 24, Pender was in the volatile city in the divided border state, which if it chose to leave the Union, might seal the fate of Washington, D.C. Of course, regardless of the actions Maryland might take concerning its political future, Pender went there to secure recruits for Southern military service. One of his first tasks was the transfer of funds for supporting his mission.

On March 25 he obtained a receipt from the president of the Baltimore Steam Packet Company for payment of $975 made to cover the costs associated with the "transportation of Sixty-five men from Balt. Md. to Charleston S.C."[26] Whatever else might be said of Pender, Cooper must have appreciated his desire to complete the appropriate paperwork for military expenditures made in his area of responsibility.

No one could question Dorsey Pender's enthusiasm for any cause to which he set his efforts. On March 26 he seemed pleased to report to Fanny, "I am sending men South to be enlisted in the Southern Army." But his duty was less the actual recruitment of these men than expediting their transfer to the Confederacy. "I merely inspect and ship them," he explained without further elaboration. Even so, he recognized the danger associated with his activities in a state that had not yet, and might not ever, leave the Union. "I do nothing that the law could take hold of if they wish to trouble me," he offered as an appeasement to any of Fanny's concerns. Besides, he felt secure in a city brimming with Southern sentiment. "The police, Marshall, and nearly all are with us." Pender's usual sense of confidence and bravado were evident as he observed, "Do not fear for me whatever you may see in the papers, for rest assured that in the first place I shall be prudent and in the second I am well backed."[27]

At the same time, the North Carolinian reiterated that his personal break with the United States was final. To be sure, he had many friends and acquaintances in the Old Army with whom he had severed ties through his actions, but his opinion was clearly expressed. "My resignation was accepted March 21st," he explained on the twenty-sixth, "which gives me twenty one days pay from Abe's *Gov.* and I had as well have it as those miserable Republican scoundrels." The fact that he set such thoughts openly on paper while serving on a covert Confederate mission in Baltimore appeared not to have troubled him, if he thought of it at all. In any event, he felt entitled to the pay that he believed he was genuinely supposed to receive, whatever his subsequent actions had been or however they might now be interpreted.

The logistics of the operation continued to be unique. In order to obtain recruits, Pender offered vague promises of a bounty for enlistment. Ever the bureaucrat, Adjutant General Cooper wanted to ensure that the proper notifications appeared on the muster rolls "under the heading of recruiting expenses" and that Pender dutifully informed General Beauregard of the nature of the promises he had made. Furthermore, Cooper wrote to the Creole in Charleston that the South was not prepared to accept just any enlistee. "Such of the sixty-two men already examined and found to be physically disqualified should be sent back to Baltimore. The others may be retained if they are capable of being made good soldiers."[28] The Confederate States of America was not yet so desperate for manpower that it would automatically accept everyone who stepped forward. Pender probably needed no prodding, for ever mindful of his reputation being on the line in whatever activity he undertook, he surely only wanted to send the best prospects forward anyway.

Pender repeated his assurances to Fanny on April 3 that "the best and larger number of the people" of Baltimore were "with us." Most importantly, the police, who monitored his actions "at the boat each time I have sent off men," did not interfere with his operations. "I sent off sixty-one in less than a week," Pender noted with pride, nearly matching the sixty-four that had left "a few days before I arrived."[29] He was determined that there would be no diminution of the recruitment effort on his watch if he could help it, but affairs in the divided city, like the nation, were fluid.

Despite this initial success and the sympathy he obtained from highly placed figures in the city, as well as assistance from Senator Wigfall, Pender met with decidedly unimpressive results overall. He was able to send a bare 126 recruits to the South, where they formed the basis for two artillery companies organized at Castle Pinckney in Charleston under Captains Charles S. Winder and Stephen D. Lee, Pender's friend.[30] The paltry numbers of recruits and the increasingly unstable political situation should have warned Pender that his secret activities might be cut short. Certainly, he ought not to have been surprised to receive a brief telegraphic message on April 10 from Cooper instructing him to suspend operations, with the directive, "Come here at once."[31]

Thus, in mid-April the captain boarded a steamer bound for home. Both he and the government must have been disappointed in the outcome of his special mission, but Pender was undoubtedly pleased to be recalled. He hoped circumstances would allow him to spend a day or so in North Carolina with his wife, but while still on the vessel, he heard the news that Union troops holding a key fort in Charleston Harbor would face imminent attack. Dorsey subsequently explained to Fanny why he would not be able to visit her as he had initially planned. "I still determined to go by Good Spring for a day, but after getting on board, Mr. [John] Forsythe [sic, Forsyth], one of the Southern Commissioners in Washington told me he had just received a dispatch to the effect that Fort Sumter would be attacked tonight and one of his colleagues told me I had better go as direct as possible, so darling I shall have to disappoint you."[32]

A fellow traveler, Alfred Belo, having just completed some business in New York of his own, met Pender aboard the vessel, and the captain "introduced me to the peace commissioners, [Andre] Ronan [*sic*, Roman], [Martin] Crawford, and Forsythe, who were on their way home from Washington having failed in their errand to secure a general peace convention." Belo confirmed Pender's source for the intelligence. "Through this Captain Pender learned that Mr. Davis had instructed General Beauregard to demand of Major [Robert] Anderson a surrender of Fort Sumter, and in case of non-compliance it was to be attacked."[33]

With hostilities likely to occur at any time between the United States and the Confederacy, and with North Carolina still in the Union, Pender realized that a visit with his family was a luxury he simply could not afford, for the moment at least. "You must not be troubled at the news, but like a brave woman as you are bear up," he instructed, adding that she should "reflect that you are not the only wife whose husband will likely be in the trouble." Once more there was no turning back for them, and the couple could "not close our eyes to the fact any longer—war exists."[34] Belo's response to the information was even less circumspect. "That seemed to me to mean a declaration of war and nothing else."[35]

For once the rumors were accurate. General Beauregard sent his counterpart at Fort Sumter, Major Anderson, an ultimatum to surrender the installation. When the Union commander would not comply, Confederate shore batteries blazed forth in the early morning hours of April 12, 1861, and, as Pender put it, a state of war thus "existed" between the United States and Confederate States of America.[36]

The firing on Fort Sumter spurred President Lincoln to call for 75,000 militia to suppress a rebellion too great for ordinary national forces to address. He expected this quota of troops from each of the remaining "loyal" states. But Sumter had also created the conditions, exacerbated now by Lincoln's actions, which would force additional Southern states out of the Union, including North Carolina on May 20, 1861.

As the emergency developed, Governor John Ellis needed his West Point–trained and combat-experienced officer to prepare North Carolina's native sons for service. Secretary of War Walker obliged by notifying Ellis from Montgomery on April 22: "The previous order to Capt. Pender to return here is recalled. He will remain on duty in North Carolina and await instructions by Col. [Theophilus H.] Holmes who leaves here tonight."[37] Thus, once more Dorsey

Pender was destined for his native state, where he hoped to find a more amenable assignment than the one he had held briefly in Baltimore.

What subsequently transpired may not have been as pleasant a responsibility as Pender had hoped for, but it was absolutely necessary. Biographer Edward Longacre explained, "Willing to serve his state in any capacity, Pender accepted the appointment, thereupon becoming a lieutenant colonel of state troops in addition to a captain in the Confederate service."[38] The path was not an unusual one for individuals in his position with West Point training and Old Army service. Historian Richard McMurry has observed, "Almost all of the active duty officers who left the United States Army in 1860–61 to go with the South went to their home states and entered military service as members of state units."[39] To be sure, Pender was pleased to contribute "in any capacity," but the elevation in rank was not lost on him and must have been a powerful incentive for him to assume the role of drill instructor, although a voucher for quarters and fuel for Pender and a servant listed him as "Capt. & Recruit Officer."[40]

Pender continued to worry about his reputation and status and was quick to grasp at any indication of his worthiness as a soldier. "The President spoke as I think complimentary of me," he informed Fanny at the end of April, "saying that I could [do] anything well, in fact he led the Col. to think that I was an Engineer." He was especially grateful that various officials seemed to covet his services. "Col. Holmes tried very hard to have me transferred to Beaufort," he explained satisfactorily, "but the Governor said that he intended to keep me."[41]

President Davis was not the only politician expressing platitudes concerning the young North Carolinian. Governor Ellis also stroked Pender's ego. In a telegram to one of his officers, the governor mentioned him favorably. "Convey to Capt. Pender the assurances of Gov. Ellis' high appreciation and entire approval of the patriotic course pursued by the Company under his command."[42] Especially early in the war, Pender lapped up such praise eagerly. But the situation in which he found himself was wearing on him. "I have been very much flattered not only by the Governor, but by others, but as the effects of that soon wear off, I have nothing but a sense of duty to sustain me and that is growing weak."[43]

There was not much to cheer Pender regarding his current circumstances. On April 28 he wrote his wife to say that he was sharing rather close quarters with the commander of the camp, Colonel Daniel Harvey Hill, and that they were subsisting on limited fare that reminded him of his days in Washington Territory. Fanny could alleviate matters with "a box of eatables," which Dorsey thought "would be more service than anything I know of," but she should not plan to send him delicacies. "Substantials, not fancies," he observed, with a drill instructor's brevity, before deciding that if the effort was too difficult, they would manage anyway.[44]

Pender threw himself into his instructional tasks at Camp Mangum near Raleigh with the zeal and determination that always characterized his efforts, but he remained mindful of where his next opportunity for advancement might appear. He wanted desperately to prove himself. Pender's twin motivations were undoubtedly interest and honor. He believed in comporting himself in such a manner as to increase his prospects for promotion while simultaneously allowing him to win the approval of others. His reputation in the eyes of others was everything to him. The way that he handled his assignments and his commands were necessary components to both of these elements.

There was no question that there was plenty of work for a person like Pender to do. William W. Holden's *North Carolina Standard* related the news of the establishment of a "military encampment" at the fairgrounds near Raleigh: "troops are pouring in every day."[45] These men required officers who knew how to mold them into soldiers. Within a week, a reporter for the same newspaper testified to his readers what Pender and others with the responsibility for that training would face. "He found the boys all hearty and eager for the fray, though military discipline goes pretty hard for some of them."[46] The same edition announced the "provisional appointment" of "Capt. William D. Pender, of the Confederate States Army, and late 1st Lieutenant and Adjutant of the 1st Dragoons, U.S. Army, to be Lieutenant Colonel. He has been assigned to duty at the Camp of Instruction."[47]

Whether Pender read this particular news item from the Raleigh newspaper is not known, but there was evidence that he was aware of what was being written in both the Southern and Northern press, whether of a broader international or national scope or more specifically about himself and his men. In the fall of 1861, he forwarded one such piece, referencing it generally in a letter to Fanny. "I send you an Article from the standard [sic] not my dear wife for the gratification of my vanity, but because I think it will give you pleasure to read it."[48] Dorsey later lamented, "In fact, I have read nothing, nor have any desire to read anything else for some time—newspapers excepted."[49]

Pender eventually revealed that of all the newspapers at his disposal, he preferred the *Richmond Sentinel*, "because it is the best edited paper in Richmond and so much more cheerful in its tune."[50] When Fanny reported that she had received the copy he forwarded to her, Dorsey responded: "I am glad you like the *Sentinel*. I think it is the best paper in Richmond. It is hopeful without being foolishly sanguine."[51]

Although Pender remained in his native state for now, he quickly became dispirited by the conditions he witnessed among the troops and, as was his habit, shared his disappointments with his wife. The recruits were enthusiastic enough but too independently minded for the likes of a professionally trained soldier. "The fact is Fanny," Dorsey complained, "we shall never be able to do anything until our Southern troops get two or three sound whippings." He was convinced that the attitudes of the men he was now responsible for training would have to be altered in order for him to be able to make any headway in converting these civilians into soldiers. "I firmly believe it would be the best thing for the South." The problem was clear. "The idea of their being brought together and having to submit to inconvenience to prepare them for service is something they cannot see the use of."[52] Pender would have concurred completely with what a later historian of the Army of Northern Virginia said about its soldiers: "To win independence Confederate soldiers must exhibit a level of discipline and sacrifice that few had known in peacetime."[53]

He was particularly frustrated by the lack of discipline and order he saw in the volunteers. "I could be a Colonel if I chose," he explained to Fanny, "but I have seen enough of Volunteers & prefer to be a Captain in the regulars." Then, quite revealingly, he admitted one of the reasons that he preferred disciplined professionals over amateur citizen-soldiers: "The general tumult & confusion, confuses me."[54]

Clearly, if he had not already experienced a transformation in this regard during his 1858 days in the Pacific Northwest, by this point in the current conflict, Pender was no longer the cadet swinging his arms while marching on the drill fields at West Point. Indeed, he was becoming increasingly intolerant of those who had not matured militarily as he had. This internal struggle between reputation and ambition lingered, but one was about to get a boost over the other.

Pender's personal ambition returned to the forefront with the possibility of the colonelcy of the volunteers he had disdained. He thought the offer of that rank, particularly since North Carolina had no immediate intention of naming any generals, might be too tempting for him to turn down. The fact that by being named colonel of the 1st North Carolina Infantry, he would be "the senior Colonel of the State" added to the allure. So he told Fanny that "with all these considerations I have determined to accept it if I can get it," but promised not to be "much disturbed" if he did not. "It is for one year, and in that time I might be a General who knows!" Then, as doubt once more crept in, he hedged. "Under all circumstances I shall hold on to my poor little Captaincy."[55]

Pender was not yet a colonel, but by early May he was working with a new set of troops. The 1st North Carolina had left for Virginia, and he took up the same duties of instruction with the 3rd North Carolina Infantry.[56] Perhaps because he had to start his efforts anew, the veteran instructor quickly became exasperated with his new charges. From the rail town of Weldon in the northern part of the state, he wrote Fanny on May 8, "It is perfectly impossible to do anything with the men here and I shall not try until I get them in camp." The proximity of the camp to sources of trouble for his recruits bothered him greatly, and he determined to move to another location to escape the effects of vice and other unwanted distractions. "Yesterday as soon as I got here I went and selected a site two miles off on the opposite side of the river so I shall be able to keep the men away from here and I hope away from liquor." Pender expected to "face a great deal of opposition in moving," he confided, but he was determined to do what was best for the command. "Sometimes I feel as if I would give up completely & let the Volunteer system go," he added almost dejectedly, "but we all must strive [in] these times."[57]

At the camp of instruction he set up at Garysburg, North Carolina, Pender settled into a mundane but important routine that alternated between drills and paperwork. He remained constantly busy and found himself torn between the numerous tasks required of him. "Just think," he explained to his wife, "I have to play Comdg. Officer, Adjt., partly Commissary, and chiefly QM [Quartermaster] and head carpenter, besides drill master and general depository of military information." The myriad assignments required enormous energy from him in a day that stretched from "five in the morning till seven in the evening," and even then he could not do enough to stifle all complaints or satisfy all parties.[58]

In his brief depression, Pender admitted that once he set his words to paper regarding his willingness to accept the colonelcy if offered, "I regretted [it] and I made up my mind nothing should tempt me again to commit myself." At any rate, he was pleased with the status he currently enjoyed. "It will be rather a fall to go back to Captain in the Confederate Army," he concluded, "for here in the state I am treated with the greatest deference. You would be amused to see how high I carry it, and I find it to be the best way." A close acquaintance had offered Pender an assessment of himself, saying, "I like the approbation of others, and let it affect me." Pender would certainly have to agree but felt justified and sufficiently humble to excuse what he was telling his wife. "Men are in some measure ranked in proportion as they rank themselves," he observed, before adding swftly, "However much I write of self to you, I have enough good sense to not show to [sic] much vanity to others."[59]

The next day he was back on the same topic, obviously having contemplated his position through a portion of the night. "Honey, you will not think me conceited writing you about myself in this way," he remarked. "I do not speak to others of myself. You know that I did not in former times put on airs, and I believe I do not now, but it makes one proud to think that my wife's husband is of enough consequence to be asked to take a Colonelcy when so many older ones are seeking it." For all of his seeming confidence, Pender was still struggling with himself over an innate sense of insecurity, noting, "Mrs. W. D. Pender's husband, altho' poor is considered a man of some merit," and that he had "always thought that you deserved something better than a poor insignificant Lieutenant." He continued to couch his position with regard to her as a measure of what he, as an officer and a man, ought to be. "I would like to be a great man for your sake," he offered, "but I have not the confidence to try. Even if I could I would be afraid to try a Regiment."

One of the individuals in the camp at Garysburg, D. A. Montgomery, authored a letter on May 14 that described Pender as "courteous and kind to all," which certainly were strange characteristics for a drill instructor to be known by. "We have about 450 men in Camp," this Confederate noted, "some as rough and uncouth as N. Carolina can produce." But the grounds were taking on a decidedly martial look, with carpenters busily engaged in erecting barracks. Additional officers and men poured into the camp, bringing the total troops accumulated to even greater numbers and creating the demand for other facilities to meet their needs. "Col. Pender has called on me for a plan for a hospital," Montgomery wrote, "and I must close and turn my mind to that subject."[60]

There was also a great deal of concern about the integrity of the organization of troops being assembled at Garysburg. Several officers from the North Carolina units there hoped to be able to remain together in any regiment created from them. Captain Alfred M. Scales of the Rockbridge Rangers, who would succeed Pender later in the year as colonel of the 13th North Carolina, was among them. "We are all satisfied as it is," he explained to Judge Thomas

Ruffin, "and I am happy to say that Col. Pender has signified his intention to accept the command of our regiment if tendered to him."[61]

Pender was desirous of advancement, but even with such demonstrations of support, his situation seemed to be precarious. "If I can get away now I shall leave in the nick of time so far as my reputation is concerned," he explained to Fanny in mid-May.[62] Dorsey had the additional and equally significant motivation that if he were able to obtain his own command, he would be allowed to exercise more personal control over his affairs. In any case, he told her that he found that he was "tired of working for other people."[63]

Ten companies accumulated at the Garysburg camp of instruction provided him with a command of his own. These organized formally as the 3rd Regiment, North Carolina Volunteers on May 16, 1861, with Pender elected as its colonel. Together the companies comprised a regiment that totaled just over a thousand men committed for a term of twelve months. When the command entered service for the war, it became the 13th North Carolina Troops.[64]

Whatever his internal misgivings and his sense of his own appropriateness for this new authority, Colonel Pender watched military developments outside of his immediate sphere with a sense of anticipation. He reported the movement of several companies from Raleigh to Virginia. "I should have been ahead of them," he noted regrettably, then realized that Fanny might not have wished so much for him to do so. "You must not be so troubled at the idea of my leaving the state," he added hastily. "It must come, and besides I do not wish to be one of the home guard."

The prospect of moving closer to the scene of active military operations was enticing, but it also caused a wave of nostalgia to sweep over him. On Sunday, May 19, he reflected "back to those pleasant times at [Fort] Vancouver when we used to walk to church together, I feeling so proud of my wife.... Honey, those were pleasant days—especially those spring days of '60." The possibility that the vagaries of war might adversely affect their lives was beginning to dawn on him. "You will say I am getting sentimental," he observed, "I own up; I do feel so this morning." But if a Sunday of reflection caused him to experience a sense of homesickness for quieter times, he saw this too as a manifestation of the better qualities of his personality. "Darling, I am not that cold and matter-of-fact individual always you seem to think," he appeared as much to be asking rhetorically as stating a fact. For the moment, the soldier felt transported, but this time to North Carolina to Good Spring and "back under *that* shade tree as the most perfectly happy time I ever spent."[65]

Of course, Dorsey Pender was not about to be transported to the arms of his loved ones just yet. Other duties called him. He was beginning to make real headway with his citizen-soldiers. "I have accomplished a [bit of] duty that I have been fearful I should have some trouble in doing," he explained to Fanny. "That is [to] make the Volunteers police [their] camp." Cleaning the grounds was the type of unglamorous, but necessary, duty that he expected relatively raw recruits to balk at undertaking, but Dorsey noted triumphantly, "I had no trouble." He had only to give the order, and the men "obeyed as completely as if they had been old soldiers."

While such gratifying steps might not be enough to satisfy Pender's ambition, advancement in rank and authority would do nicely. He certainly must have recognized the contradiction to his earlier stance concerning citizens turned into soldiers when he announced that he was assuming a new role. "Honey after all I have said I have consented to take a Volunteer Regiment," he wrote at the end of May. "It is the best Regt. yet formed," he asserted. "The election comes off tomorrow, but I was unanimously nominated last night." Pender was at last to have his own command, albeit a "Volunteer" one, but with a steady hand and a tireless assertion of discipline, they would transform into reputable soldiers.

Although Pender focused on his duties as an officer, family matters intruded in the martial atmosphere that prevailed. Young Turner was suffering from one malady or another for a period of time. Fanny kept her husband abreast of the developments, and the father dutifully inquired about his child. She was at Good Spring, under the care of her parents, but the strain of nursing Turner while enduring the final months of pregnancy was wearing on her. "Honey I am very much grieved to hear you are getting so helpless," he wrote in mid-May. With so much on his mind, he could but advise: "My own wife try to keep your health and spirits, for we all have enough to contend with these days."[66]

Fanny gave him a better understanding of her situation in a subsequent letter, causing Dorsey to become even more solicitous toward her condition. "Honey, your letter was received today, and my own precious wife how I do feel for you, in this time of suspense and suffering, and how sincerely darling, I do hope you may have a long time before you shall have to pass through the same again," he explained as tenderly as he could. "I would give anything to be with you, even for twenty-four hours about the time of your greatest suffering." Once more he admonished her to take care of herself and to "not worry yourself about Turner during the time, but let others take care of him."[67]

Pender was trying to be the "devoted Husband," the term by which he so often closed his letters, but he was undoubtedly not as aware of the circumstances that prevailed at Good Spring. His father-in-law, Augustine Shepperd, wrote Thomas Ruffin a short letter that suggested a greater level of distress than Fanny may have been willing to express to her husband directly. "I am pained to have to write to Mr. P. the extreme illness of his only child," he explained to his friend on May 26, noting also that Fanny "is staying with me" without making reference to her condition.[68] In two days' time, those circumstances would be changed dramatically with the birth of a second son, William Dorsey Pender Jr.

"Little Dorsey," as the proud father referred to him, was apparently not the daughter that Fanny had hoped for, but Pender reasoned in his first letter after the joyous occasion, "A boy will be better able to care for himself in the future." Perhaps in a way of making it easier for a mother who had gone through a difficult pregnancy, he asserted, "You must have little Dorsey for your favorite for I feel that none can ever be so dear to me as that incomparable boy Turner; the greatest boy in the world." He would certainly not turn his back on any child of his, especially one bearing his own name, but Pender had at least one compelling and revealing reason for making such a statement. "You have no idea how I love that 'man'; he is of my own raising and training."[69]

Any training Colonel Pender would be doing in the days ahead would have to be focused on his new unit and would have to be done at a different site. At the head of his troops, he finally left the relative quiet of his native state for the promise of action in neighboring Virginia. The 3rd North Carolina became part of a force of Confederate troops stationed in the southeastern portion of the Commonwealth. Some members guarded the water approaches to the region, even enjoying the occasional joust with Union gunboats, while others performed the more mundane activities of camp and the drill field, preparing themselves for a war they had yet to comprehend fully. In either case, the presence of these soldiers comforted the people of the region, allowing them a sense of security.

The move to Virginia took Pender out of familiar territory and created in him an immediate sense of unease. He had worked hard to establish himself in his own state only to be brought onto a new stage with different players. It would take a little time for him to sort things out. In the meantime, a measure of that insecurity always lurking near the surface showed itself briefly. Pender was surely pleased to have the commander in the region, Major General Benjamin Huger, come over from Norfolk with an entourage to "look round," but he also felt somewhat lost in the crowd of soldiers beginning to gather around him in the vicinity of the little Tidewater community of Suffolk. "The fact is," he admitted to Fanny, "the nearer to the scene of active operations we get the less my importance grows."[70]

Pender continued to feel uncertain of himself, compensating for the perceived deficiency by immersing himself in his books. "Honey I know you will feel disappointed when you see how short this letter is," he wrote on the night of May 31, "but really I can not write more as it is now tattoo, and I have some tactics to study before going to sleep."[71] Military demands had to take precedence for the moment over domestic considerations. Unfortunately for the happiness of the home, Pender's nagging sense of inadequacy also continued to haunt him.

The crux of the matter, as the colonel saw it, was the way in which the quality of his troops reflected upon him as their commander. "My Regiment is keeping up its reputation thus far and I only hope it will continue to do so," he wrote, without any particular indication of what he felt it had done thus far to win, much less maintain, such a "reputation."[72] So much of his personal well-being remained tied to the command, especially when the performance could be confirmed, and affirmed, by others.

The next day Dorsey wrote Fanny to say that his men were "very much complimented by the citizens for [their] general good appearance."[73] Within a few days of that letter, he would have been pleased at the description of his command by a Richmond newspaper correspondent. From the camp in Suffolk, the *Daily Dispatch* writer reported the presence of the 3rd North Carolina. "They are a fine looking body of men," he opened, before adding what surely must have sent the North Carolinian's ego soaring to new heights: "Col. Pender is admired by our citizens and loved by his command."[74]

Pender revealed a great deal about himself when he wrote home in early June: "Honey I flatter myself that thus far no one need be ashamed of me. I occupy a high position for one so young and have been able to sustain myself so far." He tried to play down any sense of conceit by noting that he felt "the terrible responsibility" of command and "the many chances for me to ruin myself in a military sense."[75]

The colonel was indeed fulfilling his obligations to his men. The troops were well situated, with their basic necessities provided and "good drill ground" on which to operate in improving their martial skills. Pender could happily report, "No sickness of any importance, and no complaining among the men of importance." To be sure, some grumbled at the life of the soldier, calling their commander "too 'damn strict,'" while others saw him as "just right." Still, the command as a whole was responding to his orchestrations in a manner that made him rather proud. "They begin to make quite a presentable appearance, much better than you would suppose," he explained. Even the presentation of a new horse prompted him to put the event in terms of personal honor. "Very few will be able to get a better mount than *your Colonel*," he told Fanny.[76]

Pender was immeasurably pleased that other reports reaching newspaper readers in the Confederate capital were overwhelmingly favorable concerning his troops. He might have feared the adverse effects of alcohol on his command while still in his native state, but in Virginia he appeared to have exorcised that demon rather effectively. Indeed, one correspondent, after noting the activity in Suffolk created by the arrival of the new troops, quickly asserted, "I mention a fact noticed by all, that there is less drunkenness and rowdy conduct than was ever seen at a place where so many soldiers were encamped." He added that on Sunday the local churches had been filled and that there was "preaching at the camp of the North Carolina Volunteers, near the splendid spring on the premises of the Rev. Mr. [William B.] Wellons, from which the soldiers are watered."[77] A subsequent account put the command at "a beautiful place for an encampment just beyond the limits of the town on the premises of Thos. J. Kilby, Esq.," but mentioned the "convenient" location of "a never failing spring of cool water."[78]

Pender was proud of the selection of ground he had made for his troops. "So far as location is concerned we have the best of any troops in this section of the state," he informed Fanny. "We are at the head of several springs, where we have plenty of good spring water and shade, and in the way of eating everything that we could wish. We could not be more comfortably situated."[79]

Even with such a suitable location, sickness was bound to be a factor for the command, brought about by the proximity of the troops and the nature of their living conditions. A member of the 3rd North Carolina complained of suffering from the "mumps awful bad" and pronounced himself "so unwell" that when the command went out for maneuvers he did not go.[80] An officer noted his own discomforts with diarrhea and observed simply, "I think all of us will have to undergo this disease." More generally with regard to the health of the command, he explained, "A good many of our boys has been sick."[81]

Apparently, various reporters and correspondents visited the camp on a regular basis and were uniformly impressed by what they saw. One feature in the *North Carolina Standard* cited a Suffolk, Virginia, newspaper indicating that Pender had found it necessary to curtail commercial activity with relation to his command. "The [Christian] *Sun* is out this morning upon the sharpers who have been speculating on the soldiers here, and I have just learned that Col. Pender has issued an order forbidding any of them to enter the camp of the North Carolina Volunteers." Whatever the men may have thought of the prohibition, the writer thought the decision "no doubt a good one."[82]

Subsequently, the *Christian Sun* of Suffolk commended the "high moral bearing of the Officers and Privates." Even the exceptions proved the rule as this newspaper account suggested, "True—we have seen some cases of intemperance and heard some profanity from some of the privates, but there is less disposition to these vices than we ever expected to find in so large a body of soldiers."[83] A correspondent from the *Goldsboro (N.C.) Tribune* also referred to the members of the 3rd North Carolina "in the highest terms." He noted for his readers similar characteristics of the soldiers from the Old North State stationed in this part of the Old Dominion: "Many in the ranks are men of position and substance, of sound morals, and many of them are pious men."[84]

In a letter from Suffolk, Dorsey shared some of this news with Fanny. He wanted his wife to be proud of him and recognize his worth; letting others say it for him seemed to be the most prudent method. "We are drilling four times a day having Regimental drill once each day," he mentioned as prelude. "In two or three months we shall make quite a presentable appearance." He then turned to his source of corroboration, lest Fanny think he was giving way to his usual vanity. "I will send you a piece from the 'Christian Sun' printed here, which had a word concerning us. I told you I intended to get dignified when I was made Colonel—recollect when we first came home."[85]

Pender not only wanted his men to reflect well on him as their commander but also wanted them prepared for duty when that time came. As such, he spared no exertion, and the rigorous pace took a mental as well as a physical toll. As necessary as it was, the routine quickly became oppressive to rank and file. John T. Hambrick probably spoke for everyone when he observed to his wife, "I am pretty worn out with drilling." The requirement for "nine hours in the sun is no small matter," he added. There was a bit of bright news, though, with the possibility of a change in the schedule that would eliminate "one drill at 3 o'clock," in the hottest part of the day, "which will make it better." Still, he expected the relief to be minimal. "If this thing is continued I shall have to snap. [O]ne drill," he wrote disgustedly with emphasis. "I can't nor want [to] stand it." As this storm passed, the officer thought better of his tirade. "But soldiers should not grumble," Hambrick observed. "[W]e are seeing a good time, when we take into consideration the soldiers of [17]76."[86]

Pender's actions while in the field were about to create new challenges for him at home, based upon the opportunities he found for social interaction between himself and a grateful local citizenry in Virginia. Almost as soon as he had gotten the men into camp, there were the first signs of a new kind of trouble about to descend upon the Carolina colonel. "There are lots of beautiful girls here," he wrote naively to his wife from Suffolk, "and [a] good many fine horses, so when I have nothing else to do, I can look at something beautiful or fine."[87] How receptive he expected Fanny to be to this line was anyone's guess. She had just delivered their second son, and the same concerns that the couple had once faced on the far northwestern frontier now surely seemed multiplied.[88] Even so, Dorsey could not resist telling Fanny all.

A few days later he followed the same theme. "I am treated with the greatest kindness by the people," he wrote on June 6. Indeed, his social calendar was coming under quite a strain. "Several invitations to dine today, as well as Sunday invitations to tea."[89] A visitor from Petersburg noticed the busy schedule and observed simply, "Col. Pender and the officers are popular."[90]

The problem was not popularity in and of itself, but it was Dorsey's tendency to put such references in his letters to Fanny. As if he simply could not contain himself, he added jauntily to his June 6 letter, "Dined today with the most beautiful girl in Suffolk—and it has [a] great many very pretty ones."[91]

Although it did not seem so on the surface, what must surely have been irritating references to an already sensitive spouse were not made deliberately. Dorsey was being thoughtless concerning her because he was so wrapped up in himself. He wanted Fanny to be proud of him, perhaps under the mistaken impression that the attentions being lavished on him by others would somehow reflect favorably on her too. These attentions also had to come from the very best of society—"the most beautiful girl" among a "great many very pretty ones."

In another few days there would be further clarification of his thinking and the motives that impelled him to write to Fanny of such things. Word had reached him that he "had a very high reputation" in Raleigh, and he could not help once more "writing of myself again." It was not that he had not asked repeatedly about his wife's health and condition or the status of the children, but the light seemed always to come back onto him. "You know however that

I like approbation," he freely confessed, "but more particularly that you should know that I am doing credit to Fanny Shepperd."[92] As he saw the situation, his status among the local populace could but redound to her credit under any circumstances.

Unfortunately for the soldier and husband, the trend of personal absorption continued on June 9. Suffolk "is the most pleasant little town I ever saw," he remarked almost casually at this time. "The kindest and most hospitable people I ever saw anywhere. The ladies keep my table covered with flowers and smile on me in the most bewitching manner." He undoubtedly saw himself as the master of his domain, accepting the accolades presented to him on such a regular basis. "The colonel is quite a lion," he concluded unabashedly. Suddenly, he must have realized how some of this might appear to his mate. "Do not be jealous," he assured her by way of instruction, "for none of them have the attractiveness of Mrs. W. D. Pender. I have not failed to let them know that I am married for *poor creatures I do not wish to destroy their rest.*"[93]

Aside from himself, Pender was also pleased with the state of his command. He felt that his "first Regimental drill" in early June had demonstrated that the men had "progressed very well" and immensely enjoyed maneuvering his troops in front of any audience that gathered to witness the occasion.[94] On June 10 he remarked to Fanny, "We have [a] great many people of both sex[es] out to see us every evening at drill & parade." Clearly, Colonel Pender was satisfied that his unit was providing such a pleasant diversion for the local residents, and obviously he was acutely aware of the image he and his men projected to the spectators. Despite the fact that his horse had "cut up considerably at first," under his deft touch the animal "tamed down before the drill was over." He could conclude only, "We shall soon be worth seeing." Then Dorsey happily explained to his wife: "Whenever [a] good many people are about looking at us, I always wish you could be [near]by. People take me to be over thirty, because as they [see] I have such a high office. I am probably the next to the youngest Colonel in the service."[95]

John Hambrick, the proud subordinate who had chafed at the routine of drill, nevertheless seemed to have appreciated the results of the hard work. Sounding very much like his commanding office, he offered a glowing assessment to his wife of the performance of his troops. "I flatter myself that I have the best drilled company in the Regiment. . . . [W]hen my company came in from Dress Parade last evening it made me proud to look at it." The captain was so pleased because, like Pender, he believed such performances reflected well on him. "I believe I pass for more than my worth in the regiment," he proclaimed, expressing his willingness to go through any trial with his men. The troops "obeyed me & acted the part of a soldier so well, I cannot praise them too much." Most importantly in his eyes, "They seem to like me, both officers and men."[96]

Colonel Pender was also extraordinarily proud of what he had accomplished and felt the support of Fanny, at least tacitly, in the undertaking. But he was less pleased with the assistance he felt was lacking from official circles in North Carolina. Politicians had appealed to his ego and offered assurances, but when it came to tangible benefits, the promises appeared to fall short. "I started to have a row with the Governor and get what we need and have been promised or give up my command in the service," an exasperated Pender wrote on June 12. "I have been fooled with long enough and am determined not to stand it any longer." Wisely, he decided to send two subordinates to Raleigh to hash out issues with Governor Ellis rather than take up the matter himself and risk a confrontation he probably would not win. Instead, he depended upon Captains Thomas Ruffin and Alfred Scales to take on the gritty task of lobbying for the regiment's supply demands. In any case, he felt his requirements must be met. "I am not Lt. Pender any longer but Col. Pender knowing my position and my worth," he stated unequivocally, promising that if drastic measures were required, there would not be inconsiderable consequences. "As an officer I know they have none who stand higher with the people," he assured Fanny, predicting, "if they force me out of the service it will be their look out."[97]

Apparently, Colonel Pender was not exaggerating the plight of his men for political purposes. A correspondent for a Goldsboro, North Carolina, newspaper who made the journey to southeastern Virginia noticed the shortages as well and prepared to bring these matters to the attentions of his readers. "I am glad to know that wherever North-Carolina soldiers have been stationed in Virginia, they have commanded the respect of all who have seen them," the newspaperman wrote. "But while the Old North State has cause to be proud of her boys, who have given up all to fight for her," the men "are thrown into the field . . . without the necessary equipments of cartridge boxes and bayonet scabbards." His criticism of "the powers that be" that allowed such a situation to prevail undoubtedly would dovetail well with the views of the disgruntled colonel.[98]

Pender was certain that the citizens would rise to his defense if need be but felt he had additional evidence of the degree to which he had demonstrated his effectiveness as an officer. When another North Carolina regiment arrived in the Suffolk area, it had to be moved out of the town and into a camp several miles away. Far from being disappointed at the less convenient proximity of his fellow Tar Heels for any possible home-state connections, Pender professed the move to be "very much to my delight as [these] men seem to be a rather disorderly lot."[99] There was always the chance that such behavior would reflect poorly on all North Carolina units, including his, and Pender wanted to avoid that possibility.

By June 18, Pender could report with full satisfaction that his lieutenants had triumphed in their mission to Raleigh. "They were completely successful, and the Regt. is now as well equipped as any in the field," he announced gleefully. As any good commander would be expected to do, the colonel had taken his stand on behalf of his men, even risking the ire of the chief executive of his state, and it had apparently paid off. "I was not light upon the Governor, for the way we had been sent off with promises, all of which had been broken."[100]

Colonel Pender had every reason to be satisfied, but he had one advantage of which he was probably not aware. Throughout this period, John Ellis was a terribly sick man. Historian John G. Barrett observed succinctly, "the demands of the office were killing him."[101] Even so, the North Carolina governor never lost his focus on the "safety and welfare of the State," as he termed it, and he seemed not to have declined in his political skills.[102] Pender noted that in reply to his ultimatum, Ellis "wrote the kindest letter you ever saw, saying to let him know what I wanted and he would attend to it in person." Yet the colonel refused to relent. "I find I am not capable of getting on with politicians who do not mind breaking their word," he observed to Fanny in the same letter. "I believe them and they deceive me."[103]

Ellis may have disappointed his young and demanding colonel, but upon its adjournment, the general assembly voted its thanks to the governor for his efforts to put North Carolina on an appropriate war footing.[104] Now the battle was largely to be one of trying to save his own well-being. In an effort to restore his health, Governor Ellis traveled to Virginia in the same month that he tackled the supply issue with Pender's representatives, but the proposition would prove to be a losing one. By July 7, the official who had promised to attend to Colonel Pender's desires personally was dead.[105]

Pender heard the news within a matter of days and was genuinely troubled by it. "I was very sorry to hear of the death of Gov. Ellis," he observed in a letter to Fanny's sister Pamela. "He was a true Southerner." But the colonel could hardly let the matter go at that, with his disappointment of just a month earlier still fresh in his mind. "I am fearful his successor will not have any more nerve or executive capacity than he had."[106]

He may have avoided his "row" with the governor and a confrontation that might have removed him from the military service by ones means or another, but in the meantime, Pender continued to lay the groundwork for a "row" in his marital relationship that would alter his life. "A lady offered to make me a cap the other day," he explained to Fanny on June 23. "I told her if she would make a net for a lady I would take great pleasure in sending it to you, whereupon she said she was not going to make anything for my wife." Dorsey was aware of the implications of what he had divulged to her but thought he had an appropriate defense for any concerns about his fidelity. "I think she goes on the principle of your Mobile acquaintance, that she had rather gain the attention of a married man than a single one. She can try on me, and see who is the loser."[107]

Dorsey had already identified the problem to Fanny in an earlier letter. "The married gentlemen have been passing themselves off for single gentlemen, that is they did not tell every one that they were married and the young ladies [assumed] that we were all single." Perhaps recognizing that this bit of information might be unsettling to his distant bride, he offered her the undoubtedly comforting assurance, "If I wanted to do [that] I could not for I can not help talking about my wife."[108]

But being the social "lion" that he had become, Dorsey did not seem to be able to avoid placing himself in compromising positions and then foolhardily, if dutifully, recording these instances for Fanny's sake. "I was at a little gathering two nights ago, and had a very nice time dancing and flirting with a very nice girl. I am trying to get her to knit you a sac for the hair, but she said that she is not going to work for my wife, but will do anything for me."[109]

The editor of the Pender letters omitted what followed from the correspondence Dorsey was sending to his wife. William Hassler worked diligently to present the young soldier, husband, and father in an unvarnished fashion, but the confession that followed was tremendously revealing about Pender's motivations, made all the more problematic from the recent birth of a second child and the difficulties that had been associated with that delivery. "Fanny, I know I am doing mean in sending this letter, for I know it will hurt your feelings and still my evil spirit forces me to send it."[110] His was an indulgence that the young husband was about to learn he could not afford.

It may not be that Dorsey realized fully what the phrase "will do anything for me" would mean to Fanny, but the fact that he admitted to an "evil spirit" suggested strongly that he had more than an inkling and took a perverse pleasure in sharing it. In any case, the letter and whatever satisfaction he may have derived temporarily from sending it dissipated shortly thereafter in a barrage as withering as any artillery or musket fire he was ever bound to face.

From her home at Good Spring, the longsuffering wife seated herself to write a reply. When her June 30 letter arrived, it began rather ominously, "Read to end."[111] Had Pender's military training given him any insight into the struggles that life would send his way, it ought to have made abundantly clear that such words were best left unread. The safest course for his immediate mental health might have been to consign the letter to a campfire, but Dorsey could no more have done that than he could prevent himself from writing as he had to Fanny in the first place. His "evil spirit" had more than a match in distant North Carolina. William Dorsey Pender was about to reap the whirlwind he had sown for himself.

Mary Frances Shepperd Pender sent her letter after enduring what must have seemed an insufferable amount of insensitive utterings in her husband's most recent correspondence. She tolerated as much as she could stand until she could take it no longer. Even so, Fanny first tried to address her own health and family matters. But as she dealt with Dorsey's prickliness when it came to the baby's christening, she began to warm to the duty that lay ahead. "I did not know, before, that you attached so much importance to the rite of infant baptism, or I should have written more at length about it." To drive the point home, she then referred to Dorsey—twice—as "Mr. Pender," and she admonished him to "remember" that if her letters were "not written exactly as you wished," it was "that I am not quite as strong as I might be, and I have a good many duties to attend to that distract my attention from the sheet before me." Indeed, she was constantly interrupting the process "to perform some little service either for the baby or someone else" or she had to attempt to go on writing "with both children screaming in my ears."[112]

Fanny's references to the baptism of their second child, her letter writing abilities, and her many domestic requirements are an indication that she was a strong-minded and strong-willed person in her own right. But the substance of that character was about to be revealed in a way that her husband would not have contemplated. She did not mince words but cut straight to the matter: "I have never in the whole course of my married [life] done anything deliberately that I knew would pain you—your will has always been my law—and I have ever tried to *obey* to the very letter the commands of my Lord and master." She quoted at length from the letter in which he had noted his joy in "dancing and flirting," focusing on the offer the Suffolk woman had made to "'*do anything for me.*'"

Dorsey must have cringed as he saw the words thrust back at him on paper. The full measure of Fanny's pent-up wrath flowed forth: "Now, I ask you candidly, in your sober senses, why you wrote me such a thing as that? Was it to gratify your vanity by making me jealous, or to make me appreciate your love still more?" But she was not going to wait for an answer to her rhetorical questions. "You are very much mistaken," Fanny noted forthrightly. "I feel indignant that any woman should have dared to make such loose speeches to my husband and that he should have encouraged it by his attentions, for you must have gone pretty far for a woman to attempt such a liberty."

Her anger vented, Fanny closed the matter with an expression of her affection. "I know you love me, my dear Husband," she observed. "I have had too many sweet and precious proofs of it to doubt it now." Her husband's carelessness had scarred, and probably scared, her too. Although she had "forgotten all the anger I felt at first," Fanny explained, "I can never forget that letter—nothing you have ever said—nothing you have ever done, nothing you have ever written in this whole of our married life—ever pained me so acutely or grieved me so deeply."[113] The depth of that pain was now something that the married couple could share, and the husband would have to endure himself in order for the marriage to have the opportunity to survive and grow stronger.

Yet even amid the turmoil that marked the greatest challenge he had experienced in his married life, William Dorsey Pender still had a war to fight and troops to prepare for their part in it. He had served his new nation in a variety of capacities, most recently as a drill instructor trying to mold a fighting command of volunteers. His hopes continued to center on his own advancement in the ranks, but the distant location his men occupied from the active seat of the war suggested that these hopes would remain deferred for now. Still, it was always best to be prepared, and Pender had demonstrated that he excelled when it came to preparation.

5

"MY DANCING DAYS ARE OVER"

(July 1861–February 1862)

I feel as if we had been laid on the shelf for the war.
—DORSEY PENDER TO FANNY

[S]o long as I am here they shall know I am Colonel.
—WILLIAM DORSEY PENDER, 6TH NORTH CAROLINA INFANTRY

Colonel W. D. Pender must have reeled from the blow that the letter from his wife dated June 30, 1861, represented. Trained to endure hardship in camp and battle, this sharpest of arrows came not from the arsenal of an opposing warrior, but from the pen of the dearest creature he knew. Dorsey was devastated. "I have loved life dearly, but tonight I feel that this war had no terrors to me," he scribbled as part of a brief reply on the original letter sent back to Fanny on July 2.

The forced introspection demanded by his wife's "Read to end" correspondence was especially difficult. "The imputations are certainly hard to bear," he explained to her forthrightly, then added, with more than a touch of understatement, "Vanity is one of my weaknesses, but God knows not to such an extent as you charge." Her letter, the soldier and husband insisted, was "the greatest blow I had ever received."[1]

Three days later Pender tried to return to the basic structure of his previous letters, minus the most egregious social references, of course. Still, he felt compelled to defend himself one more time: "Oh! Fanny, Fanny, how could you suppose a dishonorable act, for if as you say '*the young lady* acted dishonorably and I must have encouraged her,' I was acting in bad faith and again darling you accuse me of prevaricating when I said I wanted to see you but that you had better not come down, which would have been prevaricating if my intentions had been as you intimated."

Fanny's letter had achieved the desired effect, for a mortified Dorsey Pender could not sleep with its contents on his mind. Ironically, given his words in a previous communication, his actions had "destroyed" someone's "rest"—his own. "If you had simply said I do not love you I could have stood it, for I should have known that you did not mean it, but to accuse me of dishonorable acts." Finally, after trying to turn the subject to the war, he came back to the topic that most troubled him. "My own darling did you really believe I was a dishonorable man[?]" he asked cautiously. "Please say no, for it will haunt me until you say so." She would have done well to remind her husband of his pre-war admonition to her to save the "fancy dances" for only him. At any rate, the remorseful spouse declared with the certainty of one who had just been punished sufficiently for a transgression, "Darling my dancing days are over, and *that Vanity*—honey shall never lead me again." The great irony was that in writing his initial reply on her letter, it was saved to posterity. For the moment, he contritely assured her, "Honey I sent your letter back not in anger, but in grief."[2]

Employing the Penders' domestic dispute in his examination of women in the Civil War, historian George Rable observed, "Wartime separations created new uncertainties and doubts for many couples, thereby multiplying the opportunities for misunderstandings and irreparable damage." Fortunately for Dorsey and Fanny, their "misunderstanding" did not lead to permanent damage in their relationship; indeed, the brief moment of strife that constituted this Suffolk interlude appeared to have strengthened them as a couple. Rable suggested that the Penders "obviously disagreed over acceptable standards of behavior even though both seemed to operate within traditional Southern notions about male and female roles."[3] But the dispute was less about traditional roles than a failure in communication. Dorsey was less guilty of any actual sexual peccadillo than the inability to take his marriage partner as seriously as she deserved and to treat her with respect as a wife and the mother of his children. For now, he had allowed his own need for the "approbation of others," as he so often put it, to displace the recognition and appreciation of the genuine affection and devotion he could find at home.

In response to the marital crisis, Pender threw himself into his martial duties. It did not hurt that he would soon be leaving the scene of his alleged iniquities to a new camp some miles away near Smithfield. He would demand more of himself and more of his men than ever. The camp streets would be immaculate, the men sharp and crisp at drill and inspection. Pender would clutch the evidence of his unworthiness close to his heart and compensate for it in other, tangible, and creditable ways that could restore his honor and respectability. Perhaps he could eventually mend the damage he had caused in their relationship and assuage Fanny's disappointment in him.

A new location might prove a tonic, but the transfer of the 3rd North Carolina from Suffolk in July required a stringent logistical effort. The move coincided with the shifting of supplies and equipment for other units and quickly overwhelmed the transportation infrastructure in the region. This nexus of demand strained the abilities of the acting quartermaster in Suffolk to respond to all the appeals being made to him, although Pender would understandably have been most acutely concerned with his own as he supervised the movement of his command.

In any case, the Fourth of July was hardly a celebratory one for Samuel Hunt, the Confederate bureaucrat charged with assisting these efforts. The difficulty began when Captain T. M. R. Talcott sought to acquire heavy wagons for the purpose of moving artillery pieces and ammunition for a battery guarding the James River. The materials were at nearby Zuni Station, but Talcott had searched in vain for adequate transportation before turning to Suffolk, "as there are no waggons [sic] in this section capable of hauling them."[4]

Unfortunately, the application was a day late. "Yesterday I had a requisition for the moving of Col. Pender's Regiment from this Post to Pagan Creek [near Smithfield]," Hunt explained apologetically from Suffolk. Furthermore, the effort was already underway and looked as if it might take another several days' duration to complete since wagons were not available in sufficient numbers to transfer all of these troops at one time. Some of the North Carolinians had to be shuttled forward, then the wagons returned to transport the remainder.

Quartermaster Hunt advised "seeing Col. W. D. Pender of the 3rd Regiment of No. Carolina Vol. who accompanied these troops and see if he will consent to liberate the *two large wagons*," which would enable Hunt to oblige the artillery unit's requirements more swiftly. If the artillerist could convince his infantry counterpart to cooperate, the army bureaucrat promised to assist Pender "with the balance of my wagons & all the carts & wagons that can be obtained in the neighborhood."[5]

It was not known if Captain Talcott attempted to locate, much less garnered, the attention of Colonel Pender regarding his request. Pender would probably have preferred to wait until the movement of his command had been completed anyway, but the matter reached a satisfactory resolution in relatively short order. Hunt noted to Talcott on July 6 that after his last communication, he had come "in possession of some wagons and teams on their way to Norfolk, which enabled me to accelerate materially the moving of the 3rd Regiment of No. Ca. Vols." This, in turn, allowed the quartermaster to help the battery commander with his needs.[6] Hunt subsequently took the captain to task for failing to follow the proper procedures. "The Department you know is quite rigid about these things," he informed Talcott on July 15, "requesting when transportation is needed to require always the requisition [in duplicate form]."[7] Unlike his colleague, as a professional soldier who had seen his share of paperwork over his career, the North Carolinian would have understood the last requirement and complied.

Cooperation between the two branches of the Confederate military would not have been totally inconceivable or unreasonable, for Pender's regiment had the task of providing protection for such batteries along the James River. In doing so, he came under the command of Brigadier General John C. Pemberton, and his men would soon have their hands full. "We shall have plenty of hard work," Pender informed his wife, "cutting roads, making bridges, cutting ditches around our camps." When it came to social activities, the interactions were strictly businesslike and professional. The area "ladies" were still "kind," though only in providing sewing services and assistance with the sick. "They would go to the [men in the] Measles hospital regularly every day to wait on them & take them nice things to eat." Unfortunately, such duties were necessary because the disease was "prevailing in our companies to a great extent."[8]

As he worked to restore the equilibrium to his relationship with Fanny, Dorsey bemoaned the fact that his new posting required longer for her letters to reach him. He considered the site, named Camp Ruffin, as "anything but agreeable in looks or comfort," although his personal accommodations in a large and spacious tent were satisfactory. Perhaps what intrigued him most was the proximity of his position to the Union troops across the James River and the reactions his men had to them. "We can see all the movements of the enemy by water, at Newport News," he told Fanny. "It would amuse you to see the curiosity evinced by our men at every movement of theirs."[9]

Even here, the doubts continued to creep in concerning his place in the conflict. "I feel as if we had been laid on the shelf for the war. No chance for us having a fight [here] I fear," Dorsey complained to Fanny.[10] Such action as would likely take place was going to occur elsewhere. "Let it come and may God defend and strengthen the just," he explained in his next letter. "If we are worsted then we can try again and again and the result will be the same. They cannot conquer us."[11]

Such expressions of nationalism were nothing new for Pender. Nor were they simple bravado, but rather the masking of the vulnerability that his spat with Fanny had exposed so fully. There was always the enemy to do battle with, even from afar, and a God to call upon to defend the just. Yet if he could not participate in the fray, there was less chance for his redemption in the eyes of his wife, himself, and the wider world. "If I could only have some hope of getting away from here," he confided to Fanny's sister Pamela, "it would be more bearable." But such "a forsaken country" seemed to be his lot, and the fear was that it was "likely to remain [so]."

To make matters worse, Pender's command was being pulled away from him in different directions, "just when we were getting in a condition to be a little proud of our appearance." At the bottom of so much frustration remained what Fanny thought of it all, and perhaps he expected Pamela to convey the message to her sister. "Fanny says she can not appreciate my being in command of a Regiment, & I can assure her that some times I find it difficult to appreciate myself." For now, Pender's "most troublesome enemies" were "mosquitoes & Knats."[12] One could hardly win accolades doing battle with such foes.

When word arrived from the front lines of the war, it produced a mixed reaction from the North Carolinian and created an opportunity for him. First, unhappy news reached him concerning sharp fighting that had taken place in western Virginia. The Confederates had suffered a defeat at Rich Mountain on July 11 in an operation that made a captive of Pender's old West Point friend John Pegram two days later. At the same time, while supervising a rearguard action that meant to allow his command and supply wagons to escape from advancing Federals at Corrick's Ford, Brigadier General Robert S. Garnett had lost his life.[13] "It was a sad day for the South," Dorsey concluded. "Two finer men and better officers are not to be found."[14] Perhaps most of all, the news brought the reality of war home to the soldier who had only a few weeks earlier told Fanny, with more than a hint of envy: "Beaut Stuart is Colonel and also John Pegram. They have gone to the Western part of Va. with General Garnett. I should like to be with them."[15]

The second piece of intelligence to reach him was decidedly better in its outcome for the South generally and for himself personally. The antagonists had clashed south of Washington, D.C., in a large battle that became known as First Manassas (or First Bull Run). Intelligence was sketchy, but Pender expressed "no doubt" that "a general engagement took place," and the word was that Southern arms had been victorious.[16] His opportunity for advancement came with the death of the popular Colonel Charles P. Fisher in the fighting there.[17] This left the 6th North Carolina without a commander, and Pender began immediately, at least in his own mind, to angle for it.

Even so, such matters would have to wait as other personal issues took center stage for the forlorn soldier. July presented Pender with the delight of a visit from Fanny, who traveled to Virginia to be with her husband for a short time in camp. The couple spent approximately three weeks together. At the end of that time, Dorsey experienced the pain of her departure, but their time together had enhanced the rebuilding of their relationship considerably.

Sending Fanny away was only a part of the separation anxiety that Pender was feeling as he contemplated breaking ties with the men he had shaped and molded into a command. He had an attachment to the regiment that would make the transfer more difficult than it might otherwise be. "I have not made up my mind as to what I shall do about Fisher's Regt.," he explained to Fanny on August 13, "but expect to remain where I am." The choice did not seem so very clear cut. "I should like very much to get up where it is, but dislike to leave the 3rd."[18]

In Pender's mind, there were a number of reasons for remaining where he was. He had built relationships with subordinates on his staff that would have to be severed unless they too could obtain transfers. The old vanity crept forth as he contemplated the possibility of leaving one unit for another. "Capts. Ruffin and Scales talked about resigning and going with me as privates," he noted of the officers he had once sent to Raleigh to wrangle with the governor over adequate support for the command. "They talk very seriously of resigning if I leave." In addition to these staff officers, Pender believed that fully four-fifths of the men in the regiment "will hate to see me leave," all apparently telling him directly or indirectly that in his absence, the command "will go to rack."[19]

At least one of these officers agreed that the effect of Pender's departure would be catastrophic to the regiment. Captain Thomas Ruffin Jr. dashed a note to his father, for whom their camp was named. "Colonel Pender has informed me, and only me," he observed almost conspiratorially, "that a tender has been made of him, of the command of the 6th (Fisher's) N.C. Regiment, and that he intended to take it: when he does so, I feel, that this regiment has lost its only man, in it, who can render it an efficient one." Young Ruffin expressed his desire "to go, if possible, with Col. Pender." Ruffin was anxious to remain with Pender, regardless of the circumstances. Indeed, he was thoroughly enamored of his superior. "Col. Pender is a great man," he exulted, "and I would rather serve under him than any one in the world and when he quits us, I shall have lost my whole interest in the regiment, as I am fully convinced that we cannot get a successor at all up to the mark."[20]

With help from the new governor of the state, Henry Toole Clark, Pender received the coveted appointment on August 19 (to date from the seventeenth), and he was soon on his way to his new command. The officers had expressed their desire for a native North Carolinian, and Pender's selection received their "unanimous" support. By August 26 he joined the 6th and began making a thorough assessment of the regiment. "I have to announce to you that I reached here yesterday and am regularly in harness I suppose for the war," he informed Fanny. With unfeigned pleasure, Dorsey added, "My presence was hailed with joy."

Still, the new colonel had his work cut out for him. "I find the health [of] the Regt. terrible. Only about two hundred and thirty fit for duty, and a great many of the sick dangerously ill." Pender was concerned that unless he could get a handle on the situation, "we shall [have a] great many deaths before we get through." The new commander saw his role as instrumental in providing relief to the men now under his charge. "I shall do all in my power to relieve the poor fellows," he promised Fanny, but he had to conclude that the situation was not as he had expected it to be when he took on the assignment.[21]

Pender's efforts included appealing directly to Governor Clark on behalf of his new command. "I have the honor to state that I reached here last evening and have assumed command of the Regt.," he noted on August 27, adding unabashedly, "I have reason to believe that my arrival was hailed with some degree of satisfaction." The camp itself was "in excellent order," but many of the men were "without shoes [with] some of them being unable to go to drill for the want of them." Also, the colonel had "taken the liberty of ordering . . . seven Hospital Tents, which I find an absolute necessity as there is but one Tent for the sick in this Regt." Space limitations had forced many of the sick to remain in their tents, which could hardly be conducive to the health of the rest, although even these personal accommodations were inadequate against the weather. Pender's final request was that his brother-in-law, Jacob Shepperd, be appointed to the regiment. "He has been very important in raising men," the colonel observed.[22]

In a personal sense, the transition was made easier for Pender since there seemed to be a universal dislike, among the officers at least, of the regiment's second in command, Lieutenant Colonel Charles E. Lightfoot.[23] Dorsey identified this problem relatively quickly, telling Fanny less than two weeks after he had arrived how dire the situation had become just before he got there. "Strictly between us," he confided, "if Col Lightfoot had remained much longer in command, the Regt. would have been lost beyond redemption." The situation had nearly developed into a revolt, for despite being "a nice gentleman" and "a good assistant," the lieutenant colonel's greatest transgression was that, as a former military-school instructor, he could not relate to the men and alienated the officers. "My dear," Pender explained rather pointedly for a man who some labeled a martinet himself, "these conceited military school teachers are worse than good men ignorant of the first principles of drill."[24]

Colonel Fisher had been well liked as a commander, but Pender found the 6th North Carolina in poor condition, even beyond matters of health and leadership, especially given his exacting standards. This was particularly true with regard to the physical state of the men. He immediately set about shaping the regiment in a way that would reflect well upon its new commander and improve its fighting trim. "I jumped into hard work and harrowing sights," he admitted to Fanny.[25] Although never one to shrink from difficult duty, in the months ahead Pender would see "so many crosses" that caused him to reflect nostalgically on his time with the 3rd North Carolina. Yet for the headstrong officer, one fact remained certain: "so long as I am here they shall know I am Colonel."[26]

During his transition from southeastern Virginia to the vicinity of Manassas, Colonel Pender enjoyed a brief visit to Richmond. Although a shopping venture to obtain gloves for Fanny proved only moderately successful—he would send her "the next best I could get"—the opportunity to reconnect with former associates was more fulfilling. "I found Custis Lee in Richmond & was with him most of the time," he explained of his West Point classmate, while also relishing the chance to see "several other old friends."[27] Pender recognized that his previous service provided many other tangible social benefits too. He could enjoy "tea" with General and Mrs. Joseph E. Johnston, who "recollected me from Leavenworth and treated me very kindly." Aside from the comradeship and the pleasant diversions from other duties, these moments offered him opportunities to make connections that might prove useful. "[An] Old [Army] officer has an enormous advantage," Pender concluded straightforwardly to his wife.[28]

At the end of August, Dorsey informed Fanny, "We are still here & I hope we will remain for a few days more until I can get my horse & other things" that he had requested from his brother-in-law Hamilton. As usual, Pender's mind was whirling with activity. When not thinking about the condition of the men or the state of the war, he was grappling with himself and the relationship he had with the wife and family he adored. "I am hoping we shall find such winter quarters that you will be able to be with me," Dorsey professed anxiously.[29]

The colonel was also concerned about military developments in his native state. On August 27 and 28, Federal forces assailed Confederate defensive positions on the North Carolina coast. "What sad news from N.C.," Pender moaned when he learned of the loss of Forts Clark and Hatteras. "We all feel the deepest interest in her safety and to think the rascals have landed [and] commenced their ravages." From his vantage point in Virginia, it was difficult to say what those "ravages" might entail. Nevertheless, Dorsey remarked to Fanny, "Thank the Lord you are out of their reach," taking some solace in that fact.[30]

September found him still in Camp Jones, near Manassas, and just as concerned about the condition of his command. "We have not moved yet," he assured Fanny, and frankly he was not sure many of his men could move until conditions improved concerning their overall health. "Our troops are so cripled [sic] by sickness that I do not see how we could walk," he explained to her.[31] Pender revealed the ongoing nature of his worries in this regard in subsequent letters.[32] He considered the unit's morale low and saw that mentality as a key to the poor state of the men's health. "They had gotten despondent and truly they had enough to make them so." He was finding that the strain was affecting him adversely too. "I find it hard to keep up my spirits with so much sickness, and so many deaths." Other stresses remained that added to the general malaise and threatened the effectiveness of the command. Yet the colonel could take some comfort in the knowledge that with the measures he had undertaken on the men's behalf, the situation was at least improving slowly.[33]

Pender understood that morale was a fragile entity. He thought Fanny might "get up" a benefit concert "in behalf of this poor Regt." With such funds as could be thus raised, there would be some relief "for those who need it." The effort would have a humanitarian effect. "They are mostly poor men, some of them with starving wives at home," he explained. "Wives and children crying to them for bread and they unable to help them." But left unspoken, at least directly, was the role the gesture might have on limiting the excuse for the most desperate of these men to desert. The colonel felt that despite his awareness of the problem, he could not do much by himself to address it. "I sympathize with the poor fellows, but my purse is not heavy enough to help them."[34]

Yet Pender had more on his mind than the physical condition of his men or their families. Perhaps the deaths he was experiencing within his own ranks, and the loss of his West Point friend Garnett, reminded him of his own mortality. He once again contemplated life outside of the armed forces. "In fact I begin to think it impossible to be satisfied," Dorsey wrote Fanny on September 5, "but the nearest to it I could get would be out of the military and with you." Of course, he was too practical a man not to realize that any such move would only create new sources for dissatisfaction. "But then I should feel as if I ought to be serving my country," he concluded, and that particular cloud of doubt dissipated once more.[35]

Even so, Pender tormented himself as never before with the specter of eternal life without his beloved Fanny. Plagued with self-doubt and presented with a relatively quiet posting that allowed him to dwell on these feelings, Dorsey engaged in a burst of introspection that delved deeply into his own religious beliefs. "Honey, I sincerely try to be a Christian," he explained to her plaintively. "I have faith in Christ and hope for the best." Then he undermined the confidence he had just expressed in his own salvation. "Honey I am troubled because I fear I do not take that interest in reading the Bible as I should, and studying its truths." Although, he quickly added, "I read it, however, every night and try to practice [those truths] by day." Dorsey simply could not allow himself the luxury of believing that his salvation was assured. "Oh! honey the idea that when we go to our final rest you will go to everlasting life and bliss and I to everlasting damnation agonizes me." Through the means of the letter, he cried out, "Let us go together."[36]

Pender feared death less for the separation he might have from the Almighty than the one he risked from the wife he loved so dearly. She was a prime, if not the central, element of his motivation for ensuring that he would embrace the religion that she embodied for him and through her example attain the eternal "bliss" that would await them together. Yet Pender was not substituting his worldly affections for his heavenly ones. He was merely employing the earthly love he felt to propel him toward a decision he had come to realize he ought to be sure in making. If Fanny was the catalyst and a permanent reunion the reward, particularly if one's worldly journey were to be cut short as might happen abruptly during a war, then so much the better and wiser for having the certainty of a decision for salvation.

One historian has offered an interesting conceptualization of the Pender marriage and the place of religion in it. Stephen Berry has suggested that for couples such as Dorsey and Fanny, romance and religion formed complicated relationships. "William Pender's determination to become a Christian, for instance," he explained, "was less a religious quest than a romantic one." Berry added of Fanny's husband, "Each time he set out to find religion, he found only Fanny; all roads led to Romance." Finally, he asserted that Fanny, or "Mrs. W. D. Pender" as Dorsey liked to characterize her himself, "was not so much a part of his religion as the whole of it."

Certainly, such an interpretation of this complex marital relationship presented an interesting opportunity to assess the places of religion and romance amid war in mid-nineteenth-century America, but the assessment that in Dorsey's case Fanny somehow became his religion cannot be sustained. She may well have been "a suitable foundation for a religion" and a "personal intercessor with the Almighty" for her husband as her example and her prayers for him would have indicated, but he recognized that those characteristics in the woman he loved pointed him higher. No matter how much he may have worshipped her in one sense, Fanny could not be "a personal religion," even for Dorsey, or he would have lost the very eternal security for which he struggled so mightily, for her sake as well as his own.[37] Pender never would have taken that chance.

In subsequent communications Dorsey's desire to conform to his own spiritual expectations continued to exist as an underlying theme. He wished Fanny to "tell me how you felt when you joined the church" and professed his desire to undertake "my great decision to conversion."[38] Pender thought nothing more than to "be worthy to number myself amongst the sheep of his fold" and again expressed the ultimate fear that drove him. "The idea that when we separate upon this earth we may never meet is awful. It stares me in the face all the time." Pender's God would surely not reject the motivation that impelled him to act or the earthly example he would use to discover his path to righteousness. In the end Fanny was a pilot to something purer and nobler in his soul. "Darling, the desire to have true faith in Christ and reap the blessings secured to us all by his crucifixion is constantly uppermost."[39]

Nevertheless, the inner turmoil continued. Pender still felt the need to embrace the outward trappings of honor, bragging to Fanny about the "stallion" that had become "the admiration of everyone." But he struggled with the notion that his every act now carried the mark of goodness or depravity. "Every evening," he wanted her to know, "I ask myself what wrong act or thought I have done during the day and determine to do better the next." Such raw introspection also carried into daylight hours, when Dorsey seemed to be under an almost constant state of personal evaluation. These moments led to candor on other matters, such as when he predicted in the same letter, "there will be more suffering than glory this winter."[40]

Finally, at the end of a September marked with such intense personal examination, Pender announced that he was ready to take a most important step in his religious pilgrimage. "I have come to the conclusion from reading Acts that I might become a member of the Church at once, for we cannot think that all those who repented and were baptized by Paul could have been as good as they should have been." The Pender logic was in full swing. "In fact," he observed with a measure of almost palpable relief, "it seems to me that that act was about the commencement of their regeneration, for in many instances he did not perfect his work at once, but returned to them to complete it."[41] At last, Dorsey felt free to embrace his religion while accepting his depravity.

In his very next communication, Pender opened with a renewed confidence in the course he had chosen for himself. "I write particularly to let you know of a determination I have come to, that I know will give you great happiness. I have determined to be baptized as soon as I can get an opportunity." Flushed with the sense that a significant point in his life finally was being reached, he observed: "I have talked with Col. [Benjamin] Alston an old friend, & he advises me not to delay. He was very kind & offered to do any thing for me he could, will go with me if I go, to Fredericksburg, but in the mean time has written to see if the Chaplain of Hampton's Legion is with it."[42]

The would-be communicant had further assistance as he sought to "be worthy of the sacrament of confirmation."[43] The Methodist chaplain of the regiment, Adolphus W. Mangum, played a pivotal role in helping Dorsey sort through the religious elements that weighed on his mind.[44] "I talked with the Chaplain last night," he explained to Fanny at the end of September, "and told him as near as I could my feeling and the change that I thought had come over me." Fanny may have worried about the influence that a member of another denomination might exert over her husband, but Mangum assured the prospective Episcopalian that "he does not & never did wish to shake any man's preference for any particular church," an assurance Dorsey passed along.[45]

Given the novice aspect of his spiritual journey, Pender was probably not as surprised as a longtime adherent at the preacher's willingness to steer him toward religion without championing a particular denomination. Yet according to one student of religion among Civil War soldiers, he probably should not have been anyway. Historian Steven Woodworth cited examples of cross-denominational behavior by chaplains, even when those practices conflicted with their own observances and ordinances. "Such goings-on may sound trivial to many in the twenty-first century," Woodworth explained, "but they represented an unusual degree of tolerance for nineteenth-century [religious denominations and practices]."[46] The minister's neutral position on the potentially thorny issue of a supplicant's affiliation also allowed Pender to feel freer about confiding in the preacher.

Dorsey wanted Fanny to be happy about the alteration in his life. "I know that I am a changed man," he observed, while persisting in questioning his level of personal commitment. Still, he seemed satisfied that genuine progress was being made. "When I first commenced thinking seriously on this subject the idea how it would please you was uppermost," he admitted, "but now it is different." The shift in his thinking was not inconsequential to his desire to make an appropriate choice. "I think of pleasing God and saving my soul," he now sincerely believed, "and then that it will be a source of great happiness to you."[47]

Considering such important matters overnight, Dorsey returned to his letter and the subject the next day. Even so, his ambivalence had not left him entirely. On the one hand, there was the overriding desire to see and be with Fanny. On the other, there was a focus on eternity. "I feel quite reconciled now to the absence," he offered bravely, "for I believe that I have thought more of the future. If we had been together, my pleasure in being with you would have left but little chance of thinking of our Saviour." His struggles would hardly subside simply because he had reached this realization, and his doubts persisted about his worthiness, but Dorsey seemed to embrace a level of acceptance with the life-changing steps he had taken. "Today I have not had such tumultuous feelings as for the last few days," he confessed, "but I think I feel more safety, more contentment." Pender also continued to seek his wife's guidance and advice as he had done.⁴⁸

As he pondered his spiritual future, Dorsey still embraced earthly matters. Once more, he contemplated discarding his carefully orchestrated military career for civilian life with Fanny and the boys but recognized, as he had done so often before, "the duty of all who have any experience in [the] military [is] to do other [than to resign] in these times."⁴⁹

In the meantime, Pender returned his thoughts to religious matters, slowly accepting the notion that he might, indeed, be worthy enough to receive Christian baptism. "Honey, I have become perfectly reconciled in my mind to being baptized. I thought at first that I could not be worthy, but now I feel perfectly easy on the subject. I look upon becoming a member of the Church as a matter of course. Since the first night I talked to the Chaplain I have imagined at least that I have felt a peace and contentment I never knew before." Such a sense of spiritual peace was the key to any state of contentment in Pender, and both now seemed to be linked inextricably to the religious path he had chosen for himself. "If nothing happens," he closed, "I shall start to Fredericksburg tomorrow evening to be baptized the next day."⁵⁰

For all of the strains on his resolve and the personal questions of inadequacy he had worked so diligently to overcome, and despite the nagging fear that stayed with him, William Dorsey Pender took the step he had been contemplating. "I was baptized today," he dutifully reported, "in the presence of the Regt. by the Rev. Mr. Loomes Porter of Charleston." With his wife's good example as a buttress and the underlying fear that by not doing so he risked eternal separation from her, Dorsey had completed the task before him. "I was willing to have it done in the sight of all," he explained, "for with God's help I shall endeavor to live up to the vows I then took." In addition to the men of the regiment, his friends Benjamin Alston and Stephen D. Lee served as witnesses. He could only lament that he wished "my Christian wife could have been present. I know it would have caused her great joy to see her husband overcome the fear of the scoffing of the unworldly, and then bow down and acknowledge his God and Saviour."⁵¹

One of the witnesses to the "solemn scene" later recounted the proceedings that opened with hymns and a lection by Rev. A. W. Mangum. The writer noted that the "Colonel of the regiment had been for some time under deep religious conviction . . . and had selected this day and occasion, to make an open profession of his faith in the presence of the men over whom he exercised authority."[52]

Mangum himself used the occasion to develop "a lesson" that he offered years later on "The Basis of True Courage." In this reminiscence, published in the University of North Carolina's magazine, the former chaplain recalled his conversations with the young officer, often centering "on the subject of personal religion." The minister was moved by what he had witnessed of Pender's supplications: "I found that he was deeply concerned about his spiritual condition, and that he was availing himself of the lull in the storm to examine the all important question, and to secure, if possible, an assurance of his reconciliation with his God. He knew what war was, and he evidently had serious convictions that he was approaching a tremendous conflict." The colonel shared his earlier experiences in combat in the far northwest with the preacher. Mangum took from this portion of their conversation Pender's recognition of the vagaries of war and the sense of urgency such uncertainty produced in his religious journey:

> He knew that hard fighting meant wounds and death; and he knew that hard fighting was coming. He expected to do his duty; and he was sure that that would lead him where death held high carnival. If need be, he was going to die for his country; and he wished to be ready to die. A more deliberate and concentrated spiritual effort I have never witnessed. I recall him now as he came to the door of my tent with his bible in his hand, or as he sat in his own tent and buried his thoughts in the words of eternal truth. He would seek with all his mind to find the meaning of the scriptures, and with solicitude . . . he would ask me to explain what he could not understand.[53]

Perhaps Dorsey Pender was turning an important corner in his spiritual and personal development. The chaplain observed that the soldier did not seem to be motivated in this instance by the opinions of others, making no attempt to "conceal his godly purpose and effort from his officers and men" nor demonstrating "the faintest semblance of ostentation." Mangum had not known Pender long, but he obviously felt, particularly with the benefit of hindsight, that he knew him well. "In this, as in all else," the minister concluded, "his whole soul was absorbed in what he felt to be his duty."[54]

Fanny's influence upon her husband was unmistakable. The guidance she offered had steered him steadily to this result. Yet Dorsey's decision was an intensely personal one. His last steps in following the course she had helped set for him would have to be his own. "Finally he became satisfied that he was ready to connect himself with the Church of God," Mangum recalled. Again, Fanny's example led the way. "He did not appear to have any decided preference for any denomination," the Methodist chaplain explained, "but expressed himself in favor of the Protestant Episcopal Church because his wife belonged to it—speaking touchingly of their attending the house of God together."[55]

Pender had not failed to lead by example in martial matters and now obviously wished for his actions to serve as a model in spiritual ones as well. Once he had set his course, Dorsey acted. His "rapid ride" to a nearby command "miles away" to secure the services of an Episcopal minister impressed Mangum, who accompanied him, with the seriousness of his mission. Although "genial and friendly," the colonel also brushed aside the pleasantries of his friend Lee, who as an artillerist insisted upon discussing some new pieces of ordnance he had recently procured. Pender quickly turned the conversation to his reason for the visit and as a result, "not only engaged the minister, but also invited Lee to act as one of the witnesses."[56]

The images associated with the ceremony became etched in the minds of onlookers. "The Colonel," a participant explained, accompanied by "his two chosen friends, a Major and Captain of the Confederate army, advanced to the rude font where the minister was standing, when immediately the whole regiment rose to their feet and formed an unbroken circle around them." As Alston and Stephen Lee watched reverently beside the communicant, the assemblage of soldiers surrounding them grew silent. With "prayer and words of solemn exhortation," the preacher turned to Pender, received the soldier's assurance of his determination to follow a new course in his life's walk, and administered the rite of baptism. The effect was evident immediately to those around him. "As he rose from his knees, the tears were coursing down his manly cheeks, and there was scarcely a dry eye in the congregation." In the final step of the sacred process he had undertaken, Pender accepted the sacrament of the Lord's Supper.[57]

Reverend Porter knew that the public profession of faith the soldier had offered before his assembled command was actually only part of a lifelong journey that lay ahead. To aid in Dorsey's spiritual development and offer him a comfort in the inevitable times of trouble that would come, Porter presented him with a copy of *Sacra Privata: The Private Meditations, Devotions, and Prayers of the Right Rev. T. Wilson, D.D.* He inscribed the volume simply and thoughtfully: "Col. Wm. Dorsey Pender with the prayers & kind regards of the Friend & clergyman who Baptized him on Sunday 6th October, A. Loomes Porter, Rector Ch. Of the Holy Communion, Charleston, So. Car."[58] The preacher undoubtedly hoped that the gift would sustain its recipient through whatever lay ahead. But clearly, this day had been a salient and unforgettable one for a man who would never cease to hold himself to the highest personal and professional standards, and who just as often felt that he had fallen short of that mark.

Whatever he might think of his continuing frailties, others saw Pender and his public religious actions as inspirational. Although it was unclear if the soldier ever authorized or sanctioned it, the South Carolina Tract Society used his baptism ceremony as an example to others, publishing as tract "No. 129" *The Colonel Baptized in Presence of His Regiment*. The motivational pamphlet described the occasion and ended with the admonition that God would reward the person who chose to turn from sinfulness. "If you come as this officer did," it concluded, "He will make you a priest and a king unto God."[59]

In the aftermath of his baptism, Colonel Pender had more than his share of earthly concerns, but heavenly ones continued to hold a high place as well. On the way to visit a nearby artillery position, Jeb Stuart's cousin Peter Hairston ran into pickets of the 6th North Carolina who, he recalled in a subsequent letter, "stopped me, and sent me into camp. I there found Col. Pender who has just united himself to the Episcopal Church." He recorded no other subjects that passed between them during the brief stop, although the colonel also "rode down to the batteries with me" when Hairston left the camp.[60]

Pender entered this new phase of life with the assurance and contentment that come with having made a powerful and important decision. Almost immediately, his correspondence began to reflect a more positive tone. When his wife apparently unburdened her own doubts and concerns to him, he responded patiently and affirmatively. "Do not say that you are not a Christian, for Fanny, you are my earthly model." Now the roles of the two were reversed, and he was the same solid foundation for Fanny that she had so long been for him. "But honey let us fight on in the good cause, let us sustain and encourage each other, let us not faint by the wayside, for certainly He will not desert those who sincerely try. My wife, despair not, grieve not, all things are for the best, and by His arrangement."[61]

For all of his spiritual and personal developments, Pender's internal contradictions remained. He enjoyed a level of awareness and compassion for the dilemmas facing his men, but his sense of strict adherence to duty was present as well. He could explain to his wife, "Some of the poor fellows under me have wives and children who are starving," while insisting that those loved ones could "have no hope of seeing each other until this war shall close."[62] The fact that some of these men might find legitimacy in their minds for deserting to attend to family needs did not seem to dawn on him. Duty overrode all else, and fortitude in the face of privation was a virtue.

Pender continued to depend upon his wife to serve as his "earthly model" for heavenly matters, but he was also finding comfort in his new military associations. In early October Dorsey informed Fanny that he particularly enjoyed the company of the chaplain. "I like him very much," he explained, "and his society is more comfort to me than that of anyone in the Regt."[63] But within a short time, it was apparent that Mangum was not going to remain long with the unit.[64] Indeed, by early November, Dorsey informed Fanny, "As predicted, our chaplain, Mr. Mangum, has resigned." This departure left Pender more dependent than before on Fanny for his religious consultation, although he expressed the intention of locating someone else, perhaps an Episcopalian, for the vacancy. "I got a Methodist to please some of the men," he admitted. "He has left and I shall try to please myself."[65]

Writing now from Camp Fisher, but assuring Fanny that it "is the same Camp Hill that I have been at for the last month," Dorsey lamented that he had "no idea when we shall move, it may be an hour or it may be weeks. We are holding ourselves in readiness of any emergency."[66] The false alarms and rumors of imminent action continued. "We did expect an attack last week, almost hourly, but the anxiety has passed off," he explained in early November. Things had indeed "quieted down again," but the possibility of combat remained ever present. Dorsey warned his wife that she "need not be surprised to hear at any time of a big fight for it seems almost impossible to believe that after making such tremendous efforts and spending so much money, they will give up the idea of 'on to Richmond.'"[67]

While awaiting the next Union move, Pender had the occasion to see a friend who passed the camp with his unit. The moment reminded Pender of the vicissitudes of the chain of command and seniority in the Confederate service, a fact of which he remained acutely aware. Robert Ransom was at the head of a fine body of cavalry, superbly mounted, but Pender speculated that Ransom would likely be placed under the command of an officer who had finished at the academy after his friend had graduated in 1850 "and who was far below him in the same Regt. in the U.S. Army." Dorsey's conclusion of his compatriot's dilemma was likely meant as much for himself as for Fanny when he observed, "But we military men have to hold down our pride sometimes, when it is pretty hard."[68]

Pender's interest in military protocol did not diminish the many concerns of ordinary living in such extraordinary times that also consumed him. There were instructions for the boys about having young Dorsey baptized and keeping Turner appropriately dressed for the coming winter. There was the ongoing effort to keep the "mess expenses" balanced, which he took considerable pride in doing. "Rather good housekeeping I think on my part," he explained to Fanny, "but still my money goes somehow." Pender professed that he did not think about ever being rich. "I only want to pay what I owe, at least that is my feeling now."[69]

Their subsequent communications, at least if judged by the letters Dorsey sent to Fanny in mid-November, highlighted the complexity of the married relationship they enjoyed in microcosm. In one piece of correspondence, dated November 12, Pender underscored his dependency on her. "You know Honey, or at least I can tell you, that I am wanting in confidence. I have vanity enough, but singularly to say, not enough confidence, and your praise of me does me good. It makes me feel as I could do." In the same letter he illustrated a deep and abiding affection in the most tender of terms. "You say these cold nights that you do long to be in my arms. I seldom go to sleep without wishing that you were in my straw. I think to myself, altho I have nothing but blankets on straw, how happy Fanny would be to be with me on it. Good night."[70] Then in the very next letter, there was playful chiding in apparent answer to Fanny's despondent notions about death. Dorsey answered almost tauntingly: "My dear child, why do you let the future trouble you so much[?] You say sometimes you feel that death would be a relief, but then the idea of my having a second wife comes up and you think you had rather not die. What useless trouble."[71] Neither seemed to give much ground to the other. Both were more than capable of jabbing at their spouse's insecurities and vulnerabilities with almost a latent sense of pleasure at the discomfort they would create. It was as if by generating intense emotions, the pair was demonstrating to themselves and each other just how strongly they felt.

The distant warrior tried to juggle all of the responsibilities that he felt attached to his duty as an officer, husband, and father. One of the more difficult duties was a court-martial that dragged on for much of the late fall and highlighted the unsettling phenomenon of desertion. The work placed Pender in a delicate position for a man noted for his adherence to discipline and rigid acceptance of duty as he contemplated the means of battling a scourge whose most drastic remedy in the form of summary execution also challenged his sense of compassion and Christian forgiveness. Still, if military order became too lax, disorder would follow, likely to be manifested in additional unauthorized absences from the ranks, and the consequences could not help but be detrimental to the command's effectiveness. One scholar has suggested that while overall "the volume of the early desertions could hardly be deemed significant," such departures from the field nevertheless represented fractures in Confederate sentiment that were already taking place "before the real horror of war on the battlefield had occurred." Furthermore, as underscored in this instance, "no state's troops were immune."[72]

Fellow North Carolinian Lawrence O'Bryan Branch appealed to Pender for leniency on behalf of the kith and kin of some of those being charged. The request came with a petition, by which Branch assured his colleague, "Those signing do not design it as an interference with the course of discipline in your Regiment, but simply as an appeal for clemency." He noted that the young men who otherwise exhibited impeccable behavior had been misled. "Newspapers and politicians are constantly telling them that they are ill used, and exciting their jealousy towards the officers who have higher pay and more privileges." Branch added, "Whilst this does not excuse, it goes far to palliate their conduct, and I hope will be taken into consideration in meting out punishment." He understood the need for a reckoning of some form but "was quite sure that a moderate amount of punishment will have all the effect on them and their comrades, that the utmost severity of military law would have on the men of whom armies are usually composed." Branch's final effort was his most personal, calculated to reach Pender through the avenue of state loyalty, if not as a professional soldier who knew well those citizen-soldiers who served under him. "Allow me, Colonel, to appeal to you on behalf of these North Carolina boys—far from home, and from the friends whose advice would have kept them out of trouble—for all the clemency you can extend to them compatibly with your sense of duty."[73]

The problem raised by this case for Pender was an acute one, and he looked for any means of relieving him of the onus of such duty. "I am President of a General Court Martial that will take us two or three weeks. Some of the charges involve death," he wrote on Oct. 9.[74] The seriousness of the situation and his place in the drama weighed heavily on Pender's mind.

Two days later he admitted to Fanny that he would like to "run and hide myself," and he looked for Divine guidance to help him through the difficulty. Although he recognized the relative state of his "load in life in comparison with some," Pender thought "a little more would be too much sometimes." The crucial element remained the court-martial. "Putting charges against many that involve death. And then the trying of those charges." He admitted that the strain represented a "continued drag upon our tempers."[75]

By the next week, Pender could not yet point to relief on this troublesome score. "Our Court is not half through its labors," he complained to Fanny on October 19. "I am getting very tired of it, and hope some move may break it up."[76] Even when there was a respite, the circumstances proved temporary. At the beginning of November, he explained: "I am sorry to say that our court has been ordered to reassemble. It takes up all my time, or so much of it that I do not feel like doing anything after it is over." Indeed, it was not so much the time as the energy spent in performing these distasteful, though necessary, tasks. "Besides this," he added quickly, "sitting in judgement [sic] on men is not pleasant. I have [a] good many cases in my Regt. for sleeping on post and desertion."[77]

The enlisted men certainly tested Pender's patience in other ways as well, particularly with regard to squandering the already inadequate supplies provided by a strained support system. "My great trouble is the want of tools to work with," Pender complained in November. "You have no idea how scarce axes are getting in the Southern Confederacy." Additionally, those few that could be obtained were being "lost or ruined." Rather than husbanding their precious resources, the men were behaving irresponsibly and exacerbating the shortages. "It worries me some times to see how negligent these men are," he concluded. "If they had been raised so, it would not be so bad, but most of them have been raised to make everything go as far as possible."[78] The colonel was clearly struggling with the psychology of the men under his charge and was frustrated with their apparent carelessness.

One of the men who understood Pender's difficulty was Benjamin White, a lieutenant in the 6th North Carolina, who had been a schoolteacher before hostilities prompted his enlistment. His was hardly an auspicious beginning. "I have now been in camp more than six months [and] have endured a good deal of hardship and suffering," he wrote a former pupil. Doubting the youth's understanding of such conditions, he added grimly, "it is a fact that the Battlefield is far less to be dreaded than the sickness in Camp and the privations and hardships we have to undergo." The men were "now building winter cabbins

[sic], but we have so few tools that it seems like Slow business." At any rate, the scholar-turned-soldier concluded, with one eye to his letter's reader and another to himself, "the Army is no place for Boys and sick folks."[79]

Required to supervise these men, Colonel Pender relied on discipline and authority, leavened with a generous dose of paternalism. He sought to accomplish the same mix from afar in advising Fanny about domestic matters. Dorsey felt that her servant, Laura, must be dealt with firmly. "I am sorry Laura does so badly," he noted before suggesting the best solution that he could devise for controlling such behavior. "Whipping is the only remedy for children ... who unfortunately have been raised with the idea that they must be whipt."[80] Interestingly, Dorsey formulated his "remedy" without regard to race, but rather as the means a parent would use to discipline a wayward child.

Pender had a young servant of his own named Joe. On two occasions he recorded exercising corporal punishment as part of his discipline regimen. He did not couch these actions in the same terms but in response to tendencies Pender associated with race. The worst of these moments prompted him to write on October 24, 1862: "You will be surprised to hear that I gave Joe a tremendous whipping last night. I had been promising him [one] for some time and finally he got it. He is a good and smart boy but like most young negroes needs correction badly."[81]

In other respects, Pender expressed his paternalism in more benevolent ways with regard to Joe and a manservant named Harris. He wanted it understood that he would meet their basic needs. In November 1861, undoubtedly with the chill beginning to settle in the night air, Pender requested his brother David "to bring Harris an overcoat."[82] For the innovative Joe, the demands in that sense were considerably less. "The rascal seems to have plenty of money, but I have ordered him to allow me to be his treasurer," Dorsey informed Fanny in September of the following year. "He has managed to dress himself in a nice gray uniform, french bosom linen shirt—for which he paid $4—has two pairs [of] new shoes, etc. etc." Then the master realized a brighter side to the arrangement. "If he continues as he has commenced his clothing will never cost me anything."[83] At the same time, Pender put his "trust" in the older man, Harris, "entirely" with regard to the money that would keep the mess in good order.[84]

Pender believed that both men were "anxious to learn" and "desirous of doing right," but the statements themselves called into question the degree to which he considered them capable of sustaining themselves without his guiding hand.[85] Even so, Dorsey wanted to be liked by them too. "I try to be kind to them and they seem to be attached [and] are as faithful as they could be. I could not have better servants." As it turned out, Pender considered Joe something of a work in progress. He explained to Fanny that when the young man started in his position, he had a great deal to learn. "He did not know how to black boots, never had curried a horse or anything pertaining to waiting on a gentleman, but now he is quite a reputable valet."[86]

Indeed, Pender's arrangement with the men was a complex one. He expected them to provide the basic functions of servants but paid them a substantial wage for fulfilling their duties. Ever the frugal one regarding personal finance, at one point Dorsey asked Fanny to have his brother Robert find him "a cheaper boy than Joe unless his father will consent to let him stay for less." The arrangement for both Joe and Harris was costing him more money than a private soldier in the ranks earned. Apparently, Dorsey talked to the men about the subject and thought Harris the most likely to be receptive. "He is very anxious to remain but in these times when servants are so low I cannot begin to pay $15 per month for what Joe does. I shall also try to do a little better than give Harris $15. No one in the Regt. gives so much."[87]

Dorsey managed to curtail his costs. In March he informed Harris that his wage would be reduced to "$12 after this month." In the meantime, Pender sent him home "for the benefit of his health," though not before Harris promised to come back. Even so, Dorsey had his doubts, directing Fanny to "ask him if he is going to return and if not ask brother [Robert] or David to send me a[nother] cook."[88] Indeed, he struggled a bit while Harris was away. "I am getting anxious to have him back," he told Fanny a week after the man had left.[89] Finally, on April 26 he reported happily, "Harris returned yesterday bringing my shirts."[90]

Pender had admitted his lack of confidence to his wife, but he could not do so before his comrades and subordinates in arms. Not only would such a public admission be out of character, it would be anathema to the Southern conceptions of manhood, which rested so heavily on a sense of honor. Reputation meant everything.[91] He still expressed himself strongly when he felt he had to do so and retained a tendency to react when he felt imposed upon by others; only now he tempered these reactions with a desire to "do better," as he so often put it. Thus, when an individual stretched his patience to the breaking point, Dorsey told Fanny: "Today I got in a terrible passion and talked very improperly to a gentleman, but in half an hour I rode over a mile to apologize. It was all I could do and I did it." The incident left him "sorry" and "ashamed," and he determined, "I shall try to do better in the future."[92]

The North Carolinian was determined to do his duty and demanded that his officers perform theirs as well. But some of these subordinates were proving problematic. Pender noted that a number of them were "meditating resigning this winter." Such choices might make sense under some circumstances, but amid war they did not, at least to Dorsey Pender. He assured Fanny that any action of this nature "will find some difficulty if I remain in command of the Regt. for I do not think it right that officers who got their men to come [into the service], should go off and leave them."[93]

Through all of these experiences, it was clear that Colonel Pender was learning more than just about himself. His relatively short time in charge of so many men taught him vital lessons about human nature in ways that West Point had taught him about the technicalities of the drill field. This new school of the soldier provided him with glimpses into the human condition that could be difficult, for they revealed a great deal about the quality of some of his men. One such incident occurred when thieves took over one hundred dollars' worth of goods, and Pender had to solve the case. As he probed he learned that the armed services could be a refuge for those who did not fit well in civilized society. "It does appear that as soon as a man becomes a soldier he loses all honesty he may ever have had," Dorsey complained to Fanny. "There were fifty men who knew that these fellows had the goods & ought to have known they came by them dishonestly, but still said nothing about it."[94]

The professionally trained officer remained concerned about the volunteers who populated so much of the armed forces in this conflict, particularly when they lay beyond his immediate reach. Several months after his discussion about pilfering, he voiced a separate, but connected, concern. With Fanny planning a journey over some distance, he suggested that she do so in the company of his older brother Robert. He was especially worried about the number of troops congregating in the towns through which she would be traveling. "I have a horror of drunken soldiers, particularly when ladies are about," he admitted, "for it would appear that men do not act so badly until they get to be soldiers."[95]

Pender continued to receive praise from others and remained as uncertain of how to handle it. Was the sentiment genuine or motivated by some baser measure? When people he considered important deferred to him in one sense or another, the young officer swelled as surely as he had in the early days of the war. "It is very flattering to have such men . . . think so well of me," Dorsey wrote Fanny. He promised that she should not fear the praise, "for I know I have a poorer opinion of myself than many sensible people have of me. What they consider something extra I look upon as what any man with my experience and a desire to do right might do." The desire for promotion was ever present in his mind, but he disdained "aspiring" for it. "I feel as I did about the Colonelcy," he asserted. "Doubts as to my capacity to do well."[96]

Certainly, Pender continued to be conscious of and sensitive toward the status bestowed on him by others and by the rank and achievements he had accrued for himself. That sensitivity burst forth when he thought his path to advancement was once more in the hands of politicians, whom he had learned he could not trust. "Gov. Clark threw cold water upon my efforts, saying—old Foggy—that I ought to be satisfied to have risen from Lieut. to Colonel. As if my being a Lieut. was anything less in the military than a private citizen." Dorsey put as brave a face on the matter as he could, telling Fanny cavalierly: "It does not trouble me at all. I shall try to let the thing pass from my mind. If any friends pursue it, all well."[97]

Despite his internal doubts and external expressions of equanimity concerning promotion, the colonel was prepared once again to look in many directions for support. He asked Fanny to approach her father on the subject. Congressman Shepperd could certainly be of help, but Dorsey felt uneasy about seeking such assistance himself. He encouraged her to do so, "not that I would not ask him for a favor, but I really feel a delicacy in asking anyone to recommend me for such a high position." Besides, a wife could be excused for saying to her father that "her husband is capable of filling any position even if she should not think it." In any case, he hoped his record as colonel would suffice, "if merit has anything to do with it." "But," he closed the subject with a hint of despondency, "I fear merit has nothing to do in the matter."[98]

That same day General Joseph E. Johnston, the commander of the army, visited the camp. "I am told that he was much pleased with our Brigade," Pender related to his wife, "and as I have the crack Regt. in drill, discipline, [and] polish, I take something of the praise to myself." Whatever the other units demonstrated in their skills and enthusiasm, none of them "come up to mine in either of the three qualities above specified." Pender was pleased that the troops showed his leadership without having to become showy themselves. "My men are the sort who obey orders and make little fuss or pretensions."[99] A few days later he received another independent confirmation of the esteem others felt for him when "a man in the 3rd" wrote him requesting a transfer. "I do not know when anything has so pleased or stirred me," Dorsey asserted to Fanny, forwarding the letter to her so that she could see it for herself.[100]

The proud soldier reiterated his commander's comments to his wife a few days later, the impression clearly still prevalent in his mind. "Gen. Johnston said to Gen. [William H. C.] Whiting the other day while riding through my camp that it was the neatest in the Army of the Potomac." Apparently, Whiting passed along the story, for Pender hastily added that he "was very complimentary himself yesterday, saying he had chosen me for the position I occupy—left flank—and that I only had to prove myself as good a soldier in the field as in camp and he should be satisfied." The old vanity was threatening to resurface, but Dorsey now had reinforcements to call upon for aid in his time of need. "Yesterday I experienced a palpable assistance from Christ, for evil thoughts were taking possession of me," he explained to Fanny. "I prayed to Him and the temptation left me at once."[101]

After his wife had sent a letter "preaching to me about ambition," Pender found himself confronting the vice once more. "As to the Generalcy," he remarked to her, "I have given up all hope and scarcely ever think of it and then the thought passes away as soon as it sprang up unless someone is talking to me about it."[102] Obviously, he thought others were responsible for dangling the matter tantalizingly before him and only his strength of resolve and religious faith could hold such worldly preoccupations at bay.

Unfortunately, temptation of another kind threatened the tranquility of the camp. Whiting liked Pender's regiment in large part because "it gives him less trouble than any of the others." The men were, by all accounts, "remarkably orderly." But an outside agent in the form of a sutler angling to sell his wares to the troops was starting to cause the colonel "some little trouble" by selling alcohol after Pender had forbidden it. "I told him he could not bring any liquor into camp," he explained, but the fellow had done so anyway and when caught went over Pender's head to seek approval. "When I found it out," Dorsey reported to Fanny, "I ordered the clerk not to sell upon pain of being shut up and the store broken up." The angry commander confiscated some of the offending liquid for medicinal purposes at the regimental hospital and made clear his intention to take more-drastic steps to curtail the evil if required. "I will not have an authorized whisky shop in my camp," he asserted. "I am determined to break it up before it grows to such dimensions as to give me trouble."[103]

The disdain that the sutler demonstrated undoubtedly disturbed Pender. For all his claims to the contrary, his inability to obtain promotion did so as well. "If possible I get more cross and ill tempered every day," Dorsey admitted in December. Then, he turned the word to another meaning, one that would allow him to dissipate this wave of dissatisfaction. "I cannot help from brooding over and talking of my little crosses and I cannot take that interest in religious subjects that I desire."[104]

Pender had a great deal to ponder regarding his military career and reputation, but he also had family on his mind. He always asked about the boys and wanted to be remembered to them, plagued by the notion that they might never know him. Besides, they were growing up, even in his absence. "Turner must be getting on very fast in talking," he remarked after having read Fanny's description of their son in a letter. "I wish I could have been with you last Sunday evening."

Then, the mention of Sunday caused his mind to shift. "Oh! honey how anxious I feel that my parents should look to their future welfare," he observed sincerely. He was most worried about his father, who "has never taken any interest in these matters, never had any charity for God's ministers, and has lived a wicked life." Even so, James Pender was a good person and one whom a guiding hand with the right touch might reach. "Honey you must read to them," he requested of Fanny. "They have tender feelings and can be worked upon." With the proper approach, "I believe some good may be done them, and are we not bound to do that good if possible[?]" Still, Dorsey was a long distance from that field of battle and would be content to leave the fight to the one who had exerted so profound an influence over him.[105]

Fanny's presence might be enormously useful in helping convert the elder Penders to God's grace, but the wear and tear of life in isolated Town Creek, where they lived near Tarboro, was apparently having a negative effect on her at the same time. The grandparents were proving problematic with the children. Even from a distance, Dorsey admonished Fanny not to let his parents spoil the boys.[106] In addition, the rural isolation was hard for his wife to bear. As early as November 4, he inquired about her status. "I am very anxious to know how you will stand the exceeding quiet and dullness at Town Creek. I know I could not stand it and how you will I cannot imagine."[107] Perhaps the boys helped keep the issue at bay, as did visits by David Pender's wife, Mary. But the strain must have continued, for Dorsey broached the subject again near the end of the month: "My precious wife I hope you are not very lonely in the backwoods of Town Creek." Yet he missed her and the boys so much that he professed that if he could see them, "I think I should be able to be content," even there.[108]

By the end of November, the situation had hit a critical juncture. Dorsey advised Fanny to go back to Tarboro and stay with Robert. "I know it is lonely at my home," he sympathized, "so much so that I never have been able to stay there long at the time and they will not think hard of you if you [go] back to Town."[109] Finally, Fanny relented. In the first week of December, she had accomplished the move. "I am glad you have gone back to Tarboro," Dorsey wrote supportively, "for I know you will be better satisfied there and I can hear from you and you from me more regularly." He attempted to dismiss her concerns that his parents liked David's wife better, but he added an odd afterthought that must have left Fanny wondering. "Old people like child-like frankness," he observed in reference to his parents, "and that you possess to a greater degree than any grown and intelligent person I ever saw."[110] Obviously, Fanny's strong will had proven a strain on her in-laws too.

With the year winding down and so many issues with which he had to deal, Pender might be forgiven for concentrating on the present rather than anticipating the future. But such was not the case, and for the man whose connection with politics had not always been pleasing, one of his offhand comments was bound to be intriguing. The reference came amid a discussion of leadership. Pender noted that people had a tendency to blame someone else when something went wrong. "I suppose some of these days I shall be blamed for the death [from disease] in mine," he explained to Fanny, regarding his regiment. For an instant, he considered whether or not such an accusation could stand, then decided it would not. "If I am to blame[,] it is due to ignorance and not to neglect." Finally, there was the moment when he dared to think of life after the war. As was so typical, he even laced this speculation with a pessimistic twist. "You will see," he told his greatest confidant, "when I come to run for Congress all these things will be brought against me."[111]

The potential for public office lay in the future, but other political developments held promise of greater and more immediate results. Rumors had been rampant concerning cracks in the solidarity of the Northern political and military structure. Former Republican presidential candidate and current Union general John C. Frémont had created one of these apparent fissures with a unilateral proclamation of martial law and emancipation in his department in Missouri. President Lincoln had repudiated the step as inappropriate policymaking for an officer in the field, but Pender thought that the news of high-level resignations over the matter would, "if true," be "the most important event that has taken place for some time." He clung to the possibility among his opponents that "their hearts [were] changed and [they would] offer peace."[112] Certainly, the political trends seemed to be moving in a favorable direction regarding the South's fortunes.

In early December Pender expressed a guarded optimism over other recent events. "Fernando Wood, the peace candidate in New York, was only beaten by a few hundred," he observed of the colorful Democratic politician who had once advocated for the secession of New York City. At least from the North Carolinian's perspective, there seemed to be a welcome groundswell of disaffection above Mason's and Dixon's line. "These things look ominous for Lincoln and Crew," the Confederate concluded hopefully.[113] Reality was much more complicated. Wood's biographer observed, "The profound ambiguities in Wood's loyalism satisfied neither War nor Peace Democrats." They would not satisfy Pender either. Despite the seeming promise held by the "razor-thin margin" of defeat, the fact was that Wood had stressed loyalism in his campaign and insisted upon devotion to the Union cause, if not for the conduct of the war and the leadership of the country by the Republican administration.[114]

As it was, Pender waited on tenterhooks of another kind for one of two events to occur in the waning days of 1861: either for the army to move out to meet a Union threat that always seemed to be lurking but never appeared actually to materialize or for Fanny and the boys to come to Camp Fisher and take up winter quarters with him. By December 11 he declared that the command was "in a perfect state of quiescence," although he was still "waiting for something to turn up." He predicted that Fanny and the children might have to remain in North Carolina until the advent of a new year. "After the 1st of January the chances are that it will be impossible for armies to move however anxious their Generals may be to have people killed."[115]

Pender was less circumspect in a hasty note he wrote on Christmas Eve. It was clear that Fanny was on her way to him, and the anxious husband and father traveled to the railroad to meet her. A rumor had caused him to put her journey on hold, but now he was convinced that there had been nothing to it, and he urged her again to "come at once." Indeed, he had been looking for her "every day since Saturday" and pronounced, "My house is all ready." His final words betrayed his almost desperate desire to see her. "Please come as soon as possible."[116]

Fig. 1. A pencil in his possession illustrated Dorsey Pender's penchant for writing letters to his wife, Fanny, that reflected his views and values. Photograph courtesy of the Museum of the Confederacy.

Fig. 2. One of the strongest elements that characterized the young North Carolinian's life was his military service, with the dents in his scabbard reflecting his willingness to enter the fray and expose himself to danger. Photograph courtesy of the Museum of the Confederacy.

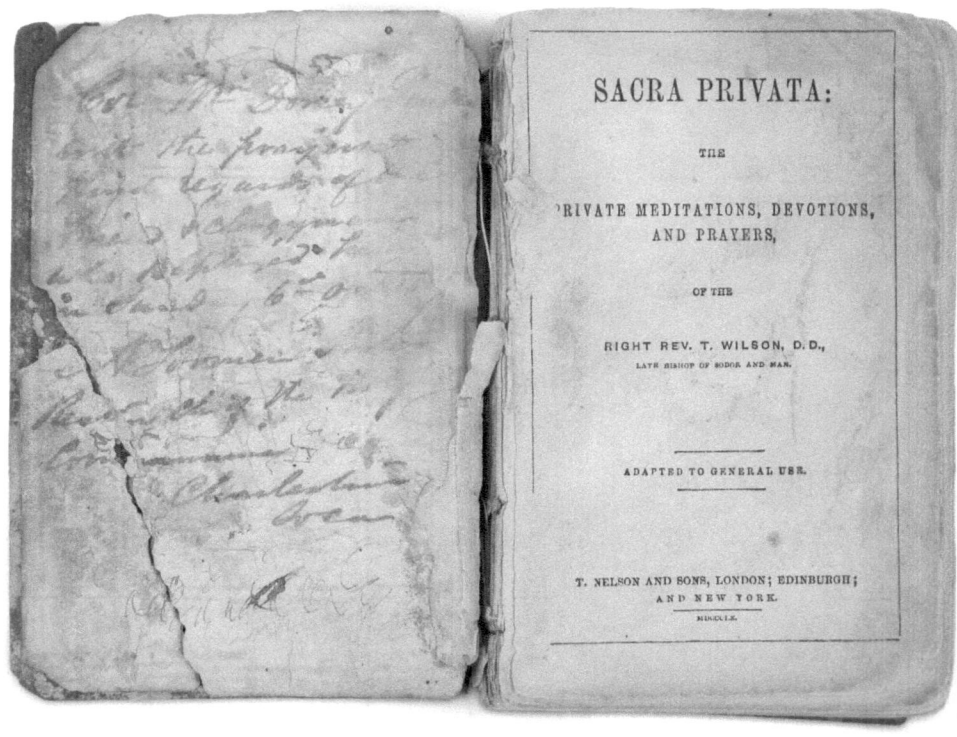

Fig. 3. Pender's quest for "glory" included the embrace of the church, which also led to his baptism before his command in the field and was reflected by sacred readings and devotions such as this book of prayer. Photograph courtesy of the Museum of the Confederacy.

Fig. 4. Fiery Ambrose Powell Hill won Pender's admiration and affection as his commander and advocate, with the North Carolinian rising as the Virginian's successor as head of the Light Division. Photograph courtesy of the Library of Congress.

Fig. 5. Pender never established a strong rapport with Thomas Jonathan "Stonewall" Jackson but respected his fighting capabilities. Photograph courtesy of the Alabama Department of Archives and History.

Fig. 6. Second Manassas (Second Bull Run) represented the type of fighting at which Pender excelled while serving under Robert E. Lee. Photograph courtesy of the Library of Congress.

Fig. 7. General Pender's frock coat from his Confederate service. Photograph courtesy of the Museum of the Confederacy.

Fig. 8. Pender, whose uniform pants were torn at the leg where a Union shell struck him on July 2, 1863, at Gettysburg, initially survived the wound only to lose his leg and life at Staunton, Virginia, on July 18. Photograph courtesy of the Museum of the Confederacy.

Fig. 9. Close-up of the bas-relief image of Pender featured on the monument to the general at Burgaw, Pender County, North Carolina. Photograph by the author.

6

A PRESIDENTIAL SALUTE
(February–June 1862)

I can manage my men in camp, on the march, and at drill, but it remains
to be seen how I can manage them on the [battle]field.
—DORSEY PENDER TO FANNY

General Pender, I salute you.
—PRESIDENT DAVIS TO COLONEL PENDER ON THE FIELD AT SEVEN PINES

Dorsey Pender was disappointed that his wife and family could not reach him before Christmas 1861. But happily, he did not have to wait indefinitely, and when they finally arrived, he had seven weeks in which to enjoy their company and bask in the glow of familial embrace. All too quickly, though, the time passed until Fanny and the boys had to depart. David Pender arrived to "fetch his brother's wife," as one of the officers in the regiment put it, who also used the opportunity to "send word to my friends by him that I was well."[1]

The parting strained Dorsey's newfound equilibrium and stretched his temper to the breaking point. Even the chance to visit again with his old friend and classmate Custis Lee did little to dull the sense of separation that pervaded his spirit. "I reached home last evening," he explained in reference to Camp Fisher, "and I can assure you it was anything but a pleasure. I do not recollect when I disliked so much to return to a place." All around him were reminders of the family's cherished moments together: a basket, a bag, young Dorsey's cradle, and the two rooms that now seemed too large to accommodate his loneliness. "I wish I had but one room," he stated plaintively. Then gathering himself as he knew he would have to do, Pender added: "Oh! darling did we not spend seven happy weeks together[?] They were as so many days, but I shall not forget them soon." The emptiness, even for a commander with responsibility for so many troops, was enormous. "My dear wife I believe I never missed you as I do now," he confessed.

There was, however, one intriguing possibility for the Penders as husband and wife returned to their separate worlds. Dorsey wanted Fanny to let him know if "your condition on the day you left Richmond turned out to be as you thought, or if it was a false alarm." Fanny's experience as a mother would certainly have caused her to be aware of the likelihood of another pregnancy. For his part, Dorsey responded in a rather convoluted fashion as he tried to temper his anticipation: "I sincerely hope it was bona fide," he observed of the possibility of a false alarm, "for we all have enough to contend with in these times even when we are free from continuous nausea and have to look forward to nine months of pain and general ill feeling." In any event, the approaching campaign season meant that it was best for Fanny and the boys to be safe among family in North Carolina. For now, his prayer was as simple as it was intensely felt: "May God protect us from all danger and allow us to meet again and not soon to be separated."[2]

Despite Dorsey's baptism and his brief reunion with Fanny during the winter lull, his personal struggles continued as he prepared himself mentally for the spring campaigning to come. In one very important sense, he had obtained the "hope of glory" he had been seeking through his spiritual advancement. In another, he had affirmation from the citizens with whom he came into contact, as well as his military colleagues and the troops themselves, of his leadership skills. Peers and superiors alike showered him with praise and admiration. But Pender had yet to achieve recognition on the battlefield, and he remained plagued by the notion that when that time and test came, he might not be up to the challenge.

One of the officers who offered an assessment of the colonel that would likely have pleased Pender was former teacher Benjamin White. "Colonel Pender is very popular with us," White wrote in February 1862. "Had he not come to us when he did, our regiment long since would have been disorganized." The lieutenant thought he understood his commander's greatest strength. "He is very rigid in discipline. Our regiment is the best drilled in this portion of the Army." White also revealed, if he failed to identify it directly, another compelling trait for the colonel, which was his willingness to apply a judicious amount of flattery for those who served under him to go with his rigidity and high expectations. "Col. Pender says he never saw a regiment anywhere drill better."³

February 1862 had proven a difficult month personally for Pender as he once again readjusted to the drabness of army life without Fanny's presence; it was also a particularly dark period for Confederate fortunes overall. An almost palpable sense of despair permeated the atmosphere, even at Camp Fisher in Virginia, where the colonel's concern for his family's safety mirrored his worries about the state of affairs generally. Union victories at Mill Springs (Logan's Crossroads) in Kentucky, Forts Henry and Donelson in Tennessee, and more significant personally, the capture of Roanoke Island, North Carolina, piled one setback on top of another and generated a crisis in confidence that tested and threatened Confederate morale.⁴

Union brigadier general Ambrose E. Burnside's successful expedition to the coast of North Carolina, culminating in a rout of the Confederate defenders at Roanoke Island, proved particularly galling to Pender.⁵ He said little to Fanny about the defeat on February 21, except to note how grateful he was that her brother had not been one of the ill-fated defenders. "Are you not glad Jake was not there, for it is generally considered to have been a disgraceful affair."⁶

The depressing theme continued several days later. "There is no use to deny the fact that our affairs look gloomy," he admitted to his wife, "but scarcely any war was ever concluded without success on both sides, much less revolution. The rebels nearly always get the worst of it & generally gain independents [sic] not by victories but by prolonging the struggle beyond the endurance of those who are fighting for conquest & power."⁷

Burnside's victory did more than widen the Union foothold on the North Carolina coastline first established with Major General Benjamin Butler's capture of Forts Clark and Hatteras the previous August; it opened the door to further operations in the state if the Federals chose to undertake them. Nevertheless, Pender tried to remain poised. "I do not fear any invasion so far inland as Tarboro," he wrote Fanny on February 26, but insisted that she not "remain if you can help it where their armies have control." Dorsey added hastily, "I do not write you this because I fear where you are, but you know I am a prudent man and always like to look out for contingencies."⁸

Pender may not have wanted to admit that he felt an immediate concern about his family's safety, but the invasion of his home state was another matter. Ironically, it was not depredations by the invaders that concerned him most, but rather some Union commanders' conciliatory policies, by which they hoped to win over Southern civilians.[9] "They are trying to wean our people from the cause by their kindness," he observed of this tactic. "I fear their kindness upon the people more than their cruelty."[10]

By this point in his life, a maturing Pender was showing evidence of a subtlety of thought and a better understanding of human nature—including his own. He recognized that in the minds of those who had yet to experience it, the notion of war was more powerful than the endurance of enemy shot and shell. "Our people are much more frightened than they would be if the enemy were nearer. Danger always looks more dangerous in the imagination than reality." He noted that Virginians who had seen the conflict at close hand had "become used to it," whereas "Our people [North Carolinians] would be frightened to death."[11]

Yet whatever sophistication he was exhibiting in his correspondence concerning others, it did not always translate to his wife. Dorsey knew the probability of her condition and praised married life and her role in "our happy union," then determined rather callously to tell her that it might be better not to have other children. "The ills of this life are too great for anyone to wish to entail it upon many of his own seed," he explained. This conclusion concerning additional offspring must have left Fanny perplexed, if not dismayed. "Two are as many as I want," he observed, knowing this was the number of children they already had.[12]

Perhaps the befuddled father and husband was only trying to protect himself from worrying about his wife's condition. He may have also sensed trouble. Fanny was not doing well with her pregnancy, and when Dorsey went a longer period of time than usual without hearing from her, he assumed the worst. After indicating his anxiety at not receiving a letter, he observed hastily, "I cannot help from thinking that my dear wife is too sick to write." He was "restless" and "uneasy," torn by what he did not know and what his worries caused him to imagine. "I pray God all my fears are groundless. Surely if anything is the matter with you, some one would write me."[13]

Two letters arrived from Fanny the next day, but they contained the sad news that she had lost the baby. Dorsey tried to be upbeat amid the tragedy, but he only exposed his lack of appreciation and understanding of what she had just gone through. "My mind was very much relieved to hear that you were not as I had imagined, very ill." But she had suffered a miscarriage, and the more he said on the subject, the less soothing the expressions were bound to be, however heartfelt and well intended he meant them.[14]

It was just as well that he shifted ground to another topic. The lack of promotion continued to rankle him. "I have given up all idea of promotion since I was in Richmond," Dorsey stated disingenuously, "not my dear that I tried to get any influence while there as you once or twice accused me." Fanny, who knew her husband so well, was surely not convinced, but he repeated his belief that he had made peace with the situation: "I shall rest perfectly satisfied with what I have."[15]

In any case, Pender would not have long to ponder such matters. On March 7 he wrote, "our long looked for orders to move are out."[16] His men were part of Joseph E. Johnston's efforts to consolidate his command and pull it back in the direction of the Confederate national capital, Richmond. This meant the necessity of destroying the winter quarters the men had built at Camp Fisher, along with such supplies as could not be carried or transported away. The immediate destination was the vicinity of Fredericksburg on the Rappahannock River, where the North Carolinian's troops took up residence at an encampment dubbed Camp Barton.[17]

While settling into camp near Fredericksburg, Dorsey informed Fanny, "We are delightfully situated here, about the right distance from Town, nice camp, lots of troops, etc." Indeed, he welcomed new recruits and anticipated the future with a newfound sense of himself. "I should be tempted to do as Col. [J. Johnston] Pettigrew, refuse promotion." That is, he could do so if such a promotion ever came his way. In the meantime, the war news also seemed to be better on other fronts. "The more we hear of the Virginia's exploits, the more brilliant it gets," he noted of the Confederate ironclad that briefly threatened the Union blockading squadron in Hampton Roads, sinking two wooden ships of war before encountering the Union ironclad *Monitor*. "What a glorious affair it was," he concluded. "It beats anything in history."[18]

In the meantime, Colonel Pender tried to keep his men sharp. The more they prepared, the more they would be ready to perform on the battlefield to the level of expectation he demanded. In the process, Pender "became exceedingly hoarse" and suffered from a "sore throat" for a time after an intense "three days, produced by drilling and cold."[19] The condition lingered. The exasperated officer complained a few days later: "I have never suffered more from cold than for the last few days. I cannot drill." Despite the soreness and coughing, he expected to get better soon.[20] Still, it was not until early April that he could finally claim, "My camp is about well & so is my cold, throat certainly so."[21]

Pender continued to try to exercise a firm control over his command and maintain its readiness for action, but the state of affairs, including his precarious health, was testing his patience and faith. His vaunted temper flared again. "I am in a precious humor," he recognized. "I got back at 11 A.M. and have done nothing but pitch into everybody and everything that has come near up to this time, 3 P.M."[22] Ironically, in these days of anticipating combat, his battles were more likely to be with himself. At the end of March, he confessed that he was still struggling mightily with these internal demons. "I feel sadly the want of true religion in my soul. That little and perverse member, the tongue, has not by any means been conquered, neither has my angry passion."[23]

Pender also persisted in waging what must have seemed to be a never-ending engagement against the unfulfilled promises of various officials for the necessary resources for his men. "I had no dinner," he explained to illustrate the level of commitment he had made to resolve the problem, "and went to see the Sec. of War and ordnance officer. I went after muskets, accoutrements, but only succeeded in getting the promise of half [of what] I wanted."[24]

The North Carolinian also began to take notice of a disturbing trend. He had recently asked Fanny for a report on conditions in his native Edgecombe County. Apparently, when she obliged, he was neither pleased nor surprised with her conclusions. "You say nearly the truth about N.C.," he observed. "She or at least her officers & soldiers have disgraced themselves. I believe it has been the fault of management and not for want of courage." Without the benefit of her assessment, it would be impossible to know precisely what she referenced to him. But the likely breakdown that threatened to bring such disgrace concerned absence without official leave or outright desertion from the ranks. Pender would become a vociferous critic of such actions, although he still believed that he could have a positive effect if given the opportunity. "I would chance a Brigade of N.C. troops if I were promoted and could be allowed," he explained to Fanny. "I feel a desire to try them anyhow."[25]

The colonel's attention to a high rate of absenteeism among North Carolina units appeared to have been warranted. Certainly from his perspective, drawn largely on anecdotal rather than empirical evidence, this seemed to be the case. He may not have distinguished in his mind between the men who left the field without intending to return and those who went missing temporarily.

Obviously, their disappearance from the ranks in either case was sufficient to reduce his number of effectives and consequently raise his ire.[26]

This period also presented Pender with an opportunity for both affirmation of his efforts to prepare his troops and anxiety over their performances under fire when the time came. "Oh, Honey, I hope my Regt. will do well when we may get into a fight," sharing his doubt once more with Fanny. He could conjure from his West Point studies and other experiences the cases of individuals who had failed to make the transition from administrators to battlefield commanders. "I can manage my men in camp, on the march, and at drill, but it remains to be seen how I can manage them on the [battle]field. They all seem to have confidence in me and I hope I shall not disappoint them." Also not far from his mind was the possibility of promotion, which he predicted would surely occur, "If I live twelve months."[27]

Once more the young colonel looked for affirmation from other sources. "Gen. Whiting had eight Regts. today in review, and mine was the largest of them all, 500 men." He explained that "after the ceremony was over," the general "rode up & said he had to compliment me on my Regt." Finally, gushing as the old Dorsey would have done, he concluded: "All said I had the best Regt. I felt very proud of it," particularly because his command included about one hundred newly recruited men.[28]

Another parade and inspection in which his men had participated garnered him additional plaudits. "One of General Johnston's staff said he had heard it complimented [a] great deal during the day," Dorsey told Fanny with enormous satisfaction on April 3. "It has the reputation of being about the best in the service." Then the nagging Pender doubt slid forward once more. "Now if we can only maintain our reputation in battle. I sometimes feel quite anxious when I think of how we should behave on that occasion."[29]

Pender placed the entire war in perspective in an extraordinary letter he drafted on April 5. In the course of his writing, he touched upon virtually every late piece of news from each of the theaters of operations that had reached him and weighed them for their respective value as gauges of success or setback to the cause. He admitted that the overview suggested that prospects for the Confederacy were currently dim, but he was determined to see things in the best light and not give way to pessimism. "I am sorry to differ with our dolorous father," Dorsey wrote Fanny candidly about his views on Union advances, "but I can not help from thinking he will be far out of it, when he thinks they will have all the country in so short a time." He may have been trying to bolster her, or himself, but Dorsey was convinced that all would be well in good course. Even when it came to lost territory, he could see something positive on which to rely. "Every inch they hold in subjugation takes soldiers from their fighting stock," he observed. "Tenn. has shown that occupation does not kill out secession, but strengthens it." Pender understood that losing the war was possible, but he remained as firmly devoted as ever to the success of the Confederacy. "I can not bring myself to imagine such an end as subjugation," he explained most sincerely. Then Pender turned to history for an example in these dark times. "Suppose our revolutionary fathers had given up when New York, New Jersey, N.C., S.C. & Geo. were in the possession of the English[?]" Fanny's father, Congressman Shepperd, seemed to have given way to the bad news prevalent in the war. Such an attitude irritated the colonel, and he gently sought to wean his wife from such a doleful influence. "Now my dear do not let your father's croaking make you despond."[30]

Prospects indeed appeared to brighten as Pender had predicted. Initial news from West Tennessee came of a "glorious victory" won at a battlefield named for a tiny meeting house located near Pittsburg Landing on the Tennessee River. Pender had learned too that the supposed victory had been dearly won with the "fall of Gen. A. S. Johnston," but he believed that coupled with success in Virginia, the negative trend might be broken, and the Federals will have had "their plans considerably disarranged again."[31]

Whatever ultimately transpired at Shiloh, Pender's focus returned to his own theater of operations. By April 10 he was at Ashland, Virginia, just north of Richmond. The colonel was in good spirits, having received both another high-level compliment and, more importantly, an intimation of possible promotion, but the movement of the command as a whole to Ashland had been chaotic. "Some of the Regts. were completely disorganized," he reported to Fanny with dismay.[32] Even so, his hard work at whipping his own regiment into shape seemed to be paying off, and he saw the distinction in the behavior of his men as additional indication of his worth as a commander.

Pender was also shepherding Fanny's younger brother Jake, who was now with him, while assuring her that her sibling was "well and shall be taken care of." The likelihood of fighting was clearly increasing, and Dorsey sought to allay her fears should she not hear from him for a time as they moved forward. In any case, he had no concerns for the outcome of such a struggle. "I think we can give them a pretty lively time," he observed, "as we have three armies concentrated." He listed the generals who would lead them and looked, as he now tended to do, to divine providence for help in the trials to come.[33]

There was no question that critical events were unfolding in the spring of 1862. Union general George B. McClellan had transported and assembled a mammoth army on the Virginia Peninsula that he hoped to take to the very gates of Richmond. Despite a tendency toward caution, his efforts were already responsible for the evacuation of Norfolk, Portsmouth, and Suffolk.

Now, Joe Johnston was scrambling to do what he could to stop the blue behemoth that threatened to descend upon the city on the James. With him in this endeavor were Dorsey Pender and his men. The colonel was anxious to test his mettle in battle with the foe. "We are all packed for the march towards Yorktown," he wrote on April 14. He anticipated action, at last seeing himself no longer confined to the sidelines of the conflict. "With the help of God we shall save the country," he explained to Fanny with a flourish, "for they are making their grand move in our front."[34]

Along the line of march, Dorsey paused to dash a note to his wife. "We are still on our way to the Peninsula but when we get there is the question," he observed, assuring her that he was "well & in fine spirits." The outcome of the great movement was a matter of course, as he saw it, with the opposing forces inevitably due to confront each other. "You may expect to hear of stirring times soon," he predicted.[35]

Finally, the martial transients arrived in the vicinity of Yorktown. "We had hard but pleasant marches to get to this place," Pender wrote, although there was grumbling that the journey had taken place on foot and not by rail. The colonel was more circumspect, understanding the vast demands made on an already groaning Confederate transportation system. "I think it was probably right for they have as much as they can do with their limited rail and water transportation."[36] Besides, the Southerners had reached the field before the Federals could launch any major attacks, which was what mattered most from his perspective.

Pender's confidence was supreme. "We have a magnificent army here," he told Fanny, "the largest and finest we have ever had at [one] place." He had confidence in the leadership as well. "We have our best Generals also. We all believe and hope we shall whip them."[37]

The possibility of an imminent engagement did not prevent him from renewing acquaintances with the troops of the old 3rd North Carolina, now designated the 13th. "I went to see my old Regt. yesterday," Dorsey informed Fanny on April 22. "My reception was truly flattering. They cheered me & stood around in groups to get a look at me." There was widespread discussion of joining Pender's current unit, which was all very gratifying to the man who constantly sought affirmation of his command capability.[38]

Despite the reception he had received, Pender did not seem able to sustain his good feelings from this due to other issues. There was mixed news from the West, where General P. G. T. Beauregard was said to "have whipt them again in Tenn." Ever the realist, Pender tempered his expectations. "Hope it is so if no more of a victory than Shiloh turned out to be." He was beginning to realize that such optimistic accounts ought to be taken cautiously. "Our people are getting to lye [sic] as bad as the yankees about fights," he concluded. Such tendencies toward propaganda and distortion rendered even the old habits less satisfying than they had been, prompting him to note exasperatingly, "I am getting so I never care to see the [news]papers."

There was also that elusive promotion to be considered, with the colonel assessing that his "chances" were "no better than they were six months ago as far as I can see." Trying to be the optimist in the face of it all, he observed, "If the war lasts & I live I shall be promoted some of these days I suppose." His obsession with advancement in rank had a basis in more than the prestige it would bring him, to hear Pender tell it. "I want promotion as much for your sake as anything else," he asserted to Fanny. "I would like for those who have known you, to know that you are the wife of a general & from supposed merit & not political influence." He wanted her to know that he was not seeking authority for its own sake. He felt he had that already as "senior Colonel of the Brigade." But if advancement were to come, "I do not want command without the rank. Too much trouble for nothing."[39]

Even with so much to consider, and much to his credit as a parent, Dorsey did not lose sight of the boys. "I suppose Turner now says any thing he pleases & that Dorsey can about stand on his own." He was missing those formative moments while serving his country. He was also doing his best to maintain at least a tenuous connection with his sons from a distance, with Fanny's indispensable assistance. "The accounts I receive about Dorsey delight; as to Turner's ability I send no confirmation," he wrote speculatively a few days later. "I know he is all a fond father could wish."[40]

As April dragged on and Pender waited for action, the opportunity for further reflection filled the void. "Fanny, it seems to me that I can want no other blessing conferred upon me in this world than to be allowed to live quietly with you and the children." If he did not always demonstrate it, she should be pleased to know that "you have inspired in me the desire at least to be better than I was when you married me."[41]

Pender soon had welcome assistance of another kind. On April 25 he informed his wife, "I have a chaplain at last." The new arrival was Kensey J. Stewart, whom the colonel deemed "eccentric but I have no doubt is an able man."[42] The minister would figure prominently in Pender's desire to reintroduce religious practices to the regiment on the eve of battle. "I hope we shall have [a] service Tuesday by Mr. Stuart [sic]," Dorsey wrote Fanny two days later. Referencing the sacrament of the Lord's Supper, the soldier observed, "I should like once more to partake of that means of grace, altho' I feel totally unworthy."[43] Reverend Stewart recalled the incongruities of the ceremony, with its row of kneeling warriors surrounding a makeshift altar "covered with a white cloth" and nestled among "old forest trees," while the occasional Union gunboat shell screamed overhead and "our music was supplemented [by] the death rattle of a soldier in a nearby tent."[44]

Near the end of the month, Pender reported that matters "militaire" were "about the same with the exception of a little activity on the part of the enemy in throwing up some dirt last night, [a] good deal nearer our works."[45] The approach of Union trenches made it increasingly clear that military action could not be deferred indefinitely. Chaplain Stewart remembered many years later, "So great was the danger that Gen. P. used to give me his watch and a letter for Mrs. P. when we retired to our bed."[46]

Finally, after a month-long "siege" of the area that George Washington had made famous in his defeat of Lord Cornwallis during the American Revolution, General McClellan hoped to write his name in the history books by reducing the Confederate works with a spectacular bombardment using the heavy artillery he had assembled for that purpose. But it was not to be, General Johnston pulling his forces back on the eve of the grand assault. A frustrated McClellan gave chase, only to become mired in the mud and experiencing a short but fearsome engagement at Williamsburg. This fighting produced over 3,900 casualties on both sides before Union forces succeeded in brushing back a stubborn Confederate rearguard effort directed by Major General James Longstreet the following day.[47]

An unsettling moment for the Confederates then took place when approximately 11,000 Union troops under Brigadier General William Franklin disembarked at Eltham's Landing near West Point on the York River. McClellan had hoped for an opportunity to strike his adversaries while they pulled back from the lower Peninsula. In response, Johnston turned to Brigadier General William H. C. Whiting, who chose Brigadier General John Bell Hood and his Texans, located in the area of Barhamsville, to redeem the situation. The aggressive Hood drove the half-hearted Union beachhead back under the protection of the Federal gunboats, producing approximately 200 casualties among the bluecoats while suffering only about a fourth as many himself.[48]

Pender's role in the action was more that of observer than participant, his regiment a part of Johnston's reserve early on. "I did not have the chance to test my courage," he lamented later to Fanny, but the role he played was more significant than perhaps he appreciated.[49] As he wrapped up his report on the occasion, General Whiting took special notice of Pender's performance. Having detached "two rifled pieces" and "two Parrott (Manassas) guns" to probe the distance to the Union vessels, Whiting assigned the task of supporting the tubes to "the Sixth North Carolina, Colonel Pender, which had been posted all the morning in advance on our extreme right." Distance prevented the Confederate gunners from doing any damage, but the Union response was more effective once a gunboat "got the range, with great accuracy and rapidity, firing exceedingly well."[50] The shelling producing minimal casualties among the North Carolinian's ranks, but it apparently caused Pender to feel that he had seen enough from his troops under fire "to satisfy me of my men's pluck."[51]

During the withdrawal up the Peninsula toward Richmond, Pender was not able to find time to write Fanny until he finally reached the area of New Kent Court House on the eighth. "I know you have been in great trouble about me," he began before insisting that he had "no possible means of sending off a letter." As it was, he was exhausted. "Up nearly all of two nights and in the saddle for two days, few hours will cover the sleep I have had in forty-eight." Dorsey had pushed his men and himself to the limits of their endurance, but they were "out of the Peninsula which was a perfect trap for us." Even with all the activity, he regretted missing the combat at Williamsburg as well as smaller skirmishes against McClellan's troops. Fanny's heart must have leapt in her throat as she read of her husband's desire for a fight, "I was seeking one all day but failed." Still, Dorsey held out hope for the chance to make his combat contribution sooner or later. "The big battle will come off yet."[52]

The following day he scribbled a hasty note "to let you know that I am still in the land of the living." Pender thought the retrograde toward the capital was almost over, speculating: "We are about done falling back, I suppose. Tomorrow or [the] next day will place us where we will make a stand for Richmond." Although approaching a point at which a climactic battle would have to be fought, the North Carolinian and his comrades were generally in good spirits.[53] But this frame of mind was eroding under the slow pace of retreat. The colonel admonished his wife not to believe the rumors that might be spreading, noting that "three-fourths of what was in the Richmond paper the other day was every word false." In the interim, he recalled nostalgically the pleasant time at Good Spring when "nearly one year ago we were under the shade tree sitting on the grass, the happiest hours of my life." He vowed: "I shall never forget it and I do not wish to. It was complete earthly happiness."[54]

Pender was heartened on the war front by word of the successful defense of Confederate batteries along the James River at Drewry's Bluff. He related the welcome news to Fanny, reveling especially in the fact that the USS *Monitor* had been "crippled in her engagement with our battery."[55] Only three days earlier he had passed along much more somber information, noting that the CSS *Virginia,* or the "*Merrimac*" as he called her from her Old Navy days, had "been blown up" to prevent her capture. At the time, he asked rhetorically, "Does it not seem a pity that she had to be lost," but concluded, "I suppose it could not be helped."[56] Now, much more satisfactorily in his eyes, the Union counterpart in the ironclad engagement that had revolutionized naval warfare looked to have been neutralized as well.

In addition to the damage sustained by the *Monitor,* Pender reported other setbacks for Northern riverine units in the fight. "The Galena Iron Clad was set afire & last word from was in a sinking condition." But from what he had learned, the engagement at Drewry's Bluff was not the wholesale victory that some had supposed the South would win while defending such formidable earthworks as Fort Darling. Ever the instructor, Pender assessed some of the defenders' actions rather harshly from his distant vantage point. "The famous Riflemen who were to kill every one who showed his head did nothing & a light Battery that might have sunk several transports refused to fire because they were afraid to show themselves." The evidence seemed clear, despite the outcome of the fight. "There is no doubt about it, our people are afraid of Gun boats."

Fortunately, the news was not all bad. Pender also felt, "we have some batteries that would fight them from the open ground." He was particularly proud of what he had heard about his old West Point classmate Stephen D. Lee. "Maj. Lee has & will fight them any time," he boasted on his friend's behalf. "Lee is considered the best artillerist in this Army." Perhaps he could only bask in the glory of victory vicariously with his colleague, especially since his own troops saw less-glamorous service and were worn out by "hard marches" and inclement weather. "I felt as tired and badly yesterday as I ever did from a march," the colonel admitted.[57]

Over the next week, Pender had comparative leisure for writing letters and contemplation. In the process, his patriotic ire soared to new heights. First, he assailed merchants, "who have refused to take Confederate notes," and considered that hanging "would not be too good for them."[58] Then he directed his anger at General Butler's "order or proclamation" in New Orleans, "in which he says if another lady dares treat a Yankee officer discourteously they shall be treated as women of the town—that is, women of bad repute." Dorsey must have thought Fanny would find the measure detestable as well, adding rhetorically: "Did you ever hear of such brutality[?] Can such people succeed[?]"[59]

Pender had developed a finely tuned sense of propriety when it came to waging war. Combatants accepted the risks of the battlefield, but he expected attitudes regarding noncombatants to reflect civilized behavior as he defined it. When others under arms violated the boundaries of such acceptable deportment, he would prove to be an unyielding critic. Thus, when Butler produced the notorious Order No. 28 for women in New Orleans, he reacted vigorously.

The North Carolinian held the same passion concerning those who remained at home while he engaged the enemy on the battlefield. These persons bore responsibility for sustaining morale, even in the face of adversity. For ultimate Southern victory, there could be no substitute for fortitude. "Everyone weakens the cause who allows himself to doubt of our success," he explained, as both an indication of his concern over his brother David's negativism and of his own stoutness in supporting that cause.[60]

Pender's determination would find its validation as George McClellan continued to deploy the mighty force he had assembled before Richmond's defenses. On May 25 the colonel assessed, "Our affairs have about come to a crisis." He anticipated: "The bubble must burst in comparatively a few hours. We all look for the all important battle to-morrow, as our troops are only a mile or so apart and there has been great activity in movement of troops on both sides today."[61]

At the same time, Dorsey informed Fanny that he had taken "the finishing step towards making myself a member of Christ's Church in this world." Expressing the hope that he would "prove myself worthy of the privilege," he explained that he "was confirmed this evening at the Monumental Church by Bishop [John] Johns." He thought that with "God's help" and the company of a new chaplain, he might do all on this earth so as to "come in the future to everlasting salvation."[62]

Two days later Pender continued to expect impending military action. "We are still going on in the usual way," he told Fanny, "two large armies lying within three miles of each other, apparently on good terms for we scarcely ever hear a gun for the last three days."[63] He languished as he whiled away the time with another letter to his beloved wife, but he would not do so for much longer. "We came out last night fully expecting to move on and attack the enemy this morning, but something prevented. I hope the attack will not be delayed many more hours."[64]

As the frustration built, Dorsey found such releases for his pent-up energies as he could. The surest outlet seemed always to be in corresponding with his wife. But even that cherished routine was not always completely satisfying under the circumstances. He continued to find fault, chiding Fanny for not letting him know initially that she had been ill. "You ask me to write or let you know if I should get sick or wounded. Why do you not set the example[?]" Then he railed against the man that Fanny's younger sister, Pamela, was considering to marry, on the grounds that the suitor had chosen to remain at home, lining his pockets, rather than risking his life at the front. "Fanny, write me no more about such a miserable degraded creature." Finally, there was the state of the Southern cause itself to consider. "My dear, never allow yourself to doubt our ultimate success. We can never be conquered." Dorsey thought her father's dismal attitude regarding the war was having too depressing an effect on her and reminded his wife of that viewpoint as well. Whatever doubts Augustine Shepperd might harbor, Pender was not prepared to confront them quietly or sympathetically.[65]

The soldier struggled with the dichotomies of a society experiencing the stresses and strains of war. Those who remained at home and demonstrated limited loyalty or outright hostility to the Confederate States threatened to offset the sacrifices he and others were prepared to make. "You love me, and think I act from a sincere conviction of the justice of our cause, and you did approve it," he noted almost caustically. "Here I am not only risking my life in battle but by any of the various camp diseases in a cause which really primarily affects me but little, while they are giving aid and comfort to the enemy by creating trouble at home, etc."

With the steam of his passion dissipated, Dorsey paused momentarily. "Erase the apparent harshness of my letter, but I say no more than I am justified in." Were she to notice, buried in the long diatribe was the admission that her husband had not slept "a wink last night and but very little for the previous 48 hours." This had caused him to feel "anything but bright today," in more ways than one, as the tone of the correspondence illustrated all too plainly.[66]

Finally, on May 31 the great engagement that Colonel Pender had been anticipating erupted in the countryside near Richmond as the Battle of Seven Pines (Fair Oaks). Initially, Joseph Johnston concocted a plan to assail his opponent's right flank, in part because he expected the arrival of heavy Union reinforcements from the north under Major General Irvin McDowell. When this concern proved as yet unfounded, the Confederate commander shifted his focus to the opposite end of McClellan's line. Union soldiers of the III Corps under Brigadier General Samuel P. Heintzelman and the IV Corps under one of Pender's Old Army colleague from the Northwest, Brigadier General Erasmus D. Keyes, held defensive positions near Fair Oaks Station on the Richmond and York River Railroad, near where a stand of pine trees marked the intersection of the Nine Mile and Williamsburg Roads. Johnston saw here an opportunity to strike made possible by the disposition of these two corps north of the Chickahominy River, separating them from the rest of the Union army. The focus of the attack would initially be on Heintzelman since his command was the closest to the Confederates, but if fortune favored Southern arms, the victorious attackers could sweep Keyes into submission against the swollen river as well.

While the heavy rains that caused the river to rise also turned each road into a morass, the inclement weather promised to increase the geographical isolation of these Federals from their comrades as much as to slow any advance against them. A decided blow might incapacitate a significant element of McClellan's massive army. Johnston biographer Craig Symonds explained that while the commander's plan was straightforward enough, its successful execution called for converging columns to arrive simultaneously by different routes. This approach required "clear orders, an efficient staff, and cooperative subordinates." Yet confused marching orders delayed the assault Johnston had planned to initiate, and instead of supporting each other as they were supposed to do, the various Confederate commands got in each other's way.[67]

Originally intended earlier in the morning, it was midday on the thirty-first before the Southern wave slammed into the Union lines. The management of the remainder of the action did not suggest much improvement in the pace of the assault. Johnston belatedly received word that the battle was joined, but the advance was in danger of losing its momentum without additional troops. After the confusion and recriminations of the morning, the Confederate commander decided to take the reinforcements in himself.

Serving on the Southern left in General Whiting's brigade of Major General Gustavus W. Smith's division, Pender was part of the force Johnston now committed to battle. The colonel's troops led a strong column down Nine Mile Road toward the depot as men from the II Corps under Major General Edwin V. Sumner arrived to bolster the defense made by their hard-pressed

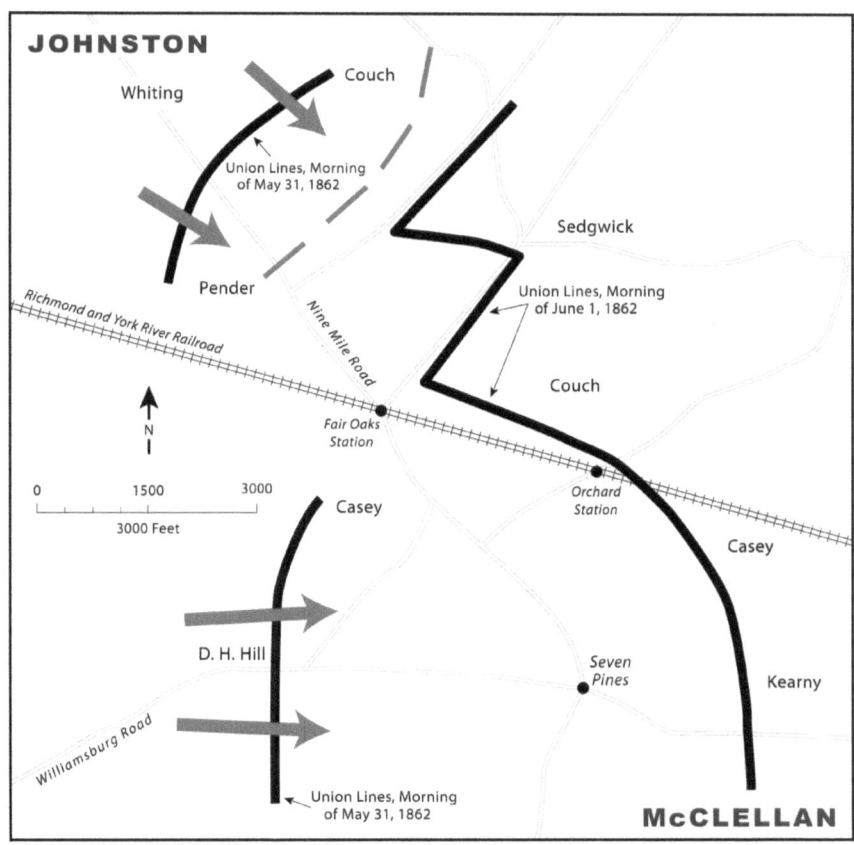

Map 3. In the fighting at Seven Pines (Fair Oaks), Pender experienced his first major action of the Civil War. Map by Heather Harvey.

Union colleagues. Historian Steve Newton observed that in sending his men forward, "Johnston was so intent upon delivering the *coup de grace* at Seven Pines that he ignored signs of Federal troops north of Nine Mile Road."[68] Pender and his men would not have such a luxury.

Initially, the Confederates on this portion of the field were unaware of how close the Federal forces had come to their position. The historian of the 6th North Carolina recalled that Pender sent his troops forward "with the assurance that he would be supported, but was led to believe that the enemy was not very near to his front." They pushed into and beyond a "dense woods" probing for the bluecoats. Then suddenly, the vanguard of Whiting's column made contact with their opponents.[69]

Despite the difficulty of the terrain and the sudden appearance of the enemy where they were not supposed to be, Pender maintained his composure, and the discipline and drill of those tedious months in camp began to pay dividends. One participant offered the assessment that his colonel remained "true to his training, obeyed orders by moving straight to the front, trusting to his superiors for support." This was not the moment to experiment or improvise, and in the matter of "a few moments," the regiment had "formed a perfect line along the road" and deployed its skirmishers.[70]

Reminiscing years later, a Pender aide was less complimentary of the moment and his commander's approach to it. Louis Young insisted that the colonel blundered in "rushing his regiment blind-fold as it were into the jaws of the enemy and had six of its companies suffer great loss, all to no purpose." Young insisted that Pender accepted the critique with the benefit of hindsight, noting, "in a conversation with me, [he] referred to this incident and acknowledged his mistake."[71]

On the field, Pender had less opportunity for contemplating his options. Union artillery played havoc with the advancing Southerners. Lieutenant Andrew Fagan of the 1st Pennsylvania Light Artillery explained that his section of two guns poured such a devastating fire at the Confederates that he quickly expended his supply of canister rounds. Undeterred, the Union artillerist ordered spherical case and finally "shell without fuse," which would explode as soon as it left the cannon tube. These explosive rounds would continue to pepper the advancing Confederates with an unrelenting rain of metal, shell fragments, and a vile, choking "yellow sulphurous smoke."[72]

Even with the steadfastness of his command under such heavy fire, Pender quickly found himself in an extremely awkward position from which he would have difficulty either attacking or extricating his men. He discovered enemy troops to his left as well as his front and wheeled his men to face the foe. Word reached him that Union flags had been sighted through the smoke. Calmly, Pender commanded that his own colorbearers furl their banners, perhaps hoping to obscure his identity from the Federals until he could rectify the situation. Then with parade-ground precision and in a voice that his comrades would later say they could hear over the din of the fighting, Pender began to shift his troops to face the new threat. "By the left flank, file left, double quick!" he barked, and the men readjusted their positions accordingly. Now with the Confederate line repositioned to confront the Federals, Pender issued another series of instructions by which he hoped to seize the initiative. "By the right flank, charge bayonets!" he called out, and the men responded as if still on the drill field. Daniel Harvey Hill noted simply that Pender's actions were instinctive and timely. "In an instant," the general noted of the North Carolinian, "his splendidly drilled and disciplined regiment changed direction, and was moving in double time to place itself across the front of its foes."[73]

According to one biographer, Pender offered these decisive orders in especially dramatic fashion. "His flanks now secure," Edward Longacre explained, "he resumed the advance, urging the men forward by twirling above his head the German-made cavalry saber (model 1840) that he had wielded in the 1st Dragoons."[74] As the troops advanced to within approximately a hundred yards of the Union position, Pender halted them. Massed in their close-order formation, they delivered a volley that staggered Sumner's line.

Nevertheless, Pender realized that his men were not sufficient in strength to hold their ground indefinitely without adequate support. He sent a staff officer rearward with instructions to "hasten the advance of other regiments," but time was of the essence. The volley his men had unleashed created enough confusion in the Union ranks to allow them to pull back from the awkward position and form alongside the other units as they appeared.[75]

Fortunately for Pender's prospects for recognition and promotion, an important figure reached the combat zone as these maneuvers took place. Confederate president Jefferson Davis liked to play a hands-on role with equal regard for office memoranda and the movement of troops. The desire to do so reflected the man's nature as well as his inclinations.[76] Consequently, he left his office and traveled to the front, where he could supervise personally the defense of the capital. The Confederate chief executive reached the scene in time to witness the execution of Pender's commands under fire. He hurried over to congratulate the harried colonel with the unexpected announcement, "General Pender, I salute you." The time to savor the verbal elevation in rank and the compliment lay ahead when the smoke of battle had cleared, but as Pender would afterward observe to his friend Stephen D. Lee, "I could have coveted no greater honor than to be promoted by the President on the field of battle."[77] Similarly, D. H. Hill later recorded Pender as telling a fellow officer, "My promotion on the field for good conduct realized the dream of my life."[78]

Even with the arrival of reinforcements to bolster the weight of their assault, the Confederate attack bogged down, and the lines settled into place for the night. On the morning of June 1, Pender remained ensconced along Nine Mile Road at an angle from the railroad and the depot that ran northwest to Richmond. To his left lay Johnston Pettigrew's brigade and to his right that of Hood. The action on this second day of the battle ended with the Southerners pulling back, their quest to annihilate the two isolated Union corps having been thwarted, with the Confederates having suffered horrendous losses, including the wounding and capture of Pender's fellow North Carolinian, General Pettigrew.

In his initial letter to Fanny about the fighting, Dorsey uncharacteristically failed to mention the encounter with the president or the compliment he had received from him. More importantly, from Fanny's perspective, he opened with assurances that he and Jake had survived the combat, although her brother had suffered "a slight wound in the back" and was recuperating in Richmond. "I merely write to tell you that Jake & myself are safe as bad rumors travel fast. I know you may have heard that I was killed as it was generally believed last night that that had been my fate."[79] Another North Carolinian demonstrated the uncertainty of such facts in the aftermath of the hotly contested fight. "Jacob Shepherd a son of Hon. Augustus Shepherd [Augustine Shepperd] and Brother-in-law of Col. Pender was wounded in the ankle," Benjamin White recorded.[80]

Having reassured her of the state of his health, Pender proceeded to describe the engagement itself, calling it "a bloody fight." His heaviest losses had come in charging an artillery position supported by infantry, and he set his losses by his best initial estimation at "about 150 killed & wounded." Even so, the command "drove the enemy" a considerable distance before expending its energy in the fruitless assaults on the Union position. Of the men's performance, Pender concluded: "My Reg. did very well until we charged a battery & three Regts. when we were badly broken. We tried a second time but failed," he explained, perhaps noting as mitigation that he had never known "that bullets & balls could fly so thick."

It was the combination of forces, infantry and artillery, which had told the difference for the Federals. "We could not get our artillery in on account of the ground," Pender explained, observing that the Confederates had nevertheless been successful in "every instance" where infantry faced infantry alone. In any event, he had survived the fray and was grateful to have been spared through the horrific fire he and his men had experienced.[81]

The colonel's actions had drawn favorable attention from his superiors. Once more, as they had done when Pender first entered Confederate service, prominent individuals added their voices to the chorus of support for his advancement. Robert Bridgers sent a letter from Tarboro in early June that emphasized, as he had done before, the North Carolinian's character, "Col. P. is about 30 years of age, a strict member of the church a moral and upright man." Bridgers also repeated the officer's military credentials and experience. "Col. P. is a graduate of West Point stood well in his class and has been regarded by the regular army officers as a young man of merit." Indeed, the fellow Tarboro native felt confident to assert that Pender had "won the confidence of every officer with whom he has come in contact." A final assurance presented the ultimate praise. "We who know him," Bridgers explained, "have high confidence in his fitness and capacity."[82] Ironically, by the time these sentiments found expression on paper, they were no longer necessary.

7

"MRS. W. D. PENDER'S HUSBAND"
(June–July 1862)

———

When you mount the enemy's works, I will be with you, if living.
—WILLIAM DORSEY PENDER TO HIS TROOPS AT MECHANICSVILLE

He asked me to tell him candidly if I thought he was fit to command the Brigade.
—PENDER AIDE LOUIS YOUNG AFTER MECHANICSVILLE

———

Dorsey Pender had experienced a religious baptism in October 1861; the following spring he received a military one on a scale he had not previously experienced. The latter came as he left the comparative quiet of winter quarters and marched to confront the hosts that George McClellan had assembled to threaten the Confederate capital. By the summer of 1862, Richmond was under McClellan's shadow, and Southern forces were scrambling to defend the city. Pender was left with the task of restoring the fighting trim of a regiment battered by combat before additional engagements ensued.

Two casualties among the higher-ranking officers in the fighting at Seven Pines would have a particular influence on Pender's subsequent career. The first of these occurred when Joe Johnston suffered wounds on the evening of May 31 that compelled him to relinquish command. The army charged with defending Richmond initially went to Gustavus Smith, but the next day it came under the hands of Pender's former West Point superintendent, Robert E. Lee.[1] Immediately, the new commander set the tone, issuing special orders that called upon the men "to maintain the ancient fame of the Army of Northern Virginia."[2] The name emanated from an earlier consolidation of departments and would win an enduring reputation that would more than "maintain" its "ancient" one under General Lee.[3]

Lee also needed immediately to replace subordinates lost in combat. Among these was the erudite James Johnston Pettigrew, who had been badly wounded and captured during the battle. Jefferson Davis instructed the commander of the Army of Northern Virginia to look to Pender as a replacement. "The uncertainty of the fate of Colonel Pettigrew, which I hope will be resolved favorably, renders me unwilling to make an appointment to his brigade," Davis explained, "therefore Col. William D. Pender (being an officer of the C.S. Army) is assigned to temporary rank as a brigadier-general."[4] Two days later, Special Orders No. 123 implemented the change and put one North Carolinian in the place of another.[5] Pender's new command consisted of five North Carolina regiments: the 13th, 16th, 22nd, 34th, and 38th.[6]

The soldiers of the 13th seemed particularly pleased to be reunited with their old chief, as they had demonstrated publicly to him with cheers on the Peninsula. A member of the regiment and author of one of its historical accounts designated the unit, without any admission of hyperbole, "one of the best brigades in the army" and deemed Pender as "one of the bravest and coolest generals in the world."[7]

The official notification of the long-awaited promotion, to rank from June 3, 1862, arrived in the form of General Orders No. 71. Davis's battlefield greeting from Seven Pines was now formalized in an appointment that provided tangible vindication for the months Pender had struggled to find his place while instructing unpolished volunteers and grappling with political and military superiors and subordinates. It was the validation that "Mrs. W. D. Pender's husband" had been seeking.

With the new position came reassignment as part of Major General Ambrose Powell Hill's "Light Division." Almost from the moment the Virginian took charge of it, Hill's command swelled in numbers until it was the largest in the army. Pender's and Brigadier General John J. Archer's brigades joined Brigadier General Charles Fields's Virginians and Brigadier General Maxcy Gregg's South Carolinians as additions to the core of Brigadier General Joseph Anderson's Georgians and Brigadier General Lawrence Branch's North Carolinians. Pender and the other commanders of these six brigades would have to get to know each other under less than ideal conditions. But Generals Hill and Pender had no trouble establishing a good working and personal relationship from the start. As Hill's biographer James I. Robertson Jr. described it, the two men "liked each other because both were ambitious, intense, and at their best in combat."[8]

Ironically, in his first letter to Fanny following what still must have been the most stirring event in his life, Dorsey barely mentioned the news. Perhaps he had already conveyed it by other means or simply did not want to seem to let vanity get the better of him one more time. Besides, the veiled reference he offered allowed him to display a bit of dry, if macabre, humor. "They heard at home that I was killed," he told his wife in an unusually low-key manner, "and David put off immediately, reaching here last night, but instead of finding me a cold corpse he found me standing in all the dignity of a Brigadier."

Dorsey was in an understandably good mood in the afterglow of the promotion, reflected in his response to an inquiry Fanny had made of his assessment of Confederate prospects. "They are in some adversity now," he admitted at the outset, "but I do not and cannot believe they can ever conquer us. Let them take Richmond, what then; we can still fight and will fight. Let them take every large town and still we are not conquered." As an illustration of his point, Pender harkened back as he had done before to the Revolution of 1776. "Did not the English have all the towns in the Revolution, and did our fathers fight on until the end was gained? We have fewer tories in our midst than they had and more facilities for conducting a war, and I do not believe that our people are one whit less patriotic now than then."[9]

Dorsey was now in full literary flower in his correspondence with Fanny. "Our men and officers showed the most wonderful bravery and determination the other day." With the support of the "ladies of the South," who have "morally speaking, done much more in this war than the men, will this struggle continue until finally our freedom will be acknowledged." Again, Pender called upon history to provide "a few examples and see how hard and almost impossible it is to subdue a people determined to be free." He was aware that greater sacrifices lay ahead, not to mention many more difficult days. "Many of us may bite the dust but our children with the help of God will be free." Finally, with regard to this subject, Dorsey closed: "I am not so brave or fearless. I wish this war could end without another shot being fired, but I will continue as long as it or I last."[10]

A byproduct of promotion was the increased set of responsibilities to which General Pender had to devote his energies and attention. "I can write but little as my mind is pretty well taken up with pickets, abatis, roads, rations, and such small sanitary details," he explained to Fanny. "My Brigade is on advance duty and I consequently have but little time to think of outside matters, but always time to think of, if not to write to, you."[11]

The "abatis" and "roads" were part of a concerted effort to shore up the defenses of the nation's capital in the face of an opposing army that could strike at any time. In addition to creating obstructions to improve the defensive works, the men labored feverishly to open up fields of fire and construct new transportation links to support the positions. General Lee himself kept a close personal eye on the developments, offering suggestions and encouragement as he deemed them necessary. The effects were noteworthy. "Forrests [sic] were felled and new roads were made, and old ones obliterated, so that the entire face of the country was changed," one of the supervising engineers noted during this period of intense activity.[12]

Under such pressure, personal conflicts were bound to arise, and Pender was not immune to them. He took special pride at the appearance his men and their work exhibited as a continuing reflection upon himself. In the course of the construction of earthworks for which he was responsible, he insisted that the efforts be made so that the end product was geometrical. Pender also planned to retain some of the trees in front of the works for the purpose of observation. A staff officer watching the efforts believed that he had a greater understanding of the utility of works that conformed to the shape of the land, not to mention the requirement for clear and entirely open fields of fire, than the general and volunteered his assistance. Pender must have seemed insufficiently grateful for the offer, stressing his own preferences and insisting that he "knew all about it." The subordinate dismissed his superior as a conceited fool.[13]

Amid these activities, practical matters were also not entirely out of his mind. Before he ended a letter on June 6 that covered the usual range of subjects, Dorsey added a postscript requesting that when Fanny's brother Jake returned from his brief furlough, he bring along "a pair of water proof boots with long legs. Size No. 6."[14] He explained that he wanted "a nice pair of riding boots" that were also serviceable and that Jake "must pay anything to get them."[15] Pender wanted to look the part of the general, and for once, he was willing to bear any expense to see that he did. Despite claiming to be "resting for what may be coming next," there was precious little opportunity for recuperation. "Here I sleep with boots and all on," he explained to Fanny two days later.[16]

Active duties did not relieve the general of family matters that troubled him deeply. Although it is unclear what David Pender had done or said, he apparently had alienated Fanny. Dorsey tried to patch the injury by defending his brother without simultaneously antagonizing his spouse. "I know he was not actuated by any mean or ungentlemanly motives and he is to me a devoted and kind brother. I know him to be a high minded, generous man." This was a delicate balancing act. "It has caused me many unhappy moments to think that my wife, the dearest object on earth, and my most beloved relative are never to get on well together, for entertaining the opinion of him that you do, the less you have to do with each other the better." Dorsey promised to "drop this unpleasant subject," and perhaps the storm passed of its own accord, for no other similar references occurred in his subsequent correspondence.[17]

The newly minted brigadier also explained more about his elevation in rank as he thought of details his wife might find interesting. "I did not tell you that I was indebted I believe to Gen. Whiting for my promotion." He speculated that his superior had taken "advantage of the first opportunity to press my promotion upon the President." In his zeal Dorsey raised the possibility that his friend Stephen Lee would enjoy the same opportunity. Then, with Lee as a potential and more suitable marriage partner for Fanny's sister Pamela, she could become "as big a lady as your ladyship." Carrying the gibe to a greater degree as he was wont to do, Dorsey admonished Fanny not to "put on the airs" and advised that she delay the purchase of new clothes for a bit longer. "Money is scarce and debts are heavy," he insisted, having obviously forgotten about his own desire for suitable apparel and missing the contradiction in his willingness to have Jake "pay anything" to obtain such items on his behalf.

If Pender thought his references to his new position sufficient to satisfy his wife, he was mistaken. Fanny's next letter to arrive chided him for not elaborating further regarding his promotion. Dorsey's insistence that she tell him everything that happened to her now came back on him. Having harped on his suitability for a promotion for so long, she was undoubtedly anxious to hear the news at the earliest opportunity and in the fullest detail. Never shy about correcting such deficiencies, Fanny must have taken him to task, and he responded as quickly as he could set writing instrument to paper.

"Your long and agreeable letter was received yesterday," he started carefully, "in which you complain that I did not let you know of my promotion." Racing to backpedal, he assured her that he had intended to tell her everything "in my first letter after it took place if I did not, for I always like to write everything that I think will give you pleasure, and I was sure that would." For now, she must accept his good-faith effort and his assurance that any neglect on his part "was not intentional, and you must not think hard of it."

On the wider front, the news was certainly not nearly as distressing as it had been for the last months. Access to a *New York Herald* led him to conclude that the Federals had suffered heavily in the recent fighting, despite their advantages in "position, preparations and artillery." Besides, he gloated, "May has passed and they have not taken Richmond yet." The spoils of victory had included personal letters, whose contents were becoming well known in the Confederate camps. "In some of the [Union] letters taken from the field they were quite facetious about marching to Richmond. Some said they had not time to write more as they were in a hurry towards the city. Others said their next [communication] would be dated in Richmond, etc."[18] Pender was proud of the role he and his men had played in helping thwart those intentions.

As a brigadier, Pender was also pleased with his increased command responsibility. "I now have five Regts., and a Battalion, in all present about 2,400," he shared with Fanny, "but the Regts. are bad off for field officers in consequence of casualties in the battle and sickness."[19] He scrambled for staff officers he considered worthy, telling his wife, "Doctor up Jake and send him back." He also explored the possibility of bringing in Fanny's older brothers Frank and Hamilton as well, the former in the Confederate navy and the latter serving with Major General Thomas J. "Stonewall" Jackson in the Shenandoah Valley. "I wish very much that Frank would come with me," he explained to Fanny. "Great many of our naval officers have been acting as staff during this war." Dorsey closed the topic, promising to "hold a position open for him for awhile."[20]

Pender's subsequent profession to "dislike these family staffs" did not prevent the new brigadier from continuing to consider his brothers-in-law for such positions.[21] In a letter home composed near the end of June, he observed, "I am very anxious to have Frank join me but from what you write I fear there is no chance." He knew from his previous experiences that the personnel surrounding him would make a difference, but the uncertainty of selections left him pondering the remaining possibilities. "I do not know who to get on my staff," he admitted at last in mild frustration.[22]

A few days later Pender was still considering the method by which he could secure his relative's services. "If Frank should by any means get away from his present position I shall always have a place for him." The current situation was by no means flush with personnel. "My staff as yet being very moderate, only one volunteer aide, and he likely to leave at any moment." Then in suitably mischievous fashion, he added rhetorically, "Do you know any real clever fellow who is desirous of serving his country at his own expense?"[23]

The general's search for staff officers took him into Richmond, where he made an appointment with Secretary of the Navy Stephen Mallory to secure

Frank's transfer. The mission ended in disappointment, although Mallory seasoned the news with the observation that Fanny's brother "was too good an officer to spare." Pender also called upon President Davis in his quest and contacted others he thought might be in a position to offer him assistance.[24]

Locating new aides was not Pender's only difficulty. A current staffer named John Hinsdale apparently was dissatisfied and sought opportunities for service elsewhere. After communicating with his father on the subject, the latter put in a direct request to Major General Theophilus Holmes, with whom young John had served initially. "I do not think John is satisfied with Genl. Pender," the elder Hinsdale explained. "He is not as well pleased with him as he was with Genl. Pettigrew." Without disparaging a fellow officer, Holmes graciously left the door open for Hinsdale's return. "Dear John," he scribbled, "If you want to come home your room is ready just as you left it and I will certainly keep [it] for you as long as you wish, or until you are promoted."[25]

Ironically, the deliberations Pender undertook regarding staff reminded him of how far he had come from the days of being considered for such a role himself. Again, in true Dorsey Pender fashion, he could not resist the chance to deem himself "less dignified" and "more lazy" in his present state, "having so many others to do for me." The circumstances prompted him to worry that he might not be able to make a transition to a simpler life once the conflict had ended. "The only fear is I shall become more helpless and too grand in my notions to retire to a small farm after the war," he explained to Fanny. Then he assured her, and himself, that only the "bribe" of "at least a Colonelcy in the Regular Army" might prevent his services from being lost to life as a civilian. The quiet existence of a country farmer remained an ideal for the warrior, who finally conceded, "I am sick of soldering and especially the fighting part, particularly as I have no desire to be killed."[26]

Of course, Pender had more to worry about than dealing with a disgruntled aide, developing a staff, or contemplating a future outside of the army. While circulating in the Confederate capital, he could not have failed to detect a sense of imminent action in the air. Near the end of June, he was starting to get his fighting blood up. "I am getting on finely," Dorsey told Fanny. "My Brigade has improved very much. I shall be able to take in the fight about 2700, and as we are preparing for marching orders which we expected tonight, it may not be long before we have to try it." Everyone anticipated the arrival of Stonewall Jackson and the opportunity for "a most decided victory."[27]

Robert E. Lee had tangled with McClellan in 1861 in western Virginia, with at best indifferent results. In the aftermath, Lee's reputation as a field commander came into question, with the derisive nicknames "Granny Lee" and "King of Spades" suggesting that whatever attributes he might have once boasted, the demands of modern warfare had now passed him by.[28] Here the stakes were larger, but the talented Confederate general now had the resources to match his fertile mind and aggressive combat nature. Pender expressed the attitude currently prevailing in the ranks regarding the new commander. "Our Generals who have access to General Lee are beginning to gain a great deal of confidence in him," he explained to Fanny. Even with a vast Union array spread out before them, he felt optimistic. "Everything, darling, around Richmond looks bright."[29]

Indeed, Lee planned to strike rather than wait and pass the initiative to his opponent. The Confederate general's greatest asset seemed to be his ability to gauge his adversary. In many ways the stately Virginian had at least one characteristic in common with his North Carolina subordinate, for Lee surely would have agreed with the sentiment, "I want one grand battle and have the thing settled."[30]

Armed with fresh intelligence from cavalryman Jeb Stuart, Pender's West Point comrade, accomplished when the horseman's troopers circled McClellan's forces in a dramatic four-day reconnaissance in mid-June 1862, Lee planned to attack an isolated portion of the Union army near Mechanicsville. The army commander wanted a fight but preferred not to fling his battalions headlong into the strength of enemy defenses. It remained to be seen if circumstances would offer him any real choice on this occasion.

Lee's determination to press the issue was part of his grander strategy for wedging a portion of McClellan's army away from its supply base and compel its surrender. Pender's part in the complex operation was quite simple: he would have to send his men forward in a frontal assault against a well-defended position. As one historian has observed, "The men of Pender's and [Roswell] Ripley's brigades had no idea how strong [Fitz John] Porter's works were, or the difficulties they would encounter while struggling across Beaver Dam Creek."[31] A direct assault in the face of an entrenched and determined foe was supposed be a matter of demonstrating sufficient élan to obtain success; it was also bound to be bloody and potentially devastating for the assaulting forces.

Wearing a red shirt to match his fighting spirit, A. P. Hill greeted the dawn of June 26 with a nervous anticipation. He was ready to send his Light Division forward in accordance with Lee's wishes. If the scheme unfolded properly, Stonewall Jackson, the hero of First Manassas and a brilliant campaign of maneuver just completed in the Shenandoah Valley, would descend upon and assault the Union right flank with troops who had hastened from the scene of their recent exploits for that purpose. That attack would be the signal to unleash the Light Division. The fiery Powell Hill had only to wait.

By midafternoon there was still no sign of Jackson and his vaunted command. The exasperation built with the humidity of the hot summer day. At last, pondering that all might be lost if he did not act soon, Hill sent his men

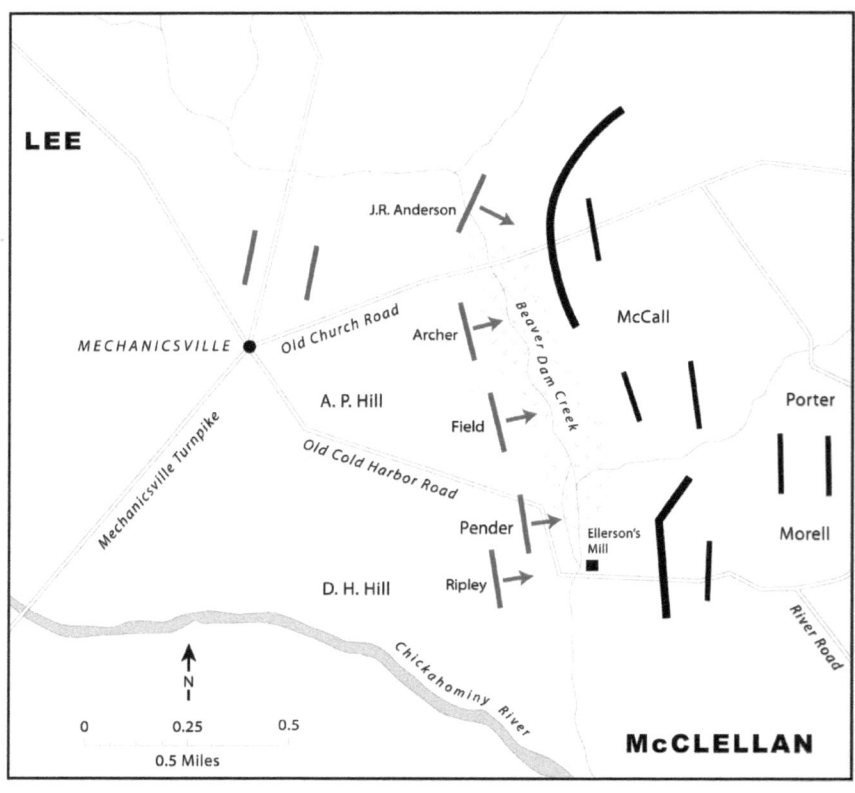

Map 4. At Mechanicsville (Beaver Dam Creek), Pender's command suffered heavily in attacks against the well-positioned and defended Union lines. Map by Heather Harvey.

forward, and they trod enthusiastically toward the blue lines. All appeared to go well as the Union pickets scattered and the whole force withdrew through the dusty little hamlet of Mechanicsville.

Pender moved off to help secure the Confederate right flank and look for any opportunities that might present themselves. But even with the troops of Major Generals James Longstreet and Daniel Harvey Hill to buttress the advance, any hope of a quick and relatively bloodless victory began to fade as two realizations set in: Jackson was not coming on this day after all, and the formidable defenses, already established for just such an eventuality along Beaver Dam Creek, loomed ahead of them.

Still anticipating Jackson's appearance on the Union flank and watching as the sun began to dip low in the sky, Powell Hill focused his attention on the Union line with the initial intention of hitting its right. If he could pry these troops from their defenses, Fitz John Porter's command would have to give way all along the powerfully constructed line. For the moment, Pender remained in the reserve as Hill sent Archer, Anderson, and Field against the objective. But as might have been expected under the circumstances, the concentrated Union firepower pulverized these units and sent the chilling and unmistakable message that any frontal attack was going to be costly in the extreme.

In the advancing darkness, it was now up to Pender to try to do what his comrades had thus far been unable to accomplish. He must have surveyed the terrain over which his men would move with trepidation. Still, his training and coolness took over. Duty called for him to try to carry the works, and if General Lee's plan worked as it should, the Federals' focus on his front would be their undoing.

Pender was nothing if not practical. He called his colonels together and, though not inclined to inspirational speechmaking, understood the value of motivation. William J. Hoke recalled that once the subordinate commanders had assembled, their general "informed them that we would be in a fight soon & that he expected everyone to do his duty." If that incentive were not enough, Hoke added, "The officers & men were informed that if this battle was lost Richmond must fall." The loss of the Confederate capital would thus likely mean the loss of the war and of the dream of the new nation's independence. Pender's words must have had the desired effect, for the commander of the 38th North Carolina concluded, "All seemed ready to do their duty."[32]

Under the circumstances, that duty would not be easy to fulfill. There was nothing quite like slogging through a swamp as one attempted to advance against a strong enemy position, all the while dodging the bullets and other projectiles being hurled against you. Yet that was precisely what Dorsey Pender and his men had to do near the end of the day. The summer heat compounded the discomfort of the troops as they surged forward, but the Union fire promised to be even hotter, as indeed it was. The Union fusillade had shredded other Southern units that had shown the audacity to push across the open expanse, through the marshy ground, and across Beaver Dam Creek against the higher ground the bluecoats held. Pender's North Carolinians did not have to wait long to experience the same reception as they entered the maelstrom. General Hill later reported: "Pender was ordered to support these brigades already engaged, and to take position on the right of [Charles] Field. This was gallantly done in the face of a murderous fire."[33]

For all of its bravery, the advance was hardly a cleanly executed and precise one. Under an intense artillery barrage and musket fire, the battlefield became swept with chaos and confusion. Men recoiled from the fire, and whole units altered their lines of advance under the effects of the weight of the metal being thrown at them. The 16th North Carolina veered off to such an extent as to take itself out of the action altogether, while the 38th North Carolina advanced in the face of the withering storm.[34] When it finally, and blessedly, dropped back, the regiment left behind more than a third of the numbers it took into the fight writhing on the ground in the agony of their wounds or resting motionless in death. A historian of the 38th noted: "About 420 men belonging to the regiment were engaged in the fight the others being on picket. The loss was 152 in killed and wounded."[35]

Looking back upon the Southern efforts to smash through the Union defenses by headlong assaults, D. H. Hill summarized the nature of the attacks by concluding, "We were lavish of blood in those days, and it was thought to be a grand thing to charge a battery or an earthwork lined with infantry."[36] Of course, just how the men felt at the time about such often-futile exercises, as this one had been, was an open question. The Union commander, General Porter, observed of the martial drama that unfolded before him, "Dashing across the intervening plains, floundering in the swamps, and struggling against the tangled brushwood, brigade after brigade seemed almost to melt away before the concentrated fire of our artillery and infantry; yet others pressed on, followed by their supports as dashing and as brave as their predecessors despite their heavy losses and the disheartening effect of having to clamber over many of their disabled and dead, and to meet their surviving comrades rushing back in great disorder from the deadly contest."[37] One of the advancing Confederates explained in understated fashion to his wife shortly after, "Charging batteries is highly dangerous."[38]

Pender tried to rectify the situation, but to no avail. His zeal—he would never lack for it on the battlefield—served him poorly at Beaver Dam Creek. More than anything he wanted to exert control over the fight and, by this painful experience, at least learned that he could not always do so. That zeal also came close to costing him his life. Staff officer John Hinsdale observed in his diary of that day's events, "Genl. Pender had his stallion shot under him by a grape shot." Had the Union ordnance hit its target a bit higher, the general could easily have been among the severely wounded or dead. When Hinsdale and another aide rushed to his side, they found Pender dazed but unhurt. Even so, the reaction of the now-dismounted warrior to his circumstances was predictable. "He hates the loss of him [the horse] very much."[39]

A. P. Hill reported that by 9 o'clock in the evening, the fighting had ceased, "my brigades resting along the creek." The feisty commander concluded that his men had carried out their duties as fully as possible that day: "It was never contemplated that my division alone should have sustained the shock of this battle, but such was the case, and the only assistance received was from Ripley."[40] As a lower-level commander, Pender's concerns were more tactical and less strategic in nature, but the sacrifices his men endured were the most tangible elements of the battle for him and them.

Once the fighting subsided, the administrator in Pender resurfaced. He knew that the men had expended much of their ammunition in their futile assaults. Now, the supplies needed to be replenished in preparation for whatever might be required of them the next day. Consequently, he detailed an officer to fulfill the necessary duty. When that man took longer to accomplish his task than Pender deemed appropriate, the brigadier rode in search of him. He would not have to travel far to determine the difficulty for himself. There was a reason for the delay—the Confederate rear was in a shambles. Even so, Pender would brook no excuses when it came to his men, and he hurried the officer along and left a courier to help him find his way back to the brigade.

But another participant was too busy taking in the grisly situation that lay before him to worry about such administrative details. This North Carolinian recalled that the harsh combat had reduced the battlefield around him to "a solitary desert of horror" as the slain lay scattered about the blood-soaked wetlands, and many of the wounded survivors continued to grapple with death or struggled to make it safely back behind their own lines. He remembered most of all the assault upon his senses in the gathering gloom. "Nothing could be heard in the black darkness of that night save the ghastly moans of the wounded and dying."[41]

The effects of the fighting reached all levels of command. General Lee's exasperation at the unfolding battle found an unusual expression for the normally stoic commander when, during the initial stages of action near Mechanicsville, President Davis and an entourage of aides suddenly appeared. "Who are all this army of people, and what are they doing here?" Lee blurted angrily. Davis observed simply, "It is not my army, General Lee." The Virginian, who was watching an engagement play out over which he could not exert any control, replied hastily, "It certainly is not my army, Mr. President, and this is no place for it." Apparently, the Confederate chief executive took the hint and rode off to find a new vantage point, away from his general's gaze and out of the thickest of the Union artillery fire.[42]

Lee had been correct that Mechanicsville was no place for an army. Pender's experience in the chaotic fighting that had occurred at Seven Pines paled in comparison to that which had taken place along Beaver Dam Creek and in the vicinity of Ellerson's Mill. But heavy fighting did not alleviate these men from the continued obligation of service as McClellan's forces remained in such close proximity to Richmond. The next day General Pender did what any commander worth his salt would do: he investigated the scene and inspected the damage the recent engagement had wrought on his troops. He wanted to assess the unit's combat capability and rekindle the soldiers' fighting spirit.

A lieutenant from the 6th North Carolina recalled that in the light of a new day, the general "rode up in our front and, taking the stump of a cigar from between his lips and holding it between his thumb and finger, thanked us for our conduct during the previous day." Pender understood his men well, and his ability as their leader to motivate them shone brightly. They might be ordered to renew the terrible advance against the well-posted Union lines. If so, he knew they would fulfill their obligations as soldiers. He paused to make one last observation: "When you mount the enemy's works," he asserted, "I will be with you, if living."[43] Then Pender turned his mount and rode off.

As Fanny would attest, her husband could be, and usually was, his own worst critic. With all he had to do in the aftermath of the battle, he might have been forgiven if he remained too preoccupied for contemplation. But Pender thrived on such internal reviews, however harsh the assessment might turn out to be. He shrank no more from critical introspection than he would from enemy bullets and shells. What plagued him now was the uncertainty he felt regarding his performance as a brigade commander. He knew how to instruct men and felt comfortable enough at the head of a regiment. But concerning a brigade, he could only wonder if he had been weighed in the balance of war and found wanting. Much of his performance had been respectable enough, yet it was hardly perfect, and perfection was the ever-present and nagging bar he had set for himself to achieve.

To satisfy his curiosity and perhaps obtain a measure of confidence in his own capabilities, Pender sought out one of his staff officers. Louis Young later recorded that the general approached him with a revealing question on the morning after the battle. "He asked me to tell him candidly if I thought he was fit to command the Brigade," the aide remembered. Despite earlier praise from President Davis, his promotion to general-officer rank, and his own actions in the recent combat, Pender's sense of insecurity caused him to make the inquiry. Of course, Young could hardly be objective toward his earnest superior regardless of what he might have actually felt. Pender needed for him to say that he had been up to the task, and the staffer obliged. Besides, as Young subsequently added, given the general's present "frame of mind," a response in the negative might have caused the distraught officer to resign his commission on the spot.[44]

It is uncertain how Pender would have responded to any negative assessment of his conduct as brigade commander. He had undergone a significant amount of maturity in the days since Suffolk, Virginia, when he had worried so much about what others thought about him. To be sure, Pender was still inordinately sensitive, especially to negative criticism, but he now tended to exercise greater control over his mood swings. Any additional doubts he might have entertained did not plague him sufficiently for him to commit his concerns to paper. In any case, Pender did not have time to write of any such self-doubts to his favorite confidant before other duties called him away and forced him to focus his attentions on more-pressing matters.

As it turned out, a final grand assault against the Union position vanished in the fresh light of a new day. The Federals had clung to their defenses long enough to buy time to conduct a staged retreat. Historian Earl Hess asserted that by doing so, "McClellan threw away a superb defensive position and all the morale advantages gained by Porter's victory."[45] Of course, the Federal commander, with his own sense of strategic vision, would not have characterized this retrograde movement as a retreat but a repositioning, which he was also trying to do with reference to securing a new base of supplies. The latter he planned to achieve by shifting from the York River to the James, establishing it at Harrison's Landing. To do so required more time, and a precipitate withdrawal from the area of Mechanicsville by Porter's exposed V Corps would not have accomplished this.

Fortunately for the "Young Napoleon," Porter had every intention of securing his command and did so by dropping back to another easily defensible position. Only a few Federals remained on the Beaver Dam Creek line to maintain the illusion that the bluecoats were still there. On June 27 Pender sent a reconnaissance in sufficient force to determine that the bulk of the Union forces were gone. The subsequent discovery of the new line, also behind a creek and protected by a swampy morass, tempered the news of the Federal withdrawal. Perhaps the Confederates could still pry these men loose and complete the destruction of Porter's corps, and once again A. P. Hill was the man with the temperament to try.

As on the day before, Pender began the engagement of Gaines's Mill in reserve and watched as others careened into the mouth of the Union guns. By this point in the fighting, a distinguished visitor had arrived to gauge the success of the attacks for himself. "The eyes of your chieftain are upon you!" Pender called in encouragement to his men as he became aware of Robert E. Lee's presence.[46] The North Carolinian had already won accolades by performing well under the watchful gaze of President Davis, now there was an opportunity to do so under his old West Point superintendent, the commander of the army itself.

When the moment came, Pender urged his men forward. What little headway the Southerners made against their opponents could not be sustained without additional troops. Federal resistance was simply too strong, and Pender, now having experienced what he later termed "a flesh wound" to his right arm, had to break off the attack. A. P. Hill reported that a portion of Pender's troops, consisting of the 16th and 22nd North Carolina, "at one time carried the crest of the hill and were in the enemy's camp, but were driven back by overwhelming numbers." Hill would be complimentary of the effort but seemed to be aware of the futility that another assault on a protected position represented. "Pender's brigade was suffering heavily," he noted, "but stubbornly held its own."[47] Pender certainly concurred with such an assessment. "My men here fought nobly, and maintained their ground with great stubbornness," he explained in his own report. Furthermore, they did so under the grueling condition of enfilading, or flanking, fire from the Federals and having been subjected to the ebb and flow of assault and retreat through the course of the engagement.[48]

As the darkness of another day descended, other Confederates under John Bell Hood managed to penetrate the Union lines and compromise the strong position, although at a heavy cost. The fighting ended with nightfall, but almost 9,000 of Pender's Confederate colleagues were killed, wounded, captured, or missing as a result of the vicious combat.

Gaines's Mill provided more than a victory for Lee and incentive for McClellan to pull back from Richmond, it also served as the first instance in an unfortunate pattern of war-related injuries Pender would receive in the conflict. One of his staff officers recorded in his diary, "General Pender was everywhere in the fight," noting that his superior had been "wounded in the arm very slightly." The physical exertion must have taken its toll as well, for the staffer also mentioned that when he "looked around sometime for General Pender," he "found him at last at the forks of the road under a large tree fast asleep." But Pender was not alone in his condition. "A. P. Hill was sleeping near[by]."[49]

Dorsey tried to soften the news of his injury to Fanny, although he knew that he could not avoid it altogether. "I did not tell you yesterday that I was slightly wounded in the right arm," he admitted on June 29. "Merely a flesh wound," he explained reassuringly, "which has not caused me to leave the field."[50]

Others in the brigade had not been so fortunate. Probably without realizing the effect of the message he was about to convey, especially given the pains he had taken to lessen Fanny's fears about the danger to himself from enemy fire, Dorsey added, "One of my aides was killed[,] the other just wrecked."[51] She could make the connection that if staff officers under her husband and in close proximity to him faced death or severe physical or mental injury, so did he, but her husband could not help relating what he had experienced.

The dead officer to whom Pender made reference was William J. Green, a former infantry lieutenant colonel who had served under the general as a volunteer aide-de-camp. The Virginia Military Institute graduate was shot in the heart during the thick of the fighting.[52] In his after-action report, Pender paid special tribute to the fallen soldier, noting that his loss "was irreparable" and terming him "an accomplished officer" who had "won the highest praise for his noble conduct."[53]

The staffer Pender described as having been "wrecked" by the fighting was John Young. The general made a rather caustic reference to the aide in his official report, noting that once the fighting for his command was over, Young apparently wanted to continue on his own. "It was now nearly night," Pender observed, "and here ended the part taken by my brigade, except so far as Lieutenant Young, my aide, was concerned, for not being satisfied with fighting as long as his general, went back, and remained principally with General Ewell until the battle was closed." Despite the show of bravado and insubordination the exuberant staffer illustrated, the general listed him subsequently as "slightly wounded on the side of the head," without further reference to his conduct. The injured aide may have had as much of the experience of battle as he wanted, for he was no longer on Pender's staff by the end of the year.[54]

The general's battle wound gained another prominent individual's attention as well. In the afternoon of June 30, Jefferson Davis ventured out of the capital to survey the scene of the fighting. One of Pender's aides noted that the Confederate chief executive and the general "had a chat." Afterward, Pender remarked that "his arm is the cause of the President being so gracious to him." In any case, the wounded limb was now "getting along pretty well."[55]

On the same day he talked with President Davis, Pender would have one more opportunity to engage the Federals, and risk death or serious injury, in fighting variously known as White Oak Swamp, Glendale, or Frayser's Farm. Once more the North Carolinian waited as other Confederates, under James Longstreet, advanced. Although not yet involved directly, Pender's proximity put him in danger. "We had hardly taken our places," a staff officer observed, "when a 12 pound shell struck in front of us . . . passing between us, we were three feet apart, Gen. Pender & I, and cutting off the head of a captain in the 16th NC who stood just behind us." John Hinsdale concluded succinctly, "It was quite a narrow escape."[56]

Dorsey was fortunate to avoid this brush with death and considered his fate as resting in the hands of a higher power. "God has spared me through another day's fight," he explained to his wife on the first of July.[57] His belief in the Divine hand on his destiny was in common with the general notions of the day. In his study of soldiers in the conflict, historian Reid Mitchell has asserted, "American Christians were particularly prone to attribute escape from death in battle to providential intervention, the result of prayer and devotion."[58] This was true of Pender, although he would have insisted that it was Fanny's prayers and her devotion on his behalf that God had chosen to answer.

In any case, he knew that she would be worried about his physical condition, and Dorsey closed his very short note with a reassurance about the injury he had sustained. "My arm is much better."[59]

In the aftermath of the fighting, one of the North Carolina Confederates did his best to try to explain what he and his men had just experienced to loved ones at home. "I have seen a good deal of hot work since I wrote you last," Robert Gray observed to his father. "Have been in four regular battles, besides several skirmishes, and thanks be to the Good Lord have escaped unhurt." Gray had assumed command of the 22nd North Carolina when its commander fell wounded in action, and his men endured heavy casualties throughout the ranks. "We have lost a good many in killed & wounded, have done some hard fighting and have killed a goodly share of Yankees," he added. Although he felt that circumstances had deprived Lee's army of a greater victory, Gray pointed out that General Pender had complimented the regiment for its conduct. Still, efforts to describe the action eluded him: "It is impossible for me to give you any description of any of the fights, as no description of a battle I have ever seen approached to anything like the reality."[60]

For all of the miscues and close calls, Pender and his comrades could also be pleased that they had propelled McClellan's army farther from the steps of their capital. "We drove them again from their position, taking one General, [George A.] McCall, and two batteries of fine rifled guns," he explained of this latest round of fighting. "My Brigade took one of them and drove the enemy until after dark, holding the field until 3 A.M. this morning when we were relieved." The Federals destroyed supplies to prevent them from falling into Confederate hands, prompting Pender to conclude that the "rout has therefore been complete."[61]

The North Carolinian had prided himself on the performance of his command in drill and parade and worried whether or not that ability would show on the battlefield too. Although they had not been in much of the later fighting that collectively came to be known as the Seven Days Campaign, Pender's men had been in enough combat to satisfy him of their merit in that terrible crucible. He could count on them in even the most severe fighting, and that meant that Pender's superior officers, including General Lee, could count on them, and him, too.

The defense of Richmond had come at a terrible cost to the armies of both sides. Some 3,286 Confederates and 1,734 Federals had paid the full price for their participation in the extensive campaigning, with 15,909 and 8,062 of their comrades, respectively, suffering wounds. Union forces had an additional 6,053 missing; their Confederate counterparts less than 1,000.[62] The staggering losses and extended combat had left the troops on both sides exhausted and required substantial reorganization to replace the line and general officers who had been among the casualties.

As part of this evaluative and rebuilding process, Pender and staff officer Hinsdale rode out in early July for an inspection of the brigade. Although it had not seen action at Malvern Hill on the previous day because "it was so late and they were so far off from the scene of action," the cumulative effects of attrition were evident. "The Brigade has been very much reduced within the last few days," Hinsdale recorded. "We numbered over twenty-five hundred when we started out. We cannot muster more than one thousand now."[63]

Much work remained to be done to rehabilitate the command's combat effectiveness, and the effort produced its share of strains on the officers too. When Hinsdale was slower returning from an assignment than Pender thought acceptable, the general chided his subordinate. "I conclude that I would like to get off from him and wish it from the bottom of my heart," the chastened lieutenant noted. Then Hinsdale added decisively, "He is the most perfect resemblance of an iceberg in the shape of a man, that I ever knew."[64]

Dorsey Pender could appear to be cold and distant to those who did not know him well, but he emerged from the experiences of the spring and summer with a renewed sense of his capabilities and confidence in his command. Other fields remained to test each of them further, but he had to look at the recent period of activity with a sense of accomplishment and satisfaction, knowing that the long hours of training and drill had paid off where matters counted most—on the battlefield.

8

"I KNOW YOU WILL HATE TO HEAR THIS"
(July–September 1862)

> Pender, do you curse in times like this?
> —JAMES ARCHER AT CEDAR MOUNTAIN
>
> I flatter myself I did good service.
> —DORSEY PENDER TO FANNY AFTER SECOND MANASSAS

After the immediate Union threat to Richmond had subsided, Dorsey Pender found an opportunity to rest and recover by spending a short time with his beloved Fanny and their children in North Carolina. Writing to her had brought him comfort, but there was no substitute for being in her arms. Unhappily for the couple, the time they had together proved terribly fleeting. By the end of July 1862, he was racing to rejoin his men as they marched toward new fields of action. "I am just in time here," he wrote in a hasty note to Fanny at the end of the month, "for my Brigade left last night to join Jackson. I shall go with Gen. Hill tomorrow night." As if understanding the full implication of what he had just told her, Pender added, "I know you will hate to hear this."[1]

Had he understood fully what the Army of Northern Virginia faced now that it had saved Richmond, Dorsey would have realized why Fanny would "hate" the news. George McClellan may have been sulking on the Peninsula, but another force, under an arrogant Union general who had won victories and a reputation in the war's western theater, was now present in Virginia. Major General John Pope had issued a circular to his Federal Army of Virginia that he felt distinguished him from his less successful predecessors. "Let us understand each other," it began. "I have come to you from the West, where we have always seen the backs of our enemies; from an army whose business it has been to seek the adversary and beat him when he was found; whose policy has been attack and not defense."

Pope was determined to instill a fighting spirit in his new command and urge the men under him to the successes that had seemed to become so common in the western theater. "Let us study the probable lines of retreat of our opponents, and leave our own to take care of themselves," he admonished. "Let us look before us, and not behind. Success and glory are in the advance, disaster and shame lurk in the rear."[2]

The new Union commander's words, undoubtedly meant to stir and inspire his command, left many who would have to serve under him with the impression that he had no respect for them. To back up such words, Pope planned to send the 47,000 men of the Army of Virginia forward with himself at their head and confident in the assurance of victory now that they were under the command of an officer who had the appropriate mindset for waging war against these Rebels.

Thus, as matters stood in Virginia in early August, Pope's army posed the most immediate threat, having reached the area of Culpeper. Stonewall Jackson's force, shortly to be augmented by Powell Hill, barred the way. Despite Pender's absence from the field, his command and the rest of the Light Division left for Gordonsville. Hill and the belatedly arrived Pender soon joined them.

Ironically, while facing a common foe, at least a portion of the Confederate high command in the Army of Northern Virginia was as equally occupied in warring with each other as they were in supposedly preparing to clash with the enemy. It was rare in the American Civil War for personal squabbles and personality clashes to work to the benefit of the command in which they occurred. But in the summer of 1862, this beneficial effect appeared to have been the case for Lee's army.

James Longstreet, destined by year's end to become known as "Lee's War Horse," and A. P. Hill had experienced a falling-out over published accounts of the Seven Days fighting. Longstreet and his staffers might have been better served not to have read the Richmond newspapers, but read them they did, and an eruption of Southern pride and emotion resulted.

A piece in the *Richmond Examiner*, under the authorship of a volunteer aide for General Hill, put forward a version of the fighting around the Confederate capital that emphasized Hill's leadership and contributions. Longstreet took offence, and a barely concealed and strongly worded response in the name of his chief of staff ensued in another Richmond newspaper. Military competition coupled with journalistic rivalry to ensure that the matter grew out of all proportion, and for all of their public attempts at decorum, Longstreet and Hill were at an impasse from which neither could, nor wanted, to extricate himself.[3]

Both men declared their mutual desire to be shed of the other. Plans even began to be entertained of a duel between the hot-headed and honor-bound officers.[4] Fortunately for the Confederate cause, General Lee found a way to allow the heat to subside while serving the country's greater interests by dispatching Hill to reinforce Jackson in Central Virginia. With its fiery commander temporarily under arrest, the Light Division soon moved off to join Stonewall, with the assurance from Lee that Jackson was receiving "a good officer" with whom he could work as long as he took the pains to include Hill in his plans, a fact the savvy army commander surely realized would likely prove problematic concerning the enigmatic Jackson.

Amid this turmoil besetting his comrades, Pender grappled with his own organizational changes and demands. Gone from his brigade were the men of the 2nd Arkansas and 22nd Virginia, who had served under him during the Seven Days Campaign.[5] His troops were now exclusively North Carolinian (the 16th, 22nd, 34th, and 38th Regiments).[6] These would be the men Pender would lead into any new engagements.

Dorsey had enjoyed the few moments he could snatch from the war for his family, but he felt that his absence from his command was having a deleterious effect that only he could remedy through his immediate presence and attention. "It was well I was in a hurry to get back," he told Fanny on August 4, "for my men were dissatisfied and deserting." He felt that the holes in the officer ranks produced by the recent campaigning were much to blame. "The Regts. were without officers, etc. etc." But the general now worked to alleviate the situation. "I have filled them up by promotions, appointments, and elections. I took it in my own hands to make appts."[7] It remained to be seen how these steps would restore morale and create the appropriate attitude among the troops, but it was highly unlikely that the next active operations would be much delayed.

A still-seething A. P. Hill would soon demonstrate that all was not completely settled in the upper echelons of command in the Army of Northern Virginia, but on Sunday, August 3, he and the officers laid aside their differences as an impressive entourage attended church services. A relatively new staff officer with Jackson, Captain Charles Minor Blackford, recorded the next day that he had accompanied "a very distinguished party" to worship. There, war and peace collided as only those powerful human elements could in the desire to experience prayerful contemplation while anticipating battle.

The group, including Pender, paused to take in a sermon before kneeling awkwardly with their military paraphernalia to engage in communion. The captain recalled the strange sensation of the noise made by the "clanking swords" that occurred "as each man managed his so as to enable him to kneel at the chancel rail." The inconvenience aside, Blackford concluded logically enough of the incongruous scene, "We were too near the enemy to lay aside our arms, even in church to worship the God of Peace."[8]

The sensation that the officer felt of the proximity of the enemy was true enough. Jackson desired to close with the Federals again, regardless of his religious preoccupations on that Sabbath day. Stonewall had made clear his preference to show his opponent the "black-flag" of "no quarter" as the only means of responding to the depredations he believed the Federals were committing against Southern citizenry. "Once more," as the general's principal biographer, James I. Robertson Jr., observed, "Jackson was advocating ruthless, uncompromising war with the enemy."[9] He and Pender would soon have opportunities to strike more blows in a hardening conflict, for their opponents were on the move.

Major General Nathaniel Banks seemed especially willing to oblige, advancing his men into a position that Jackson thought left those Union troops vulnerable to attack. The aggressive Confederate resolved to hit his old Shenandoah Valley adversary before the Federal commander could be reinforced. But Jackson ignored Lee's admonition to include his new subordinate in any maneuvers he sought to undertake. On the hot and dusty roads leading from Gordonsville, an exasperated A. P. Hill snarled at an inquiry concerning the movement: "I suppose we will go to the top of the hill in front of us. That is all I know." Perhaps by answering as he did, the general hoped to convey a message back to Jackson to stop stonewalling him when it came to his battle plans. If so, Hill was as misguided as he felt his commander now to be.

Pender was most likely to take Hill's side in any dispute, particularly with the reserved Jackson. He also found Stonewall difficult to read concerning his intentions. As a junior officer in prewar days, Pender had once taken a commander to task for not sharing plans that he expected his officers to follow. Although the North Carolinian recognized that Jackson's longstanding subordinates had come to accept this trait and adapted themselves to it, he was not tolerant of the tendency himself. "None of Jackson's old officers ever try to divine his movements," he explained to Fanny, with the telling addition that despite this, "some of the old Army like him."[10] He was "old Army" too, although he did not "like" Jackson all that much.

In addition to his martial struggles, Pender was getting a bit disillusioned again regarding his personal life. On August 6 he lamented, "Oh how I wish I could be a Christian." He agonized at how far he was from the spiritual ideal he had set for himself. Besides, as he put it to Fanny, "The life I had is becoming more and more irksome to me, for the less chance I see of getting away from the army the less hope I have of that quiet and happiness on earth and that security . . . that I so much long for." There were ample rumors of an end to the conflict, and while Dorsey knew not to trust such speculations, he noted wistfully: "I pray sincerely as I can—night and morning—for a speedy close to this war. I am tired of glory and all its shadows for it has no substance." The melancholy carried over into an assessment of his existence as a whole, in the guise of discussing the larger human condition: "We work, struggle, make enemies, climb up in rank and what is the result—nothing."[11]

Pender continued to cultivate the relationship with his wife that had grown so much stronger over the course of the previous year. "Honey, I know I appreciate you very highly and love you dearly, but I sometimes feel that my cold and unfeeling nature prevents me from feeling as much of it as I ought, or even showing you what I have." Of course, it was his inability to express himself to his satisfaction, and perhaps to hers as well, less than a "cold and unfeeling nature" that got in the way. "May Heaven bless you," he asserted with intensity, "for you are indeed dearer to me than anything on earth—now, ever was, and I hope ever may be."

Such open expressions made him feel inadequate. "You will be astonished at this outpouring of sentiment," he explained in understated fashion before coming to the core of the matter. "I am not always devoid of it, when I fail to express it," he explained, referencing the emotion he usually internalized. As for Fanny, she should allow others to assist her when needed. "You are too afraid of feeling under obligations." But as Dorsey had learned in the army, "None of us can be entirely independent."[12]

In the meantime, complications in the high command continued. Matters between Jackson and Hill came to a head just as the Confederates closed with their Union foes. Misunderstanding and inflexibility held sway over both men. Their mutual antipathy only deepened, and an antagonism developed that led to even greater stress upon the exhausted men in the ranks too.

The troops were already worn out from their exertions. A foot-worn Southerner confided in a letter to friends, "We have been marching nearly constant[ly] day and night for three weeks past and there has been a power of rain and we have taken it all." These demands had stretched them to the breaking point, leading the soldier to observe, "Much hardships such as that has worn me plum out."[13]

These difficulties were about to be replaced by others as the combatants closed with each other at Cedar Mountain on August 9, a day that would prove as brutal in meteorological terms as the previous ones had been. It was still early in the morning, with Powell Hill already in his shirt sleeves as he ordered his men out of their bivouac. Pender's command occupied the fourth place in the line of Hill's advancing Confederates. The men struggled through conditions that saturated their uniforms and choked their lungs, but by afternoon, the faint rumble in the distance told them that a battle was at hand.

Even with much of his command scattered widely along the road behind him, General Jackson did not hesitate to give battle to a foe of unknown size and strength. Perhaps part of his lack of hesitation came from the knowledge and earlier experience he had with his Union counterpart, General Banks. When Jackson's surgeon, Hunter McGuire, ventured to ask his commander's intentions, the general responded, "Banks is in our front and he is generally willing to fight." Yet Little Sorrel had hardly carried his rider more than a few steps when Jackson turned with a mischievous glint in his eye, adding, "And he generally gets whipped."

The fight started with the usual sparring of forces feeling out their positions and staking out their ground. In the subsequent battle, which also took the name Slaughter Mountain, it was not long before the opponents began to tangle more seriously with each other. A Federal assault against Jackson's left threatened to envelop the Southern position, but through the force of his own character and presence, not to mention the timely arrival of reinforcements from Hill, Jackson was able to stabilize the situation, and the Confederates held firmly to their positions.

Pender was part of this relieving force racing to the battlefield. He followed Branch's Brigade into action and adhered to its left, along with Archer's Brigade. The North Carolinians surged forward in time to assist the temporarily broken ranks of the much celebrated Stonewall Brigade. A stubborn stand by the Federals caused the momentum to stall before Pender could send his men against the Union right flank and compel them to vacate the field. A last, fleeting challenge materialized when Northern cavalry appeared late in the day, but a concentrated fire by the Southerners drove them off. The field and the battle belonged to the Confederates. Even so, Cedar Mountain had not been one of Stonewall Jackson's finest hours.

Pender probably did not know it, but in the thick of the fighting, he had something of an unofficial guardian angel by his side. At the suggestion of some of the other staffers, Captain Sam Ashe took it upon himself to "keep a good lookout on General Pender himself, and try to protect him." Pender had a well-known disposition, or as Ashe described it an "intrepidity," for throwing himself into battle wantonly, if not recklessly. Thus, Ashe stood near his general, concerned that his commander "might expose himself unnecessarily," although it was unclear what he thought he would do in such an eventuality.[14]

Ashe's proximity to Pender allowed him to see the general in action. He described his commander as "average [in] height, rather thin, weighing probably not more than 135 pounds." Ashe thought that the general's "dark complexion" accentuated his "very dark eyes," with "clear cut" features and a "countenance" that "bespoke intelligence."[15]

Pender impressed his aide in other ways too. On the battlefield at Cedar Mountain, Ashe particularly noted his superior's "coolness" under fire and characterized him as exhibiting an "entire absence of excitement or emotion," even in the chaos of combat that swirled around him. Regardless of what else was transpiring, "General Pender was entirely calm" and maintained a presence of mind that often allowed him to penetrate the fog of war.

Years later, a member of the 16th North Carolina characterized Pender similarly. "I recall his personal appearance and his conduct on the field and in battle as though it had been but yesterday," the veteran wrote. "He was a medium size man, round of body, closely knit and muscular; his movements were agile and strong; his complexion was tan, his eye gray and kindly, and his whole exterior indicated courage, nerve and power of endurance." Through the veneer of memory, but similarly to the staff officer's contemporary wartime description, the writer observed, "He was one of the coolest, most self-possessed and one of the most absolutely fearless men under fire I ever knew." The image indeed seemed burned indelibly in the man's mind. "It was by no means an uncommon thing to see him smoking a cigar and issuing commands, to all human appearance unmoved, in the heat of battle."[16]

Pender's personal performance on the field at Cedar Mountain contrasted favorably with others around him facing the same circumstances. When Maryland native James J. Archer galloped up to the North Carolinian, the former was clearly enjoying less equanimity than his colleague. In the extremes of the moment, Archer blurted, "Pender, do you curse in times like this?" Unfazed, Pender calmly replied that he did not. "Well I know it is wrong," the animated brigadier and prewar attorney retorted, "but I be d——d if I can help it." Dorsey did not remonstrate, perhaps believing that his own example would suffice; besides both men had more-pressing duties to perform.[17]

Jackson's men may have been handled roughly at Cedar Mountain, but his part in it left Pender unimpressed by what he had seen of the enemy. He reported that his men had pushed their opponents back "with heavy loss in almost the first round." Later to Fanny, Dorsey expressed a derisive view of the Federals they now confronted. "The specimen of fighting shown us the other day by the Yankees does not compare to that of the rascals around Richmond," he assessed on August 14. "Pope seems to be satisfied for the present with having caused Jackson to fall back, but let him wait a little while," he explained, "Longstreet with his Division is up and others on the way." Then recalling Pope's boastful circular, Dorsey added, "He will take to thinking about lines of retreat yet if he does not mind [pay attention]." There were lots of spoils to be had on the battlefield, including a "Yankee horse" for himself, a "Yankee saddle" for his servant Harris, and a "fine horse and equipment" for General Hill.[18] Nevertheless, the losses in the stout fight were heavy for the numbers involved: 2,381 of the 8,000 U.S. troops and 1,341 of their 16,800 C.S. counterparts.[19]

In the aftermath of the fighting, Stonewall Jackson ordered a pause to give divine thanks for the victory. At the same time, Pender received a letter from the man who had baptized him. Reverend Porter had sought to amplify the general's witness by publishing a tract "based upon the incident" that could be widely distributed. "If I had known it in time I should have objected," Dorsey told Fanny, "for I do not sincerely consider myself a fit subject for any such publication." He was not being disingenuous. Pender craved attention when he felt that it could bring him credit in the eyes of others, but on religious matters he felt a vulnerability that he could not shake. "I am a great sinner," he observed, "and not worthy to be held up to others as a light, or one to be followed." He remained disturbed about "that little member of the tongue," fearing it would "carry me to perdition."[20]

Even in the wake of a victory in which Powell Hill could take credit for having come to Jackson's assistance in a timely fashion, antagonism remained between the men. Dissension also occurred in the lower ranks between one of Pender's staff officers and General Branch. Comments the aide made with regard to the disposition of wagons led to heated exchanges that threatened to snare Pender in the imbroglio as well. The ensuing misunderstanding between the generals flared through communications that not only failed to achieve a mutually satisfying settlement of the matter but also led to a call for "satisfaction" once their military services were no longer required.[21]

Whatever the outcome of such honor-bound disagreements, a war remained to be fought. Joining his command at Gordonsville, Virginia, General Lee began to lay his own plans for John Pope's undoing. He did not want to wait while Pope swelled his ranks with reinforcements but preferred to strike him in a bold campaign of maneuver. The result was the campaign of Second Manassas (Bull Run), a series of bitter fights that ended in much the same way as the first encounter of the same name just over a year earlier, with the Federals in full retreat. But the main part of the initial battle did not start out that way.

Hill's men had enjoyed the bounty abandoned on the field at Cedar Mountain, but in the waning days of August, they became the recipients of even greater Northern largesse. The cavalry of Major General Jeb Stuart and infantry under feisty Brigadier General Isaac Trimble stormed into Manassas Junction and captured an enormous store of supplies that the Federals had gathered there. It was not until early on August 27 that Hill's men reached the scene. The famished soldiers simply could not contain themselves and, despite the existence of a token guard, fell upon the stores and helped themselves. A mortified Trimble lamented the "indiscriminate plunder" that took place, although he could hardly have been surprised by it. In any case, the troops of the Light Division were just beginning to enjoy the spoils of victory when the summons came to re-form as word of approaching Union troops reached them.[22]

Confederate artillery quickly dispersed the interlopers, and Hill's men savored the opportunity to return to the feast so ignobly interrupted. But the stern will of Stonewall Jackson intervened, at least temporarily, until he lifted the ban to allow the men to take what they could carry before consigning the remainder to the flames. By nightfall, Manassas Junction was burning brightly as the Confederates prepared to move against the Federals. Always the aggressor, Jackson expected the Union forces to withdraw. Unknown to him for the time being, however, they were actually doing the opposite. Pope was concentrating his command to seek out and destroy Jackson's pesky, isolated force.

Jackson expected some movement in response to his destruction of Pope's supply base, and he wanted some of his men poised in position to strike a surprise blow at the Federals as they marched past. He anticipated that Pope would send troops toward Centreville, thinking that the Confederates had concentrated there after wrecking the Manassas Depot. Powell Hill soon realized that Jackson faced a larger force than he had supposed, and he hastened to reach the area and render assistance to the Confederates lying in wait. His brigades were still working their way toward them when Jackson's men unleashed their assault about 5:30 in the afternoon against Brigadier General Rufus King's division as it moved along the Warrenton Turnpike near John Brawner's farmhouse in the vicinity of the 1861 battlefield. The engagement became protracted, with the opposing forces blazing away at each other at close range. The resulting bloody fight cost the Confederates dearly in commanders and alerted the Federals to their presence.

General Pope was still convinced he could "bag" Jackson and punish the celebrated Confederate for the damage he had inflicted thus far. Jackson's command was vulnerable, but the Southerners occupied strong defensive ground. Pope concentrated the next day to deliver what he hoped would be a knock-out blow against them. Hill had his men deployed in depth; Pender occupied a position in a second line between Archer and Branch. The Federals did not wait long on August 29 to advance against the Confederates. They tried to punch their way through the defenses, got hurled back by strong counterattacks, then regrouped or were reinforced and came forward again. The men of both sides exhibited courage and tenacity in the severe fighting, often characterized by hand-to-hand combat. A surge by Brigadier General Cuvier Grover's fresh brigade tore through Hill's first line, threatening the integrity of the entire Confederate left. Men moved forward to close the gap and reestablish the line. Casualties mounted in the obstinate and vicious fighting, then Hill turned to Pender to win the day.

The North Carolinians poured into the Union ranks and sent them reeling. Yet the advance exposed the troops to a severe fire. Captain Ashe recalled that Pender was conspicuous on the field, often leading his men from exposed positions. "It was no wonder that his men had unsurpassed confidence in him and devotion to him." His exposure left him vulnerable, and the general "was struck in his head" by Union fire.[23] Although slight, the wound, caused when a shell fragment grazed him, required dressing. With Pender removed temporarily, command fell to Colonel R. H. Riddick, but little more could be done than prepare for an unlikely night attack. Low on ammunition and energy, the

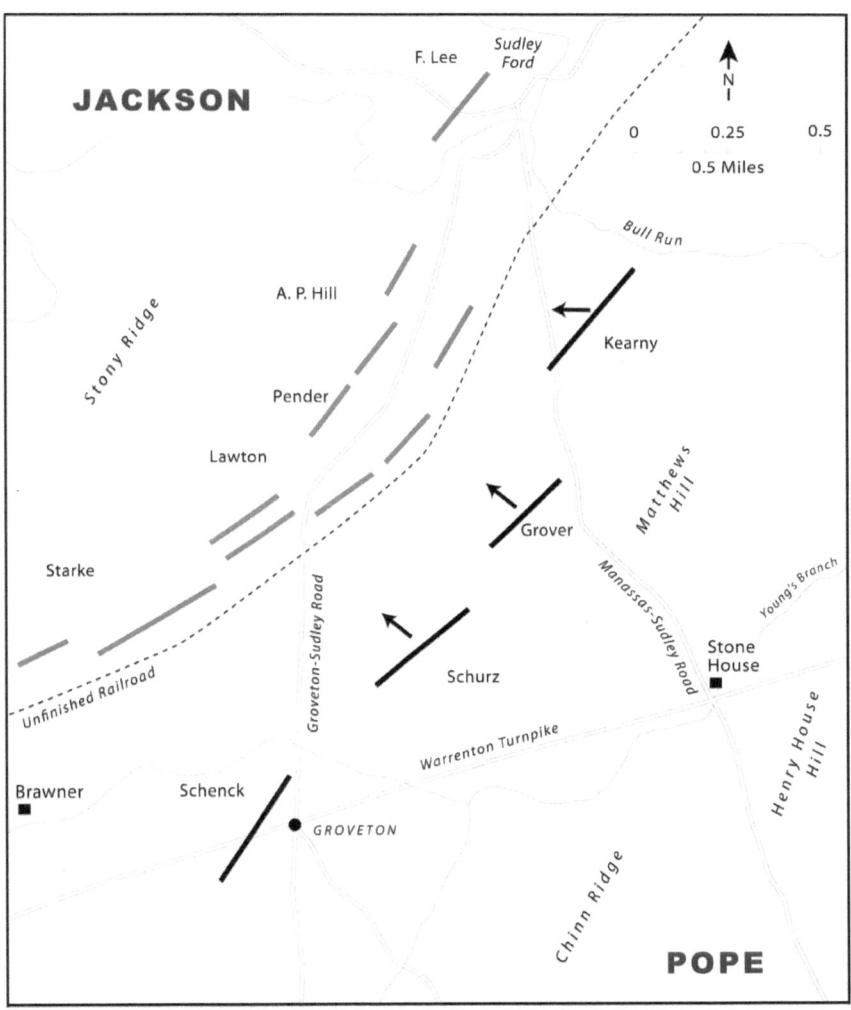

Map 5. Pender's service under Thomas J. "Stonewall" Jackson at Second Manassas (Second Bull Run) was crucial to the Confederate defense on August 29, 1862, before the Union rout the next day. Map by Heather Harvey.

Southerners were fighting exhaustion, devastating thirst, and approaching darkness as much as the bluecoats.

A temporary lull suggested an end to the major combat of the day, but it was not to be. Fresh Union troops returned to try a final drive to push the Confederates from their defenses. The Southerners clung stubbornly to the ground in the face of horrific pressure, some of them resorting to rocks when they expended the last of their ammunition. A portion of the Confederate forces shifted from another part of the field and reached the spot at the critical juncture, finally prizing the Federals away from the defenses "with great slaughter." Word reached Jackson that Hill had held against the odds, and the warrior's face at last relaxed. "Tell him," Jackson explained to the courier who had brought the welcome message with General Hill's compliments, "I knew he would do it!" It was as enthusiastic a response as Stonewall could muster, and he meant it from the bottom of his heart.[24]

Lee and Longstreet arrived as the day was coming to a close. Everyone involved in the fighting was worn completely by the exertions of the combat. Many, including Pender, were nursing wounds while tallying the dead and doing what they could to replenish ammunition and restore unit cohesion for another day of fighting. There was even time for a morsel of food, if one could be found to be consumed. An exhausted sleep finally came to men who could also look back with justifiable pride at what they had accomplished. They had held the line, as Jackson had said he knew they would.

The next day, Saturday, August 30, witnessed the end of the second struggle at Manassas. Pope believed he still confronted Jackson alone. If anything, he feared that Stonewall would retreat beyond his grasp and so moved quickly to prevent any retrograde movement or catch the Confederates in the process. Once more Powell Hill's command came under attack, and as he had done the previous day, the general turned to Dorsey Pender. Along with other regiments cobbled together for the purpose, the brigadier smashed the Union assault. One of the North Carolinians remarked pointedly and colorfully, "We slaughtered them like hogs," adding that he "never saw the like of dead men in all my life."[25]

Even amid such carnage, Pope simply would not give up in his quest to overpower the hard-pressed Confederates. In addition, he did not realize how precarious his own position was until Longstreet finally unleashed an attack that rolled the Federal left flank before it. Through the thick battle smoke, Pender recognized a weakness in the Union line that confronted them. Peering through his binoculars, he noticed that the Federals deployed before him also had their flank exposed. "If you will order the division to attack," he sent word to Hill, "the thing would be up with them."²⁶ That was all his commander needed to know, and he immediately issued the appropriate orders.

The Light Division surged forward and joined Longstreet's troops in pushing the Federals back before them. Pender's men moved out with the rest, helping capture a battery and compelling the enemy to give ground. Again the advance proved so irresistible that Pender and Archer outpaced their comrades and met with sustained resistance, which caused them to pull back. There was no doubt that a Union army was once more reeling away from Bull Run, but the Confederates had fallen short of their ultimate goal of destroying Pope's army. That knowledge tempered the celebration of a hard-fought victory, especially for General Lee. The elements also seemed to conspire against the victorious Southerners as heavy rains set in that hampered pursuit, bogging down men, animals, artillery, and wagons.²⁷

The last of the fighting connected with the Second Manassas Campaign came on September 1, 1862, at Chantilly (Ox Hill), Virginia. Amid a driving rainstorm that Pender described as "the most pelting rain I was in," the Confederates tried to close on the retreating Federals. In addition to the weather, a stiff defense by Union forces under Major Generals Isaac Stevens and Philip Kearny stymied the efforts and produced sharp casualties, among them the two Northern generals. "The Yankees had rather the best of it," Pender admitted, "as they maintained their ground and accomplished the object that was to cover their retreat." He noted candidly that in the aftermath of all of the previous combat, "none of us seemed anxious for the fight or did ourselves much credit."²⁸ A few days later Pender elaborated that "it was my luck to take a hand" in the Chantilly fight and that his men had "lost heavily," including Colonel Riddick of the 34th North Carolina, who "was wounded in two places."²⁹ Riddick was one of several senior officers who would not survive.³⁰ Still, the general felt that the overall effect was positive for the Confederates. "Their army had been totally demoralized by the recent whippings we gave them," he observed to Fanny, "and are now in and around Washington behind their fortifications."³¹

Dorsey lamented the losses, including Union general Kearny, whom he mentioned twice to Fanny as "one of their best Generals," but he was clearly pleased with the role he had played in the campaign as a whole.³² "During the fight I commanded three Brigades and parts of two others," he reported proudly to her. "I flatter myself I did good service." He also had the opportunity to enjoy the majesty of the battle itself. "I rode out in the edge of the field the enemy were formed in and never saw such a magnificent sight in my life. As far almost as the eye could reach they had one continuous line of troops, with artillery it seemed to me every fifty yards."[33] The panoply was impressive, even to a veteran of other fields in that costly spring and summer of battle. "I saw the whole army at one view Saturday, drawn up in battle array to meet our attack, we having driven back theirs," Dorsey explained a few days later, the sight still vivid in his mind.[34]

Pender left the campaign with renewed admiration for General Lee and respect for General Jackson. "Lee has immortalized himself," Dorsey wrote glowingly for Fanny, "and Jackson added new laurels to his brow," although he could not help but add, "not that I like to be under Jackson, for he forgets that one ever gets tired, hungry, or sleepy."[35]

The casualties produced by the fighting proved that Second Manassas had been another terribly bloody affair. The Confederates lost 1,481 and the Federals 1,724 killed in the weeklong fighting. Another 7,627 Southerners (including presumably Pender) and 8,372 Northerners suffered wounds. Again, as in the Seven Days Campaign, the number of missing Confederates was miniscule (89), while their routed opponents tallied almost 6,000 men (5,958).[36]

The combat had also proven to be dramatic and exciting for Pender personally. "I am safe and sound with the exception of a small cut by [a] shell on the top of the head," he explained matter-of-factly to Fanny. But the victory was worth the danger the action had posed for him since he and his Confederate comrades had "whipped them badly making almost another Bull Run affair."[37] As late as the end of September, Pender was still talking about Second Manassas in correspondence with a former staff officer now in Petersburg, Virginia. "They gave me a slight scratch at Manassas," he informed Lieutenant Lewis G. Young, "a piece of shell hitting me on the head cutting to the skull, but with a few patches I was all right next morning."[38] To his wife, Dorsey said simply of the close call, "My head is well but [a] little more bald than of yore, a small quantity [of hair] having been shaved off."[39]

Pender had much more perverse delight in telling Lieutenant Young of the plight of another of his staff officers, Sam Ashe, in the campaign just ended. "Bye the bye I did not tell you how the pretty man got himself captured & quartered in the Old Capital [Prison]," he began almost mischievously. "Late Saturday night after the fight at Manassas having left his horse & blankets & lost his bay horse—again—he went back on [R. H.] Brewers horse to get them." Apparently while in the process of attempting to retrieve his property, the aide stumbled into Union troops and became their prisoner. While Pender surely felt badly for his lieutenant, despite his jesting tone, he was particularly perturbed at what else had been taken along with the staffer. "Just to think Harris gone," he noted of the servant who had accompanied Ashe on the errand, "& the prettiest horse you ever saw that I had just captured at the [Manassas] Junction."[40]

General Pender had initially felt positively toward Lieutenant Ashe, calling him "a very nice modest young man" and telling Fanny at the end of July, "I like him very much." But within a relatively short time after making those comments, he appeared to have soured considerably on his subordinate.[41] As the command entered Maryland for a new campaign, Dorsey mentioned the incident again to his wife. "I captured the most beautiful horse at Manassas, and Harris was riding him the other night & got captured horse and all. Sam Ashe was captured at the same time and is now in the old Capital [Prison] at Washington." There was only the hint of disgust with the aide as he promised, "I shall try to get his exchange."[42] When he related the story of Ashe's capture to Young, he was more candid, noting with a touch of derision that the lieutenant "had an inclination to getting lost," obviously also holding him accountable for the other losses that had occurred as a result.[43] By October, Ashe apparently had returned to camp, but he was not destined to remain there long, for as Dorsey subsequently wrote to Fanny, the officer tendered his resignation.[44]

The ambivalent attitude Pender expressed for his ill-fated aide may well have reflected larger divisions between the general and members of his staff. As an officer, the North Carolinian could be demanding, establishing for himself and his subordinates a high level of expectation that made inadequacy intolerable. To his credit, Pender applied these demands to himself as well as to them, but if someone did not measure up, the general was bound to be unyielding in his judgment. For some, this tendency was sufficient to drive a wedge between them, and the North Carolinian was not prone to play the diplomat in an effort to seal any breach that might occur.

Such rifts included more staffers than the hapless Sam Ashe. Pender also had a prewar connection with the man whose horse the lieutenant had borrowed when he was captured. "Col. Brewer, an old friend who was Lt. in the 1st Draggons, is now on my staff temporarily," Dorsey wrote Fanny in August, just before the Second Manassas Campaign. His chief complaint then had been the old soldier's propensity for swearing, which the general noted required his "remonstrating with him about it when he came." Brewer gave the impression of "a very nice fellow and a great acquaintance," but the relationship suffered afterward, and any sense of prewar comradeship being carried over dissipated rather quickly.[45]

The situation deteriorated so that by September Pender and Brewer had finally had enough of each other. "Col. Brewer I had much rather was gone," Dorsey explained to Fanny bluntly, "for he has become so dissatisfied and talks so much about wanting to go to Richmond that it is disagreeable to have him around." Pender was pretty chagrined with another aide as well, wishing that S. S. Kirkland "ought also to be along." Attrition through combat had affected the brigade's command structure, but Pender's comments concerning these officers indicated that additional changes would be preferable as well, despite the adjustments necessitated by such departures.

If the general was not entirely pleased with every member of his staff, he was satisfied with the troops themselves. "The fact is, Hill's Division stands first in point of efficiency of any Division of this whole Army," he explained proudly.[46] Pender's handling of personnel matters was never his strong suit, but he thought that any turmoil that existed in his staff would be more than offset with the state of the command itself.

Through these eventful months, Pender underwent the extremes of combat and experienced important development as an officer. At Seven Pines he found himself under significant fire for the first time in his Civil War career. He learned much about himself as a commander of men in such conditions, aided in the confidence he developed in himself and in them by the praise of higher authorities, including President Davis. In the subsequent action of the Seven Days Campaign, he refined that knowledge and enhanced his reputation as a leader in battle. Experience in the field continued as Pender and his comrades fought and defeated John Pope at Second Manassas. If anything suggested a worrisome trend for the man who was quickly establishing himself as Lee's fighting North Carolinian, it was that he could be found where the projectiles of war flew the thickest and had a nagging tendency to attract wounds in the process. None of these had yet proven to be serious, but Dorsey Pender did not often seem to be able to leave a battle unscathed. Still, if this brought enormous anxiety to Fanny, it brought recognition and glory for the new brigadier general as well. Pender was rapidly becoming one of the Army of Northern Virginia's finest young officers. In the days and months ahead, he would have additional opportunities to test his mettle and obtain further chances for advancement through promotion. The North Carolina general with the penchant for fighting and the demand for discipline in his ranks was beginning to catch the eyes of his superiors, thereby demonstrating that his star was on the ascendancy.

9

"DRIVE THOSE SCOUNDRELS OUT"
(September–December 1862)

>Are you not surprised to find us in Md?
>—DORSEY PENDER TO FANNY

>The men seem to think I am fond of fighting. They say I give them
>"hell" out of the fight and the Yankees the same in it.
>—DORSEY PENDER TO FANNY

William Dorsey Pender might be grappling with issues relating to his troops and staff officers, his wife and family, his religious and military obligations and responsibilities, but he would soon be struggling with his Union opponents on the battlefield again in one of the highest stakes gambles of the war thus far. General Lee was prepared to do something drastic in the fall of 1862. Perhaps by taking the war into northern territory, he could put pressure on the major European states as well as the Lincoln administration and force some type of resolution to the conflict that had been raging for better than a year.[1]

"Are you not surprised to find us in Md?" Pender queried his wife on September 7, 1862. "We crossed day before yesterday and now have possession of this part of the State." Whatever Fanny might think of the military developments, and she would undoubtedly not be pleased with them, Dorsey wanted to put them in perspective and set her mind at ease. "Gen. Lee is in good earnest and the Yankees are terribly frightened," he explained. "May the Lord have mercy upon us and give us success, not for glory or conquest, but as the only way to peace."[2] The ultimate mission now seemed to be to take the war to the enemy and encourage the Federals to consider some negotiation that would end the conflict.

Pender thought that recent defeats gave the Confederates a decided edge. "Their army had been totally demoralized by the recent whippings we gave them," he observed. George McClellan was even being pressed back into service in the emergency. The circumstances looked right for a telling blow that would end in Southern independence. At any rate, Pender believed that "one more fight must settle the thing one way or the other."[3]

The general reflected the enormous confidence that the rank and file in the Army of Northern Virginia had in their chieftain. "Gen. Lee has shown great generalship and the greatest boldness," he remarked to Fanny. For the North Carolinian, the Maryland invasion paralleled the great offensive movements of history, and he compared Lee to the most notable of military lieutenants. "There never was such a campaign," Dorsey exuded, "not even by Napoleon."[4]

This theme continued in the next letter as the Confederates lingered in Frederick, Maryland. "Our army is improving very rapidly and are in fine spirits and feel confident of success," Pender observed. "We ought to succeed and I think we will. May God grant we may, in bringing them to stop this war by recognizing us." He thought that the Union response to the movement into Maryland was particularly telling in assessing the morale of their opponents. "Their delay in advancing upon us shows how totally disorganized their army must have been."[5]

Yet for all of the confidence in its commander and the élan associated with a string of recent victories, all was not well within the Army of Northern Virginia. Disciplinary problems plagued the vaunted gray ranks of Lee's command on almost every level. Generals continued to quarrel and squabble with each other. Arrests seemed almost commonplace for one infraction or another, real or perceived. The foot soldiers themselves suffered from lack of adequate footwear and poor diet. Straggling and scavenging in the ranks remained rampant.[6]

Always a hard taskmaster when it came to basic questions of discipline, Pender was especially annoyed by the lax attitudes demonstrated by some of his troops, both officers and enlisted personnel. Hard marching of the kind to which the members of the army had been subjected for months would perhaps inevitably produce straggling—he was too experienced not to expect such breakdowns—but the scourge seemed epidemic in Maryland. Historian Robert K. Krick offered a scathing assessment of these conditions in Lee's army while the Confederates traversed Maryland, noting, "North Carolina troops suffered disproportionately from this malady."[7] Such realities produced in Pender unpleasant memories that would remain in the back of his mind.

Added to this trouble came the even graver problem of requisitioning, or as the civilians who experienced the phenomenon might have labeled it, looting or stealing. This behavior embarrassed the army and its commanders, and while a common feature of ancient warfare, it was less acceptable in a modern, civilized day. Pender realized that these practices would hardly win friends among the people affected. The men "will clean out a big orchard in half an hour," he complained to Fanny. In language he normally reserved for the Federals, he denounced the looters as the most "filthy, unprincipled set of villains I have ever seen. They have lost all honor or decency," he added, "all sense of right or respect for property." The general admitted that he had even had to resort to extreme measures to restore order among them. "I have had to strike many a one with my saber." It was altogether a sad admission for a man who prided himself on maintaining decorum under all circumstances.

Conditions for the Federals were also volatile and unsettling. It would certainly have been understandable for President Lincoln to feel anxious about having to turn once more to George McClellan to thwart Confederate purposes. Yet the greatest opportunity for that general to redeem himself came in Maryland in September 1862. Lee's ragged veterans had just passed through the town of Frederick when a courier inadvertently left a small bundle behind in the encampment they had occupied. Wrapped around the unexpected treasure of several cigars was an even more significant boon: a copy of Lee's Special Order No. 191. The document revealed that the Army of Northern Virginia was divided and, with swift action by the Federals, could easily be in a position to be struck in detail and effectively destroyed.[8]

McClellan was overjoyed with the intelligence coup that had so providentially fallen into his hands. He gloated, "Here is the paper with which if I cannot whip 'Bobbie Lee,' I will be willing to go home." His counterpart at Harpers Ferry, Colonel Dixon S. Miles, did not share the same level of hope for success. Many of his troops were inexperienced, some having been in the service for only a few weeks. They were about to be tested thoroughly in their resolve by Confederate veterans who were rapidly descending upon them from all sides.

On September 13, when Major General Lafayette McLaws's men seized Maryland Heights, Brigadier General John G. Walker took Loudon Heights, and Stonewall Jackson moved up on School House Ridge near Bolivar Heights, Confederate forces created a vise that gripped the Union garrison in a desperate stranglehold. A Georgian with the approaching Southerners captured the essence of the experience for his father in a letter a week later. "We reached

Harper's Ferry on Saturday morning much fatigued and worn down from the excessive march we had taken," Lieutenant W. C. Goggans explained, noting the satisfaction of seeing the Confederate colors on the commanding heights. "We then began to wake them occasionally giving them a bum [bomb] merely to interest them, while our forces were gathering."⁹ As the officer realized, putting artillery on those various heights through the night and into the next day would prove particularly detrimental to Federal hopes for a successful defense of the historic town.

Jackson quickly closed the noose on the approximately 12,000 defenders of Harpers Ferry. At the same time, he felt pressure from other developments in Maryland. As sluggish as McClellan was capable of being, he could stir at any moment. Indeed, buttressed by the knowledge of his opponent's dispositions, the Union general was ready to take action against the Army of Northern Virginia. Harpers Ferry must fall quickly or Confederate operations against it might have to be curtailed or canceled altogether.

Stonewall Jackson clearly preferred to push for a Federal capitulation. To that end, he ordered Powell Hill to threaten the Union left by moving along the Shenandoah River toward the town's defenses. Hill called upon Pender to make a stab at one of the lightly held enemy positions of infantry behind an abatis of felled trees, with no sign of artillery. Hill augmented Pender's brigade with three others for good measure, and the North Carolinian sent his men forward. "The execution of this movement was intrusted to General Pender," Hill recorded in his report on the Maryland Campaign. "This was accomplished with but slight resistance, and the fate of Harper's Ferry was sealed."¹⁰

In his after-action report, Pender singled out "Colonel Brewer," who "was in command of the brigade at this time, and did himself great credit in the manner in which he handled it." Subsequently, he asked that Hill take note of "the distinguished gallantry and efficiency of First Lieut. R. H. Brewer, volunteer aide on my staff, whom I recommend for promotion."¹¹ The seeming discrepancy in rank aside, this was the same Old Army colleague whose relationship with Pender had deteriorated. Certainly, given the testy nature of it, such praise on the general's part was not offered lightly and suggested that performance could rehabilitate a person's reputation in his eyes. This emphasis drew Hill's attention as well. In his report for the campaign and this engagement, he mentioned Brewer as one of the colonels who deserved comment due to "especial good conduct."¹²

Pender had relinquished immediate command of his brigade temporarily so that he could focus on the larger responsibility of leading three brigades overall, including his under Brewer, Archer's, and Field's units. Upon returning to his brigade, the general promptly made readjustments in its positioning to prevent the command from being exposed unnecessarily and then allowed his exhausted soldiers to receive some much deserved rest. Others were not so fortunate. Hill's chief of artillery pushed his men through the night to get their pieces in more-advantageous positions. The effort not only provided Hill's men with security but also laid the groundwork for any final assault Jackson might order the next day. General Lee noted that this difficult work meant the placement of "several batteries on the eminence taken by General Pender."[13]

On the opposite side, Union aide-de-camp Lieutenant Henry M. Binney recorded the activities of both combatants as he saw them in the operations around Harpers Ferry. From his perspective, Binney explained how during the evening of September 14, "the enemy in strong force, composed of General Pender's brigade of North Carolinians, attempt to turn our flank, which move Brigadier General [Julius] White shrewdly anticipates and repels with much slaughter."[14] It is debatable the degree to which such "slaughter" took place among the Southern ranks in the fighting on September 14. Pender set his losses in the two days before Harpers Ferry's capitulation as two killed and twenty wounded.[15]

Understandably, given the nature of the terrain involved, it was not as much the movement of the foot soldiers as the placement of artillery that proved most decisive in bringing about a successful conclusion for the Southerners. In his entry for the final day of the siege, Lieutenant Binney noted simply, "We are surrounded by [the] enemy's batteries."[16] Georgian W. C. Goggans was also impressed with the firepower his comrades were able to bring to bear against the Union defenders at the close of operations. After resting for the "knight" in line of battle, he observed, "Early next morning a terrible fire of Artillery was opened by us soon replied to by the the [sic] enemy as the fire then opened from the Heights."[17]

A heavy mist or fog obscured the battlefield in the early morning hours until the sun burned it off to reveal the Confederates in an even more commanding position than they had enjoyed initially.[18] The Southern guns opened from positions that included, in the words of one historian, "those on the little knoll Pender had so handsomely captured."[19] There was little doubt that an assault would follow, but the bombardment rendered it unnecessary. "The enemy could not stand such terrific fire," one Confederate recalled. "The Air was rent with the missiles of death for 2 hours that morning when the enemy Hoisted the white flag and seased [sic] their fire."[20]

Unfortunately, in the confusion that followed before the surrender could be confirmed, a Confederate projectile fatally injured Colonel Miles. Through A. P. Hill, Jackson accepted the capitulation of the town and its defenders, as well as seventy-three pieces of artillery, thirteen thousand small arms, and two hundred wagons, from a successor to the fallen Federal commander.[21]

Pender remained behind as part of the force designated to complete the work at Harpers Ferry. Other units under Jackson raced off in the direction of the little village of Sharpsburg, near Antietam Creek, where Lee prepared as best he could to conduct a fight for survival against his old nemesis from western Virginian and the Peninsula.

The North Carolinian was soon under orders to march for Sharpsburg as well. His men traveled hard to cover the seventeen miles that separated them from their comrades. Pender noted that they reached the scene of battle and promptly took up a position on the Confederate right, where according to the general's report, they remained under fire but were not actively involved in the brutal fighting of September 17.[22] Hill explained that he shifted Pender's men toward the center late in the action but agreed that they were not "actively" engaged with the enemy.[23]

But at least one individual was animated by the North Carolinian's arrival on the field. "For God's sake General, hurry up! Burnside has carried the bridge and smashed our right flank to flinders," a bystander called out to Pender as he rode up. Yet the newcomer remained unperturbed at the news. "All right!" he said after digesting the scene before him, "Don't be uneasy!" Then with the self-possession he enjoyed at such moments of high drama, General Pender added quietly, "We'll straighten things out."[24] As it turned out, he did not have to "straighten things out" at Sharpsburg, but it must have been comforting to know that he and his comrades were in a position to do so if needed.

An officer (and later historian of the famed Washington Artillery) was more circumspect about Pender's arrival, though no less grateful. "None too soon did the head of A. P. Hill's column reach the battle-field, at 2:30 P.M.," William Owen recalled, with "Pender in advance." The artillerist noted that "Hill's line was immediately formed" for the purpose of holding against any Union assault that might still occur.[25]

By the time this bloodiest of all single days of combat in the war was finished, some 2,700 Confederates and 2,010 Federals lay dead in the fields, woods, and farm lanes around Sharpsburg. Another 9,024 and 9,416 men, respectively, were lying in field hospitals, local homes, and other structures in which medical personnel nursed every wound that such horrific combat could inflict upon human flesh. Some 2,000 Southerners and 1,043 Northerners would also be counted among the missing.[26] No one who had witnessed the carnage, much less participated in it, left this wholesale butchery unaffected. Replacing the numbers of casualties would be difficult, if not impossible, for once more there were enormous holes to fill at all levels in the armies that had mauled each other so savagely.

Unfortunately for the battle-worn troops, the fighting in the campaign as a whole was not over. During the night of September 19, the Federals made inroads in the Confederate lines at Shepherdstown, Virginia. The next morning Powell Hill received orders to eliminate the bridgehead and drive the intruders back across the river.[27] Consequently, he brought his division up and formed it into two lines, facing the enemy. Pender occupied the first line, sharing it with the brigades of Gregg and Thomas. In the face of a terrific fire from Union artillery, the Confederates advanced. A participant recalled that the "roar of the pieces and the howl and explosion of shells was awful." South Carolinian J. F. J. Caldwell, in Gregg's Brigade, observed the resulting carnage firsthand. "Sometimes a shell burst right in the ranks, tearing and mangling all around it," he explained. "In Pender's brigade I saw a man lifted clear into the air." Yet the Confederates plunged steadily ahead through the gathering smoke and chaos.[28]

As Pender advanced toward the Union lines, his command found itself in an increasingly awkward and hazardous position. The Charlestown Road dissected the battlefield, and the movement of the North Carolinians through the fields to the left of that artery caused a separation between them and their comrades to the right.[29]

From his position on the ground, Pender could not be aware of this development, but watching from the rear, Hill had a better vantage point and correctly interpreted the situation. The division commander also assessed the danger that Federal movements posed as they "massed in front of Pender, and extending, endeavored to turn his left." Immediately, he took steps to alleviate the crisis by ordering James Archer to move a second line of infantry up in support of Pender's assault. Subsequently, Hill recalled his admiration of the determination of his men as they rushed forward to assist their beleaguered comrades. "It was as if each man felt that the fate of the army was centered in himself."[30]

"DRIVE THOSE SCOUNDRELS OUT": SEPTEMBER–DECEMBER 1862

A number of factors appeared to have worked against the defenders at Shepherdstown. The relative inexperience and faulty weapons of some of the Union soldiers exacerbated a situation already complicated by heavy losses, poor communication, and the generally chaotic nature of the fighting. The timely assistance from General Archer for the North Carolinians created overwhelming pressure on the remaining Federals. The Confederates finally succeeded in breaking the enemy position and sent their opponents reeling in headlong retreat. The pursuing Southerners were able to fire effectively into the demoralized troops, even while themselves enduring a considerable covering fire from Union artillery.[31]

In his after-action report, Powell Hill observed that the Federals ran "pellmell into the river." Even with the killing fields of Sharpsburg fresh in his mind, he added: "Then commenced the most terrible slaughter that this war has yet witnessed. The broad surface of the Potomac was blue with the floating bodies of our foe. But few escaped to tell the tale."[32] From the rear of Pender's command, a Georgian watched the action at "ShepherdsTown" and wrote that it resulted in the Confederates having "taken between 3 & 4 hundred Prisoners killing many almost bloodying the water of the Potomac from the slain while crossing our loss was but few we routed and drove them from our side."[33] Even the usually taciturn Old Testament warrior Jackson felt moved by the scene to observe that the Confederates "drove the enemy into the river, followed by an appalling scene of the destruction of human life."[34]

Pender was less exuberant about the outcome. His men helped send the Federals "headlong into the river," he agreed, but with the exception of a detail from the 22nd North Carolina "under the gallant Major Cole," he pulled the bulk of his men back from the bank where they were being subjected to the brutal fire of artillery and musketry.[35] The Light Division had suffered 30 killed and 231 wounded, while inflicting severe casualties on their opponents. "By their own account they lost 3,000 men, killed and drowned from one brigade alone," Hill noted. "Some 200 prisoners were taken."[36] Pender's losses did not exceed the number of captives his division commander claimed to have taken, with 8 killed and 55 wounded. For the campaign as a whole, he set his brigade's casualties at 38 killed and 300 wounded.[37]

Dorsey described the fighting at Shepherdstown for Fanny shortly afterward from Virginia. "Our Division had a hard fight day before yesterday," he observed. When the Federals threatened the Confederate positions, it became "necessary for us to go and drive them back. We did it under the most terrible artillery fire I ever saw troops exposed to. They continued to shell us all day. It was as hot a place as I wish to get in." Fortunately, Dorsey had also managed to get out unscathed and left the engagement with a great pride in his association with the Light Division. "The fact is, Hill's Division stands first in point of efficiency of any Division of this whole Army." He felt that even Jackson, supervising the whole business, had been impressed.[38]

Pender was certainly pleased to be a member of the Light Division. "You have no idea what a reputation our Division has," he told Fanny. "It surpasses Jackson's old Division both for fighting and discipline." Then suddenly, he sobered, recalling the grim statistics. "But when I tell you that this Division has lost 9000 killed and wounded since we commenced the Richmond fight at Mechanicsville, you can see what our reputation has cost us." He added other numbers, including his own brigade, with between "12 and 1500" casualties to its credit. Finally, he had his fill. "Let me cease to write about war and killing."[39]

The North Carolinian especially lamented the poor examples in leadership he had witnessed. "The officers are nearly as bad as the men," he explained to Fanny. "In one of my Regts. the other day when they thought they were going into a fight, six out [of] ten skulked out and did not come up until they thought all danger over." The number of malcontents was having a decided effect. As Dorsey observed, "More than half my Brigade went off the same day."[40] For an officer who had prided himself so much on the reflection his men made upon his leadership, this type of situation was nothing short of intolerable.

The general continued to express concern about the state of the command. Skulking, straggling, looting, and the like were the bane of an army's existence and a blot on everyone else who served honorably. Subsequently, his exasperation reached new heights as he explained to Fanny, "This straggling is becoming to be the curse of the Army and unless Congress pass some law to stop it there is no telling where it will end." Then in a final fit of pique, he declared, "We will have to shoot them before it stops."[41]

Yet even with all the bloodletting and the indications of disciplinary breakdowns so starkly revealed by the recent campaign, Pender thought the Confederates could achieve success, especially if in the future they remained in defense of their own land. "My only regret," he wrote Fanny three days later of the campaign just ended, "is that we ever crossed it [the Potomac River] in the first place. They cannot drive us from any position we choose to take, by reinforcements they may cause us to draw off after the battle."[42]

Once the guns of the long campaign finally fell silent, General Pender filled at least some of his time with reading, as he had been prone to do while a cadet at West Point. His choice in this instance was not a book of tactics, though, but the controversial Harriet Beecher Stowe novel that some had attributed to helping bring on the war. Ironically, given their respective sectional connections and interests, Pender thought he had more in common with the author's views than might be expected, and the book certainly caused him to reflect on the subject of slavery and his role with regard to the South's "peculiar institution." "I am reading Uncle Tom's Cabin and really you have no idea how nearly we agree on the subject of slavery," he told Fanny. "I tried to whip Joe the other day but could go only three stripes."[43]

For Pender, slavery was more practical than political. He did not engage in the sale of slaves as chattel property or use their sale to enrich himself. In criticizing one of the would-be suitors for Fanny's sister Pamela, Dorsey exhibited his anger not only toward the willingness of the man to seek wealth and comfort over service but also "to make money by the worst calling but one—negro trading." Only the abuse of whiskey trumped slave trading and merited a greater measure of his condemnation.[44]

Still, Pender did not question the relative positions that he as master and those as slaves occupied in society. Slavery was a part of the hierarchy of life in which he had been born and raised. As such, he normally saw no reason to question or challenge, much less condemn, the institution. The exception to this laissez-faire attitude happened when the attacks came from elsewhere and his sensitivities thus became awakened.

As the general contemplated such matters, the ordinary demands of command authority also required his attention. The Army of Northern Virginia was back on the soil of its namesake when he got an opportunity to file his official report, not only of the campaign just concluded in Maryland but also of the near-constant military activity stretching back to the fighting around Manassas.

As usual, Pender singled out those he felt deserved special notice, but he took particular care to highlight the efforts of the 22nd North Carolina, for it was that regiment and its commanders, he explained, "that I usually call when any special and dangerous services are to be performed." The 22nd's commander, Major Christopher C. Cole, exhibited "coolness, courage and skill," not coincidentally attributes on the battlefield usually associated with his brigadier. Indeed, when it came to this unit, Pender must have felt almost nostalgic as he set pen to paper describing the actions of one of the junior officers.

Second Lieutenant David Edwards drew his special attention and undoubtedly reminded him something of himself in Washington Territory at the same stage in his career. In a stunt of bravery and daring that came at the height of the fighting at Second Manassas, Edwards and two other comrades "rushed ahead of their regiment and captured a piece of artillery when it was on the eve of escaping, having a hand-to-hand engagement with the enemy."[45]

Frustrations with the conditions of his command had always been a factor in shaping Pender's sense of well-being. In the aftermath of the campaign, such concerns presented him with challenges that had a painful familiarity. On October 1, 1862, the general forwarded a list of names from one of the regiments in his brigade for appearance in a Raleigh newspaper. Under the heading "Thirty-Eighth Regiment—Absentees," the item was intended to put pressure on the ninety men Pender had identified as "absent without leave" through incentives for assistance from civilians and jailors who might become involved in their apprehension and return to duty. "A reward of $30 will be paid for their delivery (or any one of them) to any Confederate officer," with a bounty of $15 each to jailors. Most of the men had left the command in the late summer months of August and September, but a handful had disappeared from the ranks in the spring. One, a fellow named A. C. Wike of Company F, had been gone since the previous December and was the individual listed with the longest-standing absence from his unit. Undoubtedly, the brigade commander was anxious to have them all back in the ranks, for the notation appeared that the advertisement was to run "twice, weekly, and send bill to Gen. Pender."[46]

Wanting to stop the depletion of the ranks through desertion just as he had hoped to tackle the issue of straggling in the recent Maryland Campaign, Pender nevertheless recognized the underlying symptoms of despair that drove some men to become fugitives. He had only been back in Virginia a short time when he found an opportunity to put his Christian virtues to work in a manner that would help ease such situations. He knew well how severely his men suffered from wartime deprivations, but he was also aware that civilians endured hardships that in many ways were worse. Pender felt an obligation to his soldiers, but he was solicitous of destitute citizens and sought a means to try to offer them assistance too. Among a list of the donors of "sums for relief of the poor" that appeared in the *Daily Dispatch* of Richmond, Virginia, in mid-October was a notation for ten dollars from "Gen. W. D. Pender" of "Major General A. P. Hill's Division."[47]

Pender also had an interlude in which to enjoy some socializing if he were so inclined. He remained a bit skittish, but apparently Hamilton, Fanny's older brother, was less circumspect. "Ham" went out to perform in a band for some of the local residents and made a favorable impression on one of the listeners. According to Dorsey, "one of whom I was sorry to hear had fallen in love with him, being under the impression that he was single." Single or not, the whole event reminded him of his own previous flirtations in Suffolk, and although he did not mention those particulars by name, there was no doubt about his allusions to them. "I do not know how she is," Dorsey explained snidely, "but my wife would hold me responsible for such weakness on the part of any lady. The fact is, my wife is so particular that I hardly dare go where young ladies congregate."[48]

Another individual with a reputation for having a flare with women was back in the headlines and in Pender's letters. His old West Point friend Jeb Stuart was once again busy. "What do you think of Stuart's last raid?" Dorsey inquired of Fanny. "It was nip and tuck with him." He felt there was more at work here than the typical military operation. "Beaut is after a Lieut. Generalcy." Stuart's quest for promotion put Pender in mind of his own. "I did not write you that Gen. Hill proposed the other day to write and recommend my promotion and told me to use all my political influence."[49] Three days later he broached the subject of advancement again. "My name has been mentioned in army circles and it has been several times reported that I had been promoted, but I am too young and have no one in Richmond to push my claims."[50]

Opportunities would continue to present themselves. In a short time it became apparent that neither the recent hard-fought campaign in Maryland nor the difficult retreat back into Virginia was going to deter General Lee from seeking another confrontation with his Union opponents. In late October Pender thought he had identified the signs of impending military action. He explained to Fanny on the twenty-ninth, "Everything looks promising particularly as I have just received an order that no furloughs will for the present be granted except on [a] surgeon's certificate." Pender considered himself a candidate for such a release, based upon one malady or another. "Any pretext for a leave would be taken advantage of," he assured her. "I do want to see you so much. It seems to me more than I ever did." His mind whirling with possibilities, Dorsey explained almost conspiratorily, "My dear wife if you knew how often I resolve the various ways of getting a leave in my mind and how much I think about it, you would not for one moment suspect me of missing any chance to see you."[51]

Dorsey seemed to have gotten his chance to visit briefly with Fanny in mid-November. Interestingly, this stickler for discipline when it came to others was less demanding of himself in this instance. On November 15 Colonel Alfred M. Scales noted in a letter to his future wife, Kate, "Gen. Pender left on a sick furlough and I was placed in command of the Brigade consisting of five Regiments."[52] If the "sick furlough" was a subterfuge to allow Dorsey to see Fanny for a few moments, the irony was that Scales, lovesick in his own right, did not penetrate through it.

Of course, Pender may have been ill or using poor health to mask the opportunity to visit his wife; he may also have had a third mission in mind. James Archer was convinced that whatever else he might be trying to accomplish, Pender was going to be in the Confederate capital on other, professionally oriented business. In a "confidential" aside, Archer wrote on November 5, "Pender has gone home on sick leave—I have no doubt he stopped long enough in Richmond to make some enquiries of his friends as who are likely to be made Maj. Gen."[53]

While its general was absent, the brigade had a brief firefight with Federal troops near Winchester. Scales assessed the men as being "in fine spirits though the foot fellows are without tents, badly clothed & badly shod." He could not help admiring them under the circumstances. "Such self sacrificing devotion deserves & will be rewarded & with the help of God we will drive the invader from our soil."[54] The colonel also apparently did not realize the slight that such comments suggested for the commander who had slipped away to see his wife.

By November 22, Pender was back in Richmond, where he dashed off a quick note to Fanny that provided a short update. In it he included the fact that his friend Stephen D. Lee had received a promotion and had gone to the western theater.[55] No such transfer or advancement seemed likely for Pender, although his stock remained generally high.

From distant Wilmington, North Carolina, his former commander, W. H. C. Whiting, sent a special request for Pender's Brigade to be sent to him if circumstances allowed. Pender thought well of Whiting, in large measure because the general thought so highly of him. But a transfer to North Carolina was not going to occur, and the promise of pending action made it even more unlikely.[56] "Gen. Lee is very anxiously awaiting a fight," Dorsey explained to

Fanny on December 3. "He told me to-day that he believed he would be willing to fall back and let them cross for the sake of a fight." Pender may have been surprised at the army commander's exuberance, but the troops under him thought he shared the same characteristics as Lee in that regard. "The men seem to think that I am fond of fighting," he observed to Fanny. "They say I give them 'hell' out of the fight and the Yankees the same in it." But his soldiers seemed ready to fight too. "One cannot imagine the degree of confidence and high spirits displayed by the men," Dorsey remarked to Fanny, sharing his troops' high regard for Lee.[57]

Yet for the time being, all there seemed to be to do was to wait. "They throw up their works and we throw up ours," Pender noted with exasperation on December 5. Melting snow had turned the roads into quagmires, limiting military operations as was common in the winter. But even in the case of the pickets, there appeared to be little activity or desire on either side for it. The quiet allowed Dorsey to ponder many things from his personal finances and his matrimonial plans for Fanny's younger sister and his best friend, Stephen Lee. He got mischievous when he thought of Abraham Lincoln's announcement of a preliminary emancipation proclamation. "What do you say to selling our negro property to old Abe and quitting the war?" he asked. The playful question about the "old villain" aside, Dorsey closed his thoughts as he always did these days, telling Fanny, "I love you more dearly every day and think more about you than I once thought it possible."[58]

The probability for promotion also remained in his mind, although advancement to major general looked as elusive as ever. "General rumor and general feeling both have pointed me out to be Gen. Hill's successor," he explained, if his superior and friend Powell Hill became a lieutenant general. "He told me the other night that he hoped I would soon be a Major General." Almost sheepishly this time, given Fanny's usually blunt assessments of such comments, Dorsey added, "I had no idea that I was a man of reputation in the army until I got back."[59]

Whether centered on promotion or other elements, Pender's thoughts would not be entirely his own in the days to come. Ambrose Burnside, the bewhiskered Union general who had brought unsettlement to Pender's mind when he led his troops into eastern North Carolina in early 1862 and who had threatened Lee's position across Antietam Creek in Maryland later that same year, was the man who now faced Lee across the Rappahannock. Known by most as a genial fellow, Burnside was determined to prove anything but that to his adversaries. By mid-November he had occupied Stafford Heights, across the river from Fredericksburg. Delays in the arrival of pontoons prevented the Federals from crossing the Rappahannock before Lee could shift to block such a move. It would be well into the next month before the Army of the Potomac challenged the increasingly strong Southern position.

Confronted with the certainty of a stout resistance to any crossing at Fredericksburg, Burnside forged ahead anyway. Brigadier General William Barksdale's riflemen made the work of the Union engineers, finally begun on December 11, difficult at best and prompted a bombardment by Federal artillery to clear the Mississippians from the town. Even so, the Confederates burrowed into the rubble and awaited new targets.[60]

General Pender reacted strongly to the shelling of Fredericksburg. The cannonade had "commenced about 6 A.M." and continued through the morning. "The barbarity of the thing is unheard of," he insisted. "To shell an unfortified town is against [military] usage." Then resignedly, he noted that such laws were meant "for nations to suit their own convenience."[61]

As distasteful as some of them may have been for Pender and other Southerners, these actions ensured the ability of the Union troops to cross the river and occupy Fredericksburg proper. A day of preparation and fairly indiscriminate plundering preceded the assault Burnside now planned to make directly into the face of the main Confederate position along the heights beyond the town. Even amid the ensuing bloody carnage, as wave after wave in blue crashed futilely against the Confederate defenders poised confidently in a sunken road behind a stone wall at Marye's Heights, the chance for Union victory remained; it just did not likely exist there. Instead, the greater potential for success rested with the efforts to wrest the Confederate right flank from its moorings alongside the Richmond, Fredericksburg, and Potomac Railroad. Here, under the overall command of Major General William B. Franklin, Major General George Gordon Meade thrust his Pennsylvanians forward at midday on December 13 after a section of Confederate horse artillery under Major John Pelham held up their advance for a time.

Pender's Brigade constituted a portion of the Confederate defense of that sector of the lines. According to one of the participants, the men were "in position before daylight on December 13th." Suffering severely in the wintry conditions, they shivered under a blanket of snow, watching for any action that might occur on this day. As it turned out, they would not have to wait long.

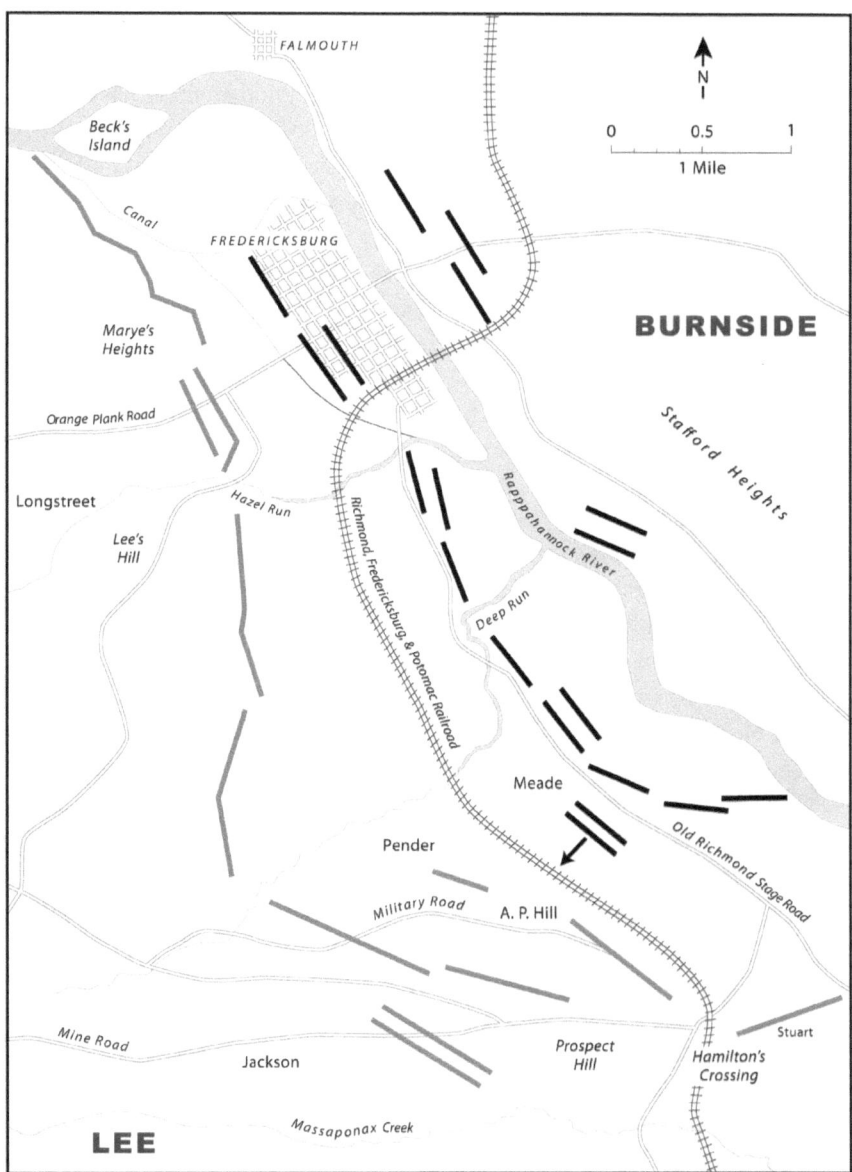

Map 6. Fredericksburg's most vulnerable point was along the Confederate right, where Pender helped limit Federal penetrations of the line and secure victory for Gen. Robert E. Lee. Map by Heather Harvey.

A thick fog added to what must have been an almost surreal atmosphere. "One could not see eighty paces away," a Confederate recorded. Such conditions also would provide cover for an assault, and the men must have peered anxiously into the thick swirls of mist for any sign that a movement was afoot. At approximately 9:30 A.M., their ears detected the first shots from the pickets, who fell back after having performed their important duties in this regard and reported that an advance was underway.

Shells began to fall among the defenders. The 13th's position near a Southern battery meant that they received counterbattery fire meant for their artillery comrades. "The shells came in showers," a participant recalled. He ventured to peek above the snow-covered ground to ascertain the effect and watched as a shell struck a comrade "in the breast and explode." The unfortunate victim was blown "all to atoms," while another lost the upper portion of his skull to another round. The stunned soldier immediately went into shock before "finally he sank down on his face in the snow." The witness concluded that his regiment endured some twenty deaths "within ten minutes" from the hail of missiles that descended upon them.[62]

Other North Carolina troops took their share of punishment as well. General Jackson noted that the batteries of Greenlee Davidson and Joseph W. Latimer, "acting in conjunction with Major [Chris C.] Cole, of the Twenty-second North Carolina, [succeeded] in dispersing the cloud of skirmishers and sharpshooters that hung all day upon that part of the line." Prior to this welcome development, Jackson observed, "that brigade received much of the fire that was directed at these guns, and suffered severely."[63]

The matter was perhaps hardest on the 16th North Carolina, which took the brunt of a surprise blow as Federal troops emerged unexpectedly. "At 3 o'clock in the afternoon," according to Brigadier General Evander Law, who threw his men forward to help, "a force of the enemy defiled from the wood on Deep Run, and forming into line of battle advanced upon Latimer's battery, which was posted in the plateau on General Pender's left and supported by one of his regiments."[64] Jackson explained that these North Carolinians "became warmly engaged with a brigade of the enemy, which had advanced up Deep Run under cover," before the supporting units came up and drove the attackers back.[65]

It certainly must have seemed as if the Federals would punch through the Southern defenders with ease. But Meade's men represented only a fraction of the troops Franklin had available had he chosen to employ his full might to compromise the Southern line. Even so, the Northerners began to make headway, although in a sporadic and chaotic movement that limited the effectiveness of the blow. In the smoke and disorder, some of the defenders were unsure of the identity of the men who approached them until it was too late. The resulting maneuver widened a gap that already existed in A. P. Hill's line, but the limited numbers of attacking blue coats prevented any further exploitation of the breach. Disjointed even in success, the Federals lost momentum at the very instant they stood poised to sever Lee's line. Still, the situation was a precarious one for the endangered Southern flank, especially as in the early afternoon, Brigadier General John Gibbon pushed his men into the fight in support of Meade's efforts. Some of the Confederates had broken, shattered by frontal and flank attacks, but others managed to cling to their positions, limiting the damage to that section of Jackson's lines.

Pender was in reserve to the left and rear of other North Carolinians under General Lane when Meade struck.[66] The bulk of the fighting before him initially fell to these troops. They took severe punishment and had almost expended their ammunition before Pender came up to assist them, adhering to their left flank. His brigade's arrival was timely and effective. The fresh troops poured fire into the opposing masses, assisted by rounds of double canister from two batteries that pummeled the Federal ranks crowded before them. Casualties mounted on both sides as men fought ferociously against each other for possession of the embattled flank. At length, lack of support and Confederate success on the other side of the breach compelled the Federals to withdraw under fire, and Pender's troops were among those who hurled Gibbon's hard-fighting units rearward.[67]

The outcome had by no means been a sure thing. Union pressure sent some of the Confederates scurrying for the rear. According to one witness, while watching these troubling developments, "Pender who was standing by at the time immediately leaped on his horse and accompanied by his aide attempted to rally the skirmishers on the right of the Battery." Apparently, he had begun to succeed in this critical task when, "in less time than it takes me to tell it, General Pender was wounded and his aide killed." The wavering troops lost heart and left the artillerists "out in the open field to contend unaided against the advancing column which was now on the south side of the railroad and within a stone's throw of my guns; dashing at us at a full run." However dire the circumstances appeared, the Federals never reached the Southern tubes.

The North Carolinian's gallant effort had garnered just enough time for the Confederates to mount a successful defense, with the artillery pieces belching double canister, sweeping the ground before them, and driving back the attackers. When the smoke cleared, the effect was the utter devastation of the assailants and the ground over which they had come. The officer who had seen the drama unfold before his eyes concluded succinctly, "Canister from a Napoleon gun is a terrible engine of destruction."[68]

Pender had indeed suffered a wound in the action when a Union Minié ball struck his left arm. The artillery officer recorded that the general had to be assisted from the field, but another witness with the 13th North Carolina explained that in the course of the fighting, "General W. D. Pender came riding down his line among the hail of shot and shells, his left-hand hanging down and the blood streaming down his fingers." Pender must have been favoring the injured limb enough as he rode to have the wound dressed that he caught the attention of Colonel Scales. "General, I see you are wounded," that officer observed. "Oh, that is a trifle," Pender fired back, "no bone is broken." There was still work to do, and he ordered Scales "to send at least two companies down to the railroad and drive those scoundrels out." His main concern was neither his own safety nor the condition of his troops, but the toll being exacted on the battery he was charged with supporting. "They are killing Colonel Cutts' men and horses," he noted as his reason for his vehemence.[69]

An incident related to Pender's wounding at Fredericksburg revealed that not everyone thought so highly of the North Carolinian. One of Archer's colonels was with Pender in the fighting on the thirteenth when the Union round caused the general's wound. Subsequently, when the officer related the incident to his superior, Archer's response was immediate and sharp, "I wish they had shot him in his damn head," he blurted, the colonel concluding with the understatement that the outburst by the Marylander meant, "He didn't like him."[70]

Archer had been seething for some time over the possibility that Pender might be elevated over him before he could gain promotion himself. When he happened to stumble on Pender's medical officer in the Confederate capital "electioneering for Pender," as Archer explained, and having "succeeded in getting the North Carolina delegation interested in the case," the revelation unleashed a torrent of expression from the disgruntled general that he subsequently shared at some length in a letter to his brother.

Probing for a weakness in Pender that he thought he might have found, Archer instructed his sibling to point out to anyone who would listen "that a difficulty may be raised on account of Pender's seniority." He wanted to be sure that someone in authority knew "that on the same day I was appointed to the *full* rank of Brigadier Pender was appointed to the *temporary* rank of Brigadier from which it appears to me conclusive that it was intended I should rank him." Unhappily from Archer's perspective, Pender had earlier benefitted from "an interview by him with the President about the 2nd July" and was "appointed to the *full* rank of a Brigadier to date from 3d June the date of both our original appointments—and as his *Colonelcy* was older than mine he became the ranking officer by virtue of former commission—although I was a *brevet* Major in 1847 before he entered the Army." For good measure, Archer added hastily, "I forgot to say that my rank as captain when I resigned was about six years old while he [Pender] was only a 1st Lt."[71]

At length, Pender became aware of Archer's attitude toward him and commented on it to Fanny. "I fear my promotion has caused Archer to be cool towards me," he explained the following June as the army moved into Maryland and Pennsylvania. "His manner the last time we met was not as cordial as heretofore, and he seemed very much embittered and rather down on Gen. Hill and I suppose because I will not join him in the latter he grew cool towards me." It mattered greatly to Pender what others thought of him, but he was oblivious to the personality clash and the apparent disregard of protocol that prompted Archer's feelings. Still, the ever-sensitive Dorsey regretted the situation. "I am sorry for it," he concluded to Fanny, "but I know I have done nothing to forfeit his good opinion or will."[72] Ever focusing on his own position, Pender had failed to see the violation of that time-honored military tradition of seniority through his colleague's eyes.

Pender knew that he could come across negatively to others, although he may never have realized the extent to which such attitudes existed with some of his men. South Carolinians seemed especially ready to castigate their North Carolina neighbor. In one instance a member of the Pee Dee Light Artillery inquired of an infantryman, "Pender is pretty hard on you boys isn't he?" Joseph W. Brunson was convinced that the general could behave "unfairly."[73] Fellow South Carolinian J. R. Boyles viewed him as sufficiently "cruel" in reputation as to shake the confidence of men who were to serve under him.[74] James Fitz James Caldwell simply labeled him as not "very popular with our brigade."[75]

Pender had established a reputation for courage under fire that few other young officers could surpass; unfortunately, he was continuing to demonstrate an attraction for enemy missiles. Indeed, Fanny had already come dangerously close to losing her husband on more than one occasion, but his escape from serious injury did not prevent her from experiencing another terrible personal loss. Prior to the war, Fanny's brother, and Dorsey's close friend, Samuel Turner had died from an illness. Lieutenant Jacob "Jake" Sheppard, another of her brothers, having recovered from a previous wound, was likely the aide that the cannoneers saw fall when Pender suffered his wound. Jake had only recently obtained the staff position he held during the engagement and died as he rode forward to rally the troops faltering under heavy Union fire. Dorsey would not have the time at the moment to mourn the loss of his brother-in-law or to feel regret for having brought him back into harm's way. That time would come, and the most difficult aspect of the tragedy would be breaking the terrible news to Fanny.

Jake Shepperd was not the only officer Pender lost that day. Another perished in the fighting, and seventeen more suffered wounds of various types. Fourteen of Pender's enlisted men were also killed in action and 136 wounded. All of the regiments took losses, the 16th North Carolina's being the heaviest.[76]

Pender tried to remain dispassionate and professional in the report on the battle he produced a few days later, but undoubtedly the personal losses were still fresh. "In the death of Lieutenant Shepperd," he wrote simply at the close of the document, "I have to lament the loss of a brave and promising young officer."[77] If the general masked in his official report whatever private grief he harbored concerning the loss of his young relation, Dorsey also felt the need to be stoic with regard to his brokenhearted wife. She would need his strength in this sad moment, just as they had needed and helped each other through the sudden illness and death of her older brother and his dear friend and West Point classmate Samuel back in prewar Leavenworth, Kansas.

Settling into winter quarters at a camp named for another recently fallen general, Maxcy Gregg, and located below the Rappahannock River, Pender and his men continued to process recent events and prepare for future ones. In the quiet that transpired after the buzz of activity of constructing cabins subsided, Dorsey also tried to console Fanny as best he could. He had gotten several letters from her, and although he was happy to receive them, he noted, "it makes me feel sad to have you write in such a sad and despondent tone." He knew that there was nothing that he could say that would lessen the blow she had sustained and promised not to "reason" with her "on the subject" of her depression, "for you will at once say that it is my want of feeling." He could not help but be deeply moved, especially as he thought of the efforts he had taken to get Jake the staff position that had brought him back on the battlefield.

"Honey, the more I think of you and your letters the more sad I am. I feel like shedding tears."

Yet Dorsey was nothing if not practical. He carefully shifted to other topics, including the arrangements he was making for accommodating her pending visit, now that the army was demobilized for the season. There were always the boys to think of too, if one or both of them accompanied her. Perhaps the servant Joe would be of help in that regard. "Rather than not see you I would say bring both," Dorsey concluded of the children, "but if you could be satisfied to leave them it would be better for there is no telling how long before or when we may move."

He reminded Fanny gently that her sister Pamela must also have taken their brother's death hard. By doing so, he could encourage her to support her younger sibling, who had "loved him better than anyone else," and perhaps assuage some of her own grief in the process. In the meantime, Dorsey had a final duty to perform. "I will send Jake's horse home by the first good chance," he explained, assuring her that the animal would be well cared for in the interim.

There was little of a cheering nature to Dorsey's last letter to Fanny in 1862. With Jake's death still so fresh and the enormous cost of a bitter year of fighting, perhaps there was no reason to feel upbeat. But to his credit, Dorsey would not let the letter go without a stab at a positive expression. She must have noted her desire for the war to end, a feeling that her husband certainly shared, for his closing was couched in such terms. "As for peace," he observed before offering his usual invocation of God's blessing and last words of affection for her and the boys, "it depends a great deal upon the impending battles in the West." In the meantime, their reunion awaited. "Come quick Honey."[78]

10

"YOU MUST HOLD YOUR GROUND, SIR!"
(January–May 1863)

⸺•⸺

Thus far we have whipt them beautifully.
—DORSEY PENDER TO FANNY REGARDING CHANCELLORSVILLE

All that I saw behaved as heroes.
—GENERAL PENDER'S CHANCELLORSVILLE REPORT

⸺•⸺

Fanny Pender spent almost two months with her husband while the winter weather and bad roads kept the army transfixed. Even so, the time they shared together was not entirely carefree. General Burnside contemplated another crossing of the Rappahannock which he hoped would redeem the blood spilled at Fredericksburg. By mid-January 1863, the Federal commander seemed prepared to take his chances, but then even the weather appeared to conspire against him. Rain that turned first to sleet and then to snow bogged the operation in the morass that the roads swiftly became. Burnside's "mud march," as it derisively came to be known, floundered in the wintry mix, and with it the Union general's reputation and status. Before the roads were dry, the Army of the Potomac had a new commander, Major General Joseph Hooker, with a stirring nickname, "Fighting Joe."[1]

Ironically, about the same time Fanny was making the long journey from North Carolina to be with her husband, he was coming close to being transferred back to his home state. The pressure was mounting for bringing some of the North Carolinians in the Army of Northern Virginia back to their native soil. Events went so far as the issuance of orders for the move, only to have them placed in abeyance. General Lee expressed his amazement to President Davis, not so much regarding the ultimate decision, but at the reaction it generated among the Carolinians. "I was surprised to learn from General A. P.

Hill on my return that the other two North Carolina brigades, Pender's and Lane's, which had been ordered off, were delighted at the suspension of their orders," he explained. Then without further elaboration, the army commander observed, "They did not wish to go to North Carolina."[2] It is difficult to know the extent of such sentiment in the ranks, either among officers or enlisted men, but with Fanny close by, and the efforts he had taken to put himself on a more active front, Pender certainly must have been as relieved as anyone to be able to remain in Virginia with Lee.

The respite in active campaigning also contributed to an increase in calls for leaves of absence in the officer corps. In the latter part of February, with Fanny having departed, Dorsey took up their correspondence once more and addressed the dissatisfaction of one subordinate . "Col. Scales it would appear does not think 20 days long enough to marry & have his honey moon in." Then realizing that he had said more than he ought on the subject, he added quickly, "Do not [let] any one know he is going home for that purpose." Of course, Alfred Scales was not alone. "Major Englehard sent up an application this evening for 10 days to go to see his wife & babies." As a person who knew well the pains of separation from loved ones, Dorsey was sympathetic, but as General Pender, he had to maintain discipline and prevent the tide of requests from inundating him or leaving the command shorthanded. It must have seemed like a losing battle. He explained almost dejectedly, "The mania for leaves still stays & I believe is on the increase."[3]

In the meantime, the same weather that played havoc with Burnside's post-Fredericksburg intentions provided the Confederates with a chance for a release of passions in a different sense. At Camp Gregg, Pender's men took advantage of the conditions for a bit of sport. "The only battle we had that winter," one soldier recalled, "was with General McGowan's Brigade of South Carolina." Heavy snowfall provided the ordnance for the engagement, state bragging rights the incentive, as Pender's North Carolinians took on their counterparts from the neighboring state. When McGowan's men advanced, waving their colors antagonistically, the "Tar-heel boys" responded in kind. The adversaries tangled with more than a bit of good-natured rivalry, which the witness described as "a hard fight" that ended when "finally the Tar-heels charged them, ran them into their quarters and on through camp, demolished a goodly number of shanties, and returned to their own quarters with but one casualty—that was the red-headed Adjutant of the 13th North Carolina, who was struck in the eye with a snow-ball nested with a flint rock."[4] There is no indication that the brigade commander who preferred good order and discipline tolerated such shenanigans, but the chance for such nonlethal military action surely proved a tonic for the men against the dullness and routine of winter-camp life.

A North Carolina soldier offered a much more general description of the situation in a February 25 letter to his sister. Burwell Cotton of the 34th North Carolina explained: "We have plenty snow here and the soldiers appear to enjoy themselves finely snowballing each other. Penders Brigade & Greggs had a powerful time yesterday." Cotton assured his sibling that both units "held their ground" and then concluded that the snowball fight "imitates a battle as much as anything I ever saw." But for all of the diversion such moments provided, there were serious consequences over other matters to sober the atmosphere. "I saw one man shot to death this week for desertion," he explained. "Several have been branded in our reg. for desertion."[5] Pender might have perceived of the snowball battle as more than an outlet for pent-up energy, particularly if he had felt it reflected poorly on his leadership and authority, but the comments of his fellow North Carolinian suggested that discipline remained a top priority.

With one eye focused on the state of his command, the always curious general apparently continued to keep abreast of affairs on other fronts as well as on international developments. The war had lasted long enough so that the chance of immediate intervention on the part of one or more of the European nations had largely dissipated. But he held out hope that such a development might yet occur, placing particular faith in one crowned head of state. "I am a full believer in Louis Napoleon's good intentions," Dorsey wrote to Fanny. "I can not think him so silly as to make himself a laughingstock all over the world by offering his advice when he could not have but known it would not be rejected. I look confidently now to recognition & possibly more. May God grant us a speedy peace."

Of course, peace meant his being at Fanny's and the boys' sides once more. Always prone to nostalgia when in a pensive mood, Dorsey speculated what that moment would be like. "I think I could for a few moments at least be happy. Will that day ever come? I hope & believe so then won't we be happy[?]" For the time being, though, there was their correspondence to provide a solace, but even that contained an unsettling aspect that he felt compelled to bring to her attention. Apparently, Fanny had chided him for filling his letters so often with martial affairs rather than marital or familial ones. Dorsey decided to defend himself and what he considered a reasonable practice that he wanted to continue. "But darling some of my happiness if that is to be, you will not enjoy

& that is fighting my battles over. You either are annoyed when I talk about my feats . . . or laugh at what you call my conceit. You must learn to listen to my stories of war, at least, with patience." Fanny surely understood the nature of his profession by now and knew she had to accept the effect his experiences had upon him. "How can it be helpt making a strong impression on me, & how can one help talking when he thinks so much about these things[?]"[6]

Dorsey also remained consumed with the possibility of promotion and looked with disdain on behaviors that might challenge or threaten him in that regard. Happily for him, another opportunity for advancement came in February 1863, when Daniel Harvey Hill received an appointment to serve in North Carolina. In response, a group of Confederate congressmen from the state petitioned the president to consider Pender to fill the vacancy created by Hill's departure. Signed by a dozen of these political figures, the recommendation lauded Pender and reminded the chief executive of the heavy presence of North Carolina troops in Stonewall Jackson's corps, to which this appointment would be made. The statesmen were also aware of Davis's well-known sensitivity regarding interference in such matters, imploring him not to consider "this recommendation obtrusive." As a final endorsement, they noted their candidate's personal qualifications. "Permit us to add, what you already know, that Gen. Pender is an accomplished officer, a Christian, and a gentleman of the very first order."[7]

Pender would have been pleased to know of the depth of support his advancement had from such officials, but he always thought his prospects were dim. That attitude relaxed somewhat in his first letter to Fanny after their winter rendezvous. Writing on February 21, he focused on the views of his friends in the service. "Gen. [A. P.] Hill came back yesterday & I find I have a most kind & energetic friend in him," Dorsey informed her. His commander was exerting assistance where he could, including urging "Custis Lee to lay my claims before the President." Nor was Hill alone in his actions on Pender's behalf. "In [Brig.] Gen. [Stephen D.] Ramseur I also have a warm friend." His fellow North Carolinian had written "Hon. Wm. Landes who got up a petition signed by every member for the state both in the Senate & House which petition has [also] been laid before the President." Pender was pleased and grateful for the support. "So you see," he told his wife, "I am of some importance to have so much fuss made about me. I hope I shall get it for many reasons."[8]

Even with the aid of important and influential friends, Pender knew that advancement in rank was always going to be a complicated matter. "My promotion hangs as it did and really I do not expect it for months at all," he observed to Fanny a few days later. "Gen. Jackson is in my way having recommended another man," he noted, adding somewhat caustically, but understandably, "I never will vote for his being President."[9] He would later relate that in addition to support from the secretary of war, Jackson actually had recommended him too.[10] A relative thought that no North Carolinian would prevent his promotion, but Pender observed "that it will be between Gen'l. [Robert E.] Rhodes [Rodes] and myself."[11]

The test of his patience probably did him much good; certainly, his constant personal reevaluations did. In early March he confessed to a change in lifestyle that Fanny surely found pleasing. He was doing his best to watch his temper, and he had "also stopped taking that occasional toddy." He had made the resolution while in Richmond, "and altho' very much pressed since, have kept to it."[12] Dorsey made no reference to other vices, such as those he had written about from the Pacific Northwest in 1860 regarding a "good appetite for eating, smoking, & sleeping," but Fanny would surely be proud of his efforts in any case.[13] A contemporary later attested to Pender's success in controlling such evils. "A Christian, he mastered a high temper and transformed it into a virtue."[14]

Fanny was central to his motivations for these personal improvements. "I always want to be not only a Christian—which I cannot—but a husband whose habits his wife may approve of."[15] Dorsey described himself now as being "in a loving mood" as he contemplated her beauty and the miles that kept them apart. Interspersed in his closing with inquiries about the children and other family members, he added: "Darling, did you think about yesterday being the anniversary of our marriage? Four years, how short they seem." Speaking of the two of them figuratively as the old married couple that he felt they had become during that short time, he observed somewhat mischievously, "We are more violently in love by far than the sweethearts."[16]

Dorsey continued to be worried about what he deemed to be Fanny's delicate health as well as the frailties of his own character. But he was less concerned about the fate of the nation. He shared his notion that Napoleon III might yet "interfere in this war" but remained realistic about even such a bold initiative by a foreign power ending the conflict in the short term, having "made up my mind to a year or two more of it." Optimistically, he tried to focus on the most positive possibility. "If it comes sooner so much the better." But the toll of war had been terrible, and he assessed, "we cannot well have such another year as the last."[17]

A few days more and the general's mood lightened. "My Brigade is still increasing," he told Fanny on March 10. "I have now 2150 and will have one or two hundred more." As for the Army of Northern Virginia, it was "large and in fine condition." Probably without realizing that he was doing so, Dorsey employed the same description he had used on previous occasions when he observed, "We have never had such an army before as this."[18]

But Pender was not alone in such an assessment. Even before 1862 was out and the men had the recuperation and recreation that a winter's rest could bring them, another member of Pender's command observed to his wife, "Our army was in better fighting trim at the battle of Fredericksburg than at any other time since the war began, and it is still in the same condition." Hopes for success looked as high as ever too. "It does not seem possible to defeat this army now with General Lee at its head," Spencer Welch concluded confidently.[19]

Such observations demonstrated that Pender and his comrades had departed significantly from the dark and difficult days of the Maryland Campaign, when everyone seemed plagued by the sense that straggling and shortages were ruining the army's combat effectiveness. The general was now clearly more optimistic about the conditions he felt prevailed, but any notion that the army's problems with these maladies were behind it could be undone quickly in the next campaign. Besides, he had reason to focus on another priority beyond the state of the troops for which he was responsible.

It was becoming increasingly clear to him that the cause for Fanny's delicate condition was that she was expecting once more. "Indeed I did sincerely hope that you had escaped this time," he explained on March 13, using a euphemism for her pregnancy, "but darling it must be the positive and direct will of God that it should be so."[20] Dorsey had hinted at the possibility as early as December, offering on the third, "I suppose you know by this time how things will be for the next *nine months*."[21]

The subject remained on his mind in the next days as well, although Dorsey exposed an ambivalent attitude that could not have provided much support for Fanny. "How glad I should be to hear that you had again escaped," he noted almost plaintively. "You have no idea nor would believe from my past conduct, how much I think about it."[22] These suspicions followed him into the new year. "Altho' you wrote as if you were well, still I cannot but feel some uneasiness about you, supposing you to be in a condition that might give you some trouble provided you took cold."[23] The cryptic references were the best that Dorsey could make as he considered the likelihood that they would bring another child into a family separated by the circumstances of his profession and the state of the war.

As he contemplated what might otherwise have been joyous personal developments, Pender teetered on the brink of depression. In keeping with so much that happened in his world, the fact of his wife's pregnancy turned on him. "If I had not gone to Richmond I should have had no trouble. It cannot be helped and I have been in low spirits more than I usually allow myself." He considered approaching A. P. Hill with a request for leave, even speaking to him about the subject, before they both decided he probably would not get one and thus it was best not to try. "So that miserable visit to Richmond comes back upon me," he groused self-centeredly. Then as an indication to her of the extent to which he had been willing to try for a furlough, he added, "You have some idea how much it was when with my notions about leaves, etc., I went to Gen. Hill merely to get the slightest encouragement."[24]

It would be hard to say, absent the letter that Pender received with what should have been glad tidings, why he reacted as he did. Fanny had experienced a difficult childbirth with their last son and had endured complications that ended another pregnancy prematurely, so he may well have feared more trouble in that regard. But his reaction also reflected the apprehension that he might not be able to assist her with their growing family if he should fall in combat. The idea weighed heavily on his mind and apparently on hers as well. "My dear, if your worst fear should be realized, try to bear it as well as you can and that is as well as any one could do." Wisely seeking to diminish her concerns while validating her strength in confronting the many challenges of life as his spouse, Dorsey added, "honey the amount of suffering you have borne since we have been married and so uncomplaining too, I could not bear it, I am sure."[25]

As the now-expectant father closed his emotion-filled letter, he admonished Fanny, "Write me often, not only once in six days." Then his usual farewell came on this night with even greater vehemence. "May God bless you and the boys and may [we] be preserved at last to a long, Christian and happy life. My love to all. Kiss the dear boys."[26]

It was probably inevitable that these two strong-willed and emotionally intense individuals would experience more turbulence. Fanny had been for some time taunting Dorsey with an earlier love interest. He responded strongly each time that he simply did not want to discuss the matter any further. Yet the jousting between spouses continued unabated. In a March 15 letter to "My own dear Wife," Dorsey alluded heavily to old sweethearts of his own. In each case, he tried to allay Fanny's fears that he harbored any affection for these old flames, or indeed, that he had ever even loved them in the first place. Painfully written, and as painful to read, he dismissed these past relationships curtly with the insistence, "if there ever was a husband who adored his wife and thought her so near perfection as flesh can attain, it is yours." What was most important to him was that he had chosen her "because I wanted you for my wife." He was certain that this choice, as with most that he had made, reflected well upon him. "My judgement [sic] sustained me," he argued, making reference to the year they first met, "a decision [was] reached in 1854 and maintained up to this moment, and I fear not that it will ever be shaken."[27]

Although factors that ranged from Pender's recent time away from the ranks, the prospect that the Union army might become active at any time, and the likelihood that General Jackson would turn down the request in any case rendered the issue of obtaining another furlough moot, Dorsey did not want Fanny to think that he had neglected her in preference to anyone or anything else, even his duty. He tried to turn the subject by reminding her that he had professed the desire for a girl as further evidence of his devotion to her. She could name this child whatever she wished, but he teasingly added, "do not forget that I want an F in it."[28]

Despite so much personal excitement, the dullness of camp continued, interrupted by the occasional rumor of impending action or a tragedy that only added to Pender's dark mood. "I am very well but find my time hanging on me like a millstone," he wrote Fanny on March 21. Undoubtedly, one of the reasons for his "blue" mood was the unsettling task of having to write to the widow of one of his subordinates, Colonel R. H. Gray, of Pender's favorite 22nd North Carolina. Apparently, the colonel lost his battle with alcoholism, and the general suffered the loss personally. "He was a fine soldier and a nice gentleman," Dorsey observed. Then in a quiet moment of reflection tinged with regret, he added, "If his officers had let me know of his condition I could have stopped his drinking in time probably to have saved him." At the very least, the general was sad that amid so much death through the profession they all had chosen, Gray's end had come "without even the satisfaction that his death accomplished anything except to show how soon one can kill themselves with whiskey."[29]

On March 26 Pender had to communicate trouble of a different nature to his wife. Powell Hill had "preferred charges against me." These stemmed from a communication that Pender posted outside of the proper channels. When the order reached Richmond, "it got to the Sec. of War," who dutifully "returned" it to General Lee. The army commander issued instructions of his own to Hill to prefer charges against Pender for the unauthorized activity. Hardly a matter of supreme hazard to the republic, it was nevertheless a violation of military protocol. Referring to the charges, Pender explained that "Gen. Hill sent them up, but disapproved them, stating that the letter was only semi-official, so Gen. Lee sent them back authorizing Gen. Hill to withdraw them." Hill did so and went beyond by "taking the paper out of the general packet so it would not be made public." Pender would be spared any further embarrassment because Hill had "acted most kindly and delicately" in the matter. "I cannot feel too kindly towards him," Pender observed, although the same could not be said for the individual who had sent the letter to the War Department in the first place and thereby initiated the unsettling process.[30]

Two days later the rollercoaster of emotions within Pender took another turn. "The news we got yesterday was truly encouraging. I cannot but feel that this war is near its close," he observed to Fanny. "More fighting we must have of course, but not as severe or as much. How I do long for peace and quiet enjoyment with you."

Dorsey may have ached for peace as he frequently told Fanny and recognized that any new military operations might result in his death, but the quiet of camp life was becoming nearly unbearable for him. A court-martial on which he sat provided some diversion from the mundane. "Anything to be employed," he explained to his wife as the tedium of the martial routine took its toll. "I cannot bear to be idle."

The time away from active campaigning also allowed him to contemplate once more on his professional advancement. This was all the more so when word reached him that his friend Stephen Lee would become a major general. Dorsey could not help but revisit his own situation, and Fanny again became his confidant. "I think if claims were considered I should be promoted, too," he remarked, but as he had insisted so often before, he professed this time to have "given up that idea." Indeed, Dorsey observed that he thought he could be as content if the war were to end and his status remained as it now stood. "You will think me just as much a hero as if I were a full General and love me just as much," he speculated rhetorically, "and what more need I care for, and then I know I stand high to those who know me."[31]

Early in April, Pender noted the feeling among the fighting men concerning the war. "In the army the impression prevails that in six months the war will be virtually over." But he had also to allay Fanny's concerns about a troubling presentiment that she had apparently shared with him in one of their communications. "You say you dreamt that you were riding in a hearse and that it was a bad sign." Then, perhaps as much to hold his own fears at bay while mitigating hers, he concluded, "I thought dreams were interpreted by contraries; that hearses indicated a wedding or something of that sort."[32]

Whatever his future prospects, Pender understood one imperative: he needed more men. Replenishing the numbers lost to combat, disease, and desertion was critical for the effectiveness of the depleted units in any upcoming campaigning. Despite its foundation on individualism and states' rights, the Confederate States of America had resorted to conscription, or a draft, implementing the measure on April 16, 1862, and revising it on September 27 of the same year.[33] Debates would rage in hindsight over the effectiveness of the policy as well as the nature of desertion for Confederate forces in the field, but Pender welcomed the opportunity to swell his ranks.[34]

The influx of recruits was indeed propitious, and Pender's Brigade was one of the beneficiaries. As a result, the general could tell his wife that his command was "increasing very rapidly." He noted enthusiastically: "They are sending me conscripts now. I have nearly 2,500 present, and they are coming in every day." Pender seemed not to have worried that these individuals entered the ranks with less zeal than most of the original volunteers had possessed. Nor did he seem troubled that they lacked the extensive training and drilling he had demanded from their predecessors. He remained convinced that if given time, he could prepare the new arrivals for useful service. "I shall have more men than I ever did," he concluded. "The more the better, if I can get them drilled any."[35]

General Pender was pleased with the accessions to the military rolls and confident of his ability to turn these civilians into soldiers. But he remained deeply disturbed by those who deserted their posts and the stain he felt North Carolina endured as a result. Pender wrote directly to General Lee to express his concerns. The letter made its way, with the army commander's endorsement, to Secretary of War James Seddon, who forwarded it to Governor Zebulon Vance. The war secretary appealed to North Carolina's leader to heed the situation and do what he thought best to apply a remedy. "The subject is one of great importance," Seddon explained, "and I respectfully urge that you will aid in arresting the progress of desertion among the North Carolina troops, which, unless promptly checked, will be destructive of the discipline and morale of our army."[36]

A clerk in the War Department recorded the Pender communication in his diary the following day. "General Pender had sent up a letter disclosing a most disgraceful spirit of desertion among the North Carolina troops, which he attributed to a dictum of Judge [Richmond] Pearson that the conscript law is unconstitutional." Robert G. H. Kean noted of the deserting soldiers, "They think when they get there [to North Carolina] they will be safe from re-arrest and desert in squads, with their arms."[37]

North Carolina Supreme Court chief justice Richmond M. Pearson stood in a unique position to interpose his judicial authority between the Confederate conscription law of 1862 and the soldiers who sought refuge from it in his state. In the absence of a national supreme court, the Southern state institutions held special status.[38] By issuing writs of habeas corpus to deserters, the justice ran afoul of Pender's equally strongly held views on patriotism and loyalty. The general was adamant in his condemnation of the rulings and his belief that they emanated from the pen of the basest of traitors.

Surprisingly, Pender's initial assessment of such influences upon the men suggested that he thought they might withstand the onslaught. In early April he observed, "It is a very remarkable fact that all the complaining and disaffection at home does not produce any bad effects upon our soldiers."[39] But later in the month, with the evidence mounting that the troops were not as impervious to enticements from the rear, Pender's confidence began to erode, and he changed his tune considerably on the subject. "I am very much worried of late about desertions," he told Fanny, "Our N.C. soldiers are deserting very rapidly." For the man who was convinced that the actions of the troops under his command reflected for good or ill on their commander, Pender was especially alarmed. "I have had about 30 [desert] in the last 20 days," he moaned, "and all due to those arch traitors [William W.] Holden and Pearson and Co." His indictment of these men did not yet apply to his home state as a whole, but the trend was decidedly negative and personally worrisome. "Poor old N.C., she will disgrace herself just when the worst is over, and after two years of faithful service." As he had done with reference to Federals he found particularly pernicious, Pender employed the term "rascaly" to the newspaper editor and the politician and declared them as next "to a Yankee," a "most loathsome sight."[40]

As before, one of the chief reasons that the general had his eye on desertions was how it reflected upon him as a commander. Pender also knew that spring would bring with it the drier conditions that made offensive operations probable. "I think the sooner the campaign opens the better both for the army and the country. Our people always get gloomy when they have no excitement and there is too much disposition to desert from the army."[41]

The status of his commanding general's health was on Pender's mind too. "General Lee has been quite sick but is better," he informed his wife. Then Pender allowed himself to contemplate what it would mean if his superior's condition took a turn for the worst. "I do not know what we should do if he were taken from us."[42]

Robert E. Lee was showing the strains of the hard winter, the constant pressures, and the demands on his time and energies. His illness forced him to spend a period sequestered in a local home until he could recover his stamina sufficiently to return to his duties.[43] Dorsey was more optimistic when he informed Fanny on April 3: "I was glad to learn that Gen. Lee is better and able to be up. The loss of his services would be irreparable to us just now."[44] It would not be until the end of the month that he could report the news that the Virginian was back at headquarters. "Gen. Lee is about attending to business much to the gratification of all."[45] As it turned out, Pender had reason to worry. Lee remained weak, and according to biographer Emory Thomas, would never fully recover from the bout that occurred in the spring of 1863.[46]

In early April the Confederate capital itself erupted into violence that required intervention from Richmond mayor Joseph Mayo, Virginia governor John Letcher, and President Davis himself as well as the threat of force to quell.[47] Dorsey read of the event in the newspapers and expressed an informed opinion of what had occurred to Fanny. "Bread, alias plundering, riots are becoming common," he explained. "Some of the rioters in Richmond will probably get sick of it before they get through with it."[48] The fact that pilfered goods included more than foodstuffs made the behavior especially suspect.[49]

The dire situation that played out so dramatically in Richmond affected the troops in the field as well. To remedy these supply shortages, among other competing missions, General Lee authorized the detachment of a portion of his forces to areas of southeastern Virginia, where foodstuffs could be obtained. Soldiers under the command of Lieutenant General Longstreet trudged from their camps north of Richmond toward one of Pender's old stomping grounds: Suffolk. The Federals had occupied the town and its environs for a year and had the area heavily fortified and well defended. The Confederates generally contented themselves with containing the garrison while elements fanned out through the neighboring countryside and bordering counties of North Carolina to secure the badly needed resources.[50]

For Pender, still stationed at Camp Gregg, the return of Suffolk to the news dredged up unpleasant personal memories as well. "If you did not fret about my absenting myself and not staying with you all day when we are together, I should feel that something is wrong." Even so, Dorsey admitted, "I like it, and I like the little touches of jealousy you show sometimes, but Darling you carried it a little too far to be very pleasant about Suffolk matters. Bless my dear little wife if she did not abuse me a little occasionally [or] I should think she did not love me so much as she used to."[51]

Perhaps Fanny felt she had touched a nerve with her expression of jealousy, or she may simply have missed her husband, but apparently she wrote rather affectionately to him on a subject that, if his reply were any indication, was a source of importance to him. "Honey, are you in earnest when you say you are proud to bear the name of Pender and that you want your children to be Penders in all respects?" She could not have said anything more dear to him or more powerful in its representation. "I am much more sensitive about the name than might be supposed," Dorsey admitted, and although he claimed "no particular fancy for it," considered his name important enough to "do all in my power to make it respected and one not to be ashamed of, and if I can help it you never shall regret bearing my name in particular." He felt that his name represented a personal marker that stood "well in the Army" and expressed his belief "that I have more reputation than any Brigadier in this Army." Whatever anyone else might think, and he insisted not to care much on his own behalf, Dorsey Pender was content "to be able to cause your husband to be one that you can claim with some pride officially speaking."[52]

Dorsey had expressed a similar type of pride several days earlier, using essentially the same phraseology he had employed as a colonel. "I had Brigade drill yesterday," he told Fanny on April 11, "and it came off beautifully. I am getting a splendid Brigade. Good size, fine drill, and discipline." This latter point continued to be the key, as Pender had now learned from the battlefield as well as the many intervening encampments from the summer of 1861. "My men say I am hard on them, but that I treat all alike. It would worry me very much if I had a reputation for injustice. I try to be impartial."[53]

A fellow North Carolinian noted in a letter home that Pender had been around to visit with him recently. "I have not seen him before in two years," Francis Marion Parker explained, "he is looking very well." The general also had a reputation that had preceded him. "He is regarded as a no. one soldier, by those who know him. Edgecombe [County] has cause to feel proud of him." Indeed, Pender's visit left Parker with only a greater desire to serve under him directly, as he observed wistfully to his wife, "I wish very much, that my Regt. was in his Brigade."[54]

Pender would have been pleased by this endorsement from a comrade of another Carolina regiment, but he remained in a nostalgic mood when he sat to write to his wife two days later. "I often think darling that when we get together again I will not be cross and look mad and refuse to talk as I used to do. I know you won't believe me, and I do not blame you." The hope that the war might end soon and allow husband and wife to "get together" sustained them both. "I think the papers contain very strong indications of a letting down on the part of Lincoln, but we have refreshed ourselves so often upon false hopes that I will only say that this war as anything, must have an end and that each day brings that desirable result nearer to us."[55]

Apparently, Fanny had broached the idea of the family establishing a home when the conflict ended. Dorsey had even thought about purchasing a farm. "Bless you my dear wife it is all for your sake, for I know how much you would like to have a home where we could live quietly together." Even so, he continued to hedge about the future that neither of them were yet free to attempt to determine. "I fear I began to feel that there is no alternative for us but the army for life. If I could get a position, it will be better than anything else I could do, probably. It will certainly be a gentlemanly position."[56]

In the previous year Pender expressed concern that the North's conciliatory policy would tempt Southerners to stray from the cause. He need not have worried. As the war continued, many Union soldiers and their commanders became less interested in winning back their straying Southern brethren than in offering them a dose of the "hard hand of war."[57] Renewed campaigning promised to offer more opportunities for this new mode of warfare.

The North Carolinian's response to such measures was predictable. He could have as dedicated an approach to warfare as anyone, but he believed that rules governed military practices for civilized nations and had been determined to abide by these limitations as much as possible. Nevertheless, the temptation to offer object lessons of their own was great. "Our people have suffered from the depredations of the Yankees," Dorsey explained to Fanny on April 19, "but if we ever get into their country they will find out what it is to have an invading army amongst them." General Lee might prefer not to follow such a course, but Pender found that even "some of our chaplains are telling the men they must spoil and kill." Union policies had certainly taken a toll. "Our endurance has almost worn out," he admitted. "Sometimes when I think of their rascality I get furious." The fury and the transition to a harsher state of war melded for him. "They have gone systematically to work to starve us out and destroy all we have, to make the country a desert. I say let us play at the same game if we get the chance." Then without the notice of any contradiction in spirit, Dorsey bade his spouse the usual closing of God's blessing to "my own dear wife. Kiss the boys. Love to all."[58]

Indeed, Dorsey reacted strongly to the expressions of Northern determination and the chance to settle scores. "This spring will be our time to strike them," he told Fanny in late April, and may we pay them for some of their devilish acts. I almost get beside myself sometimes," he admitted, "when I get to thinking about the way they treat our people in their lines." He expressed an understandable reluctance to exhibit the same policy toward those who sympathized with the Union and frustration at what might be done to the "devils incarnate." "Surely the just God will punish them," he righteously concluded, leaving the matter of retribution to a higher power. "Granting that we were wrong morally and politically, it could not have justified such treatment as they have been guilty of towards especially our families. They are merely giving us a taste of what we might expect if they should conquer us."[59] For Pender, such a "taste" was sufficient reason to stay in the fight until it had been won.

While still waiting for the promotion to come through that he was unconvinced would, Pender learned that Stonewall Jackson was not nearly so implacable toward him as he had thought. When A. P. Hill's recommendation reached his camp desk, "Old Jack" took new notice of the young up-and-comer from North Carolina. "I understand Gen. Jackson has been making some inquiries about me and said he was sorry he did not know more of me personally— the old humbug," Dorsey wrote Fanny. Jackson had "asked an officer of his staff in whom he has great confidence, the other day who was the best Brigadier in the Corps and I think he told him I was." Still, Pender was skeptical as to the veracity of the story or the likelihood that it would make any difference in his case.[60]

"Col. Scales is trying to get on foot a general petition from the officers of our N.C. Regts. here that I be promoted, but I have no idea it will succeed." Pender was certain that old animosities would prevail. "I do not believe Gen. Jackson will have me promoted because I have been recommended by Gen. [A. P.] Hill." Then as if to cover all possibilities, he speculated that Jackson "wants someone in place who will feel under obligation to him."[61] Pender was even more dejected on the subject when, upon visiting army headquarters, he learned that Edward Johnson and William H. C. Whiting were being nominated as major generals. "Johnson was my competitor," he told Fanny, "so you see my hope is gone." Once again he professed not to be surprised or disappointed in the outcome, "as I have expected it for some time." He saw "two drawbacks" in his case, and "heavy ones, too." As a North Carolinian and a friend of Powell Hill, he figured his chances were doomed. "The first will work against me with Mr. Davis, and the latter with Gen'l Jackson."[62]

All of these concerns disappeared when Pender finally obtained the promotion he had sought so eagerly and earnestly. He would have been particularly gratified by the high esteem that General Lee and President Davis seemed to hold for him. "I felt the high commendation you bestowed upon Pender to be fully due to him," the Confederate chief executive observed to Lee on May 26, "having marked his conduct in the campaign before Richmond with peculiar admiration."[63] Davis's recollection of the momentous Seven Days' Battles in defense of the Confederate capital the previous year would have pleased Pender enormously.

Any time to savor the honor would have to be of short duration, for the complexion of the situation in Central Virginia for Lee and the Army of Northern Virginia changed dramatically in May when Joseph Hooker at last shook the Army of the Potomac into action. The Confederates labored under some significant disadvantages, most telling the absence of the battle-hardened veterans under Longstreet who were still in southeastern Virginia and northeastern North Carolina sparring with Union forces there and collecting supplies.

Hooker's army started into the Wilderness near a crossroads known as Chancellorsville in a maneuver designed to outflank the Confederates. The situation forced Lee to be at his creative best, for the Federal forces outnumbered his own by two to one. Historian Robert K. Krick has called the disparity "the largest imbalance of any major battle in Virginia during the Civil War."[64] Counting on his trusted lieutenant Thomas J. Jackson to bolster him, Lee rose to the challenge.

General Lee used a portion of his command to halt the Federals and convince them to relinquish the initiative. "Fighting Joe" obliged. In the meantime, the Confederate leader prepared to send Jackson on a march by which he willingly gambled the fate of his army. Those troops were to move along a route of some twelve miles that would bring them onto the right flank of the Union position. A sudden thrust and the disparity in numbers could be offset in the panic and disorder that would surely ensue in the Union ranks.

Following the planning session that generated the audacious scheme, Jackson set out to implement it. As the afternoon slipped away on May 2, the Confederates tramped into place near the corps of Union major general Oliver Otis Howard, Pender's old West Point classmate. The sun was dipping low in the western sky when the Southerners surged from the woods, wildlife scurrying before them as the men sounded the vaunted "Rebel yell," at once a cathartic release and a powerful psychological weapon against their opponents. Union cohesion melted away before the tide of butternut and gray.

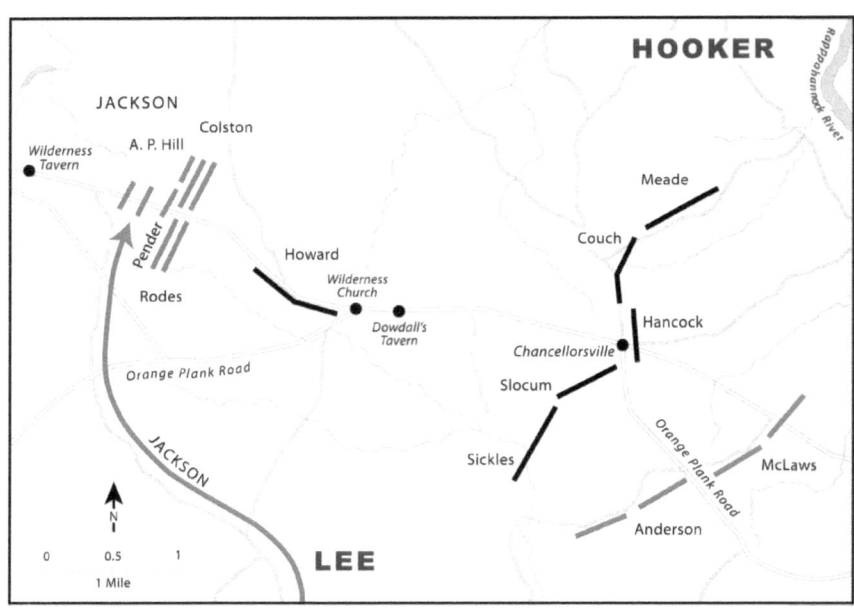

Map 7. Lee's boldness at Chancellorsville featured a dramatic flank attack on the first day by Stonewall Jackson that included Pender's command. Map by Heather Harvey.

Even with the benefit of this initial success and the fact that Jackson had presented Lee with the opportunity for a greater one, several factors weighed against the Confederates. Daylight was rapidly vanishing, and Southern unit integrity itself was breaking down in the course of the attack. Complicating factors further was the possibility that the Southerners might also become the victims of an unexpected Union counterattack that would reverse the momentum and cost them all that they had achieved thus far.

In the gathering darkness, the Confederates paused to regroup, and individual commanders took steps to achieve as much security as circumstances permitted without sacrificing the momentum they enjoyed. James H. Lane, who later wrote that his most pressing concern was "preparing for a night attack," placed his brigade "across the plank road & [it] was the only one in line of battle." He knew that the Federals still had enormous numbers of troops that could be brought to bear if they chose to do so, and Lane alerted his men to this possibility. "I had warned the command to keep a sharp look out," he recalled, "as they were confronting the enemy & would soon be ordered forward."[65]

General Lane and his men could not know that any movement taking place in their vicinity would not just be from enemy combatants. Thomas Jackson and some of his staff members had ridden out to reconnoiter the Union lines. Intermittent firing caused them to alter their course and brought them back in the darkness toward soldiers on a portion of the Southern lines who were unaware of the entourage's presence in their front. Tragedy struck when these troops responded, "under the impression that it [Jackson's party] was a body of Yankee Cavalry," and in his hour of success, Stonewall fell to fire from his own forces.[66]

Jackson took two rounds in the left arm that caused the damaged limb to hang uselessly. A third round also struck him in the right hand. The shots staggered not only the legendary general but also his staff and that of Powell Hill, who was one of the first persons to reach Jackson. To add insult to grievous injury, the general's warhorse, Little Sorrel, broke free and bolted into Union lines. It would be another few weeks before Jeb Stuart's cavalrymen were able to retrieve the animal from the enemy.

The night erupted in chaos and madness. Blind shelling from artillery screamed through the dark sky, and sporadic musket fire from confused men on both sides threatened everyone and made the job of removing the wounded general infinitely more difficult than it would otherwise have been. A staffer sent by Hill to locate a doctor stumbled into Dorsey Pender as he came forward to make his own assessment of what had happened. Fortunately, Pender had a surgeon, Richard R. Barr, handy for any circumstance, and he soon appeared.

General Hill felt a proprietary interest over the general with whom he had previously feuded so frequently and spent his time attending to Jackson as well as he could. When Stonewall asked quietly if Barr, whom he did not know personally, was reliable as a doctor, Hill responded, "I don't know much about him, but he stands very high with his brigade." In any case, he reassured the injured man, nothing significant was going to be done barring an emergency until Jackson's own surgeon, the young but trusted Dr. Hunter McGuire, could reach him.[67]

In the meantime, Pender hastened to the stricken commander's side. "Oh, General, I hope you are not seriously wounded," he offered as a small indication of his own concern. But there was more to be worried about than the fallen general. The circumstances of Jackson's wounding had been an indication of the confusion left from the day's hard fighting. Prudence called for realignment and the reestablishment of command and control. "I will have to retire my troops to re-form them," Pender explained to Jackson as he lay there, "they are so much broken by this fire." The North Carolinian had an unquestioned reputation for staunchness on the battlefield, but he was undoubtedly taken aback when Jackson gathered himself sufficiently to blurt out, "You must hold your ground, General Pender! You must hold your ground, sir!"[68]

Whatever thoughts may have raced through his mind at the moment, the circumstances did not require Pender to say more on the subject. Jackson's directive was clear and unequivocal. His troops were to stay where they were and hold against whatever enemy might materialize to challenge them. As the general surely knew, Pender was a fighter who would do all he could to adhere to the directive. He could be counted on to implement this last field order that Stonewall Jackson would ever issue.

By one account, Pender acted quickly in obedience to the instructions. A member of the 13th North Carolina, serving with the pickets that evening as the sudden burst of firing rattled the night air, remembered that as first "one loose horse came from the direction of the shooting" and then "another," he "slid down into the road" and met a party returning to the Southern lines. The identity of the man borne in the litter was pronounced only to be "a Confederate officer," but the soldier afterward deduced that it had likely been the stricken Jackson. While this encounter was unfolding, he also recalled hearing Pender distinctly instructing his men to move forward.[69]

Pender and Hill realized that despite the successes of the flanking assault and the tragic aftermath of that fateful night, much fighting remained to be done before the battle could or would be decided. Other command changes remained to be felt in the near future. Hill himself would be wounded in the fighting to come, and Pender's West Point friend Stuart would have to be summoned from his cavalry responsibilities and pressed into command of infantry.[70]

Through the remainder of the night following Jackson's wounding, men slept fitfully as they pondered the next day's events. One soldier harassed a comrade with a working timepiece for updates on the hour until he finally deemed it near enough to day for them to prepare for action. "Let's get up and get ready," the anxious soldier called out, "for hell will be to pay as soon as it gets light." The other recorded that all of the men were soon awakened and answered an impromptu morning roll call. "Just as we could see day was opening, while it was red in the east," he explained, "I heard that keen, shrill voice of General W. D. Pender, down on the right of the brigade, scream out, 'Attention, forward, guide center.'"[71] The time for renewed fighting had come.

This combat would be as difficult as any at Chancellorsville. Federal troops under Major General Hiram G. Berry and Brigadier General Alpheus S. Williams occupied strong positions across the Orange Plank Road and were supported by artillery. Berry would not survive the day, shot from his horse while directing the action. Behind him, William Hays next felt the brunt of Pender's attack and ended the day the North Carolinian's captive, alongside staff members caught in the same situation when the Confederates struck the Union brigade's flank.[72]

Pender noted that on that day, May 3, the fighting was particularly intense as the opposing forces jockeyed for the key ground. "After five terrible hours commencing 5 A.M. Sunday, 3rd, we drove him from his position," Dorsey crowed to Fanny. "I was in the front line to start at them and went through to the last." As the chaotic fighting unfolded, he found himself leading other troops as well. "Fought my Brigade until the final repulse," the general explained to his wife, "and then took command of other troops as they came up."[73]

One of his men remembered the engagement vividly. The Federals in the initial line they confronted had improved the works overnight. Even so, the early hour and close proximity of the two lines allowed the Confederates to overwhelm the defenders. For much of that morning, or at least from approximately 5:00–8:30 A.M., the pattern continued as positions fell to the Southern attackers. When reinforcements finally reached Pender's men, the timing could not have been better. The North Carolinians and their ammunition were exhausted, the ranks devastated by the repeated charges and by the cumulative effects of the casualties that they had suffered. R. S. Williams observed that as the 13th pulled back to the last Union line they had overrun and replenished their ammunition, the unit also took roll, to which "one hundred and thirty-nine men answered to their names" out of the "three hundred and forty-two good men" who would have been heard from earlier that morning. The 22nd North Carolina also lost heavily in officers and men and, consequently, in experience. Colonel C. C. Cole fell in the fighting, and the regiment lost twenty-six of thirty-three officers and 219 men killed or wounded.[74] A staff officer concluded succinctly, "We have lost some valuable and brave officers."[75]

As much of a fighter as he was, Pender was still a professional soldier who sought to hone his craft, even in the midst of an engagement. One fellow North Carolinian explained in the aftermath of the heavy fighting that the general summoned his subordinate brigade commanders to a meeting. Based upon the orders he had issued through the day, he presented critiques on their performances. "As the officers of the different regiments came before him he praised or blamed them as they deserved." Such an exercise might have been awkward for some, but the drill instructor in Pender appeared to have won out, and with the likelihood of critical fighting yet to come, it must have seemed necessary to him, even under such circumstances. "General Pender was a West Pointer," the witness explained, "and was a strict disciplinarian, and, as we thought, a rigid drill-master; but after a few battles, when in the most trying circumstances the regiment was able to keep an unbroken front, the wisdom of General Pender was fully justified."[76]

In the bitter affair that swirled around the Virginia crossroads, the men not only benefited from the general's rigorous demands for their preparation but also from his personal inspiration. Powell Hill recalled Dorsey Pender's valorous example later for General Lee in presenting his subordinate's name for a promotion. "At Chancellorsville, he seized the color," the Virginian noted of his North Carolina subordinate, "and on horseback led his Brigade *up to* and *in to* the Federal intrenchments."[77]

As commanders in the engagement on both sides learned, victory could be a fragile enterprise. In his moment of triumph, Lee was rapidly facing the prospect of being caught in a vise himself. "Fighting Joe" remained in his front, but when Major General John Sedgwick finally succeeded in driving Major General Jubal Early's Confederates from Marye's Heights at Fredericksburg, he could be expected to make for Lee's rear at Chancellorsville. The remnants of the Fredericksburg defenders and troops the Confederate commander dispatched to reinforce them countered the Union move at Salem Church, halting Sedgwick's progress and preventing disaster for the Army of Northern Virginia.[78]

Monday, May 4, marked another day of the drama as Hooker sought to regain the momentum on these bloody fields. Pender once again put himself at the front. Afterward, he related what happened with an almost clinically detached quality to the wife who so desperately dreaded such moments. "I was hit . . . while standing behind the entrenchments in a miserable skirmish, but it is only a very slight bruise by a spent ball which killed a fine young officer standing in front of me." The injury occurred "on the right arm near the shoulder."[79]

Pender had softened the incident so as not to alarm his wife unduly. But the situation was worse than he had indicated. A staffer for General Stuart, who happened upon the North Carolinian to deliver a message at about the time the wounding occurred, found Pender "spitting blood" and noticed that at his feet lay the dead subordinate. "A bullet had passed through the latter's head and struck him [Pender] in the breast," the courier recalled. Deeming Pender to be "among the most splendid looking soldiers of the war," the messenger attested that the general had been fortunate that the officer who perished deflected the round before it struck its second target.[80]

Another witness chose to accentuate the positive in an account offered for a North Carolina newspaper's readership. "Gen. Pender was slightly wounded through the right shoulder by a minie ball," D. M. McIntire observed, "but did not give up the command [except] only long enough to have the wound dressed."[81]

In the meantime, General Lee continued to wrest the initiative from "Fighting Joe" Hooker. Heavy rain and the need to reposition the troops prevented an attack from occurring before darkness fell on May 5. Now, on the soggy morning of the following day, Lee prepared for what he hoped would prove to be a final, decisive assault against the Federals at Chancellorsville. His inclination, as ever, was to strike, and he wanted his troops poised to do so before Hooker could consolidate his position, or worse, pull out of the way altogether. The Confederate chieftain did not know that it was already too late, and it was Pender's misfortune that he was the one who proved to be the bearer of the news that the Federals had escaped. Consequently, he was the individual who felt the wrath of the commanding general's first response to this unwelcome development. Pender had no sooner passed along the information when a frustrated Lee lashed out at the unwitting messenger. "Why General Pender!" the venerable soldier blurted uncharacteristically, "That is what you young men always do. You allow those people to get away. I tell you what to do, but you don't do it."[82] Lee may have thought that he could still catch the Federals in the open or may simply have wished to impart a lesson for an officer he knew would do whatever fighting was required of him in the future. "Go after them," the proud Virginian commanded, waving his hand in frustration concerning the chance for a final blow, "and damage them all you can!"[83]

For a man of Pender's sensitivity, the commanding general's outburst must have been tremendously mortifying. Lee had been his superintendent at West Point and was now a mentor. Even more disturbing, no doubt, there was nothing the North Carolinian could do to retrieve the situation either for his exasperated chief or for himself. For the man who claimed to inform his wife of "everything," Pender wrote nothing that survives of the incident or his reaction to it in letters to her after the engagement.

In his first postbattle letter to Fanny, Dorsey complained that he had "not had time to write before." He was ready to provide a capsule of the fighting at Chancellorsville but offered few specific details. "We had on the 2nd & 3rd the hardest fight we have ever had. They had great odds against us & a strongly fortified position, but about 5 hours hard fighting on the morning of the 3rd found us in possession." The general considered the outcome of the contest satisfying. "Thus far we have whipt them beautifully," he explained. But Dorsey had to know that Fanny would be most pleased that he was safe, if not unscratched. "I have had better luck than usual having only been bruised a little by a spent ball."

Pender also wanted her to know that his authority had expanded. "I now have command of four Brigades & will probably [keep] them at present as Gen. Hill is disabled having received a slight wound on the leg which prevents him from walking." Still, the preparations leading to the battle and the demands of the fighting itself left Pender exhausted as he grumbled gently to her. "I have no time to write darling & if I don't I could not for I have had you may say no sleep for nearly a week."[84]

Two days later Dorsey took up his writing implement again, but his physical and mental state remained under duress. "We are back at the same old camp after eight memorable days," he observed. "The enemy are all once more on the other side of the river," he remarked, again omitting any reference to the exchange Lee had with him on that subject, "and may God grant that they may go still further." He recounted the price of the victory and promised to "write more of the fight in my next for I am very tired and sleepy now."[85]

Others in his command shared similar views. Assistant Adjutant General McIntire noted the return of "Pender's brigade" to "our old 'Camp Gregg,' where we spent the past hard and dreary winter." Yet the difficulties of those earlier months now faded under the light of the harsh experiences of "10 days marching and fighting."[86] The quiet of camplife seemed less onerous to the battered survivors of Chancellorsville as they worked to count the costs and restore themselves to fighting trim.

In addition to writing Fanny, the general also had the opportunity to complete the official paperwork for which he had responsibility. His drafting of a May 14 after-action report focused on the positive aspects of the recent campaign and engagement. There was no acknowledgment of failures, placement of blame, or apology for missed opportunities. Indeed, Pender had nothing but praise for his troops. "I can truly say that my brigade fought May 3 with unsurpassed courage and determination," he noted matter-of-factly. "I never knew them to act universally so well."[87] Only a year earlier he had been so uncertain of what he and his men would do in the heat of battle. Now he could say with a justifiable pride, "Our N.C. troops behaved most notably."[88] They had responded to his exacting demands and performed to his satisfaction under the pressures of the battlefield.

Dorsey was sufficiently satisfied to tell Fanny that he felt that through his performance he had secured elevation to a higher rank. "If not before, I won promotion last Sunday and if it can be done I think I shall get it." He was effusive in his commendations, doling out plaudits to his friend Stephen Ramseur, "who covered himself and Brigade with glory," as well as to his own brigade, which "behaved magnificently [but] got cut up terribly."[89]

"Terrible" was a word that Pender employed repeatedly to describe Chancellorsville.[90] Not often known for hyperbole, the general found himself affected profoundly by the viciousness and consequences of the combat he had witnessed. His losses in the battle were severe by any measure, though particularly so in the number of officers struck down. "Six out of 10 field officers were killed or seriously wounded," Pender recorded. He set the total casualties for his command at 116 officers and men killed, 567 wounded, and 68 missing or captured.[91] Of course, such losses, especially in the leadership ranks, were hardly exclusive to his brigade alone. One student of Lee's celebrated command noted simply, "The attrition rate for officers in the Army of Northern Virginia was simply disastrous."[92]

Among the leaders who fell were the lieutenant colonel and the major of the 22nd North Carolina upon whom General Pender had so often depended over the past year. "Two finer soldiers or more gallant men were not to be found in the army," Pender explained for the record. "They never failed me on any occasion."[93] For the regiment that he had already indicated he turned to when things got especially rough the deaths of these officers must have been hard indeed.

The *Daily Progress,* located in Raleigh since coming to the state capital from New Bern in 1862, carried a full tally of the losses Pender's Brigade had experienced, confirming for the public what the general already knew concerning the costs of the engagement. Each of the regiments in the brigade had suffered, but the 13th and the 22nd North Carolina led the others substantially, with 219 and 221 total casualties, respectively. Twenty-seven of these men of the 13th were listed among the killed, with the 22nd matching its dead to its regimental number. The 34th North Carolina was not far behind, with 155 total men lost, and the 35th and 16th experienced a hardly inconsequential 114 and 97 respective casualties. Altogether, the numbers coming out of brigade headquarters at Camp Gregg brought the tally to just a few less killed (113) and missing (63) but more wounded (680) than the accounting Pender provided in his official report.[94]

Dorsey had promised to write Fanny a longer letter after he had gotten some badly needed rest. On May 9, two days after making that compact, the circumstances of his shoulder being "a little stiff" forced him to break it, at least in terms of length. He mentioned that he was taking medicine that eased the pain and lamented the news that Stonewall Jackson was "thought to be in a very serious condition." Pender understood that the fallen warrior had contracted pneumonia and knew what that was likely to mean to his chances for survival. "He will be a great loss to the country," Dorsey related, softening his stance toward the man with whom he had occasionally expressed strong antipathy prior to the battle, "and it is devoutly to be hoped that he may be spared to the country."[95] Others, from Robert E. Lee on, were offering the same devout wishes, but the struggling soldier would enter his reward the following day, fittingly a Sabbath, and leave a difficult void to fill.

Jeb Stuart was one of the individuals who had already accepted more command responsibility during the battle. Initially, Pender took pains to celebrate the achievements of his friend. "Stuart commanded the Corps in the Sunday fight, Gen. Hill being unable to ride horseback and right noble did Stuart do."[96] Yet this attitude quickly soured. Although Pender always enjoyed reconnecting with his West Point cronies, by the end of May, he was becoming perturbed with "Beaut" Stuart. "It seems that Gen. Stuart has been in Richmond trying to oust Genl Hill out of his corps," he explained to Fanny. "He is a scheming fellow as ever you saw. I do not like him over much & would not have him command the corps for any thing in the world. I should want to leave it [instead]." Fortunately for the proud North Carolinian, he could add, "Genl Lee is on Hill's side."

Jefferson Davis was another matter. Pender felt that the president might not wish to adhere to the recommendations of even such a trusted commander as Lee. "It has come to a pretty pass," he concluded to Fanny, "when he can not do as Gen. Lee wishes about the General's own Army." Besides, whatever commendable might be said of the cavalryman's recent performance at Chancellorsville, Dorsey explained, "Stuart lost as much with the Army as he gained in the fight, for all saw that he was so totally deficient in dignity that all his fighting qualities could not overcome it."[97]

Pender's scathing critique of his comrade also revealed his concern that someone might vault into a position at the expense of a friend and highly regarded superior. Such an interloper might not prove as helpful to his own cause for advancement as another was already known to be. Pender knew that he and the others who had survived the carnage of the spring had more campaigning to come. Those who had fallen were ever-present reminders of the duty that lay ahead. General Lee and the Confederate nation would need their services as much now as at any time in the young country's existence, and William Dorsey Pender would be expected to answer the call as he had proven himself willing and capable of doing since the war had begun.

11

"I AM TIRED OF INVASIONS"
(May–July 1863)

⎯•⎯•⎯

Pender is an excellent officer, attentive, industrious, and brave.
—ROBERT E. LEE

Tell my wife I do not fear to die. . . . My only regret is to leave her and our children. I have always tried to do my duty in every sphere of life in which Providence has placed me.
—WILLIAM DORSEY PENDER AS HE LAY IN A HOSPITAL
AT STAUNTON, VIRGINIA

⎯•⎯•⎯

Robert E. Lee had been too long around history himself not to understand the odds that were gathering against him in waging a successful revolution. The Confederate general had noted with exasperation, "I wish I could get at those people over there."[1] Earlier in the spring, even before the miraculous and dearly bought victory at Chancellorsville, Dorsey Pender exposed his military instincts with regard to another Southern invasion of Northern soil. On April 8, 1863, he had noted plainly to Fanny: "I am inclined to think that will be the move we make, march for Md. turning the Yankee Army and force them to fall back upon Washington. I am now in favor of going straight through Md. into Penna. and I believe we can do it. Gen. Lee undoubtedly has some bold plan upon foot."[2] When Fanny expressed reservations, Dorsey reiterated his view with the stark declaration that he could see no other choice "but to go," adding quickly: "This is a very different army than the one we marched into Maryland last year, and they have not as good a one to meet us. I am for going."[3] His determination had not subsided two days later when he observed: "You say you hope we will not go into Md. I hope we will pass through it into Penn. and believe the large majority of the Army would like to."[4]

Now, in the aftermath of Chancellorsville, the way seemed to be open for the Army of Northern Virginia to march northward with confidence that a second invasion might garner extraordinary results. "We have nothing new in the world, but all feel that something is brewing," Dorsey confided to Fanny, "and that Gen. Lee is not going to wait all the time for them to come to him."[5]

Pender also wanted his men to understand the confidence he had in them. On May 13 he issued General Orders No. 38, announcing his return to active service following his wounding. He commended the brigade for its performance in the recent engagement. "Upon resuming command of the brigade, it affords me great pleasure to express to you my high appreciation of your conduct and services in the late battle of Chancellorsville," he began. Noting the gallantry with which they had fought, the odds they had faced, and the severe losses they had sustained, he concluded, "I may be exacting, but in this instance you may rest assured that I am perfectly satisfied." Perhaps most importantly, he felt that the brigade had reflected with credit upon his leadership. "I am proud to say that your services are known and appreciated by those higher in command than myself."[6]

In the meantime, the general continued to recover, assuring his wife on May 14 that he was now in "excellent" health and promising her that he would "take as good care" of himself "as possible." He had much to look forward to in returning home when the war ended, as eventually it must. "Rest assured that I value my life too highly to throw it away uselessly," Dorsey observed, but the demands of the conflict might still call upon him to make that sacrifice, as both of them knew in the recesses of their hearts and minds.

In any case, he was returning to some of the feistiness of old. If Stonewall were dead, the old Jackson–A. P. Hill feud yet lived. "Do not believe all you see about the last words of Jackson," Dorsey insisted to Fanny in mid-May, "for some designing person is trying to injure Gen. Hill by saying that he frequently said that he wanted [Richard S.] Ewell to have his Corps." Pender was certain that a delirious Jackson was hardly in shape to make such definitive statements, but in any event, Powell Hill was still his man. "It is strange what a jealousy exists towards A. P. Hill and this Division, and for what cause I cannot see, unless it is because he and it have been so successful." He remembered the efforts Hill had made on his behalf and was determined to exhibit loyalty to his superior and friend. "I hope to stick to him," Dorsey asserted to Fanny, "for he sticks to me."[7]

Since his early days as a colonel instructing his men in North Carolina and Suffolk, Virginia, Pender had come a long way in learning to navigate the torturous path of army politics effectively. Whereas he had once dispatched junior officers with strong words of encouragement to one North Carolina governor, to another he sent a more acceptable token and tangible symbol of fortitude in the form of a sword taken from Union general William Hays at Chancellorsville.[8] Having had the item "presented to me," Pender decided to forward it to Zebulon Vance "to be kept at Raleigh [along] with a very patriotic letter." He was obviously pleased with the gesture. "That is the way to make glory tell," he concluded.[9]

Pender had always appreciated public notices of his conduct and performances on the field, but he had begun to realize that such recognition could be fickle as well as fleeting. "Did you see a little notice in the *Journal* of your husband," he observed with some of the old verve, "but I am getting to care very little for newspaper compliments; I feel that they [are] worth but little compared to the good opinion of my superiors."[10] Perhaps he was only jaded by the constant stream of hyperbole and misinformation that populated the pages of prominent news organs. Only days before, he had lamented, "Our [news]papers in Richmond made themselves disgustingly ridiculous."[11]

At the same time, Pender suffered a slight setback with his battered limb and shoulder. "It is getting on very well," he explained on May 23, "but last Sunday it was very painful. It has turned out to be a little deeper than it appeared at first, but still it is but trifling." He was not likely to let the injury impair his duties, although he still contemplated using it as a reason to obtain a furlough to see Fanny and the boys. Then his conscience pricked him, and he decided to remain at his post.[12]

The battle between duty and family remained powerful. As long as the campaigning season was in full swing, it was doubtful that he would be successful in obtaining leave, and as it turned out, he was not. At the end of the month, Dorsey regretfully informed Fanny that he could not get away. "Gen. Lee says from information he has received, it would be preferable for me to go to Richmond [where he planned to see Fanny] some other time, as my command may be needed very soon." From this, Pender deduced that the commanding general "anticipates another fight." The tug-of-war between these internal forces pulled him considerably. "The damper to my hopes of seeing you is very grievous to bear," he admitted. With no chance for furlough, Dorsey contemplated a quick visit by Fanny herself, but the possibility of active operations squelched that scheme as well. "I almost hope you may have left home before you get my dispatch not to come," but he knew that there would be no opportunity for enjoying her presence. "I have not much doubt but that a fight is on hand."[13]

Although many uncertainties remained for the North Carolinian, once again through the attrition of the battlefield, the way opened for him finally to obtain advancement in rank. Rumors abounded that President Davis preferred to promote Virginians over others; Pender certainly believed this to be so. A surgeon in the 3rd North Carolina had heard of even a worse possibility than his comrade's failure to obtain promotion. Thomas Fanning Wood suspected that Pender, "who is acknowledged a fine Brigadier, and who was senior Brigadier in command of A. P. Hill's Division, has been removed." He was convinced that this decision came "because he was from N.C. and would succeed A. P. Hill." Nevertheless, Wood expressed the hope that all would work out appropriately in the end. "I am confident," he explained to his father, "that Genl. Lee is doing all of this for the best."[14]

Surgeon Wood need not have worried. Hill left a meeting with Lee in which he learned of his own elevation in rank to lieutenant general and composed a letter concerning his replacement atop the Light Division. Two serious candidates emerged for consideration: Henry Heth and William Dorsey Pender. Hill viewed both men positively and considered Heth to be "a most excellent officer, and a gallant soldier." But Heth had not been with the command as Pender had, and the North Carolinian's record was impressive on any account. Following his remarks on Heth, Hill added, "On the other hand Gen. Pender has fought with the Division in every battle, has been four times wounded and *never* left the *field*, has risen by death and wounds from fifth Brigadier to be its senior, has the best drilled and disciplined Brigade in the Division, and more than all, possesses the unbounded confidence of the Division." Pender's bravery under fire was unquestioned, and Hill believed this perception of his character among the troops was essential to future success. "The effect of such examples of daring gallantry at critical moments is incalculable," the new corps commander observed of his potential replacement. "I am earnest in this matter, for I know that 10,000 men, led by a Commander whom they know, and have fought with, may turn the tide of battle." Dorsey Pender was Powell Hill's choice. "Hence," he emphasized, "as much as I admire and respect Gen. Heth, I am conscientiously of [the] opinion that in the opening campaign, my Division under him, will not be *half* as effective as under Gen. Pender."[15]

Hill continued to endorse Pender's promotion enthusiastically, noting to Lee on June 3, "I have the honor to call to your attention the uniform good conduct and gallantry of Brig. Gen. W. D. Pender and to recommend him to you for promotion." He felt that his subordinate's record provided ample evidence to support this position. "Since under my command he has fought his Brigade, and uniformly with success," Hill observed, reeling off the battles from Mechanicsville to Fredericksburg that he believed substantiated his point concerning Pender's leadership qualities. "He has been conspicuous for gallantry, skill, and promptness. Has been wounded three times, and never left the field, save for the time necessary to bandage his wounds and eminently deserves promotion."[16]

The twenty-nine-year-old Pender was indeed one of the beneficiaries when General Lee completed the reorganization of the Army of Northern Virginia necessitated by the death and incapacity of so many, especially Stonewall Jackson. As Powell Hill moved up to fill the slot in charge of one of the three corps into which Lee now organized his army, Pender stepped into Hill's shoes as commander of the Light Division. "Pender is an excellent officer, attentive, industrious and brave," Lee reported to President Davis in late April, especially noting that the North Carolinian "has been conspicuous in every battle, and I believe wounded in almost all of them."[17] After the war, one of Lee's aides, Colonel Walter Taylor, responded to a query about the commander's assessment of Pender's suitability to fill Jackson's place. "I cannot confirm this report," he began, "but I can say that Genl. Lee had the highest opinion of Genl. Pender, and regarded him as one of his most able Division Commanders, as I know from expressions which fell from his lips."[18]

Army and state politics presented another hurdle to Pender's advancement in the form of fellow North Carolinian Robert Ransom. This matter ceased to be a problem when Ransom replaced Major General Samuel G. French, who had departed for another command himself, "and thereby," according to Douglas Southall Freeman, famed student of Robert E. Lee and his generals, "clearing the way for Pender."[19]

Pender's promotion also raised questions in some circles. As always in the turbulent world of martial politics, there were those who did not view such choices in the most positive light. Obviously, some felt themselves to be more correctly suited for the position than the one who had received it. British-born Confederate colonel Collett Leventhorpe was the individual in this instance. "Gen. Pender is promoted, & though it was the unanimous wish of the officers, that *I* should have *that* Brigade, you will see that a different arrangement will be made," he wrote home dejectedly on June 4.[20]

"I AM TIRED OF INVASIONS": MAY–JULY 1863

Pender did not have to send word of this important moment by mail. Historian William Hassler noted, "Fanny and the boys fortuitously were visiting Pender at the time of his long-cherished promotion."[21] Freeman argued that in any case, Pender would not have treated the event differently than he had other promotions in the past. "It was his nature to desire, to strive, to achieve," the historian concluded of the soldier, "and, having reached his goal, to minimize what he had gained."[22]

The newly appointed major general had barely seen Fanny and the boys on their way back to North Carolina when military action beckoned. "The enemy crossed here Friday afternoon," Dorsey wrote from near Fredericksburg on June 7, "so you see you did not get off much too soon this time." He chided General Hill's wife for remaining longer and praised Fanny for being "too good a wife to have given me as much anxiety and trouble as she gave the general." At any rate, they were safely away, and Pender was once more "in line of battle" to face the enemy. "The campaign has commenced at last," he concluded, "and now we expect sharp work."[23]

Another North Carolinian serving under Pender had a similar message to a family member, though a different anticipation of the future. "We are in line of Battle near the place where we fought last winter," Thomas Cotton explained to his sister. "The Yankees have crossed the river. We have had some skirmishing but no regular engagement. I do not think they will attempt us here but probably they will some where else." Wherever the Federals might "attempt" them, the soldier predicted, "I am afraid we will have some hard marching to do before long." As far as his own family was concerned, Cotton told his sister, "I want to see you all very bad but there is no chance."[24]

Cotton did not have the luxury of visiting directly with his loved ones, but even for those who did, like General Pender, the subsequent separation was as difficult to bear. Dorsey had to console Fanny after she apparently wrote him from Tarboro, having had time on the journey to reflect following their emotional adieu. "My dear wife," he began, "you need not have made so many excuses for yourself for you did nothing that required it. You hated to leave and thought I was hurrying you off and very naturally expressed yourself, but I knew that in your heart you did not blame me for doing what you knew I thought was best."[25]

Always a relationship marked by powerful emotions that were seldom contained by the Victorian sense of control and decorum, the Penders had a marriage in which feelings flowed freely, and both partners shared strong stances that did not give way easily. This departure had apparently been no exception, for as Dorsey concluded his letter, he returned to the point he had made when he opened it. "Be assured, Darling, that I was not mad nor did I think that you did not love me, as you should, for I know it was that very love that made you dislike so much to leave."[26] It may well have been that Fanny also thought, as she had done before, that this could be the last time she would ever see him.

Of course, Pender also had to face the war, or at least the portion of the Union forces that remained in his front. He expected that the bulk of the Federals had moved off to find General Lee and the rest of the army while these troops remained in place outside Fredericksburg watching his division. Both sides were working diligently to discover the intentions and dispositions of their opponents, but this state of affairs left Pender with little to do but wait while he carried out the duties of his new command.

One of these tasks was to consider the requests of subordinates for promotion. Pender was obviously not the only officer for whom advancement was an issue. He took particular delight in having the colonel of the 55th North Carolina approach him privately for his assistance in moving up in rank. At the very least, John Kerr Connally wanted a transfer and was boisterously threatening everything from bringing the matter directly to Governor Vance to resigning his commission. "In fact, he has made himself very ridiculous," Pender explained, perhaps forgetting his own early war ruminations of a similar nature about putting state officials in their proper places if they did not meet his exalted expectations. Then the general added a final word of condemnation that probably explained his attitude toward the matter, describing Connally as "a most conceited fellow." Perhaps with that assessment in mind, Dorsey confessed to Fanny, "It was a source of great pleasure to me to have him ask a favor of me." With the army on the move, it was highly unlikely that anything would be done with the colonel's case for the time being, but Pender gave his assurance that he would do what he could at the proper time. "He left with the determination to try to get his Brigade in my Division in which [effort] I will try to help him and then try to teach him his place."[27]

General Pender's potential subordinate certainly had a fiery history in the South's service. Earlier that spring, Connally had been one of several disgruntled officers who engaged in a duel with each other over the loss of a battery of artillery outside Suffolk. The duel amounted to little since the participants ultimately resolved the matter amicably, but Pender would do well to steer clear of the volatile colonel.[28]

"I AM TIRED OF INVASIONS": MAY–JULY 1863

In mid-June Pender was still at Hamilton's Crossing, picking up such war news as he could. "We are occupying the same position we took last Saturday morning," he wrote irritatingly on the twelfth. The Federals were making a big show of building earthworks, but to Pender this was an indication of weakness rather than strength. The fight, if one were to occur, would obviously happen elsewhere. "I am getting tired of it," he stated with regard to the sedentary nature of his present duty, "and shall be glad to move up." What bothered him most was the amorphous situation: "We are in a very unsettled state, neither one thing nor the other."[29]

The Confederate advance that he and the Federals at Fredericksburg watched from afar seemed to unnerve the bluecoats. Dorsey reported to Fanny on June 15, "Tomorrow morning we start as I suppose for Penna., the enemy having left the vicinity of Frederick[sburg] during the night apparently in great haste and fear." Taking his cue from Powell Hill, whom he was certain knew Lee's intentions, Dorsey added, "Thus far, General Lee's plans have worked admirably." He was not privy to such high-level intelligence, but he felt he "could see far enough to look into Md."[30]

Pender continued to be anxious about the risks, as well as the potential for great rewards, that lay before them. With an eye cast to the previous September across the Potomac, he quietly observed, "May God in his goodness be more gracious than in our last trial," and he thought that there might be reason to hope for a better result "as our mission is one of peace altho through blood." Perhaps most comforting, he concluded that the vastly exaggerated reports of Confederate combat strength "will scare them so badly they will be half whipt before they commence the fight." At any rate, he was certain that there would be no action of any consequence before the Southern forces crossed the river.[31]

Two days later the outlook appeared decidedly to have moved in the Confederates' favor. "We have a grand race on hand between Lee and Hooker," Dorsey told his wife with satisfaction. "We have the inside track, Hooker going to Washington and we by Winchester." Pender recognized that the Union forces had the responsibility to shield the national capital first and foremost. He continued to believe that "[e]verything this far has worked admirably" for the South, and "if the campaign goes on as it has commenced it will be a telling one." Just as if he were back in the wilderness of Washington Territory writing to his young bride in those heady, prewar days, Dorsey tried to remain practical as well as upbeat. "We will get North for a few months but we shall have to come back by September or Oct.," he explained to her, "for their force will be increasing while ours will be decreasing, but by that time we shall probably give them such a taste of war that they may be willing to quit."³²

He repeated his cheery assessment of Confederate fortunes almost verbatim on June 21. "Since I wrote you I have had some hard marching and some grumbling, but the boys are in fine plight and spirits." Lee's army had fanned out, and Pender reiterated that all was working "admirably." "I would not be surprised if we went into Penna.," he speculated, with much more justification this time than earlier. Dorsey warned Fanny that if she did not hear from him for a period that she should not "be uneasy." He was tired but in otherwise peak condition for all of the marching and any of the fighting that might lie ahead. He closed with an admonition, "Keep in good spirits, honey, and hope that this summer's work will tend to shorten the war."³³

Dorsey continued to try his best to accentuate the positives in his correspondence with Fanny as the campaign progressed. "I think our prospects here are very fine," he wrote her from the vicinity of Berryville, Virginia, on the twenty-third. "The General seemed yesterday in fine spirits," he noted of Lee, "but he said he was going to shoot us if we did not keep our men from straggling." In his good humor Lee revealed the concern he no doubt harbored from his previous invasion of the North, when straggling had depleted the army's numbers so badly and limited its combat effectiveness accordingly. Although he believed the men had "marched finely coming up here," Pender responded with an interesting extension to the point. "I told him if he gave us the authority to shoot those under us he might take the same privilege with us."

There was no question from Pender's account of his encounter with the commanding general that spirits and confidence on all levels were high. "Gen. Lee has completely outgeneraled Hooker thus far," Pender assessed, and any fight ought to be a fair one since "our numbers are more equal than they have been." Indeed, if all transpired as it appeared it might, the "prospects for peace" appeared to the young general at least to be "very fine" indeed. "Our army is in splendid condition and everyone seems hopeful and cheerful. Cheer up my dear little girl and hope for good things ahead."³⁴

On the same day Dorsey had written Fanny his upbeat message, another North Carolinian was looking at the situation from a more sobering aspect. "Well, you see now," F. M. Parker explained to his wife in a letter composed in camp in Pennsylvania, "that we are an invading army, instead of one for defence."³⁵ Another footsore warrior paused at the same time to dash off a letter to friends at home, telling them that while he was in relatively "common health," he was also "wearied by so much marching." From his perspective, George Job Huntley felt that he had plenty of room for complaint. "Something like 10 days ago we left Fredericksburg," he explained. "We have been marching ever since that time till this morning. We have stopped, but I don't know how long."[36]

By the next morning, Pender himself was more circumspect in his enthusiasm for the operation. "Tomorrow I do what I know will cause you grief," he observed on the twenty-fourth, "and that is to cross the Potomac." Almost certainly Fanny remembered the terrible human toll of Lee's last invasion of the North less than a year earlier. She knew that in all likelihood, an even more dreadful engagement would ensue as the Federals moved to block the Confederate advance and defend their own territory and capital. It would have been highly uncharacteristic of her not to recognize the danger the operation posed for her husband, but she had faced down such fears created by military expeditions that dated back to his prewar career in the Far West.

Dorsey saw the advance as another opportunity for the war to end sooner and thus bring him closer to a reunion with Fanny and the boys. "May the Lord prosper this expedition and bring an early peace out of it," he observed optimistically. Still, despite the show of faith he bravely put forward, he harbored doubts of his own. "I feel that we are taking a very important step," he explained, "but see no reason why we should not be successful." He was confident in his men, the army was "in splendid condition and spirit," and in its military leadership the Army of Northern Virginia had "the best Generals of the South." All appeared calculated for success. "Hope and pray for the best," he at last requested of his beloved spouse. "This is a momentous time but at the same time we are in better condition to meet it than we have ever been."[37] Lee was right to roll the dice and let them fall however they might.

Pender's fellow North Carolinian Stephen D. Ramseur agreed with this last sentiment in particular. He was already in Pennsylvania on the twenty-third when he informed his wife: "I take advantage of the first opportunity since leaving Culpeper to write you. Our advance has been wonderfully rapid and gloriously successful." More importantly, the men were "in the finest spirits and when we meet the enemy's horde we will give a good account of ourselves."[38] Like Dorsey Pender, Dod Ramseur realized all too well that the numerical odds were stacked against them. Still, the two men, like so many of their comrades in this enormously important military enterprise, shared a confidence that they expressed eloquently in their letters.

Apparently, the generals were attempting to instill the same type of confidence in their enlisted men and subordinates. One member of the 34th North Carolina wrote on June 25: "We have moved within 4 miles of the Potomac. We will commence crossing the river into Maryland in a few hours." But he also wanted friends at home to know, "General A. P. Hill has informed his men that we are going to carry the war into the heart of the enemy country." That message was undoubtedly meant to inspire, but for this infantryman at least, it provided a stark reality. "What luck we will have, I am unable to tell." Either way, G. J. Huntley expected a fight and the risk that combat always brought to those who participated in it. "This may be my last lines to you."[39]

On June 28 Pender was at Fayetteville, Pennsylvania. He and his men were resting briefly after long, grueling marches that had taken them from near Fredericksburg in just twelve days. Dorsey was worn out but ready for action. For now, there was the opportunity for liberal requisitioning in hostile territory, although the men "have done nothing like the Yankees do in our country." The general had even "bought a few articles" to send Fanny and anticipated obtaining more items for her "before we leave."

"I am tired of invasions," Dorsey confessed openly to his wife. Even his desire for retribution appeared to have tempered somewhat. He noted that "altho' they have made us suffer all that people can suffer, I cannot get my resentment to that point to make me feel indifferent to what you see here." Still, the prospects were great that this invasion might prove a decisive one for the struggle for Southern independence. "We might get to Phila. without a fight, I believe, if we should choose to go."[40]

Despite the physical wear and tear he had undergone in the push northward, Pender's fighting spirit was certainly intact. "I hope we may be in Harrisburg in three days," he noted. "What a fine commentary upon their 90 days crushing out, if we should march to the Capital of one of their largest states without a blow," he remarked, referencing the timeframe President Lincoln had used in his initial call for ninety-day volunteers to suppress the rebellion. "I never saw troops march as ours do," Pender stated proudly, observing that "they go 15 or 20 miles a day without leaving a straggler and hoop and yell on all occasions." Unlike the previous fall's campaign, the Army of Northern Virginia appeared to be in fine fettle this time. "Confidence and good spirits seem to possess everyone," the general concluded, presumably including himself.

But Pender would not have been himself without making a more realistic assessment of so great a military venture as this. Perhaps when he should have left well enough alone and allowed Fanny to grasp at his optimistic picture of the command and its good spirits, it was almost as if he could not help himself. "I wish we could meet Hooker and have the matter settled," he observed, coupling these wishes with the word that good news appeared also to be coming from the besieged defenders of the Mississippi River town of Vicksburg. "This campaign will do one of two things: viz—to cause a speedy peace or a more tremendous war than we have had, the former may God grant."[41] For Fanny, back in distant North Carolina, it might yet be that "a more tremendous war" would still demand the sacrifice that she had feared it might exact from her and the children all along.

The demands on General Pender, as on all of the general officers in the invasion Lee had launched into Maryland and Pennsylvania, were significant. The troops needed the basic necessities to function, and access to Union resources was bound to prove irresistible. General Lee tried to anticipate the likelihood that excesses would take place on Northern soil with General Orders No. 72, issued on June 21, 1863. In this directive he admonished, "While in the enemy's country, the following regulations for procuring supplies will be strictly observed, and any violation of them promptly and rigorously punished." Private property was to be left unharmed as a general rule, with vouchers and market prices promised for those items that fell under Confederate supply demands. Whether honored more in the breach than in reality, given all of the associated difficulties for enforcement during an active campaign, Lee's intentions were clear: there was to be no retaliatory ravaging of noncombatant property by his army in hostile territory.[42]

Lee's awareness of the challenges of preventing depredations continued to find expression in the days that followed. On June 25 he wrote President Davis, "It is plain to my understanding that everything that will tend to repress the war feeling in the Federal States will inure to our benefit." Although the general's specific reference was to Copperheads in the North, as Peace Democrats tended to be known widely, the principle applied elsewhere. "I do not know that we can do anything to promote this pacific feeling, but our course ought to be shaped as not to discourage it."[43]

On June 27, General Orders No. 73 was a tacit admission that the excesses he had hoped to avoid were occurring at any rate. Lee praised the general behavior of his command but added, "There have, however, been instances of forgetfulness, on the part of some" when it came to the hands-off policy he had set in place. "The commanding general considers that no greater disgrace could befall the army . . . than the perpetration of the barbarous outrages . . . and the wanton destruction of private property, that have marked the course of the enemy in our own country." For Lee and subordinates like Pender who cherished order in their ranks, the approach was less about what Northerners deserved based upon the behaviors visited upon Southern civilians than it was about lawless activity being broadly counterproductive and worse, "subversive of the discipline and efficiency of the army."[44]

Ironically, Pender's best procurement officer in the campaign had not been an aide or a staff officer, nor even an official member of the Confederate military structure. His most successful agent was his black servant. "Joe enters into the invasion with much gusto," he told Fanny on June 28, "and is quite active in looking up hidden property." Dorsey had complained that the locals were proving most proficient at denying the Confederates easy access to their property. "The rascals have been expecting us and have run off most of their stock and goods." That is, they had attempted to do so, until Joe worked to ferret out those items. The general had learned an interesting lesson and had to acknowledge that "the negroes seem to have more feeling in the matter than the white men and [I] have come to the conclusion that they will press horses, etc., etc. to any amount."[45]

Fellow North Carolinian Alfred Belo addressed the same phenomenon in his postwar memoirs and suggested that Joe would not have been alone in carrying out this form of activity. He noted that some of the men of the 11th Mississippi "had their servants with them, who up to this time were always foraging for their masters."[46]

The extent to which the campaign produced other effects for people of African descent was less clear. Pender did not indicate if some of the white Southerners were taking the opportunity of the invasion to sweep free blacks into bondage as slaves as one historian has asserted, but the prospect of doing so may have existed whether he was aware of it or not.[47]

Pender certainly seemed to have agreed with General Lee's dictum that the soldiers themselves ought to be restrained from engaging in general pillaging. There was to be no repetition of the loss of control exhibited during the 1862 Maryland Campaign. One of the men in Pender's Division noted his superior's position on such matters in a letter home. "Our Maj. Gen. has issued such strict orders about straggling and plundering that the people have not suffered from us."[48] Even so, historian Steven Woodworth has argued that the degree of Confederate depredations in Pennsylvania was "no better or worse than the Union armies that marched through various parts of the South at different times during the war."[49]

Pender's men approached Cashtown on June 30, following in the wake of Harry Heth's division. Unfortunately, with the fateful battle of Gettysburg about to transpire, their corps commander, A. P. Hill, was suffering from an illness that confined him to bed for part of the morning of July 1. With the lieutenant general unwell, Heth and Pender both new to division command, and General Lee tactically blind without immediate access to much of Stuart's cavalry, the situation was rife for trouble. That trouble came from Brigadier General John Buford's blue-coated cavalrymen, aided by infantry under Major General John F. Reynolds, as these soldiers hastened to support the horsemen once they became engaged in a firefight.

Heth plodded toward the tiny Pennsylvania crossroads town of Gettysburg oblivious to the strength of the opposition he faced. With the initial contact, he deployed his men but took disproportionate losses from the Federal defenders. Before the fight was over, a Union bullet felled Heth from his horse, and command devolved to Johnston Pettigrew. The Confederate soldiers were also rapidly becoming disorganized in the face of the heavier-than-expected resistance. Having arrived at the front to supervise the action, Hill turned in Pender's direction.

It is curious why Hill dispatched Heth to lead the way to Gettysburg from Cashtown when he knew that the Southerners were likely to run into Union cavalry at the very least. By historian Robert Krick's assessment, he could easily have detailed Pender for that critical assignment since the North Carolinian commanded "Hill's four best brigades, which had fought shoulder-to-shoulder through a spectacularly successful year of victories." Furthermore, Heth's more pedestrian regiments included Colonel John J. Archer, who bore such a distinct and decided distaste for Pender that it might render cooperation difficult if any were required.[50]

As it was, Heth ran into more than he had bargained for, and Archer quickly became a prisoner of war as he led his men into a trap along a deep railroad cut. Pender's services would have to be called upon, and he was, as ever, ready to respond with his characteristic energy and zeal. Certainly, he was not one to dawdle, and whatever he may have thought of Hill's initial dispositions, it was his turn now, as it had been on earlier fields such as Mechanicsville and Fredericksburg.

In this instance, time was becoming critical. The afternoon of July 1 was beginning to slip away. Anyone with a timepiece and the inclination to glance at

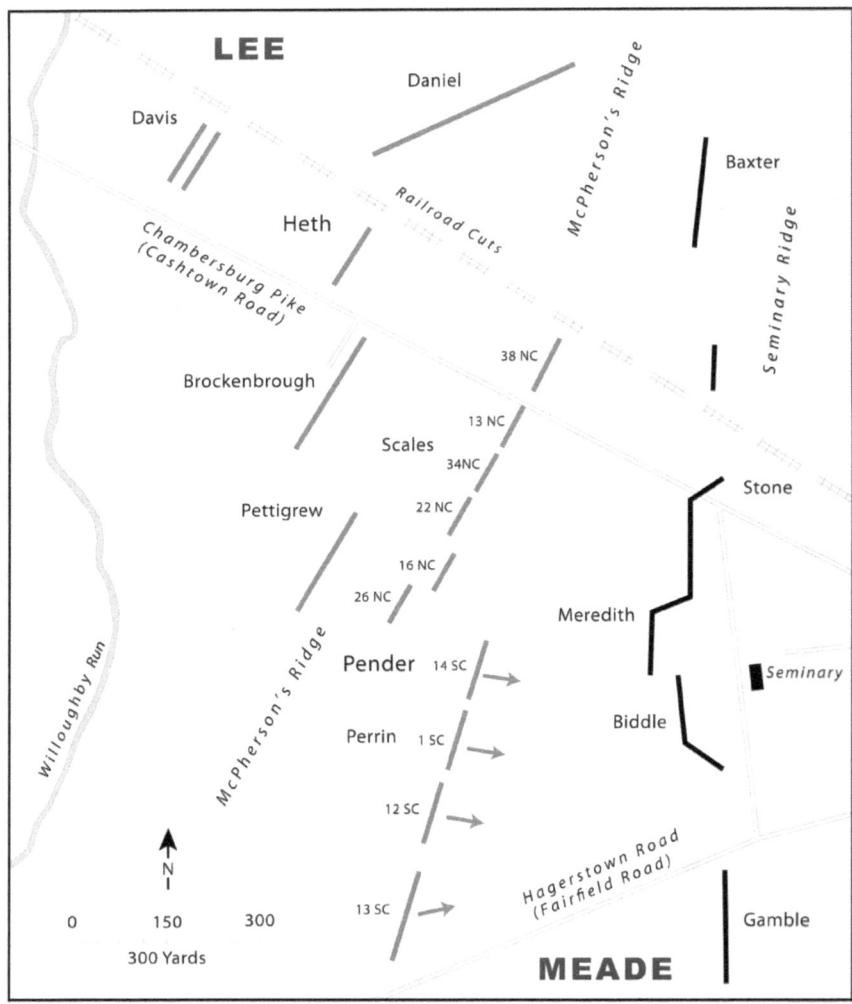

Map 8. On the first day at Gettysburg, July 1, 1863, Pender's attacks in tandem with other Confederate assaults drove Union forces through the town and onto the high ground beyond. Map by Heather Harvey.

it under the circumstances would have noted that the hour was approximately 4:00 P.M.[51] General Pender quickly had his men on the move. As it turned out, the movement itself was as crucial as the hour to the hopes for Confederate success. One of his brigadiers recalled that as the men approached their comrades in Heth's exhausted and bloodied ranks, the "poor fellows could scarcely raise a cheer for us as we passed." Pender's subordinate, Colonel Abner Perrin, would soon find out why.

Pender's men went into the fight with the determination to push the Federals from Seminary Ridge and back into and through the town of Gettysburg. Supporting Heth's troops after their success in driving the stubborn Federal defenders from McPherson's Ridge, Pender came up in the face of withering Union fire to finish the task. The regiments of Brigadier General Alfred Scales and Colonel Perrin led the way across the fields bracketed by Chambersburg Pike on one side and Hagerstown Road on the other, with Perrin's South Carolinians having the advantage of discovering the Union infantry's left flank. Scales's North Carolinians stood to his left, facing the Northerners who clung stubbornly to their positions around the brick Lutheran seminary that gave the rise of ground its name. Across the Hagerstown Road, Brigadier General James Lane deployed his North Carolinians. Brigadier General Edward Thomas's Georgians remained in the rear to be used as circumstances dictated. They could be thrown forward to exploit a breach or to respond to any unforeseen threat that might arise. Their adversaries included some of the Union's finest fighters, the "Black Hats" of the Iron Brigade.[52]

The officers urged the men forward following a brief rest for reorganization. Witnesses recalled Perrin riding among the troops and exhorting them to do their duty. The Confederates soon surged ahead over the sloping ground to their front. "Their bearing was magnificent," an opponent noted in awe as he recalled the spectacle that played out before him. Harassing fire from Union cavalry under Colonel William Gamble compelled Lane to respond, and the Confederate charge lost some of its steam, now largely being limited to the brigades of Scales and Perrin.

Undeterred, Scales threw his 1,350 men against the Union defense and was immediately answered by a withering fusillade that decimated his ranks. The general himself fell with a severe wound from shrapnel, and the advance almost literally disintegrated. Perhaps the most poignant scene that day occurred when a lone Confederate staggered through the smoke and chaos toward the Union artillery pieces arrayed against them. He managed to reach for the muzzle of one of the Union tubes and called out triumphantly, if prematurely, "This gun is mine." A blue-coated cannoneer was unimpressed with the show of bravado. "D—n You, Take it then," the artillerist yelled in response as he tugged the lanyard and the foolhardy Southerner disappeared in a red-tinged, vaporous mist.[53]

From his position in the rear, Pender could not witness such dramatic instances. He busied himself with the greater task of trying to hold the attack together in the face of the devastating losses. With Scales out of action and his men staggered by the Union blasts of canister and bullets that tore through their ranks, many of the troops were understandably reluctant to continue forward. The urge to return fire overcame the need to advance as a means of suppressing it. Then, into the void Perrin came forward to urge his men on, and the superior numbers and positioning of the Confederates began to tell. Even so, the fighting was so intense that Southern colorbearers dropped as soon as they advanced. Indeed, one lad, with the fortitude that can only be explained by shock, calmly shifted the flag he had been carrying to his left hand when a Union shell carried away his right arm, all the while urging his comrades forward.[54]

There were plenty of heroics from the men on both sides. But the Federals simply did not have enough of these staunch defenders to secure their flank. The rolling retreat that followed left the Confederates in possession of this ridgeline, though in such disorder and chaos from the fighting and the heavy losses that they could do little to exploit the opportunity for pushing ahead decisively.

In these chaotic moments Pender remained uncertain concerning the outcome of the engagement or the condition of his troops. He could not have been heartened by the sights he encountered as he rode forward amid the shredded forms of the dead and dying or watched as bloodied survivors stumbled toward the rear. Considering the issue still in doubt, he stopped one junior officer to ask him of the status of the assaulting forces. The soldier assured his superior that despite appearances, the command had not been annihilated completely in the assault. "No," the fellow replied calmly, pointing back in the direction of the ridgeline, "it is over the hill yonder."[55]

If Pender was puzzled, he did not remain so for long, and a sense of euphoria began to replace the deep concern that had occupied him earlier.[56] One participant observed that as the general reached the town, he began "pulling off his hat to our regimental colors" as a sign of respect and admiration for their accomplishments and "said our Regiment had done enough for one day." Pender could see the disorganization that plagued the victorious troops and realized that with all unit cohesion in disarray, it would be best to allow the men to consolidate and replenish their ammunition and energy.[57]

Planting the Confederate flag in the embattled little Pennsylvania town seemed enough, and with the day closing and the men exhausted, that was as good as it was going to get. Two other brigades, those of Lane and Thomas, stood poised to move against the Federals if ordered to do so, but the chance slipped through Southern fingers, and what might have been would never be for the Confederate cause on July 1, 1863, at Gettysburg.[58]

As in so many other engagements in which his troops fought, General Pender's demand for the greatest exertions produced appalling casualties. The historian of the 38th North Carolina noted simply, "Every officer in Scales' Brigade except one, Lieutenant Gardman, upon whom the command devolved, was disabled, 400 men killed, wounded and missing." As for his regiment, the writer set its loss at 100 men.[59]

While his men recuperated from the difficult and bloody work of the afternoon, Pender prepared for more action the following day. The overall scheme called for the Confederates to test the Union flanks in the areas of Culp's Hill and Cemetery Hill on the Union right and the round tops on the Union left. Pender's position, with the rest of the III Corps, was on the right of the force assigned to try the Culp's Hill/Cemetery Hill defenders. On his left was Major General Robert Rodes of Lieutenant General Richard Ewell's II Corps, and on his right, fellow III Corps division commander Major General Richard Anderson. Pender was the link between the two corps. If the attack became general, as it was supposed to do, Pender would move in support of Rodes and Ewell's overall effort against that portion of the Union line in coordination with Anderson. Scheduled to take place early in the day on July 2, the assault failed to materialize as time wore on into the evening.[60]

In the meantime, Pender determined to pave the way for any advance and clear his front of pesky Union skirmishers with a probe of his own. One of the participants of the effort recalled: "On the day of the 2nd of July 1863 we were in line of battle on Seminary Ridge to the right and not very far from a theological Seminary, Genl. Pender who commanded our Division came up to Col. I. W. Avery who commanded our Regt. which was the 38th N.C. State Troops and asked Col. Avery if he could pick out 75 men from his Regt. with two officers who could take a certain point in a road in our front that was held by some Federal troops." Colonel Avery responded immediately, producing the requisite number for the special mission. Years later the officer called upon to lead the detail remembered that Pender pulled him aside to gauge his ability to carry out the assignment. "Can you take that road in front?" the general wanted to know. When the officer responded doubtfully, Pender's countenance changed, and he "became a little angry, and said if you can't take it say so and I will get someone who can." The fellow needed no further incentive. He recalled that the gibe "touched me up and I replied to him [we] can take it if any other 75 men in the Army of Northern Virginia can." That was the reply that the general had been seeking, and "he remarked that is the way I love to hear you talk."

Pender had instructed the men to move rapidly toward the objective, holding their fire for as long as possible. The attackers formed up and set out across the open ground in full view of the Union forces on the high ground in the distance. The men raced forward, yelling fiercely. A portion of the defenders in their front turned and fled, while some two dozen surrendered. Yet the conclusion did not come before a volley at close range cost the life of one of the Southern officers, who dropped in the hail of gunfire. Under the continuing fire, the Confederates took additional casualties. "We had 12 men killed and wounded out of the 75," the surviving officer remembered, although none of them could be extracted until nightfall brought them under the cover of darkness.[61]

General Pender was never able to take advantage of the extraordinary valor and sacrifice of these men. At some point after the small but sharp fight with the skirmishers, he rode out along the lines to familiarize himself better with the lay of the land before them. His troops were now all up, and he expected at any time to receive the order to engage the enemy. It was best to know what they would be facing by examining the ground and assessing conditions with his own eyes.

The general dismounted and perched atop a boulder, from which he hoped to give himself a better vantage point. While doing so, he noted an intensification in nearby Union artillery fire. Pender turned to his staff officer, Joseph Englehard, and observed, "Major, this indicates an assault, and we will ride down our line."[62]

A Union shell suddenly burst nearby, splintering into fragments as it was intended to do. One of the jagged pieces tore into Pender's thigh, ripping a ghastly gash in the limb. According to one source, the shell fragment that struck the general included the fuse plug, a solid piece of metal that would have created still greater damage to flesh and sinew, arteries and nerves. Indeed, some two inches of Dorsey's thigh had been sliced open.

The wound was worse the next day due to the swelling that set in, and weak and stiff, Pender found that he could not ride his horse. If he were going to return to Virginia to recuperate, it would have to be by another conveyance. From there, he would perhaps be healed sufficiently to travel to North Carolina for a joyous reunion with his wife and family, if also having at the same time to endure a painful and extended period of recovery before he could return to the service.

Afterward, one of Pender's men produced a concise overview of the campaign that began with the crossing of the Potomac and the march "through Maryland into Pennsylvania to a town called Gettysburg." It was at that point, he explained: "we met the enimy and fought them for three days and fighting each day. We whipped and drove them back the first two days but they got a position the third day that our men could not drive them from." His final assessment was as grim as it was succinct. "We lost a great many men in kill[ed] and wounded."[63]

Pender's men participated in that final charge on July 3 against a copse of trees at the heart of Cemetery Ridge, though without the benefit of their dynamic leader. Isaac Trimble, Johnston Pettigrew, and George Pickett sent their troops against the center of the Union line only to see them hurled back in defeat. North Carolina soldiers reached farther than those from any other state, a fact of which Pender would have been immeasurably proud, but to no avail. Shattered in the face of a withering fire, the men dropped dead or wounded, found themselves prisoners, or somehow managed to limp back to their starting point across the wide, blood-soaked, and debris-filled field.

General Pender was just one of many men who suffered death and wounds in the three-day conflagration. The Battle of Gettysburg produced appalling casualties on both sides that depleted the ranks and destroyed whole units. A member of the 13th North Carolina reported that his unit lost 155 of the 180 men who entered the battle.[64] One student of the aftermath of the engagement noted that "there were nearly forty Confederate hospital and ambulance depot sites in or near Gettysburg caring for more than 15,000 wounded and nearly 5,000 sick officers and men."[65]

Assessments of various elements in the multiday engagement began almost immediately and have continued since. Concerning the action on the second day, or rather the lack thereof, Southern zealot Edmund Ruffin confided his thoughts to his diary with his usual vigor. Excoriating the inability of some of the Confederate commanders to move their forces on July 2, Ruffin concluded, "This failure was alleged as the reason why Pender's division did not advance—& that, for the like failure of Heth's division." Thus, he contended, thousands of troops lay inactive, depriving the Confederacy of a chance for victory.[66] Pender's wounding undoubtedly contributed to the situation that darkened the prospects for Southern success on the second day at Gettysburg and helped set the stage for the dramatic close. The last moments of the battle came as Robert E. Lee anticipated a counterattack on his position, while undertaking the initial steps toward withdrawing his men from the protracted engagement they had endured. Near the front of the line of men and vehicles now turned toward Virginia was one that carried the badly injured William Dorsey Pender.

Despite the enormous discomfort and the disability the injury represented, Pender sought to keep himself apprised of the state of his command, especially while it remained in close proximity to the enemy. Major David T. Carraway, the Light Division's commissary of subsistence, met with his chief before the wagons rolled for Virginia. According to the staffer, Pender understood his plight, but the sharp paroxysms of pain did not prevent him from making "minute inquiry into the quantity of supplies on hand" and pressing his subordinate for a detailed assessment of the "condition" of his men. Not much more could be done for the general beyond embarking on what he hoped would be the long road to recovery, but he wanted as much done as possible to see to the "comfort of his soldiers" as they prepared for their trek back to Virginia.[67]

The swelling in Pender's damaged limb still prevented him from being able to ride, and his best chances for recovery probably demanded that he remain inert for a longer period, but he did not wish to be left behind to the tender mercies of even those "rascals" with whom he had been on good terms at West Point or in the Old Army. He preferred to accept the extreme discomfort of being loaded into the back of a wagon for transportation southward than to submit to capture and an indefinite period in a Union hospital or prison camp. He simply did not think that he could abide being separated so completely from Fanny and the boys as he would be if he fell into Northern hands.

For a time, Pender shared his temporary accommodations with another wounded compatriot, General Scales, who had suffered his injury on the first day of the great battle. Like Pender, he did not wish to be left behind. An escort from George Imboden's 18th Virginia Cavalry rode along to provide an element of protection.

At about noon on July 5, General John Imboden stopped to offer the wounded generals "a little bread and meat" as sustenance for the difficult journey that lay ahead. One account noted that after the meal, the two officers "waited patiently for hours for the head of the column to move."[68] At last the caravan of shattered bodies started forward, creaking and moaning over indifferent roads, the occupants no doubt wondering if the waiting had not been less painful than the trip now at long last under way.

The Federals were prepared to do their part to prevent a safe arrival from occurring for their war-torn adversaries, although not as prepared as detractors would afterward insist they should have been. The elements were less ambivalent. Rain plagued the retreating columns, turning roads into quagmires and rendering movement at any pace difficult. One Confederate noted simply, "The march was awful."[69]

Pender had survived many scrapes in his short Confederate career. He was still strong enough to endure the long and torturous trip from Gettysburg in the bed of a springless wagon. The wounded soldier had even begun to show signs of recovery. But the injured leg was simply too damaged to sustain the work that had been done to repair it and began to hemorrhage badly. Dorsey saved himself from death in this instance through his own quick thinking and reactions. He used a towel and a hairbrush to fashion a tourniquet and squeezed the bleeding limb into submission.[70]

The North Carolinian's return to Virginia soil garnered attention as the entourage of ambulances and wagons passed. Winchester resident Mary Greenhow Lee entered a brief reference to Pender's presence, "in town, wounded," in her diary for July 6.[71] On July 14 the *Richmond Whig* cited a report, also from Winchester and dated six days earlier, listing him as one of several wounded generals to reach the vicinity, although it considered "none of them [hurt] dangerously." The *Staunton Vindicator* informed its readership on July 10 only that the general was "among our wounded."

At Staunton, a surgeon attempted to assess Dorsey's physical needs while an "attendant" addressed his spiritual ones. "General, the hemorrhage is serious, and may prove fatal," the latter recalled explaining to the patient. "I beg, therefore that you will communicate with me freely, and especially about the state of your soul." Pender remained lucid, reflected momentarily as if composing his thoughts, and replied, "Tell my wife that I do not fear to die. I can confidently resign my soul to God, trusting in the atonement of Jesus Christ."

William Dorsey Pender's journey was rapidly reaching its end. Still, he was loath to "resign" himself just yet, focusing again on those he cherished most on earth. "My only regret is to leave her and our two children," he observed quietly of Fanny, not knowing that a third son would soon be part of his growing family. "I have always tried to do my duty in every sphere of life in which Providence has placed me."[72]

Dorsey's favorite sibling, David, was able to reach his stricken brother's side, but he was powerless to do more than provide the comfort of his companionship. Repairs to the artery in the leg were not holding, and the difficult decision had to be made about the viability of the injured limb. The surgeon determined that Pender's best chance, perhaps his only one, was for the leg to be removed. In a procedure that had been done countless times before, the doctor accomplished his grim task, but the prognosis for the general remained bleak.

For a time, Pender's mind focused sharply on what was going on around him. He inquired about the state of the army and was naturally distressed to learn of the death of fellow North Carolinian Johnston Pettigrew, struck down during the retreat to the Potomac. Dorsey certainly could not have remained conscious for long but in his extremis continued to reflect the themes he had developed over his short life: duty, family, and Christian faith.[73]

How much agony Pender endured in this final period could not be known. Perhaps in the fog of his fading life, he did not suffer much. Obviously, that was what Fanny would have wished for her beloved, if sometimes exasperating, husband. She had been a catalyst for his desire to experience a religious conversion. He had embraced faith as sincerely as he knew how, and on July 18, 1863, he took the final step into the eternity for which he had been so assiduously preparing himself.

Epilogue

A "GOOD FIGHT" FINISHED AND REMEMBERED

I have fought a good fight. I have finished the course. I have kept the faith.
—2 TIMOTHY 4:7

Gen. Pender died at Staunton. I am sorry for his poor wife—write to her.
—JEB STUART TO HIS WIFE, FLORA

Poor Pender, so full of every noble and manly spirit.
—STEPHEN DODSON RAMSEUR TO HIS WIFE

The mortal remains of William Dorsey Pender reached the Confederate capital late on July 19, 1863. Several Richmond newspapers took note of the body's arrival by way of the central train and its repose in a place of honor in the Capitol.[1] The *Daily Dispatch* added that although the general's wound was known, his death had not been expected. "At the time his wound was received it was not regarded as mortal, but when he reached Staunton it was found necessary to amputate his leg, under the effects of which he died."[2] This was undoubtedly the first news that reached the general public of Pender's ultimate fate. Gettysburg had tallied another fatality to its already impressive casualty count.

Friends and compatriots reacted to Pender's death with appreciation for him as a Christian soldier and a noble warrior. From his "old stomping grounds" near Culpeper, Virginia, fellow West Pointer and friend Jeb Stuart hurried a quick note to his wife, Flora. After telling her that he was "well & in fine fighting trim," he broached the sad tidings. "Gen. Pender died at Staunton," he stated. Then, perhaps remembering the happier times at the Shepperd household after he and Dorsey had graduated from the academy and the pretty young girl with the sweet singing voice who entertained them that summer, he added, "I am sorry for his poor wife—write to her."[3]

As for the invasion itself, there were mixed feelings among the survivors. General Stuart was positively exuberant in a letter to his wife posted five days before Pender died. "I had a grand time in Penna.," he wrote her from Maryland, then inexplicably added, "& we return without *defeat* to recuperate & reinforce when no doubt the role will be reenacted." Indeed, "Beauty" was certain that another offensive north of the Potomac was in order. "We must invade again, it is the only path to peace," the cavalryman insisted. "Genl. Lee's maneuvering the Yankees out of Va is the grandest piece of strategy ever heard of."[4]

One of the haggard survivors who had served under Pender at Gettysburg was less enthusiastic about the campaign just ended. "You have heard a great deal about our trip in Pennsylvania but you have not heard half, I know," the fellow explained in a home-bound letter to Georgia. "We have been marching for more than one month, and have seen hard service I assure you. I thought we saw hard times last year but we certainly seen harder service this summer than we did last." Labeling the recent engagement at Gettysburg "the hardest Battle that we ever fought," the soldier was almost at a loss for words in describing what he had experienced. Finally, he gave up the effort and concluded, "I am sure that I shall never forget much that I have seen, heard and felt since we crossed the river."[5]

Another member of Pender's division, W. G. Thompson, was also of a very different frame of mind than Stuart as he wrote his family from Virginia at the close of the campaign. Offering a short but accurate overview of the fighting at Gettysburg, he proceeded to tell how badly his unit had been roughed up in the engagement. Now that they were safely back in Virginia and he remained in "the land of the living yet," Thompson observed, "I hope we never will cross the Potomac again for I don't believe we ever made anything by crossing it yet."[6]

Fanny Pender would have agreed far more with her perceptive North Carolina neighbor in the ranks than the musings of the bold dragoon she had met and entertained so long ago. In less than a year, "Beauty" Stuart too would be gone, mortally wounded at Yellow Tavern just north of Richmond on May 11, 1864; Jeb died the next day, leaving behind a war widow and the legacy of another life cut short tragically by the conflict that had produced so much misery for so many. Yet Fanny would derive small comfort from the knowledge that she did not suffer alone.

EPILOGUE: A "GOOD FIGHT" FINISHED AND REMEMBERED

Stephen D. Ramseur, destined to lose his own life in October 1864 at Cedar Creek, Virginia, could barely contain his emotions as he calculated the cost of the Gettysburg Campaign. "I am sad, my sweet one," he explained to his wife. "I lost some of my dearest friends in the last battle." The first he recalled was his fellow North Carolinian. "Poor Pender, so full of every noble and manly spirit. . . so brave and glorious in battle!! I can but shed tears over his fall." To an even greater extent than had Stuart, his next thoughts went to Fanny. "And his poor wife! May the God of the Fatherless and the widow sanctify this affliction to her and give her strength to bear it."

Ramseur poured his grief over the letter for others as well, not the least for "those among the humble Soldiers—heroes all." The recent campaign, so "admirably planned & admirably executed up to the fatal days at Gettysburg," had to be set down as a failure. Then in words that would have echoed his fallen comrade's sentiments entirely, Dod asserted, "But my Hearts Darling, though sad and greviously disappointed, do not dream for a moment that my confidence in the final success of our cause the complete and glorious triumph of our arms has abated one jot or one tittle." For now, Ramseur would have to "look the thing square in the face" and be "prepared to undergo dangers and hardships and trials to the end."[7] Such an expression represented the kind of spirit that Pender would have appreciated most in the dark days that lay ahead for the South as the Confederacy and the soldiers who survived to continue its fight to the end of the struggle.

A surgeon in the Light Division explained to his wife in August that the officers and men "feel the loss of General Pender in our division." His final assessment of his fallen superior reflected both the uniform praise and occasional ambivalence about Pender's personal and professional character. "He was a very superior little man," Spencer Welch observed, "though a very strict disciplinarian."[8] At about the same time, Burwell Cotton, a junior officer in the 34th North Carolina, observed simply to his brother: "I am very sorry we lost Gen. Pender. He was a great Gen. and as brave a man as ever lived."[9]

At about the same time these outpourings of grief found their way to paper, an extraordinary session of officers gathered at the headquarters of Brigadier General Scales to draft resolutions concerning Pender's loss. Generals Scales and Lane were two of the five-man committee selected for the task on behalf of the Light Division, Major Joseph Englehard, a third. The expected sentiments of "irreparable loss" to the command and profound sadness for "his military family" and Dorsey's "widow and orphans" gave way to that suffered by "the cause in which we are all engaged and for which he so freely gave his life." Pender's attributes as a soldier had been well known. He would be remembered as "brave," "obedient," "impartial," "just," "skillful," and "vigilant." But his "character as a Christian and a man" surpassed even these "military virtues" he had embodied. In addition to the expression of these sentiments, the attendees resolved to "raise a fund in the Division for the erection of a monument to Major Gen. Pender." With that determination, and a sense of obligation to the fallen leader fulfilled, the meeting came to a close, and the men returned to their duties.[10]

Pender's superiors certainly lamented his death and heaped laudatory comments on him as the occasion allowed. Twice Robert E. Lee put tribute to paper for the North Carolinian. At the end of July, the Confederate chieftain forwarded a report to Adjutant General Samuel Cooper on the Gettysburg Campaign in which he acknowledged Pender's wounding. "General Pender has since died," he noted mournfully. "This lamented officer has borne a distinguished part in every engagement of this army, and was wounded on several occasions while leading his command with conspicuous gallantry and bravery." But Lee also recognized in Pender the qualities of the whole man. "The confidence and admiration inspired by his courage and capacity as an officer were only equaled by the esteem and respect entertained by all whom he was associated for the noble qualities of his modest and unassuming character."[11]

Lee continued to feel the loss of his fighting North Carolinian into the new year, if another assessment of the Pennsylvania expedition were to serve as an indication. "The loss of Major-General Pender is severely felt by the army and the country," he observed in January 1864. Noting his service "from the beginning of the war," Lee explained that as an integral part of the Army of Northern Virginia, Pender "took a distinguished part in all its engagements." The Confederate commander emphasized his subordinate's willingness to confront the dangers of the battlefield. "Wounded on several occasions, he never left his command in action until he received the injury that resulted in his death." But as he had done earlier, Lee continued to appreciate the character of the man. "His promise and usefulness as an officer were only equaled by the purity and excellence of his private life."[12]

Likewise, A. P. Hill, Pender's friend and predecessor in command of the Light Division, also expressed his regrets in the form of a short eulogy included in his official report of the campaign made in November 1863. After describing the early phases of the fighting around Gettysburg, Hill turned to the action on July 2. "On this day also," he noted solemnly, "the Confederacy lost the invaluable services of Maj. Gen. W. D. Pender, wounded by a shell, and since dead." Hill especially lamented the passing of his young protégé. "No man fell during this bloody battle of Gettysburg more regretted than he, nor around whose youthful brow were clustered brighter rays of glory," he added, without the intention of hyperbole.[13]

Later at Petersburg, an acquaintance had occasion to ask Hill who he considered to be "the best officer *of his grade* he ever knew." The lieutenant general apparently paused to reflect on the question before offering a response, and when he did, it was concise and clear: "General Pender."[14] Hill's own death in the waning days of the war outside Petersburg prevented any further elaboration over the years that followed, but this glimpse that came late in the war was nevertheless revealing.

In November 1864 Major Joseph Engelhard generated a report on the campaign for Pender's division. That final duty gave him the opportunity to eulogize his fallen chief, and he did not neglect the chance. "Seldom has the service suffered more in the loss of one man than it did when this valuable officer fell," he concluded. "Gallant, skillful, energetic, this young commander had won a reputation surpassed only by the success and ability of his services."[15]

The life of Lee's fighting North Carolinian had indeed been snuffed out, as had a great deal of the fighting spirit with which the Army of Northern Virginia had won its laurels. A British officer captured the essence of the harsh reality that Lee's command now faced. The conduct of the Confederates had been extraordinary, as had the terrible price paid for such gallantry. The observer then listed the names of the fallen, including Pender, before concluding that the South could not continue to do as it had done thus far on too many battlefields. "Don't you see your system feeds upon itself?" he explained. "You cannot . . . fill the places of these men. Your men do wonders, but every time at a cost you cannot afford."[16] The drain in leadership and experience, not to mention in sheer manpower, particularly of young and dynamic officers like W. D. Pender, would sap the Confederacy of many of its best men throughout the ranks.

In the meantime, Lee and his intrepid army returned to Virginia to carry the fight on its journey toward Appomattox. Pender returned to North Carolina, spared of that outcome, if also denied of the chance to experience the peace that would result. He was laid to rest at Calvary Episcopal Church in Tarboro. The words that would adorn his final resting place symbolized many of the most important elements of his life: "Patriot by nature, soldier by training, Christian by faith." A complete description would have included a reference to his devotion as a husband and a father.

As the war continued, Pender's death was not entirely lost amid the ever-expanding casualty lists. One soldier who passed through the region in the spring of 1864 recorded his thoughts about his fallen comrade. "This is the home of the lamented Pender, whose life was opening with such brilliancy for himself and [his] country," South Carolinian David Logan noted of Tarboro, "but also whose youthful form now lies resting in his native soil, but mangled by the missiles of the enemy."[17]

In the wake of her husband's death, Fanny was left to fend for herself, but in doing so she demonstrated the strength of character and fortitude of spirit that Dorsey had always seen in her. After a period of formal mourning, she turned her attentions and devotion to the happier task of raising their three sons, including Stephen Lee Pender, born after the death of his father and named for Dorsey's West Point friend.[18] Congressman and kinsman Robert R. Bridgers apparently worked to help Fanny secure funds from the Confederate Treasury Department for what the government still owed her husband when he died. A receipt dated January 30, 1864, cleared the way in typically bureaucratic fashion, the form stipulating that William D. Pender, major general, C.S.A., "alleged died in Hospital July 18th 1863."[19] With this official confirmation, "Mary F. Pender the Widow of William D. Pender, deceased, late Maj. Gen., C.S. Army," obtained an allowance of $240.60 in February that covered the last eighteen days of her husband's life and service. Of this sum, $180.60 constituted his regular pay, based upon a monthly salary of $301.00 per month, and $60.00 was essentially a hazardous-duty supplement, based upon $100 per month, "Additional for Commanding in the field."[20]

In the postwar years she established a school, exhibiting an aptitude for teaching that rendered "Miss Fanny" popular with her students. She left that avocation for the position of postmistress in Tarboro.[21]

Frances Shepperd "Fanny" Pender never remarried, joining her husband in death finally in 1922. She was interred, as ought to have been expected, at his side in the Calvary Episcopal Church cemetery.[22]

One contemporary lamented that in his visit to the general's resting place in July 1886, he found "no memorial to indicate or distinguish the resting place of this gifted and resourceful soldier save heaps of cannon shot strewed over the simple mound beneath a window of the modest but tastefully conceived structure."²³ In later years veterans and friends of the Penders sought to indicate their devotion to their memories in more tangible ways. His wartime comrades, her postwar students, and some of their family members gathered in Tarboro to witness the unveiling of a monument in an elaborate ceremony carried out under the auspices of the United Daughters of the Confederacy. A dinner and a memorial address preceded the march to the graveside, where wartime flags from Pender's division received salutes and flowers garnished the burial sites. "These last," the account of the events indicated, "were placed by thirty-six of her former pupils." Two of the general's nieces supervised the unveiling, and the festivities closed with "the singing of 'Rock of Ages,' one of General Pender's favorite hymns."²⁴

Dorsey Pender continued to be remembered in other ways as well. During the Second World War, he was one of a number of North Carolinians whose names were selected for designation for a Liberty ship. A Wilmington shipbuilding firm produced the vessel as one of 126 constructed and turned over to the U.S. Maritime Commission from February 17, 1942, to August 28, 1943.²⁵ For the celebration of the Civil War Centennial almost twenty years later, North Carolina also erected a historical marker drawing attention to Pender's birthplace.²⁶

Through his service in the American Civil War, William Dorsey Pender established a solid reputation as one of Robert E. Lee's best-fighting subordinates. He served with distinction at Seven Pines and played the critical role in preventing further damage to the Confederate right flank at Fredericksburg that might have changed the outcome of that battle and as a result the reputation of its Union commander.

Yet Pender was only one of many outstanding young military officers who rose quickly in the ranks and demonstrated exceptional prowess on the battlefield. For instance, it is remarkable how closely the lives of two North Carolinians in the Confederate service paralleled each other. Pender and Stephen Dodson Ramseur both exhibited powerful ambitions that took them to the heights of command and responsibility at relatively young ages. Both were West Pointers, although Pender's earlier period at the academy allowed him to pursue a military career and experience combat before the Civil War, whereas Ramseur had not. Even so, both started their Confederate careers at the lower- to mid-level range before advancing to become general officers. Wounded on numerous occasions, the two never failed to put themselves in the thick of the fighting, as circumstances required, despite the risks to personal safety.

Both men sought status, appreciated and even craved approval from others, and sought diligently to perfect the craft they had chosen to pursue of preparing men for, and leading them into, battle. Superlatives came easily to these officers from those who observed their actions and demeanors. In the end, both Dorsey, sometimes "Dorse," and Dodson, or "Dod," died in defense of the cause they cherished, with the final comfort and equanimity they had obtained from their beliefs in the Christ they had also chosen to serve.

Pender and Ramseur shared other characteristics as well. Both sought comfort through their family connections and longed for the time when they would be able to enjoy the full experience of them. Ramseur could be found to muse about peace and a quiet life as a small planter in ways that Dorsey and Fanny Pender would have understood and appreciated when they embraced the vision of a future life at Good Spring. Ramseur's biographer characterized his subject in terms that applied as accurately to Pender: "driving ambition and intense pride," a "tough disciplinarian and drillmaster," with a "fearlessness in combat" and a desire to provide for the needs of his troops. The North Carolinian from Lincolnton exhibited other traits that mirrored his counterpart from Tarboro: "Devoutly religious, loyal to friends and devoted to family," and a love of his section and state for which he was ultimately willing to sacrifice all.[27]

In the final analysis, it would be impossible to know how Pender would have responded to the events that followed Gettysburg had he been fortunate enough to recover from his wound, as it appeared at one time that he might. From what could be known of his life, he would surely have followed the Confederacy to its end and contributed on other fields as he found the opportunity. He would have done so for Fanny and the boys and for the North Carolina he loved as dearly. He would also likely have done so because he felt he had no other viable choice. Dorsey surely would have continued to pursue both "the hope" of an earthly and a heavenly "glory" as he had done throughout his adult life, dedicated to achieving a point as close to perfection as it was possible for him to achieve. Like his friend Ramseur, Pender had come to the point in his mortal journey and martial career from which he could not realistically have departed. As the other North Carolinian had once observed to a friend in 1855, "Who knows, but that I may write my history with my sword?"[28] William Dorsey Pender could not have said it much better for himself.

NOTES

Abbreviations

Ashe-Pender, CWC	S. A. Ashe, Reminiscences, "Wm. Dorsey Pender," Folder 45, Box 71, CWC
Clark, *North Carolina Regiments*	Walter Clark, *Histories of the Several Regiments and Battalions from North Carolina in the Great War 1861–'65*, 5 vols. (Raleigh: E. M. Uzell, 1901; reprint, Wendell, N.C.: Broadfoot, 1982)
CWC	Civil War Collection, NCSA
DU	William R. Perkins Library, Duke University, Durham, N.C.
Hassler, *The General*	William Dorsey Pender, *The General to His Lady: The Civil War Letters of William Dorsey Pender to Fanny Pender*, ed. William W. Hassler (Chapel Hill: University of North Carolina Press, 1965)
NA	National Archives, Washington, D.C.
NCSA	North Carolina State Archives, Division of Archives and History, Raleigh
OR	*The War of the Rebellion: The Official Records of the Union and Confederate Armies in the War of Rebellion*
Pender-CWC	Folder 45, Box 71, Maj. Gen. William Dorsey Pender Papers, Civil War Collection, NCSA
Pender-PC	William Dorsey Pender Papers, Private Collections, NCSA
SHC-UNC	Southern Historical Collection, University of North Carolina, Chapel Hill
USMA	U.S. Military Academy Library, West Point, N.Y.
VHS	Virginia Historical Society, Richmond
WDP	William Dorsey Pender

Introduction

1. R. E. Lee to Jefferson Davis, Sept. 23, 1863, *OR*, 29(2):743.

2. Gallagher, *Lee*, 432. Early rather diplomatically explained, "There was enough glory won by the Army of Northern Virginia for each state to have its full share and be content with it, and there is no occasion to wrangle over the distribution of honors." Quoted in ibid.

3. McWhiney and Jamieson, *Attack and Die*, 15.

4. See Gallagher, *Stephen Dodson Ramseur*; and Carmichael, *Lee's Young Artillerist*; and *Last Generation*. Carmichael's young Virginians constituting the "last generation" before the Civil War demonstrated many of the character elements that Pender exhibited.

5. Carmichael, *Last Generation*, 164.

6. The statement appeared in an 1894 address by Raleigh attorney and historian William A. Montgomery, who attributed it to Confederate general G. C. Wharton, "in the shape of an extract from a letter written from Radford, Va., on September 5, 1893, to James M. Norfleet, Esq., of Tarboro." Wharton observed, "After explaining his wishes and giving the necessary orders [concerning troop dispositions] I was about leaving General Lee's headquarters, when Gen. A. P. Hill, an old friend and school-mate, rode up." He overheard the conversation that developed between the two men "in regard to the movement of the troops and the result of the recent campaign in Maryland and Pennsylvania, specially in regard to the ill-fated battle of Gettysburg." Wharton recalled that "General Lee said with sadness, 'I ought not to have fought the battle of Gettysburg; it was a mistake.' Then, after a short hesitation, he added: 'But the stakes were so great I was compelled to play; for if we had succeeded, Harrisburg, Baltimore and Washington were in our hands; and' (with emphasis) 'we would have succeeded had Pender lived.'" Quoted in Montgomery, *Life and Character of Pender*, 26. D. H. Hill related the same basic scenario and Lee's admission and assessment of Gettysburg in *North Carolina*, vol. 4 of Evans, *Confederate Military History*, 337. See also Ashe-Pender, CWC, 10.

7. Tucker, *High Tide at Gettysburg*, 389, 391–92.

8. Freeman, *Lee's Lieutenants*, 3:xxx.

9. Foote, *Civil War*, 2:520.

10. Barton, *Goodmen*, 43.

11. "In Memoriam," newspaper clipping, n.d., Blackford Family Papers, Special Collections, Alderman Library, University of Virginia, Charlottesville. Reprinted in *Tarboro (Va.) Southerner*, Sept. 19, 1863.

12. Hassler, *The General*, 261. The phrase or variations of it have been popular among students of Pender because it reflects the values the North Carolinian embraced so fully. See Samito, "'Patriot by Nature, Christian by Faith'"; and Simpson, "'Patriot by Nature, Soldier by Training, Christian by Faith.'"

Chapter One

1. This composite sketch of Pender's birth and family comes from Hassler, *The General*, 3, 265; Diket, *wha hae wi'*, 1; S. T. Pender, "Life of General Pender," Pender Papers, SHC-UNC, 1; and Williams and Griffin, *Bible Records of Early Edgecombe*, 199.

2. WDP to My dear Wife, Camp 5 miles of Richmond, Va., June 8, 1862, SHC-UNC; Hassler, *The General*, 154. Unfortunately, a rift between Fanny and David prompted the remark. Nevertheless, Hassler described David on two occasions as Dorsey's "favorite brother." Ibid., 22, 260.

3. Samito, "'Patriot by Nature, Christian by Faith,'" 167.

4. Turner and Bridgers, *Edgecombe County*, 194–95.

5. S. T. Pender, "Life of General Pender," 1.

6. WDP to My dear Wife, Camp Fisher, Va., Nov. 4, 1861, SHC-UNC; Hassler, *The General*, 93.

NOTES TO PAGES 8–13

7. WDP to My dear Wife, Camp Hill, Va., Oct. 19, 1861, Hassler, *The General*, 84.
8. Hassler, "Religious Conversion," 171.
9. WDP to My dear Wife, Oct. 19, 1861; Hassler, *The General*, 84.
10. WDP to My dear Wife, Camp Fisher, Va., Nov. 18, 1861, SHC-UNC; Hassler, *The General*, 94.
11. WDP to My precious Wife, Camp Gregg, Va., Apr. 26, 1863, SHC-UNC; Hassler, *The General*, 230–31.
12. WDP to My dear Wife, Camp near Richmond, Va., June 25, 1862, SHC-UNC; Hassler, *The General*, 158. Hassler noted that Robert's wife died on June 20, 1862.
13. Longacre, *General Pender*, 17–18.
14. S. T. Pender, "Life of General Pender," 1. In a postwar address, a North Carolina attorney and historian concurred with this assessment of the young Dorsey Pender, observing simply, "This employment was distasteful to him from the first." Montgomery, *Life and Character of Pender*, 7.
15. Quoted in Carpenter, *Sword and Olive Branch*, 6.
16. J. R. J. Daniel to G. W. Crawford, Washington, D.C., Apr. 26, 1850, M688, Roll 182, NA. Biographer A. L. Diket credited Rep. Thomas Ruffin with the appointment. Diket, *wha hae wi'*, 2.
17. WDP to Secretary of War, Tarboro, N.C., May 6, 1850, M688, Roll 182, NA.
18. The U.S. Military Academy's list of officers and cadets gave Pender's age as sixteen years, four months at the time of his admission. *Official Register* (1851), USMA, 15.
19. Shepperd was older than Pender, listed at the time of his entrance into the institution as nineteen years, two months. Ibid.
20. Morrison, *"Best School in the World,"* 64.
21. Ibid., 66–68.
22. Ambrose, *Duty, Honor, Country*, 147.
23. Montgomery, *Life and Character of Pender*, 7.
24. Green, *Recollections and Reflections*, 70.
25. Simpson, "'Patriot by Nature, Soldier by Training, Christian by Faith,'" 10.
26. Longacre, *General Pender*, 20.
27. Clark, *North Carolina Regiments*, 1:765.
28. WDP to My dear Wife, Camp near Yorktown, Va., Apr. 27, 1862, SHC-UNC; Hassler, *The General*, 139.
29. Howard, "Campaigns and Battles of Gettysburg," 345.
30. Green, *Recollections and Reflections*, 70.
31. Ambrose, *Duty, Honor, Country*, 147.
32. J. E. B. Stuart to My dear Cousin, Camp Gaines, West Point, N.Y., Aug. 17, 1850, J. E. B. Stuart Letters, VHS. Gaines was one of the three rising U.S. Army generals after the War of 1812, despite being court-martialed for unauthorized activities during the Mexican-American War. Skelton, *American Profession of Arms*, 110–11, 334; Matloff, *American Military History*, 168 (see also 159–60, 162). The next summer's cantonment was known as Camp Brady, for War of 1812 and Mexican-American War participant Maj. Gen. Hugh Brady. J. E. B. Stuart to Dear Cousin, Camp Brady West Point, N.Y., Aug 13, 1851, quoted in Stuart, "Stuart's Letters to his Hairston Kin," *North Carolina Historical Review* 51 (July 1974): 271 and notes. Brady had died tragically in 1851 when his horse became frightened, and he tumbled from the carriage in which he had been riding, Skelton, *American Profession of Arms*, 213–14. The last of these encampments for the Class of 1854 was named for the new secretary of war, Jefferson Davis, also a veteran of the war with Mexico and a product of West Point.

33. Stuart, "Stuart's Letters to his Hairston Kin," 263. Stephen Ambrose mentioned the schedule of Henry A. du Pont in the summer of 1856. It was a rigid regimen that the harried cadet termed "too much like slavery to suit me." Quoted in *Duty, Honor, Country*, 148.

34. Stuart appeared to be particularly enamored with the tradition. See, for example, J. E. B. Stuart to Dear Cousin, Camp Brady, West Point, N.Y., Aug. 13, 1851; and Stuart to My Dear Cousin, Camp Jefferson Davis, West Point, N.Y., June 29, [1853], in "Stuart's Letters to his Hairston Kin," 271, 296.

35. Morrison, *"Best School in the World,"* 70–71.

36. J. E. B. Stuart to Dear Cousin, West Point, N.Y., Mar. 6, 1851.

37. Morrison, *"Best School in the World,"* 73.

38. *Official Register* (1851), 15. The irony was that West Point had such a terrible reputation for failing to teach French with adequacy, at least for some of its graduates. Ambrose, *Duty, Honor, Country*, 142–43.

39. *Official Register* (1851), 15.

40. *Official Register* (1852), USMA, 11.

41. Morrison, *"Best School in the World,"* 74.

42. *Official Register* (1853), USMA, 9.

43. *Official Register* (1854), ibid., 15.

44. Demerits, Pender, William D., 1853–54, USMA.

45. Demerits, Shepperd, Samuel T., 1853–54, USMA; *Official Register* (1854), 7.

46. Patterson, *From Blue to Gray*, 9.

47. Circulation Record Books, Pender, 1849–55, USMA.

48. Howard, *Autobiography*, 1:48.

49. Ibid., 53–54. Stuart quoted in Skelton, *American Profession of Arms*, 349.

50. J. E. B. Stuart to Cousin George, West Point, N.Y., Apr. 13, 1853.

51. Quoted in McFeely, *Yankee Stepfather*, 31.

52. Demerits, Pender, William D., 1853–54, USMA.

53. Emory Thomas observed that even a tested veteran like Robert E. Lee commented on the severity of that season. See *Robert E. Lee*, 158.

54. Edward Hartz to Dear Father, West Point, N.Y., Apr. 10, 1854, Edward L. Hartz Papers, Library of Congress, Washington D.C.

55. Longacre, *General Pender*, 23.

56. Demerits, Pender, William D., 1853–54, USMA.

57. Utley, *Frontiersmen in Blue*, 33.

58. Morrison, *"Best School in the World,* 101.

Chapter Two

1. George Cullum listed Pender as a brevet second lieutenant of artillery upon his graduation from West Point on July 1, 1854. *Biographical Register*, 2:586.

2. Commission of 2nd Lt. William D. Pender, Jan. 10, 1855, Pender-PC; Cullum, *Biographical Register*, 2:586.

3. WDP to Sir [Col. W. G. Freeman], Fort Myers, Fla., Feb. 13, 1855, Correspondence, Letters Received, Office of the Adjutant General, 1822–60, M567, Roll 524, NA.

4. The Shepperd siblings were, in order of birth: William Henry "Willie" (b. 1830), Samuel Turner "Sam" (b. 1831), Francis E. "Frank" (b. 1834), Hamilton "Ham," (b. 1836), Mary Frances "Fanny" (b. 1840), Pamela "Pam" (b. 1844), and Jacob "Jake" (b. 1845).

5. Hassler, *The General*, 4, 265.

6. Hassler, "Religious Conversion," 177.

7. J. E. B. Stuart to Dear Cousin P——, Salem, N.C., Aug. 3, 1854, quoted in Stuart, "Stuart's Letters to his Hairston Kin," 313–14.

8. Post Returns, Fort Myers, Fla., Oct.–Nov. 1854, Jan.–Mar. 1855, Returns for U.S. Military Posts, 1800–1916, M617, Roll 827. For a brief description of Fort Myers, see Prucha, *Military Posts*, 93. Prucha did not include Fort Thompson in his compendium.

9. Quoted in Coffman, *Old Army*, 67.

10. WDP to Hon. J. C. Dobbin, Fort Myers, Fla., Apr. 14, 1855, M567, Roll 524, NA. Thomas Ruffin held various judicial positions, including chief justice of the North Carolina Supreme Court. Described as "a Jeffersonian Democrat, [and] an ardent Southerner," Ruffin "had no toleration for Northern Aggression." Quoted in McCormick, *Personnel of the Convention of 1861*, 70-71.

11. WDP to Sir [Col. S. Cooper], Fort Myers, Fla., May 18, 1855, M567, Roll 524, NA.

12. Cullum, *Biographical Register*, 2:586.

13. Jefferson Davis to 2nd Lt. William D. Pender, Washington, D.C., May 25, 1855, Pender-PC.

14. WDP to Sir [Col. S. Cooper], Fort Myers, Fla., June 21, 1855, M567, Roll 524, NA. The June returns for Fort Myers listed him under "Transferred." Post Returns, Fort Myers, Fla., June 1855, M617, Roll 827, NA.

15. Missall and Missall, *Seminole Wars*, 214–20. In Pender's portfolio George Cullum noted, "Hostilities against the Seminole Indians, 1854–1855." *Biographical Register*, 2:586.

16. George W. Cullum, Circular, Charleston, S.C., July 1, 1855, reply by Lt. J. E. B. Stuart, 1st Cavalry, ("Lt. Shepperd, died of cholera at Fort Leavenworth, K.T. June 27th 1855,") Stuart Files, 1643, USMA; McIver, "North Carolinians at West Point," 21.

17. Post Returns, Fort Leavenworth, Kans. Terr., Sept. 1855, M617, Roll 611, NA. No record for this immediate period exists for Jefferson Barracks, Mo. (see M617, Roll 547).

18. George Cullum placed Pender at Fort Thorn in 1856. *Biographical Register*, 2:586.

19. Post Returns, Fort Thorn, N.Mex. Terr., Feb. 1856, M617, Roll 1271, NA.

20. Frazer, *Forts of the West*, 104; Prucha, *Military Posts*, 112.

21. J. E. B. Stuart to Lizzie Peirce, Fort Leavenworth, Kans. Terr., June 6, 1856, Stuart Letters, VHS.

22. Utley, *Frontiersmen in Blue*, 152–54.

23. Apparently, the lesson that the army had hoped to impart did not succeed, for when the Mogollon Apaches struck again later in the year, the response proved no greater "than the usual ineffectual pursuit." By that point, Pender had transferred elsewhere and was not involved. Ibid., 154.

24. Cullum, *Biographical Register*, 2:586; Post Returns, Fort Thorn, N.Mex. Terr., Mar. 1856, M617, Roll 1271, NA.

25. Post Returns, Fort Thorn, N.Mex. Terr., May 1856, M617, Roll 1271, NA. The April returns placed Pender on detached service as previously indicated on a scouting mission.

26. Frazer, *Forts of the West*, 105; Prucha, *Military Posts*, 113. For a fuller discussion of the post and its history, see Utley, *Fort Union*.

27. Post Returns, Fort Union, N.Mex. Terr., June–Aug. 1856, M617, Roll 1305, NA.

28. Frazer, *Forts of the West*, 32; Prucha, *Military Posts*, 111.

29. Cullum, *Biographical Register*, 2:586. Correspondence put Pender at Fort Tejon in April 1857. See Special Orders No. 1, Hd. Qrs. Fort Tejon, Calif., Apr. 19, 1857, Box 12, Correspondence, Reports, Etc., Letters Received, Department of the Pacific, 1854–58, RG 393, NA.

30. "Earthquake," *Los Angeles Star*, Jan. 10, 1857; "The Earthquake," ibid., Jan. 17, 1857; "The Earthquakes," *Santa Barbara Gazette*, Jan. 15, 1857. For a detailed assessment of the damage at the post, see "From Fort Tejon," *Los Angeles Star*, Jan. 24, 1857.

31. Post Returns, Fort Tejon, Calif., Jan. 1857, M617, Roll 1257, NA.

32. "Earthquakes Again," *Santa Barbara Gazette*, Jan. 22, 1857.

33. Post Returns, Fort Tejon, Calif., Jan. 1857, M617, Roll 1257, NA.

34. "Lieut. Col. B. L. Beall," *Los Angeles Star*, Jan. 24, 1857.

35. "Arrival of U.S. Troops," ibid., Jan. 31, 1857.

36. Post Returns, Fort Tejon, Calif., Feb.–Mar. 1857, M617, Roll 1257, NA.

37. "U.S. Troops," *Los Angeles Star*, Feb. 7, 1857.

38. Post Returns, Fort Tejon, Calif., Jan.–Mar. 1857, M617, Roll 1257, NA.

39. Frazer, *Forts of the West*, 29; Prucha, *Military Posts*, 101; Schlicke, *General George Wright*, 95–96. Joseph Mansfield recorded his impressions of these sites on an inspection tour he conducted in 1853–54. See *Condition of the Western Forts*, 116, 191–92.

40. Cullum, *Biographical Register*, 2:586. Records noted that Pender transferred to Fort Reading under departmental orders dated May 4, 1857. Post Returns, Fort Tejon, Calif., May 1857, M617, Roll 1257, NA. See also Post Returns, Fort Dalles, Ore. Terr., 1857–59, ibid., Roll 285, NA; Post Returns, Fort Walla Walla, Wash. Terr., 1857–59, ibid., Roll 1343; and Post Returns, Fort Vancouver, Wash. Terr., 1857–59, ibid., Roll 1315.

41. Frazer, *Forts of the West*, 176; Prucha, *Military Posts*, 113; Mansfield, *Conditions of the Western Forts*, 114–15, 170–75.

42. Frazer, *Forts of the West*, 177; Prucha, *Military Posts*, 114.

43. Frazer, *Forts of the West*, 127–28; Prucha, *Military Posts*, 70. For a fuller description of Fort Dalles, its history, and its architecture, see Knuth, "'Picturesque' Frontier." See also Mansfield, *Condition of the Western Forts*, 116, 175–79.

44. Special Orders No. 1, Hd. Qrs. Fort Tejon, Calif., Apr. 19, 1857, Box 12, RG 393, NA.

45. J. E. B. Stuart to Miss Lizzie Peirce, Fort Riley, Kans. Terr., July 9, 1857, Stuart Letters, VHS.

46. John B. Floyd to 1st Lt. W. D. Pender, Washington, D.C., Sept. 29, 1858, Pender-PC; Cullum, *Biographical Register*, 2:586.

47. Post Returns, Fort Walla Walla, Wash. Terr., May 1858, M617, Roll 1343, NA.

48. WDP to Major [W. W. Mackall], Fort Walla Walla, Wash. Terr., July 16, 1858, RG 393, Box 12, NA; Pender to Mackall, Fort Walla Walla, Wash. Terr., Aug. 14 1858, ibid.

49. A biographical sketch of the two officers appeared in Manring, *Conquest of the Coeur D'Alenes*, 275–80.

50. Composite of the "Steptoe disaster" drawn from Dunn, *Massacres of the Mountains*, 284–88; Glassley, *Pacific Northwest Indian Wars*, 144–46; Hunt, *Indian Wars*, 19–30; Manring, *Conquest of the Coeur D'Alenes*, 67–143; and Schlicke, *General George Wright*, 144–53. Garrett Hunt cited a participant as observing that only Captain Taylor's body was able to be recovered and interred before the command left the scene, and in the effort another trooper fell to hostile fire. *Indian Wars*, 29.

51. Kip, *Army Life in the Pacific*, 23–24.

52. Keyes, *Fifty Years' Observation*, 265–66.

53. Schlicke, *General George Wright*, 155.

NOTES TO PAGES 31–36

54. Hunt, *Indian Wars*, 57–58.
55. Post Returns, Fort Walla Walla, Wash. Terr., Aug. 1858, M617, Roll 1343, NA.
56. Hunt, *Indian Wars*, 53–54, 56; Manring, *Conquest of the Coeur D'Alenes*, 182–83; Schlicke, *General George Wright*, 159–61.
57. Erasmus Keyes recalled that the command "crossed the river on the 25th and 26th days of August—the men, baggage, provisions for 40 days, and ammunition in boats, of which there was a great scarcity, and about 700 mules and horses swimming the rapid stream, with Indians alongside the leaders to keep them headed towards the opposite shore." *Fifty Years' Observation*, 267. Garrett Hunt suggested that the storm prevented a crossing "until late in the afternoon of the 26th." *Indian Wars*, 57. Carl Schlicke noted, "On the twenty-fifth the Third Artillery began crossing at 5 A.M.," and the remainder did so through "the next day." *General George Wright*, 162. B. F. Manring concurred that severe winds and rainy conditions delayed the operation until "5 o'clock in the morning of the 25th," and the effort continued the next day. *Conquest of the Coeur D'Alenes*, 184–85.
58. Kip, *Army Life in the Pacific*, 55; Keyes, *Fifty Years' Observation*, 265–89. Garrett Hunt provided a useful sketch map of the area and extensive discussion of the two major engagements. See *Indian Wars*, 61–72 (map, 62). Carl Schlicke used the work of a contemporary, Capt. John Mullan, to produce an excellent map of the region and to trace the routes taken by Steptoe in his ill-fated expedition and Wright in his subsequent one. *General George Wright*, 142–43.
59. Kip, *Army Life in the Pacific*, 57.
60. "The Late Victory of Col. Wright!," *Olympia (Wash. Terr.) Pioneer and Democrat*, Sept. 24, 1858.
61. Kip, *Army Life in the Pacific*, 57.
62. Quoted in Ruby and Brown, *Indians of the Pacific Northwest*, 162.
63. Kip, *Army Life in the Pacific*, 57.
64. Keyes, *Fifty Years' Observation*, 269.
65. Ibid.; Kip, *Army Life in the Pacific*, 57; "Late Victory of Col. Wright!"
66. Kip, *Army Life in the Pacific*, 58.
67. Burns, *Jesuits and the Indian Wars*, 293.
68. Report, Headquarters, Expedition against Northern Indians, Camp at the "Four Lakes," Wash. Terr., Sept. 2, 1858, RG393, NA. Robert I. Burns described the effort dismissively as a "lyrical effusion Wright now composed in lieu of a report," given his apparent "state of high euphoria" in the aftermath of the engagement. *Jesuits and the Indian Wars*, 293.
69. "Another Indian Fight!!" *Olympia (Wash. Terr.) Pioneer and Democrat*, Sept. 17, 1858. See also "Late Victory of Col. Wright!" (which credited the superior firepower of the U.S. forces for their lack of casualties in the engagement).
70. Keyes, *Fifty Years' Observation*, 270; Kip, *Army Life in the Pacific*, 58.
71. Kip, *Army Life in the Pacific*, 65.
72. Report, Headquarters, Expedition against Northern Indians, Camp on the Spokane River, Wash. Terr., Sept. 6, 1858,RG393.
73. "Continued Brilliant Success of the U.S. Troops under Col. Wright," *Olympia (Wash. Terr.) Pioneer and Democrat*, Oct. 8, 1858.
74. Kip, *Army Life in the Pacific*, 67.
75. Keyes, *Fifty Years' Observation*, 271–72.
76. Kip, *Army Life in the Pacific*, 66.
77. Ibid., 67; Hunt, *Indian Wars*, 70; Manring, *Conquest of the Coeur D'Alenes*, 209–12. See

also Dunn, *Massacres of the Mountains*, 302–303; Glassley, *Pacific Northwest Indian Wars*, 149; and Schlicke, *General George Wright*, 176.

78. Keyes, *Fifty Years' Observation*, 272–73.

79. Quoted in Hunt, *Indian Wars*, 77.

80. Keyes, *Fifty Years' Observation*, 274–75; Hunt, *Indian Wars*, 77, 79–80; Manring, *Conquest of the Coeur D'Alenes*, 219–24.

81. Keyes, *Fifty Years' Observation*, 279. The artillery officer long remembered the effect of the hangings on him but seemed not to have charged the matter to any darker purpose on the part of Colonel Wright other than the duty required of him to maintain peace and order.

82. Colonel Wright recorded simply, "Qualchew came to me at 9 o'clock and at 9:15 A.M. he was hung." Quoted in Hunt, *Indian Wars*, 83. Erasmus Keyes described Qualchin as "one of the most desperate murderers and villains on this coast" and insisted that the warrior "came in [to camp] on his own accord, when Wright ordered his arrest and execution." *Fifty Years' Observation*, 277–79.

Second lieutenant in the 3rd Artillery and future Confederate general Hylan Lyon considered such draconian measures far more controversial. In his recollections, Lyon labeled the capture and killing of Qualchin as "the basest piece of treachery on the part of the commander of the expedition ever charged against an intelligent American." He noted that Colonel Wright issued a challenge for "Qualshem [Qualchin], the war chief of the North Western Indians," to "come into Camp." The next day the chieftain appeared with his wife and another warrior and spoke briefly to Wright, who quietly summoned soldiers to arrest him. Although the Indian leader did not resist, the commander immediately ordered his adversary's execution. Coffman, "Memoirs of Hylan B. Lyon," 36–38.

A third account suggested that the warrior rode into the camp after having watched the departure of the troops tasked with recovering remains and the buried howitzers from Steptoe's expedition, apparently thinking that the "entire detachment of dragoons was gone." Michael Morgan, a lieutenant of artillery in 1858, recalled many years later that the "notorious Indian murderer named Qualchen" rode into camp, was taken into custody, and "was sentenced by Colonel Wright to be hanged that day, and Capt. James A. Hardie, who succeeded Capt. Keyes as officer of the day, was charged with the execution of the unpleasant duty." Quoted in Hunt, *Indian Wars*, 101.

83. Kip, *Army Life in the Pacific*, 109, 111–12.

84. "Continued Brilliant Success of the U.S. Troops."

85. G. Wright to W. W. Mackall, Headquarters Expedition against Northern Indians, Camp on the Nedwhauld (Laktoo) River, Wash. Terr., Sept. 25, 1858, M567, Roll 586, NA.

86. Utley, *Frontiersmen in Blue*, 208.

87. Kip, *Army Life in the Pacific*, 123. See also Hunt, *Indian Wars*, 88; and Manring, *Conquest of the Coeur D'Alenes*, 260. Manring noted that several years after their burial at Walla Walla, Captain Taylor and Lieutenant Gaston were reinterred at West Point. Ibid., 261.

Chapter Three

1. WDP to My darling wife, In Camp, June 19, 1860, SHC-UNC.

2. [WDP] to My dear Wife, Camp Jones, Va., Sept. 8, 1861, SHC-UNC; Hassler, *The General*, 57.

3. Burns, *Jesuits and the Indian Wars*, 308. The competition for limited opportunities to obtain leaves may account in part for Pender's subsequently expressed hostility toward Smith.

4. In his letter Pender noted that his leave of absence had "commenced Oct. 8th, 1858." WDP to Col. [S. Cooper], New York, Nov. 30, 1858, Correspondence, Letters Received, Office of the Adjutant General, 1822–60, M567, Roll 586, NA. Post Returns for October 1858 set the beginning of the leave of absence on the eleventh, and various returns showed Pender absent from the post through the subsequent winter and spring months. The June 1859 returns indicated that he reported back on June 25, 1859. Post Returns, Fort Walla Walla, Wash. Terr., Oct. 1858–June 1859, Returns from U.S. Military Posts, 1800–1916, M617, Roll 1343, NA.

5. WDP to Col. [S. Cooper], New York, Dec. 1, 1858, M567, Roll 586, NA.

6. WDP to Col. [S. Cooper], Tarboro, N.C., Feb. 1, 1859, ibid., Roll 609.

7. WDP to Col. [S. Cooper], Tarboro, N.C., Feb. 15, 1859, ibid.

8. The marriage notice read: "Married. On Thursday morning, the 3d inst., at the residence of the Hon. A. H. Shepperd, by the Rev. Mr. Haughton, Episcopal Minister at Salisbury, Lieut. William Dorsey Pender, U.S.A., a native of this county, to Miss Mary Frances, daughter of the Hon. A. H. Shepperd, of Salisbury." *Tarboro (N.C.) Southerner*, Mar. 12, 1859. Edward Longacre erroneously gave the date for the ceremony as February 3, 1859. *General Pender*, 34. In a sketch of his father, son Samuel T. Pender stated the marriage of his parents occurred on March 3, 1859. William Hassler also used March 3 in his introduction to the Pender letters. *The General*, 4–5. In a March 4 letter to Fanny, Dorsey made reference to their anniversary having occurred "yesterday." WDP to My dearest, Camp Gregg, Va., Mar. 4, 1863, SHC-UNC; Hassler, *The General*, 201.

9. Hassler, "Religious Conversion," 171.

10. W. G. Lewis to Donald Gilliam, Camp Vanderbilt, Ecusta, Transylvania Co., N.C., Oct. 21, 1893, William Gaston Lewis Papers, SHC-UNC.

11. WDP to My dear Wife, In Camp near Richmond, Va., June 22, 1862, SHC-UNC; Hassler, *The General*, 156.

12. WDP to Col. [L. Thomas], Washington, D.C., Mar. 14, 1859, M567, Roll 609, NA. Edward Longacre described Smith as "one of the Pender family slaves" and explained that she was likely meant to "attend Fanny." *General Pender*, 35. William Hassler noted that Smith was "a young Negro servant girl who attended Fanny." *The General*, 13.

13. WDP to Col. [L. Thomas], Mar. 14, 1859.

14. WDP to My dear Wife, Baltimore, Md., Apr. 3, 1861, SHC-UNC; Hassler, *The General*, 13.

15. WDP to Col. [L. Thomas], Mar. 14, 1859.

16. Hassler, *The General*, 5, appendix.

17. Post Returns, Fort Walla Walla, Wash. Terr., June, Aug.–Oct. 1859, M617, Roll 1343, NA; Cullum, *Biographical Register*, 2:586; Post Returns, Fort Vancouver, Oct. 1859, M617, Roll 1315, NA.

18. Post Returns, Fort Vancouver, Wash. Terr., Jan.–Apr. 1860, M617, Roll 1316, NA.

19. Utley, *Frontiersmen in Blue*, 115–20. After an arduous journey from the East Coast, Harney arrived in California on October 16 to learn that the Indian uprisings he had been sent to address were largely ended. Adams, *General William S. Harney*, 186–87.

20. Schlicke, *General George Wright*, 197–205; Adams, *General William S. Harney*.

21. WDP to My dear Wife, In Camp—Oregon, June 26, 1860, SHC-UNC.

22. Schlicke, *General George Wright*, 205–8.

23. WDP to My darling wife, In Camp, June 19, 1860, SHC-UNC.

24. WDP to My dear wife, Camp on Eight Mile Creek, May 15, 1860, SHC-UNC. The captain in Pender's 1860 correspondence was the Pennsylvanian and West Pointer Andrew Jackson Smith,

a future Union general who served prior to the Civil War as an officer in the 1st Dragoons from 1845 and as captain since 1847. Warner, *Generals in Blue*, 454.

25. WDP to My darling wife, June 19, 1860.
26. WDP to My dear wife, May 15, 1860.
27. WDP to My darling wife, June 19, 1860.
28. WDP, Columbia River, Oregon, May 17, 1860, SHC-UNC.
29. WDP to My dear Wife, June 26, 1860.
30. WDP to My darling wife, June 19, 1860.
31. WDP to My dear Wife, June 26, 1860. Cullum listed Pender as participating "in Oregon Hostilities, 1859–60, being engaged in a Skirmish near Harney Lake, May 24, 1860—and Skirmish near Owyhee River, June 23, 1860." It was this latter fight of which Dorsey wrote Fanny. Cullum, *Biographical Register*, 2:586.
32. WDP to My dearest wife, Indian River, Oregon, Aug. 1, 1860, SHC-UNC.
33. WDP to My dear Wife, June 26, 1860.
34. WDP to My dearest wife, Aug. 1, 1860.
35. Ibid.
36. Ibid.
37. "August 2nd," in ibid.
38. "August 3," in ibid.
39. Ibid.
40. For a discussion of prewar politics in the region, see Johannsen, *Frontier Politics*.
41. WDP to My dear Wife, June 26, 1860.
42. "August 2nd," in WDP to My dearest wife, Aug. 1, 1860.
43. WDP to My dear wife, In Camp 300 miles from Ft. Dalles, Aug. 18, 1860, SHC-UNC.
44. Ibid.
45. WDP [to Fanny], "August 23rd," SHC-UNC.
46. Post Returns, Fort Walla Walla, Wash. Terr., Sept. 1860, M617, Roll 1343, NA.
47. Ibid., Oct. 1860.
48. Cullum, *Biographical Register*, 2:586.
49. WDP to Col. [L. Thomas], San Francisco, Calif., Nov. 27, 1860, M567, Roll 630, NA.
50. Cullum, *Biographical Register*, 2:586.
51. Lincoln, "Inaugural Address," Mar. 4, 1861, *Lincoln Papers*, 4:265, 271. President Lincoln's initial language would have proven more incendiary, for he employed the term "treasonable" for "revolutionary" and offered the rhetorical "Shall it be peace, or a sword?" Ibid., 253, 261.
52. S. T. Pender, "Life of General Pender," Pender Papers, SHC-UNC, 6.
53. WDP to My dear Wife, High Point, N.C., Mar. 4, 1861, SHC-UNC; Hassler, *The General*, 9.
54. WDP to Colonel [L. Thomas], Salem, N.C., Mar. 9, 1861, Correspondence, Letters Received, Office of the Adjutant General, 1861-70, M619, Roll 45, NA.
55. WDP to Hon. Sec. of War, Tarboro, N.C., Mar. 9, 1861, ibid. George Cullum placed the resignation on March 21, 1861. *Biographical Register*, 2:586.
56. WDP to My dear Wife, Montgomery, Ala., Mar. 14, 1861, SHC-UNC; Hassler, *The General*, 9.
57. S. T. Pender, "Life of General Pender," 6.
58. Post Returns, Carlisle Barracks, Pa., Mar. 1861, M617, Roll 184, NA
59. WDP to Colonel [L. Thomas], Mar. 9, 1861.

Chapter Four

1. WDP to My dear Wife, Montgomery, Ala., Mar. 14, 1861, SHC-UNC.
2. Powell, *North Carolina*, 129.
3. Longacre, *General Pender*, 43; Gallagher, *Confederate War*, 102. Edward Longacre disputed Gallagher's assertion about the focus of Pender's loyalties.
4. Samito, "'Patriot by Nature, Christian by Faith,'" 163.
5. Longacre, *General Pender*, 43.
6. T. L. Clingman to C. G. Memminger, Asheville, N.C., Sept. 11, 1861, in Compiled Service Record, David Pender, 13th North Carolina Infantry, Compiled Service Records of Confederate Volunteers Who Served during the Civil War, North Carolina, M270, Roll 217, NA.
7. R. R. Bridgers to the Secretary of the Treasury, Raleigh, N.C., Sept. 11, 1861, in ibid. The file contains similar letters from others and a petition that endorsed David for positions in the Confederate service.
8. WDP to My dear Wife, Baltimore, Md., Apr. 3, 1861, SHC-UNC.
9. WDP to My dear Wife, Mar. 14, 1861.
10. Thomas, *Confederate Nation*, 86–87.
11. Powell, *North Carolina*, 130.
12. WDP to My dear Wife, Mar. 14, 1861; Hassler, *The General*, 9.
13. WDP to Hon. L. P. Walker, Montgomery, Ala., Mar. 14, 1861, M331, Roll 196, NA.
14. McIver, "North Carolinians at West Point," 35.
15. A. H. Shepperd to [Jefferson Davis], Good Spring, N.C., Mar. 1861, M331, Roll 196, NA; Robert R. Bridgers to Thomas Ruffin, Tarboro, N.C., Mar. 12, 1861, T. Ruffin, *Papers*, 140.
16. John W. Ellis to Sir [Jefferson Davis], Raleigh, N.C., Mar.12, 1861, M331, Roll 196, NA.
17. WDP to Gen. S. Cooper, Montgomery Ala., Mar. 19, 1861, Pender-PC.
18. WDP to My dearest wife, Montgomery, Ala., Mar. 16, 1861, SHC-UNC; Hassler, *The General*, 10.
19. WDP to My dearest wife, Mar. 16, 1861; Hassler, *The General*, 11.
20. WDP to My dearest wife, Mar. 16, 1861.
21. Ibid., 9 P.M.; Hassler, *The General*, 11.
22. Weinert, "Confederate Regular Army," 104.
23. S. Cooper to WDP, Montgomery, Ala., Mar. 21, 1861, Pender-PC.
24. L. P. Walker to Hon. L. T. Wigfall, Montgomery, Ala., Mar. 21, 1861, OR. 1:278.
25. S. Cooper to Brig. Gen. G. T. Beauregard, Montgomery, Ala., Mar. 21, 1861, ibid., 279.
26. Receipt, Baltimore Steam Packet Company to Capt. W. D. Pender, Mar. 25, 1861, Pender-PC.
27. WDP to My dearest wife, Baltimore, Md., Mar. 26, 1861, SHC-UNC; Hassler, *The General*, 12.
28. S. Cooper to Brig. Gen. G. T. Beauregard, Montgomery, Ala., Apr. 1, 1861, OR, 1:284.
29. WDP to My dear Wife, Baltimore, Md., Apr. 3, 1861, SHC-UNC; Hassler, *The General*, 13.
30. Weinert, "Confederate Regular Army," 104–5.
31. S. Cooper to Capt. Wm. D. Pender, Montgomery, Ala., Apr. 10, 1861, Pender-PC.
32. WDP to My dear Wife, On board of Norfolk Steamer, Apr. 11, 1861, SHC-UNC; Hassler, *The General*, 14.
33. Belo, *Memoirs*, 4.
34. WDP to My dear Wife, Apr. 11, 1861; Hassler, *The General*, 14.
35. Belo, *Memoirs*, 4.

36. Alfred Belo concluded his recollection of these events with the notation, "On our arrival at Norfolk next morning, we heard of the bombardment of Fort Sumter the night before." Ibid.
37. Leroy P. Walker to John W. Ellis, Montgomery, Ala., Apr. 22, 1861, Ellis, *Papers*, 2:660.
38. Longacre, *General Pender*, 49.
39. McMurry, *Two Great Rebel Armies*, 94. McMurry specifically cited Pender.
40. Voucher 21, Compiled Service Record, WDP, M331, Roll 196, NA. The voucher covered the period March 24–April 10, 1861.
41. WDP to My dear Wife, Raleigh, N.C., Apr. 26, 1861, SHC-UNC.
42. John W. Ellis to Marshall D. Craton, Raleigh, N.C., Apr. 17, 1861, Ellis, *Papers*, 2:619.
43. WDP to My dear Wife, Garysburg, N.C., May 14, 1861, SHC-UNC; Hassler, *The General*, 21.
44. WDP to My dear Wife, [Raleigh, N.C., Apr. 28, 1861], Hassler, *The General*, 16–17.
45. "The Military Encampment," *North Carolina Standard*, Apr. 27, 1861.
46. "The Encampment," ibid., May 4, 1861.
47. "Appointments by the Governor," ibid.
48. WDP to My dear Wife, Camp Fisher, Va., Nov. 3, 1861, SHC-UNC. Numerous letters addressed broader events that he had learned from printed sources, often Northern newspapers. See, for example, WDP to My precious Wife, Camp Fisher, Va., Feb. 26, 1861, SHC-UNC; Hassler, *The General*, 115; WDP to My dear Wife, In Camp near Richmond, Va., June 22, 1862, SHC-UNC; Hassler, *The General*, 157; WDP to My dear Wife, Summit Point, Va., Oct. 29, 1862, SHC-UNC; Hassler, *The General*, 187; WDP to My dear Wife, Camp Gregg, Va., Apr. 5, 1863, SHC-UNC; Hassler, *The General*, 220; and WDP to My dearest Wife, Hamilton's Crossing, Va., June 9, 1863, SHC-UNC; Hassler, *The General*, 244.
49. WDP to My dear Wife, Camp Fisher, Va., Dec. 4, 1861, SHC-UNC; Hassler, *The General*, 104.
50. WDP to My dear Wife, Camp Gregg, Va., Apr. 8, 1863, SHC-UNC; Hassler, *The General*, 220.
51. WDP to My dear Wife, Camp Gregg, Va., Apr. 23, 1863, SHC-UNC; Hassler, *The General*, 229.
52. William Hassler cited this letter as being from Pender's "new post" at "Camp Mangum on the Old Fair Grounds just outside Raleigh," dating it April 28. *The General*, 15 (quote, 16).
53. Glatthaar, *General Lee's Army*, 128.
54. WDP to My dear Wife, Raleigh, N.C., Apr. 26, 1861, SHC-UNC.
55. WDP to My dear Wife, Wilson, N.C., May 8, 1861, SHC-UNC. Hassler cited this letter erroneously as being from Raleigh, N.C., May 4, 1861. *The General*, 19 (quote, 20).
56. Hassler, *The General*, 19.
57. WDP to My dear Wife, May 8, 1861; Hassler, *The General*, 20–21. Undoubtedly, Pender meant Weldon rather than Wilson, as he wrote in his letter, for the former fit the geographical references he made in the letter and the proximity to his new camp at Garysburg "two miles off."
58. WDP to My dear Wife, Garysburg, N.C., May 14, 1861, SHC-UNC; Hassler, *The General*, 21. Pender's service record in the National Archives placed him "as Colonel commanding Camp of Instruction at Garysburg" on May 16, 1861. Compiled Service Record, WDP, 6th North Carolina Infantry, M270, Roll 165, NA.
59. WDP to My dear Wife, May 14, 1861; Hassler, *The General*, 22.
60. D. A. Montgomery to Thomas Ruffin, In Camp, Garysburg, N.C., May 14, 1861, in T. Ruffin, *Papers*, 155–56.
61. Alfred M. Scales to Thomas Ruffin, [Garysburg, N.C.], May 24, 1861, in ibid., 159.
62. WDP to My dear wife, Garysburg, N.C., May 18, 1861, SHC-UNC.
63. Ibid.; Hassler, *The General*, 23.

64. Clark, *North Carolina Regiments*, 1:653–54.

65. "Sunday, 19th," in WDP to My dear wife, May 18, 1861; Hassler, *The General*, 24. In this and all following instances, any emphasis is Pender's.

66. WDP to My dearest Wife, May 8, 1861; Hassler, *The General*, 20.

67. WDP to My dear Wife, May 14, 1861; Hassler, *The General*, 22.

68. Augustine H. Shepperd to Thomas Ruffin, Good Spring, May 26, 1862, in T. Ruffin, *Papers*, 160.

69. WDP to My dear wife, Suffolk, Va., May 30, 1861, SHC-UNC; Hassler, *The General*, 25. For a discussion of Pender in Suffolk, see Wills, *War Hits Home*, chap. 3.

70. WDP to My dear wife, May 30, 1861; Hassler, *The General*, 25.

71. WDP to My dear wife, Suffolk, Va., May 31, 1861, SHC-UNC; Hassler, *The General*, 26.

72. WDP to My dear wife, May 30, 1861; Hassler, *The General*, 26.

73. WDP to My dear wife, May 31, 1861.

74. *Richmond Daily Dispatch*, June 5, 1861.

75. WDP to My dear wife, Suffolk, Va., June 2, 1861, SHC-UNC; Hassler, *The General*, 27.

76. WDP to My dear wife, June 2, 1861; Hassler, *The General*, 26–27.

77. *Richmond Daily Dispatch*, June 3, 1861. The man to whom the articled referred, William B. Wellons, was a local Methodist minister who became famous for his fiery, pro-Confederate messages before eventually being forced out of Suffolk once Union troops arrived in the spring of 1862. Wills, *War Hits Home*, 57–58.

78. "GULIELIMAS," "Correspondence of the Standard," Suffolk, Va., July 13, 1861, *North Carolina Standard*, July 17, 1861.

79. WDP to My dear wife, Suffolk, Va., June 9, 1861, SHC-UNC; Hassler, *The General*, 31.

80. L. R. Moore to Dear Mother, Suffolk, Nansemond Cty., Va., June 15, 1861, L. Robert Moore Letters, VHS.

81. J. T. Hambrick to Dear Wife, Suffolk, Va., June 6, 1861, Hambrick and Paylor Papers, Private Collections, NCSA.

82. "North Carolina Troops in Virginia," *North Carolina Standard*, June 16, 1861.

83. Quoted in "Our Regiments at Suffolk," ibid., July 3, 1861.

84. Quoted in "Third N.C. Regiment," ibid., June 20, 1861.

85. WDP to My dear wife, June 9, 1861; Hassler, *The General*, 32.

86. J. T. Hambrick to Dear Wife, Camp Suffolk, Va., June 24, 1861, Hambrick and Paylor Papers.

87. WDP to My dear wife, May 30, 1861; Hassler, *The General*, 25.

88. Hassler, *The General*, 3–6.

89. WDP to My dear wife, June 6, 1861; Hassler, *The General*, 30.

90. "Brock," correspondent with the *Petersburg Express*, quoted in "State news," *North Carolina Standard*, June 16, 1861.

91. WDP to My dear wife, June 6, 1861; Hassler, *The General*, 30.

92. Ibid.

93. WDP to My dear wife, June 9, 1861; Hassler, *The General*, 30–31.

94. WDP to My dear wife, Suffolk, Va., June 3, 1861, SHC-UNC; Hassler, *The General*, 28.

95. WDP to My dear wife, Suffolk, Va., June 10, 1861, SHC-UNC; Hassler, *The General*, 33.

96. Hambrick to Dear Wife, June 24, 1861.

97. WDP to My dear wife, Suffolk, Va., June 12, 1861, SHC-UNC; Hassler, *The General*, 35.

98. Quoted in "Third N.C. Regiment," June 20, 1861.

99. WDP to My dear wife, June 12, 1861.

100. WDP to My dear wife, Suffolk, Va., June 18, 1861, SHC-UNC; Hassler, *The General*, 37–38.
101. Barrett, "North Carolina," 142.
102. Ellis, *Papers*, 1:c–cii.
103. WDP to My dear wife, June 18, 1861; Hassler, *The General*, 38.
104. Barrett, "North Carolina," 142.
105. Ellis, *Papers*, 1:c–cii.
106. WDP to My Sweet Sister, Camp Ruffin, Va., July 10, 1861, SHC-UNC.
107. WDP to My dear wife, Suffolk, Va., June 23, 1861, SHC-UNC; Hassler, *The General*, 39.
108. WDP to My dear wife, Suffolk, Va., June 15, 1861, SHC-UNC.
109. WDP to My dear wife, Suffolk, Va., June 26, 1861, SHC-UNC; Hassler, *The General*, 40.
110. WDP to My dear wife, June 26, 1861.
111. Fanny to My dear Husband, Good Spring, N.C. June 30, 1861, SHC-UNC; Hassler, *The General*, 42.
112. Fanny to My dear Husband, June 30, 1861; Hassler, *The General*, 43.
113. Fanny to My dear Husband, June 30, 1861; Hassler, *The General*, 43–44.

Chapter Five

1. WDP to Fanny, Suffolk, Va., July 2, 1861, SHC-UNC; Hassler, *The General*, 45.
2. WDP to My dear wife, Old Town, Va., July 5, 1861, SHC-UNC; Hassler, *The General*, 45–46.
3. Rable, *Civil Wars*, 60–61. George Rable leaves the impression of a greater transgression on Dorsey's part than a flirtation, suggesting that the colonel was "referring to his sexual needs" when he mentioned in a subsequent letter that his posting was "lonely enough to satisfy a monk." While certainly possible, a more convincing explanation for this remark is his determination after the "Read to End" letter from Fanny to avoid any further concern on her part over his desire to carry on, much less consummate, any additional flirtations with Suffolk-area belles.
4. Capt. T. M. R. Talcott to the Quartermaster at Suffolk, Day's Gap Battery, Va., July 4, 1861, Talcott Family Papers, VHS.
5. Samuel J. Hunt to Capt. T. M. R. Talcott, Suffolk, Va., July 4, 1861, ibid.
6. Samuel J. Hunt to Capt. T. M. R. Talcott, Suffolk, Va., July 6, 1861, ibid.
7. Samuel J. Hunt to Capt. T. M. R. Talcott, Suffolk, Va., July 15, 1861, ibid.
8. WDP to My dear wife, Old Town, Va., July 5, 1861, SHC-UNC.
9. WDP to My dear wife, Camp Ruffin, Va., July 9, 1861, SHC-UNC; Hassler, *The General*, 46.
10. WDP to My dear wife, July 5, 1861; Hassler, *The General*, 46.
11. WDP to My dear wife, July 9, 1861; Hassler, *The General*, 47.
12. WDP to My Sweet Sister, Camp Ruffin, Va. July 10, 1861, SHC-UNC.
13. Garnett was the first general officer on either side to die in the war. Newell, *Lee vs. McClellan*, 138–39.
14. WDP to My dear Wife, Camp Ruffin (near Smithfield), Va., July 20, 1861, SHC-UNC; Hassler, *The General*, 49.
15. WDP to My dear Wife, Suffolk, Va., June 28, 1861, SHC-UNC; Hassler, *The General*, 40.
16. WDP to My dear Wife, July 20, 1861; Hassler, *The General*, 49.
17. Richard Iobst illustrated the popularity of the fallen officer, particularly in the reaction of the crowd when Fisher's casket arrived in Raleigh. See *Bloody Sixth North Carolina Regiment*, 24.

NOTES TO PAGES 87–95

18. WDP to My dear wife, Aug. 13, 1861, SHC-UNC.
19. WDP to My dear Wife, Weldon, N.C., Aug. 16, 1861, SHC-UNC; Hassler, *The General*, 49–50.
20. Thomas Ruffin Jr. to Thomas Ruffin Sr., Camp Ruffin, Aug. 16, 1861, in T. Ruffin, *Papers*, 181.
21. WDP to My beloved Wife, Camp Jones—near Manassas, Aug. 27, 1861, SHC-UNC; Hassler, *The General*, 50.
22. WDP to His Excellency Gov. Clark, Camp Jones near Manassas, Va. Aug. 27, 1861, Clark Letterbooks and Papers, NCSA.
23. To Governor Clark, Pender noted that Lightfoot "stands very high with Gens. Johnston & Whiting" and had other qualities, but he insisted, "From some reason however I can see that he would not have been acceptable to the Regt." Ibid. See also Iobst, *Bloody Sixth North Carolina Regiment*, 29–30.
24. WDP to My dear Wife, Camp Jones, Va., Sept. 14, 1861, SHC-UNC. William Hassler noted that Lightfoot had taught at Tew's Military Academy in Hillsboro, North Carolina. *The General*, 60.
25. WDP to My beloved Wife, Aug. 27, 1861; Hassler, *The General*, 50.
26. WDP to My dear Wife, Camp Hill, Va., Oct. 21, 1861, SHC-UNC; Hassler, *The General*, 85.
27. WDP to My dear Wife, Suffolk, Va., Aug. 13, 1861.
28. WDP to My dear Wife, Aug. 27, 1861; Hassler, *The General*, 50.
29. WDP to My dear Wife, Camp Jones, Va., Aug. 30, 1861, SHC-UNC.
30. WDP to My precious Wife, Camp Jones, Va., Sept. 1, 1861, SHC-UNC; Hassler, *The General*, 53.
31. WDP to My precious Wife, Sept. 1, 1861.
32. For example, see WDP to My dear Wife, Camp Jones, Va., Sept. 5, 1861, SHC-UNC; Hassler, *The General*, 54; and WDP to My dear Wife, Camp Jones, Va., Sept. 14, 1861, SHC-UNC; Hassler, *The General*, 60.
33. WDP to My dear Wife, Sept. 5, 1861; Hassler, *The General*, 54.
34. WDP to My dear Wife, Camp Jones, Va., Sept. 22, 1861, SHC-UNC; Hassler, *The General*, 65.
35. WDP to My dear Wife, Sept. 5, 1861; Hassler, *The General*, 54.
36. WDP to My dear Wife, Camp Jones, Va., Sept. 8, 1861, SHC-UNC; Hassler, *The General*, 56–57.
37. Berry, *All That Makes a Man*, 92–93. In addition to these arguments concerning the Penders, Berry insisted that with regard to a Divine, Dorsey could not "really be expected to love another male, to surrender to Him," and that such a notion "violated something fundamental to Pender's basic being." The affection Dorsey demonstrated for a number of different males suggested that he actually could do so without compromising his feelings for Fanny or for God and that he could grasp the differences in the types of such affections available for him to express.
38. WDP to My dear Wife, Camp Jones, Va., Sept. 11, 1861, SHC-UNC; Hassler, *The General*, 58.
39. "Sept. 15th," in WDP to My dear Wife, Sept. 14, 1861; Hassler, *The General*, 62.
40. WDP to My dear Wife, Camp Hill, Va., Sept. 26, 1861, SHC-UNC; Hassler, *The General*, 67–68.
41. WDP to My precious Wife, Camp Hill, Va., Sept. 28, 1861, SHC-UNC; Hassler, *The General*, 70.
42. WDP to My dear Wife, Camp Hill, Va., Sept. 30, 1861, SHC-UNC; Hassler, *The General*, 71.
43. WDP to My dear Wife, Sept. 30, 1861; Hassler, *The General*, 72.
44. Manarin and Jordan, *North Carolina Troops* 4:269; Brinsfield et al., *Faith in the Fight*.
45. "Oct. 1st, 1861," in WDP to My dear Wife, Sept. 30, 1861; Hassler, *The General*, 72.
46. Woodworth, *While God Is Marching On*, 224–25.
47. WDP to My dear Wife, Sept. 30, 1861; Hassler, *The General*, 72.
48. "Oct. 1st, 1861," in WDP to My dear Wife, Sept. 30, 1861; Hassler, *The General*, 72.
49. "Oct. 1st, 1861," in WDP to My dear Wife, Sept. 30, 1861; Hassler, *The General*, 73.

50. WDP to My precious Wife, Camp Hill, Va., Oct. 4, 1861, SHC-UNC; Hassler, *The General*, 74.

51. WDP to My dear Wife, Camp Hill, Va., Oct. 7, 1861, SHC-UNC; Hassler, *The General*, 76–77.

52. Anonymous, *The Colonel Baptized in the Presence of His Regiment*, tract 129 (Charleston: South Carolina Tract Society, n.d.), 2. Copy in personal collection of John Bass.

53. [Magnum], "Basis of True Courage," 216–17.

54. Ibid., 217.

55. Ibid.

56. Ibid.

57. *The Colonel Baptized*, 2–3. Mangum's account suggested that he led the opening phases of the ceremony, which included hymns and prayers, as well as the sermon, "'*The inconstancy of human fortune*'; or '*The law of change*'" (emphasis his). "When the discourse was finished, the Rev. Mr. Porter took charge of the exercises and proceeded to administer the holy Rite." [Magnum], "Basis of True Courage," 217–18.

58. Inscription in *Sacra Privata: The Private Meditations, Devotions, and Prayers of the Right Rev. T. Wilson, D.D.*, copy in Religious Works Collection, Eleanor S. Brockenbrough Library, Museum of the Confederacy, Richmond, Va. Pender mentioned the work in a letter to Fanny: "Mr. Porter brought me some nice books. 'The End of the Controversial Converted.' 'Double Witness of the Church.' 'Confession of Sins' by Dr. Lewis of Brooklyn, 'Sacra Pravata' and two others, but I am sorry to say, no Prayer book. He has written in three of them, presenting to me." WDP to My dear Wife, Camp Hill, Va., Oct. 26, SHC-UNC; Hassler, *The General*, 87.

59. *The Colonel Baptized*, 1, 4.

60. Peter W. Hairston to My Dear Fanny, Camp Beverly, Oct. 11, 1861, Peter W. Hairston Correspondence, SHC-UNC.

61. WDP to My dear Wife, Camp Hill, Va., Oct. 9, 1861, SHC-UNC; Hassler, *The General*, 77.

62. WDP to My dear Wife, Oct. 9, 1861; Hassler, *The General*, 78.

63. WDP to My dear Wife, Camp Hill, Va., Oct. 11, 1861, SHC-UNC; Hassler, *The General*, 80.

64. WDP to My dear Wife, Camp Fisher, Va., Oct. 29, 1861, SHC-UNC; Hassler, *The General*, 88.

65. WDP to My dear Wife, Camp Fisher, Va., Nov. 3, 1861, SHC-UNC; Hassler, *The General*, 90. Even in religious affairs, Pender could be as blunt as he was on martial matters. He wrote the Episcopal bishop "to recommend someone for Chaplain," telling him "that the pay was poor, [there were] some hardships, and not much encouragement in the spiritual benefit to his charge manifested, but that it was a duty I thought some one ought to take upon himself." William Hassler omitted the latter phrase from the published version. WDP to My dear Wife, Camp Fisher, Va., Nov. 4, 1861, SHC-UNC; Hassler, *The General*, 92. The next chaplain listed for the regiment was Kinsey (Kensey) J. Stewart, appointed May 9, 1862. Manarin and Jordan, *North Carolina Troops*, 4:269.

66. WDP to My dear Wife, Oct. 29, 1861; Hassler, *The General*, 88.

67. WDP to My dear Wife, Nov. 3, 1861; Hassler, *The General*, 90.

68. WDP to My dear Wife, Oct. 29, 1861; Hassler, *The General*, 88. Since Pender uses the spelling "Stewart" it is unclear to whom he is referring in this instance. Hassler indicates that the commanding officer was G. H. "Maryland" Steuart, an 1848 graduate of West Point. Jeb Stuart graduated four years after Ransom in 1854 Hassler, *The General*, 88n.

69. WDP to My dear Wife, Nov. 3, 1861; Hassler, *The General*, 90–91.

70. WDP to My dear Wife, Camp Fisher, Va., Nov. 12, 1861, SHC-UNC; Hassler, *The General*, 94.

71. WDP to My dear Wife, Camp Fisher, Va., Nov. 18, 1861, SHC-UNC; Hassler, *The General*, 95–96.

72. Weitz, *More Damning than Slaughter*, 43.
73. L. O'B. Branch to Colonel [WDP], Raleigh, Oct. 2, 1861, Branch Family Papers, DU.
74. WDP to My dear Wife, Oct. 9, 1861; Hassler, *The General*, 78.
75. WDP to My dear Wife, Oct. 11, 1861; Hassler, *The General*, 79.
76. WDP to My dear Wife, Camp Hill, Va., Oct. 19, 1861, SHC-UNC; Hassler, *The General*, 83.
77. WDP to My dear Wife, Nov. 3, 1861; Hassler, *The General*, 91.
78. WDP to My dear Wife, Camp Fisher, Va., Nov. 24, 1861, SHC-UNC; Hassler, *The General*, 100.
79. Benjamin F. White to James J. Philips Jr., Camp Fisher, Va., Dec. 3, 1861, James J. Philips Papers, Private Collections, NCSA.
80. WDP to My dear Wife, Nov. 3, 1861; Hassler, *The General*, 91.
81. WDP to My dear Wife, Camp near Bunkerville, Va., Oct. 24, 1862, SHC-UNC; Hassler, *The General*, 186. The other recorded occasion took place in late September 1862, at the same time Pender was reading Harriet Beecher Stowe's novel and declaring himself in close agreement with her "on the subject of slavery." WDP to My dear Wife, Camp Branch near Martinsburg, Sept. 25, 1862, SHC-UNC; Hassler, *The General*, 177.
82. WDP to My dear Wife, Camp Fisher, Va., Nov. 22, 1861, SHC-UNC; Hassler, *The General*, 99.
83. WDP to My dear Wife, Sept. 25, 1862; Hassler, *The General*, 177–78.
84. WDP to My dear Wife, Camp Fisher, Va., Dec. 7, 1861, SHC-UNC; Hassler, *The General*, 109.
85. WDP to My dear Wife, Nov. 22, 1861; Hassler, *The General*, 99.
86. WDP to My dear Wife, Dec. 7, 1861; Hassler, *The General*, 108–9.
87. WDP to My dear Wife, Camp Fisher, Va., Mar. 4, 1862, SHC-UNC; Hassler, *The General*, 117.
88. WDP to My dear Wife, Camp Barton, Va., Mar. 11, 1862, SHC-UNC; Hassler, *The General*, 121.
89. WDP to My dear Wife, Camp Barton, Va., Mar. 21, 1862, SHC-UNC; Hassler, *The General*, 126.
90. WDP to My dear Wife, Camp near Yorktown, Va., Apr. 26, 1862, SHC-UNC; Hassler, *The General*, 137.
91. For a thorough discussion of this subject, see Wyatt-Brown, *Southern Honor*.
92. WDP to My dear Wife, Nov. 18, 1861; Hassler, *The General*, 95.
93. WDP to My dear Wife, Nov. 3, 1861; Hassler, *The General*, 91.
94. WDP to My dear wife, Camp Fisher, Va., Nov. 17, 1861, SHC-UNC.
95. WDP to My dear Wife, Camp Barton, Va., Mar. 15, 1862, SHC-UNC; Hassler, *The General*, 124.
96. WDP to My dear Wife, Nov. 18, 1861; Hassler, *The General*, 95.
97. WDP to My dear Wife, Camp Fisher, Va., Nov. 21, 1861, SHC-UNC; Hassler, *The General*, 97.
98. WDP to My dear Wife, Camp Fisher, Va., Nov. 25, 1861, SHC-UNC; Hassler, *The General*, 102.
99. WDP to My dear Wife, Nov. 21, 1861; Hassler, *The General*, 97.
100. WDP to My dear Wife, Nov. 24, 1861; Hassler, *The General*, 100.
101. WDP to My dear Wife, Nov. 24, 1861; Hassler, *The General*, 100.
102. WDP to My dear Wife, Camp Fisher, Va., Nov. 28, 1861, SHC-UNC; Hassler, *The General*, 103.
103. WDP to My dear Wife, Camp Fisher, Va., Dec. 4, 1861, SHC-UNC; Hassler, *The General*, 105–6.
104. WDP to My precious Wife, Dec. 7, 1861; Hassler, *The General*, 108.
105. WDP to My dear Wife, Nov. 22, 1861; Hassler, *The General*, 98.
106. WDP to My dear Wife, Nov. 18, 1861; Hassler, *The General*, 96.
107. WDP to My dear Wife, Camp Fisher, Va., Nov. 4, 1861, SHC-UNC; Hassler, *The General*, 93.

108. WDP to my dear Wife, Nov. 21, 1861; Hassler, *The General*, 97.
109. WDP to My dear Wife, Nov. 28, 1861; Hassler, *The General*, 103.
110. WDP to My dear Wife, Dec. 4, 1861; Hassler, *The General*, 105.
111. WDP to My dear Wife, Nov. 28, 1861; Hassler, *The General*, 103–4.
112. WDP to My dear Wife, Nov. 4, 1861; Hassler, *The General*, 92. For a brief description of the Frémont-Lincoln squabble over emancipation, see McPherson, *Battle Cry of Freedom*, 352–58.
113. WDP to My dear Wife, Camp Fisher, Va., Dec. 9, 1861, SHC-UNC; Hassler, *The General*, 110. A standard interpretation is that Wood had contemplated ideas of secession as mayor of New York City in early 1861. See, for example, McPherson, *Battle Cry of Freedom*, 247. For a fuller discussion, see Mushkat, *Fernando Wood*.
114. Mushkat, *Fernando Wood*, 119 (see also 123–24).
115. WDP to My dear Wife, Camp Fisher, Va., Dec. 11, 1861, SHC-UNC; Hassler, *The General*, 112.
116. WDP to My dear Wife, Brook Station, Va., Dec. 24, 1861, SHC-UNC; Hassler, *The General*, 113.

Chapter Six

1. Benjamin F. White to James J. Philips Jr., Camp Fisher, Va., Feb. 28, 1862, James J. Philips Papers, Private Collections, NCSA.
2. WDP to My dear Wife, Camp Fisher, Va., Feb. 21, 1862, SHC-UNC; Hassler, *The General*, 114.
3. White to Philips, Feb. 28, 1862.
4. Wiley, *Road to Appomattox*, 49–50.
5. Emory Thomas termed Roanoke Island "a classic Confederate disaster" for its illustration of deficiencies in preparation, leadership, communication, and cooperation. *Confederate Nation*, 120–23. In addition to 1,500 prisoners and thirty artillery pieces captured, the Confederates lost 23 killed and 62 wounded to the Federals' 37 killed, 214 wounded, and 13 missing. Long, *Civil War Day by Day*, 168.
6. WDP to My dear Wife, Feb. 21, 1862.
7. WDP to My precious Wife, Camp Fisher, Va., Feb. 26, 1862, SHC-UNC.
8. Ibid.; Hassler, *The General*, 115.
9. Concerning the shift in policy by the Union military toward white Southern civilians, see Grimsley, *Hard Hand of War*.
10. WDP to My precious Wife, Feb. 26, 1862; Hassler, *The General*, 115.
11. WDP to My precious Wife, Feb. 26, 1862; Hassler, *The General*, 116.
12. WDP to My precious Wife, Feb. 26, 1862; Hassler, *The General*, 116.
13. WDP to My dear Wife, Camp Fisher, Va., Mar. 4, 1862, SHC-UNC; Hassler, *The General*, 116–17.
14. WDP to My dear Wife, Camp Fisher, Va., Mar. 6, 1862, SHC-UNC; Hassler, *The General*, 118.
15. WDP to My dear Wife, Mar. 6, 1862; Hassler, *The General*, 118.
16. WDP to My dear Wife, Camp Fisher, Va., Mar. 7, 1862. SHC-UNC; Hassler, *The General*, 120.
17. Hassler, *The General*, 120–21.
18. WDP to My dear Wife, Camp Barton, Va., Mar. 11, 1862, SHC-UNC; Hassler, *The General*, 121.
19. WDP to My dear Wife, Camp Barton, Va., Mar. 13, 1862, SHC-UNC; Hassler, *The General*, 122.
20. WDP to My dear Wife, Camp Barton, Va., Mar. 18, 1862, SHC-UNC; Hassler, *The General*, 125.
21. WDP to My dear Wife, Camp Barton, Va., Apr. 3, 1862, SHC-UNC.

22. WDP to My dear Wife, Mar. 18, 1862; Hassler, *The General*, 124.
23. WDP to My dear Wife, Camp Barton, Va., Mar. 30, 1862, SHC-UNC; Hassler, *The General*, 129.
24. WDP to My dear Wife, Mar. 18, 1862; Hassler, *The General*, 124.
25. WDP to My dear Wife, Camp Barton, Va., Mar. 25, 1862, SHC-UNC; Hassler, *The General*, 129.
26. Contemporaries and historians alike have long asserted that more North Carolinians left the ranks than the troops of other Southern states, but subsequent examinations have suggested that the numbers have been exaggerated. For traditional assessments relating to North Carolina and desertion, see Bardolph, "Inconstant Rebels"; Coulter, *Confederate States of America*, 464–65; and Lonn, *Desertion during the Civil War*, 19, 24, 32, 62, 65. See also Moore, *Conscription and Conflict*; Tatum, *Disloyalty in the Confederacy*; and Yates, *The Confederacy and Zeb Vance*. For a challenging evaluation, see Reid, "Test Case."
27. WDP to My dear Wife, Mar. 18, 1862; Hassler, *The General*, 125.
28. WDP to My dear Wife, Mar. 25, 1862; Hassler, *The General*, 128. In this letter Pender also referred to sending all of the letters he had received from Fanny back to her. "You must not destroy one for I sent them to you for safekeeping." Unfortunately, with the exception of the "Read to End" Suffolk letter, this side of their correspondence (if any more of it survives) has remained unpublished.
29. WDP to My precious Wife, Apr. 3, 1862; Hassler, *The General*, 131.
30. WDP to My precious wife, Camp Barton, Va., Apr. 5, 1862, SHC-UNC.
31. WDP to My dear Wife, Camp Barton, Va., Apr. 7, 1862, SHC-UNC; Hassler, *The General*, 133. Shiloh did not turn out to be the "glorious victory" for the South that Dorsey had assumed it was initially.
32. WDP to My dear Wife, Ashland, Va., Apr. 10, 1862, SHC-UNC.
33. WDP to My dear Wife, Ashland, Va., Apr. 14, 1862, SHC-UNC.
34. Ibid.; Hassler, *The General*, 134.
35. WDP to My dear Wife, Townstate Depot, Va., Apr. 16, 1862, SHC-UNC.
36. WDP to My precious Wife, Camp near Yorktown, Va., Apr. 19, 1862, SHC-UNC; Hassler, *The General*, 135.
37. WDP to My precious Wife, Apr. 19, 1862; Hassler, *The General*, 134.
38. WDP to My dear Wife, Camp near Yorktown, Va., Apr. 22, 1862, SHC-UNC.
39. Ibid.
40. WDP to My dear Wife, Camp near Yorktown, Va., Apr. 25, 1862, SHC-UNC; Hassler, *The General*, 135.
41. WDP to My dear Wife, Camp near Yorktown, Va., Apr. 27, 1862, SHC-UNC; Hassler, *The General*, 139.
42. WDP to My dear Wife, Apr. 25, 1862; Hassler, *The General*, 135.
43. WDP to My dear Wife, Apr. 27, 1862; Hassler, *The General*, 138.
44. Kensey Johns Stewart to Right Rev. & Dear Sir, Washington D.C., Sept. 16, 1894, Cheshire Papers, NCSA.
45. WDP to My dear Wife, Apr. 27, 1862; Hassler, *The General*, 139.
46. Stewart to Right Rev. & Dear Sir, Sept. 16, 1894.
47. Long, *Civil War Day by Day*, 207.
48. McMurry, *John Bell Hood*, 38–40.
49. WDP to My dear Wife, Camp near New Kent C.H., Va., May 8, 1862, SHC-UNC; Hassler, *The General*, 140. Noted historian Douglas Southall Freeman obviously found Pender compelling,

citing oblique reports of the North Carolinian's presence at Eltham's Landing before concluding, "There was nothing to suggest [yet of] the picture of a rising professional soldier with high aptitude for combat." *Lee's Lieutenants,* 1:199.

50. W. H. C. Whiting report, Camp near New Kent Court House, Va., May 8, 1862, OR, 11(1):629–30.

51. WDP to My dear Wife, May 8, 1862; Hassler, *The General,* 140.

52. WDP to My dear Wife, May 8, 1862; Hassler, *The General,* 139–40.

53. WDP to My dear Wife, May 9, 1862, SHC-UNC; Hassler, *The General,* 140.

54. WDP to My dear Wife, May 11, 1862, SHC-UNC; Hassler, *The General,* 141.

55. WDP to My dear Wife, Camp 5 miles from Richmond, May 17, 1862, SHC-UNC; Hassler, *The General,* 143.

56. WDP to My dear Wife, Camp near Baltimore Store, Va., May 14, 1862, SHC-UNC; Hassler, *The General,* 142.

57. WDP to My dear Wife, May 17, 1862; Hassler, *The General,* 143.

58. WDP to My dear Wife, May 14, 1862; Hassler, *The General,* 142.

59. WDP to My dear Wife, Camp near Richmond, Va., May 21, 1862, SHC-UNC; Hassler, *The General,* 144.

60. Hassler, *The General,* 144–45.

61. WDP to My dear Wife, Camp near Richmond, Va., May 25, 1862, SHC-UNC; Hassler, *The General,* 147.

62. WDP to My dear Wife, May 25, 1862; Hassler, *The General,* 146. Reverend Stewart recalled assisting Pender with the arrangements for the confirmation. Stewart to Right Rev. & Dear Sir, Sept. 16, 1894.

63. WDP to My dear Wife, Camp near Richmond, Va., May 27, 1862, SHC-UNC; Hassler, *The General,* 147.

64. WDP to My dear Wife, 5 miles from Richmond, Va., May 29, 1862, SHC-UNC; Hassler, *The General,* 149.

65. WDP to My dear Wife, May 29, 1862; Hassler, *The General,* 148–49.

66. WDP to My dear Wife, May 29, 1862; Hassler, *The General,* 149.

67. Symonds, *Joseph E. Johnston,* 165, 166–68. Of the Confederate commander's performance, Symonds concluded, "Johnston had bungled a splendid opportunity," 174.

68. Newton, *Battle of Seven Pines,* 76.

69. Clark, *North Carolina Regiments,* 1:350.

70. Ibid., 351.

71. Young, "Reminiscences of Pender," Pender-CWC, 1–2.

72. Newton, *Battle of Seven Pines,*77.

73. Clark, *North Carolina Regiments,* 1:351. D. H. Hill described Pender's actions here similarly and maintained that the effort reflected a "born soldier's quickness of perception and promptitude of action." *North Carolina,* vol. 4 of Evans, *Confederate Military History,* 68.

74. Longacre, *General Pender,* 95.

75. Clark, *North Carolina Regiments,* 1:351.

76. Davis, *Jefferson Davis;* Woodworth, *Davis and Lee at War,* 5. Herman Hattaway and Richard Beringer noted "Davis's propensity to enmesh himself in mountains of minutiae." *Jefferson Davis, Confederate President,* 108.

77. Hassler, *The General*, 149. After the fighting, Davis was supposed to have observed to Pender: "Your commission as Brigadier bears date of to-day. I wish that I could give it to you upon the field." Walter Clark provided a corroborative account of Davis's expression cited above and Pender's response to Stephen D. Lee noted in the text. *North Carolina Regiments*, 1:352. A contemporary newspaper clipping added hearsay confirmation: "Promoted in the Field." The *Raleigh State Journal* reported: "We learn on good authority, that Colonel W. D. Pender, of the 6th NC Troops was promoted to the rank of Brigadier General on the field of battle, for gallant and heroic conduct in the late battle of Richmond." Henry T. Clark Scrapbook, Private Collections, NCSA. S. A. Ashe also referred to the incident through what he had heard regarding it just prior to joining the general's staff. Ashe-Pender, CWC, 1.

78. Hill, *North Carolina*, 69. D. H. Hill reversed the Davis statement: "I salute you, *General Pender*" (emphasis in original).

79. WDP to My dear Wife, 4 miles from Richmond, Va., June 6, 1862, SHC-UNC; Hassler, *The General*, 151.

80. Benjamin F. White to Dr. James J. Philips, June 6, 1862, Philips Papers, NCSA.

81. WDP to My dear wife, In Camp, June [?], 1862, SHC-UNC.

82. Robert R. Bridgers to Thomas Ruffin, Tarboro, N.C., June 2, 1862, in T. Ruffin *Papers*, 245–46.

Chapter Seven

1. Special Orders No. 126, Richmond, Va., June 2, 1862, *OR*, 11(3):571.
2. Special Orders No. 22, June 1, 1862, ibid., 569.
3. Joseph Glatthaar produced an updated study of the principal Confederate command in Virginia in 2008. See *General Lee's Army*.
4. Jefferson Davis to Robert E. Lee, Richmond, Va., June 2, 1862, *OR*, 11(3):569.
5. Special Orders No. 123, June 4, 1862, ibid., 574.
6. Ibid., 11(2):487.
7. Clark, *North Carolina Regiments*, 1:663.
8. Robertson, *A. P. Hill*, 59–61.
9. WDP to My dear Wife, 4 miles from Richmond, Va., June 6, 1862, SHC-UNC; Hassler, *The General*, 151.
10. WDP to My dear Wife, June 6, 1862; Hassler, *The General*, 152.
11. WDP to My dear Wife, June 6, 1862; Hassler, *The General*, 153.
12. Quoted in Hess, *Field Armies & Fortifications*, 110.
13. Quoted in ibid., 110–11.
14. WDP to My dear Wife, June 6, 1862; Hassler, *The General*, 152.
15. Postscript in WDP to My dear Wife, June 6, 1862.
16. WDP to My dear Wife, Camp 5 miles of Richmond, Va., June 8, 1862, SHC-UNC; Hassler, *The General*, 153.
17. WDP to My dear Wife, June 8, 1862; Hassler, *The General*, 154.
18. WDP to My dear Wife, In Camp 5 miles from Richmond, Va., June 14, 1862, SHC-UNC; Hassler, *The General*, 155.

19. WDP to My dear Wife, In Camp near Richmond, Va., June 22, 1862, SHC-UNC; Hassler, *The General*, 157.

20. WDP to My dear Wife, June 6, 1862; Hassler, *The General*, 152.

21. WDP to My dear Wife, In Camp, Va., June 20, 1862, SHC-UNC.

22. WDP to My dear Wife, June 22, 1862; Hassler, *The General*, 157.

23. WDP to My dear Wife, Camp near Richmond, Va., June 25, 1862, SHC-UNC; Hassler, *The General*, 159.

24. WDP to My dear Wife, June 22, 1862.

25. W. Hinsdale to Dear Genl., Fayetteville, [N.C.], June 24, 1862, Theophilus Hunter Holmes Papers, DU; Holmes reply in ibid. Holmes continued to press the case after his assignment to Arkansas. T. H. Holmes to General [Samuel Cooper], Little Rock, Sept. 6, 1862, ibid.

26. WDP to My dear Wife, Camp near Richmond, Va., June 25, 1862, SHC-UNC; Hassler, *The General*, 159.

27. WDP to My dear Wife, June 25, 1862; Hassler, *The General*, 158.

28. Thomas, *Robert E. Lee*, 210, 225.

29. WDP to My dear Wife, June 25, 1862; Hassler, *The General*, 158–59.

30. WDP to My dear Wife, June 25, 1862; Hassler, *The General*, 159.

31. Hess, *Field Armies & Fortifications*, 122. Earl Hess observed that while the defenses were formidable, "the works themselves were modest by later standards." Ibid., 120.

32. "Organization and Movements of the Thirty-Eighth North Carolina," Hoke Papers, SHC-UNC.

33. Ambrose P. Hill report, Feb. 28, 1863, *OR*, 11(1):835.

34. William D. Pender report, July 16, 1862, ibid., 899.

35. Clark, *North Carolina Regiments*, 2:680–81.

36. D. H. Hill, "Lee's Attacks North of the Chickahominy," in *Battles and Leaders of the Civil War*, 4 vols., ed. R. U. Johnson and C. C. Buel (1887–88; reprint, New York: Century, 1956), 2:352. See also Hill, *Bethel to Sharpsburg*, 2:106.

37. Fitz John Porter, "Hanover Court House and Gaines's Mill," in *Battles and Leaders*, 2:337.

38. Quoted in Burton, *Extraordinary Circumstances*, 74.

39. John W. Hinsdale Diary, Thursday, June 26, 1862, DU, 32.

40. Hill report, Feb. 28, 1863, *OR*, 11(2):836.

41. Clark, *North Carolina Regiments*, 1:756.

42. Burton, *Extraordinary Circumstances*, 71.

43. Clark, *North Carolina Regiments*, 1:756–57.

44. Young, "Reminiscences of Pender," Pender-CWC, 4, 5. In his study of Pender, Paul Rakes was unsparing of the general on this occasion, observing that he "mishandled his role in the assault," but that his "aggressive spirit remained unaffected by the mistake of the attack." "Military Career of Pender," 125, 126.

45. Hess, *Field Armies & Fortifications*, 122.

46. Quoted in Longacre, *Pender*, 118.

47. Hill report, Feb. 28, 1863, *OR*, 11(2):837.

48. Pender report, July 16, 1862, ibid., 900.

49. Hinsdale Diary, Friday, June 27, 1862, 41, 42.

50. WDP to My dear Wife, June 29, 1862, SHC-UNC; Hassler, *The General*, 142.

51. WDP to My dear Wife, June 29, 1862; Hassler, *The General*, 142.

NOTES TO PAGES 147–156

52. R. E. L. Krick, *Staff Officers in Gray*, 142. See also Hinsdale Diary, Friday, June 27, 1862, 41.
53. Pender report, July 16, 1862, *OR*, 11(2):900–901.
54. Ibid., 900, 901; R. E. L. Krick, *Staff Officers in Gray*, 311. Krick listed the officer as being wounded in the hand, not the head as Pender had indicated.
55. Hinsdale Diary, Monday, June 30, 1862, 55–56.
56. Ibid., Friday, June 27, 1862, 55.
57. WDP to My dear Wife, July 1, 1862, SHC-UNC; Hassler, *The General*, 161.
58. Mitchell, *Civil War Soldiers*, 78.
59. WDP to My dear Wife, July 1, 1862; Hassler, *The General*, 161.
60. R. H. Gray to My Dear Father, Camp near Richmond, Va., July 10, 1862, Gray Letter, Eleanor S. Brockenbrough Library, Museum of the Confederacy, Richmond, Va.
61. WDP to My dear Wife, July 1, 1862; Hassler, *The General*, 161. Ezra Warner described McCall as "one of the oldest West Point graduates to perform active field duty during the Civil War," noting that he was captured on June 30 at Glendale (Frayser's Farm), which may account for why Pender singled him out in the letter. *Generals in Blue*, 289.
62. Figures from Long, *Civil War Day by Day*, 235.
63. Hinsdale Diary, Wednesday, July 2, 1862, 61–62.
64. Ibid., Friday, July 4, 1862, 68–69.

Chapter Eight

1. WDP to My dear Wife, Richmond, July 29, 1862, SHC-UNC; Hassler, *The General*, 161.
2. John Pope to the Officers and Soldiers of the Army of Virginia, July 14, 1862, *OR*, 12(3):473–74. Variously viewed as "bombastic" and "insolent," Pope's supposedly inspirational speech generated ill will, particularly among supporters of George McClellan, and according to one historian, "followed him doggedly, taunting him every moment, for the rest of his life and beyond." Union general Fitz John Porter's assessment has perhaps become the most famous: "I regret to see that General Pope has not improved since his youth and has now written himself down as what the military world has long known, an ass." See Hennessy, *Return to Bull Run*, 12–13.
3. Wert, *General James Longstreet*, 153–54; Robertson, *General A. P. Hill*, 95–97.
4. Robertson, *General A. P. Hill*, 97.
5. "Organization of the Army of Northern Virginia, Hill's Light Division, Sixth Brigade," *OR*, 11(2):487.
6. "Organization of the Army of Northern Virginia, General Robert E. Lee commanding, during the Maryland Campaign," ibid., 19(1):807.
7. WDP to My dear Wife, Camp near Gordonsville, Aug. 4, 1862, SHC-UNC; Hassler, *The General*, 164.
8. Blackford, *Letters from Lee's Army*, 97.
9. Robertson, *Stonewall Jackson*, 514–15.
10. WDP to My dear Wife, Aug. 4, 1862; Hassler, *The General*, 164.
11. WDP to My dear Wife, Aug. 6, 1862, SHC-UNC; Hassler, *The General*, 165.
12. WDP to My dear Wife, Aug. 6, 1862; Hassler, *The General*, 166.
13. G. J. Huntley to Dear Friends, Camp near Gordonsville, Va., Aug. 15, 1862, in Cotton and Huntley, *The Cry Is War*, 96.

14. Ashe-Pender, CWC, 5. For a biographical sketch of Archer, see Warner, *Generals in Gray*, 11.

15. Ashe-Pender, CWC, 1–2.

16. Clark, *North Carolina Regiments*, 1:764–65.

17. Ashe-Pender, CWC, 5.

18. WDP to My dear Wife, Aug. 14, 1862, SHC-UNC; Hassler, *The General*, 167. Robertson indicated that Hill "acquired a gray stallion, which he named Champ and rode exclusively thereafter." Robertson, *General A. P. Hill*, 109.

19. Figures from Long, *Civil War Day by Day*, 249–50.

20. WDP to My dear Wife, Aug. 14, 1862; Hassler, *The General*, 168.

21. Ashe-Pender, CWC, 3–4. See also Rakes, "Military Career of Pender," 133–34. Dorsey remained silent on this matter to Fanny. Branch's death during the Sharpsburg (Antietam) Campaign prevented any necessity for a duel that might have occurred during the lull in operations.

22. Quoted in Robertson, *General A. P. Hill*, 113.

23. Ashe-Pender, CWC, 7.

24. Robertson, *General A. P. Hill*, 123.

25. Ibid., 124.

26. Ibid.

27. In addition to Robertson's coverage of the campaign as it related to Hill and Pender, for an excellent examination of the Second Manassas Campaign, see Hennessy, *Return to Bull Run*.

28. WDP to My dear Wife, Near Fairfax C.H., Sept. 2, 1862, SHC-UNC; Hassler, *The General*, 170.

29. WDP to My dear Wife, Near Frederick City, Md., Sept. 7, 1862, SHC-UNC; Hassler, *The General*, 172.

30. Clark, *North Carolina Regiments*, 2:585. The historian of the 34th North Carolina described Riddick's loss as "irreparable," noting that he "had been in the Mexican war and was a fine disciplinarian."

31. WDP to My dear Wife, Sept. 7, 1862; Hassler, *The General*, 172.

32. WDP to My dear Wife, Sept. 7, 1862; Hassler, *The General*, 172. Pender called Kearny "one of their brave Maj. Generals." WDP to My dear Wife, Sept. 2, 1862; Hassler, *The General*, 171.

33. WDP to My dear Wife, Sept. 2, 1862; Hassler, *The General*, 171.

34. WDP to My dear Wife, Sept. 7, 1862; Hassler, *The General*, 173.

35. WDP to My dear Wife, Sept. 2, 1862; Hassler, *The General*, 171.

36. Figures from Long, *Civil War Day by Day*, 258.

37. WDP to My dear Wife, Aug. 31, 1862, SHC-UNC; Hassler, *The General*, 169.

38. WDP to My dear Mr. Young, Bunker Hill, Va., Sept. 30, 1862, Robert Gourdin Papers, Woodruff Library, Emory University, Atlanta, Ga.

39. WDP to My dear Wife, Sept. 2, 1862; Hassler, *The General*, 171. Five days later he repeated the same information: "My head is well, but I am minus the hair, it having been shaved off." WDP to My dear Wife, Sept. 7, 1862; Hassler, *The General*, 173.

40. WDP to My dear Mr. Young, Sept. 30, 1862.

41. WDP to My dear Wife, Camp near Gordonsville, July 31, 1862, SHC-UNC; Hassler, *The General*, 163.

42. WDP to My dear Wife, Sept. 7, 1862; Hassler, *The General*, 172.

43. WDP to My dear Mr. Young, Sept. 30, 1862.

44. WDP to My dear Wife, Camp near Bunker Hill, Va., Oct. 24, 1862, SHC-UNC; Hassler, *The General*, 186.

45. WDP to My dear Wife, Aug. 14, 1862, SHC-UNC; Hassler, *The General*, 168.
46. WDP to My dear Wife, Near Martinsburg, Va., Sept. 22, 1862, SHC-UNC; Hassler, *The General*, 176.

Chapter Nine

1. Speculation on the strategic influence of the campaign has been rife since 1862. For contemporary historical assessments, see, for example, Gary W. Gallagher, "The Autumn of 1862: A Season of Opportunity," in *Antietam*, 3–8; Harsh, *Taken at the Flood*, 25–27; McPherson, *Crossroads of Freedom*, 93–95; Sears, *Landscape Turned Red*, 41, 166–67; and Slotkin, *Long Road to Antietam*.
2. WDP to My dear Wife, Near Frederick City, Md., Sept. 7, 1862, SHC-UNC; Hassler, *The General*, 172.
3. WDP to My dear Wife, Sept. 7, 1862; Hassler, *The General*, 173.
4. WDP to My dear Wife, Sept. 7, 1862; Hassler, *The General*, 173.
5. WDP to My dear Wife, Frederick, Md., Sept. 8, 1862, SHC-UNC; Hassler, *The General*, 174.
6. Harsh, *Taken at the Flood*, 117–19; Glatthaar, *General Lee's Army*, 166–67, 174–85, 196–97; Robert K. Krick, "The Army of Northern Virginia in September 1862: Its Circumstances, Its Opportunities, and Why It Should Not Have Been at Sharpsburg," in Gallagher, *Antietam*, 45–46.
7. R. K. Krick, "Army of Northern Virginia," 45.
8. For an overall assessment of the Army of the Potomac, see Wert, *Sword of Lincoln*.
9. W. C. Goggans to Dear Father, Camp Jackson near Martinsburg, North Virginia, Sept. 23, 1862, W. C. Goggans Letters, Hargrett Library, University of Georgia, Athens.
10. Ambrose P. Hill report, Feb. 25, 1863, *OR*, 19(1):980. J. F. J. Caldwell of Gregg's Brigade concurred, noting that "Pender gained his position with little difficulty." Caldwell, *Brigade of South Carolinians*, 71.
11. William D. Pender report, Oct. 14, 1862, *OR*, 19(1):1004, 1005. Joseph Harsh pointed out the discrepancy in rank and noted the unusual step of Pender handing over command to a voluntary aide rather than the senior regimental officer. *Sounding the Shallows*, 68.
12. A. P. Hill report, Feb. 25, 1863, *OR*, 19(1):982.
13. Robert E. Lee report, "Capture of Harper's Ferry and Operations in Maryland," [Aug. 19, 1863], ibid., 147.
14. Henry M. Binney report, Sept. 18, 1862, ibid., 538.
15. Pender report, Oct. 14, 1862, ibid., 1005.
16. Binney report, Sept. 18, 1862, ibid., 539.
17. Goggans to Dear Father, Sept. 23, 1862.
18. Frank Vandiver thus described the conditions: "Heavy morning mist blotted out the target for a while." *Mighty Stonewall*, 387. Dennis Frye employed the phrase, "Dense fog blanketed the area." "Drama between the Rivers: Harpers Ferry in the 1862 Maryland Campaign," in Gallagher, *Antietam*, 33. In either case, the elements had to clear for the artillerists to be effective, and the bombardment seemed to have waited until they could do so.
19. Vandiver, *Mighty Stonewall*, 387.
20. Goggans to Dear Father, Sept. 23, 1862.
21. Frye, "Drama between the Rivers," 33. James Robertson noted that in addition to the war materiel captured, there were "quartermaster stores too multitudinous to be inventoried,"

especially under the circumstances of an active campaign in enemy territory. Robertson, *General A. P. Hill*, 138–39.

22. Pender report, Oct. 14, 1862, *OR*, 19(1):1004.

23. A. P. Hill report, Feb. 25, 1863, ibid., 981.

24. Quoted in Diket, *wha hae wi'*, 81.

25. Owen, *In Camp and Battle*, 153–54.

26. Figures from Long, *Civil War Day by Day*, 267–68.

27. Joseph Harsh attributed the Confederate success at Shepherdstown to Stonewall Jackson, labeling the engagement "a small gem of tactical execution" and noting that "Stonewall ended any thought the Federals had of exploiting a confused Confederate army in retreat." Harsh, *Taken at the Flood*, 465. Thomas McGrath was more circumspect, contrasting the Confederate view of "an important and decisive victory" with the reality of a "reconnaissance" from which the Federals "were in the process of withdrawing upon enemy contact." He labeled A. P. Hill's rendering of the engagement "the most overblown and widely circulated account of the battle" and attributed it to a remaining bitterness toward Jackson and pride in "his division's brilliant fighting at Sharpsburg and Shepherdstown." *Shepherdstown*, 198.

28. Caldwell, *Brigade of South Carolinians*, 82.

29. McGrath, *Shepherdstown*, 117.

30. A. P. Hill report, Feb. 25, 1863, *OR*, 19(1):982. Jackson noted the same threat and the reaction to it in his report. Thomas J. Jackson report, Apr. 23, 1863, ibid., 957. James Lane couched his description of the fighting in terms that suggested he had found Pender's command "sheltered behind the hill in front of the residence near the ferry," had recognized the threatened turning movement, and had taken the decisive steps to counter it. James H. Lane report, Nov. 14, 1862, ibid., 986.

31. McGrath, *Shepherdstown*, 139, 143–44, 148–49, 168–69.

32. A. P. Hill report, Feb. 25, 1863, *OR*, 19(1):982. The historian of the 38th North Carolina employed similar language, obviously relying on Hill's report. Clark, *North Carolina Regiments*, 2:686.

33. Goggans to Dear Father, Sept. 23, 1862; Fox, *Red Clay to Richmond*, 122.

34. Jackson report, Apr. 23, 1863, *OR*, 19(1):957.

35. Pender report, Oct. 14, 1862, ibid., 1004–5.

36. A. P. Hill report, Feb. 25, 1863, ibid., 982.

37. Pender report, Oct. 14, 1862, ibid., 1005. For each of the engagements, Pender noted the following casualties: Near Warrenton Springs, August 20, 1 killed, 3 wounded; Manassas Junction, August 27, 1 killed, 3 wounded; Manassas, August 29 and 30, 12 killed, 145 wounded; Ox Hill, September 1, 12 killed, 46 wounded; Harpers Ferry, September 14 and 15, 2 killed, 20 wounded; Sharpsburg, September 17 and 18, 2 killed, 28 wounded; Sherpherdstown, September 20, 8 killed, 55 wounded.

38. WDP to My dear Wife, Near Martinsburg, Va., Sept. 22, 1862, SHC-UNC; Hassler, *The General*, 176.

39. WDP to My Dear Wife, Camp Branch near Martinsburg, Va., Sept. 25, 1862, SHC-UNC; Hassler, *The General*, 178.

40. [WDP to Fanny], Sept. 19, 1862, Hassler, *The General*, 175.

41. WDP to My dear Wife, Bunker Hill, Va., Sept. 28, 1862, SHC-UNC; Hassler, *The General*, 179.

42. WDP to My dear Wife, Sept. 28, 1862; Hassler, *The General*, 180.

43. WDP to My dear Wife, Sept. 25, 1862; Hassler, *The General*, 177.
44. WDP to My dear Wife, 5 miles from Richmond, Va., May 29, 1862, SHC-UNC; Hassler, *The General*, 149.
45. Pender report, Oct. 14, 1862, *OR*, 19(1):1005.
46. Newspaper clipping, *Raleigh State Journal*, with receipt from WDP to John Spelman, Oct. 1, 1862, Pender-PC.
47. *Richmond Daily Dispatch*, Oct. 18, 1862.
48. WDP to My dear Wife, Camp near Bunkerville, Va., Oct. 11, 1862, SHC-UNC; Hassler, *The General*, 181.
49. WDP to My dear Wife, Oct. 21, 1862, SHC-UNC; Hassler, *The General*, 183–84.
50. WDP to My dear Wife, Camp near Bunkerville, Va., Oct. 24, 1862, SHC-UNC; Hassler, *The General*, 185.
51. WDP to My dear Wife, Summit Point, Va., Oct. 29, 1862, SHC-UNC; Hassler, *The General*, 187.
52. Col. A. M. Scales to My Dear cousin Kate, Camp near Winchester, Nov. 15, 1862, Alfred M. Scales Papers, Private Collections, NCSA.
53. J. J. Archer to My dear Bob, Clark County, Va., Nov. 5, 1862, in "James J. Archer Letters," 137.
54. Scales to My Dear cousin Kate, Nov. 15, 1862.
55. WDP to My dear Wife, Richmond, Va., Nov. 22, 1862, SHC-UNC; Hassler, *The General*, 189–90.
56. W. H. C. Whiting to Gustavus W. Smith, Nov. 21, 1862, *OR*, 18:782.
57. WDP to My dear Wife, Camp near Fredericksburg, Va., Dec. 3, 1862, SHC-UNC; Hassler, *The General*, 190, 191.
58. WDP to My dear Wife, Camp near Fredericksburg, Va., Dec. 5, 1862, SHC-UNC; Hassler, *The General*, 193.
59. WDP to My dear Wife, Dec. 3, 1862; Hassler, *The General*, 191.
60. Sutherland, *Fredericksburg & Chancellorsville*, 34–37.
61. WDP to My dear Wife, Dec. 11, 1862, SHC-UNC; Hassler, *The General*, 193–94.
62. Clark, *North Carolina Regiments*, 1:664.
63. Thomas J. Jackson report, Jan. 31, 1863, *OR*, 21:633–34.
64. E. M. Law report, Dec. 19, 1862, ibid., 623–24.
65. Jackson report, Jan. 31, 1863, ibid., 634.
66. Rable, *Fredericksburg! Fredericksburg!* 508n14.
67. Ibid., 244, 248.
68. Davidson, *Diary and Letters*, 64, 67.
69. Clark, *North Carolina Regiments*, 1:665.
70. Quoted in Robert K. Krick, "Three Confederate Disasters on Oak Ridge: Failures of Brigade Leadership on the First Day at Gettysburg," in Gallagher, *First Day at Gettysburg*, 98.
71. J. J. Archer to My dear brother, Near Guinea Station, Va., Feb. 15, 1863, in "James J. Archer Letters," 144–45.
72. WDP to My dear Wife, Hamilton's Crossing, Va., June 10, 1863, SHC-UNC; Hassler, *The General*, 245.
73. Brunson, *Pee Dee Artillery*, 20.
74. Boyles quoted in R. K. Krick, *Stonewall Jackson at Cedar Mountain*, 66.
75. Caldwell, *Brigade of South Carolinians*, 143.

76. W. D. Pender report, Dec. 20, 1862, *OR,* 21:663.
77. Ibid.
78. WDP to My dear Wife, Dec. 31, 1862, SHC-UNC; Hassler, *The General,* 196.

Chapter Ten

1. For an examination of the "Mud March" and its fallout regarding the army command, see Rable, *Fredericksburg! Fredericksburg!* 410–24.
2. Robert E. Lee to Mr. President, Jan. 23, 1863, *OR,* 18:856.
3. WDP to My dearest, Feb. 21, 1863, SHC-UNC.
4. Clark, *North Carolina Regiments,* 1:666.
5. B. T. Cotton to My Dear Sister, Near Fredericksburg, Va., Feb. 25, 1863, in Cotton and Huntley, *The Cry Is War,* 131.
6. WDP to My dearest, Feb. 21, 1863.
7. Petition to Jefferson Davis from North Carolina Congressmen, Richmond, Feb. 16, 1863, M331, Roll 196, NA.
8. WDP to My dearest, Feb. 21, 1863.
9. WDP to My dearest Wife, Richmond, Feb. 25, 1863, SHC-UNC; Hassler, *The General,* 197.
10. WDP to My own Dear, Mar. 5, 1863, SHC-UNC; Hassler, *The General,* 202.
11. WDP to My dearest Wife, Camp Gregg, Va., Feb. 28, 1863, SHC-UNC; Hassler, *The General,* 198.
12. WDP to My dearest, Camp Gregg, Va., Mar. 4, 1863, SHC-UNC; Hassler, *The General,* 199.
13. WDP to My darling wife, In Camp, June 19, 1860, SHC-UNC.
14. Henry E. Young, "Reminiscences of Pender," 1907, Pender-CWC, 7.
15. WDP to My dearest, Mar. 4, 1863; Hassler, *The General,* 199.
16. WDP to My dearest, Mar. 4, 1863; Hassler, *The General,* 200, 201.
17. WDP to My own Dear, Mar. 5, 1863, SHC-UNC; Hassler, *The General,* 201–2.
18. WDP to My dear little Wife, Camp Gregg, Va., Mar. 10, 1863, SHC-UNC; Hassler, *The General,* 203, 204.
19. [T. F. Welch to Wife], Camp on Rappahannock River, Spotsylvania County, Va., Dec. 28, 1862, in Welch, *Confederate Surgeon's Letters,* 39.
20. WDP to My dearest, Mar. 4, 1863; Hassler, *The General,* 199.
21. WDP to My dear Wife, Camp Near Fredericksburg, Dec. 3, 1862, SHC-UNC; Hassler, *The General,* 192.
22. WDP to My dearest, Near Fredericksburg, Dec. 5, 1862, SHC-UNC; Hassler, *The General,* 193.
23. WDP to My dearest, Mar. 4, 1863, SHC-UNC; Hassler, *The General,* 199.
24. WDP to My dear Wife, Camp Gregg, Va., Mar. 13, 1863, SHC-UNC; Hassler, *The General,* 204, 205.
25. WDP to My dear Wife, Mar. 13, 1863; Hassler, *The General,* 205.
26. WDP to My dear Wife, Mar. 13, 1863; Hassler, *The General,* 206.
27. WDP to My own dear Wife, Camp Gregg, Va., Mar. 15, 1863, SHC-UNC; Hassler, *The General,* 206–7. This letter contained the names of several women whom Dorsey had courted. There were no dates associated with these relationships in order to be able to determine their connection to his courtship with Fanny. In trying to be honest, undoubtedly as a representation of his sincerity, Dorsey once again said too much. Likely his most problematic statement was the fol-

lowing: "Fanny indeed you may rest assured of the truth of what I have so often told you, that I never saw but two women who I would in a cool moment and in which my judgement [sic] would have allowed me to [be] married. One I never loved and the other I married, and do love with all my heart and soul." WDP to My own dear Wife, Mar. 15, 1863; Hassler, *The General*, 206.

28. WDP to My dear Wife, Camp Gregg, Va., Mar. 19, 1863, SHC-UNC; Hassler, *The General*, 208, 209.

29. WDP to My dear Wife, Camp Gregg, Va., Mar. 21, 1863, SHC-UNC; Hassler, *The General*, 210. The historian of the 22nd North Carolina noted only that the officer's "services . . . were lost to the regiment at this time." Referring to Gray, he concluded, "Always a man of delicate health, he died 16 March, 1863." Clark, *North Carolina Regiments*, 2:170.

30. WDP to My dearest Wife, Camp Gregg, Va., Mar. 26, 1863, SHC-UNC; Hassler, *The General*, 211–12.

31. WDP to My Dearest Wife, Camp Gregg, Va., Mar. 28, 1863, SHC-UNC; Hassler, *The General*, 213.

32. WDP to My dearest Wife, Camp Gregg, Va., Apr. 1, 1863, SHC-UNC; Hassler, *The General*, 216.

33. Thomas, *Confederacy as a Revolutionary Experience*, 61–62; Long, *Civil War Day by Day*, 271.

34. Emory Thomas has argued that "without conscription, the Confederacy could never have endured the campaigning season of 1862, much less the remaining years of the war; and with conscription, the Confederacy did manage to mobilize, however imperfectly, just about the entire Southern military population." *Confederate Nation*, 155. Gary Gallagher maintained, "At the least, historians should avoid portraying Confederate desertion as a linear problem of constantly increasing gravity." *Confederate War*, 32.

35. WDP to My Dearest Wife, Mar. 28, 1863; Hassler, *The General*, 213.

36. James A. Seddon to His Excellency Z. B. Vance, Richmond, Va., May 5, 1863, *OR*, 51(2):702. See also Hilderman, *They Went into the Fight Cheering!* 109–10.

37. Kean, *Inside the Confederate Government*, 55.

38. Weitz, *More Damning than Slaughter*, 141–42.

39. WDP to My dearest Wife, Apr. 1, 1863; Hassler, *The General*, 215.

40. WDP to My precious Wife, Camp Gregg, Va., Apr. 21, 1863, SHC-UNC; Hassler, *The General*, 227. Holden was the outspoken editor of the *North Carolina Standard* in Raleigh and organizer of the Conservative Party, which helped put Zebulon Vance in the statehouse in 1862. For more on these men, see Harris, *William Woods Holden;* and Glenn Tucker, *Zeb Vance: Champion of Personal Freedom* (Indianapolis: Bobbs-Merrill, 1966). See also Barrett, *Civil War in North Carolina;* and "North Carolina," 148–49.

41. WDP to My dearest Wife, Camp Gregg, Va., Apr. 3, 1863, SHC-UNC; Hassler, *The General*, 218.

42. WDP to My dearest Wife, Apr. 1, 1863; Hassler, *The General*, 215.

43. Thomas, *Robert E. Lee*, 278.

44. WDP to My dearest Wife, Apr. 3, 1863; Hassler, *The General*, 217.

45. WDP to My precious Wife, Apr. 21, 1863; Hassler, *The General*, 227–28.

46. Emory Thomas noted, "Whatever the precise diagnosis, the illness in March 1863 signaled the onset of cardiovascular problems that would become more serious and eventually provoke a stroke, the complications of which proved fatal [after the war]." *Robert E. Lee*, 278–79.

47. See Thomas, "Richmond Bread Riot," 41–44; *Confederate Nation*, 203–5; and *The Confederate State of Richmond: A Biography of the Capital* (Austin: University of Texas Press, 1971), 119–20.

48. WDP to My dear Wife, Camp Gregg, Va., Apr. 5, 1863, SHC-UNC; Hassler, *The General*, 219.

49. The looters apparently took jewelry and clothing in addition to food items. Thomas, *Confederate Nation*, 203.

50. For examinations of Longstreet's expedition to the region, see Wills, *War Hits Home;* and Cormier, *Siege of Suffolk*.

51. WDP to My dear wife, Camp Gregg, Va., Apr. 11, 1863, SHC-UNC; Hassler, *The General*, 223.

52. WDP to My dear wife, Camp Gregg, Va., Apr. 19, 1863, SHC-UNC; Hassler, *The General*, 225.

53. WDP to My dear Wife, Apr. 11, 1863; Hassler, *The General*, 222–23.

54. [F. M. Parker] to My dear Wife, Headquarters 30th Regt. N.C.T., Apr. 19, 1863, in Parker, *To Drive the Enemy from Southern Soil*, 238.

55. WDP to My dear wife, Apr. 21, 1863; Hassler, *The General*, 227.

56. WDP to My dear wife, Apr. 21, 1863; Hassler, *The General*, 228.

57. Grimsley, *Hard Hand of War;* Slotkin, *Long Road to Antietam*.

58. WDP to My dear Wife, Apr. 19, 1863; Hassler, *The General*, 226.

59. WDP to My dear wife, Camp Gregg, Va., Apr. 28, 1863, SHC-UNC; Hassler, *The General*, 232.

60. WDP to My dear Wife, Camp Gregg, Va., Apr. 8, 1863, SHC-UNC; Hassler, *The General*, 221.

61. WDP to My dear Wife, Apr. 11, 1863; Hassler, *The General*, 222.

62. WDP to My dear Wife, Camp Gregg, Va., Apr. 23, 1863, SHC-UNC; Hassler, *The General*, 218–19.

63. Jefferson Davis to R. E. Lee, Richmond, Va., May 26, 1863, *OR*, 51(2):716.

64. Robert K. Krick, "Chancellorsville Campaign: April–May 1863," in Kennedy, *Civil War Battlefield Guide*, 197.

65. James H. Lane to Mr. Chas. E. Jones, Auburn, Ala., Oct. 26, 1898, James H. Lane Letter, Hargrett Library, University of Georgia, Athens.

66. Ibid.

67. Robertson, *Stonewall Jackson*, 728–31.

68. Ibid., 733–34. William Hassler provided a slight variation of Pender's remarks: "Ah, General, I am sorry to see you have been wounded. The lines here are so much broken that I fear we will have to fall back." *The General*, 234. These were the same words found in Vandiver, *Mighty Stonewall*, 481–82. Ernest B. Furgurson offered a third variation: "Ah, General, I hope you are not seriously hurt. I will have to retire my troops to re-form them, they are so much broken by this fire." *Chancellorsville, 1863*, 205–6. Jackson's reply was the same, except as quoted by Stephen Sears: "General Pender, you *must* keep your men together, and hold your ground." *Chancellorsville*, 297. R. L. Dabney had the stricken general reply in the same manner (including the emphasis) after Pender had informed him, "My men are thrown into such confusion by this fire, that I fear I shall not be able to hold my ground." *Life and Campaigns of Lieut.-Gen. Thomas J. Jackson*, 690.

69. Clark, *North Carolina Regiments*, 1:667–68.

70. Robertson, *General A. P. Hill*, 189–90; Thomas, *Bold Dragoon*, 210.

71. Clark, *North Carolina Regiments*, 1:668–69.

72. Sears, *Chancellorsville*, 320–23.

73. WDP to My dear Wife, Camp Gregg, Va., May 7, 1863, SHC-UNC; Hassler, *The General*, 135.

74. Clark, *North Carolina Regiments*, 1:669–70, 2:171. Colonel Scales was one of the men compelled to leave the field with wounds as a result of these vicious morning assaults.

75. D. M. McIntire, "Headqrs. Pender's Brigade," Camp Gregg, Va., May 17, 1863, in *Wilmington Daily Journal*, May 26, 1863.

76. Clark, *North Carolina Regiments*, 1:697.

77. Quoted in Freeman, *Lee's Lieutenants*, 2:698 (emphasis in original).

78. Long, *Civil War Day by Day*, 347.
79. WDP to My dear Wife, May 7, 1863; Hassler, *The General*, 135.
80. Robertson, "Reminiscences," 15.
81. McIntire, May 17, 1863, in *Wilmington Daily Journal*, May 26, 1863.
82. Quoted in Furgurson, *Chancellorsville, 1863*, 317–18. Stephen Sears offers a slight variation: "This is the way that you young men are always doing. You have again let these people get away. I can only tell you what to do, and if you do not do it it will not be done." Sears, *Chancellorsville*, 430.
83. Jedediah Hotchkiss, *Virginia*, vol. 3 of Evans, *Confederate Military History*, 392. See also Stackpole, *Chancellorsville*, 353. The quotation varies slightly in Sutherland, *Fredericksburg & Chancellorsville*, 179.
84. WDP to My dear wife, Chancellorsville, May 5, 1863, SHC-UNC.
85. WDP to My dear Wife, May 7, 1863; Hassler, *The General*, 235.
86. McIntire, May 17, 1863, in *Wilmington Daily Journal*, May 26, 1863.
87. W. D. Pender report, May 14, 1863, *OR*, 25(1):936.
88. WDP to My dear Wife, May 7, 1863; Hassler, *The General*, 235.
89. Ibid.
90. For example, in his May 7 letter to Fanny, Dorsey stated: "We have had a terrible time of it. . . . We had the most terrible battle of the war." WDP to My dear Wife, May 7, 1863.
91. Pender report, May 14, 1863, *OR*, 25(1):936–37. Pender made the same reference to Fanny. See WDP to My dear Wife, May 7, 1863; Hassler, *The General*, 235.
92. Glatthaar, *General Lee's Army*, 198.
93. Ibid., 936.
94. "Pender's Brigade after the Fight," *[New Bern] Daily Progress*, May 29, 1863. Similar figures appeared in McIntire, May 17, 1863, in *Wilmington Daily Journal*, May 26, 1863.
95. WDP to My dearest Wife, Camp Gregg, Va., May 9, 1863, SHC-UNC; Hassler, *The General*, 236.
96. WDP to My dear Wife, May 7, 1863; Hassler, *The General*, 235
97. WDP to My dear wife, Camp Gregg, Va., May 22, 1863, SHC-UNC. Stuart biographer Emory Thomas suggested that while the cavalryman indeed desired promotion, he may have been of "a divided mind on the matter" in this case, as such an elevation in rank and responsibility would likely take him away from the cavalry. *Bold Dragoon*, 214–15.

Chapter Eleven

1. Quoted in Freeman, *Lee's Lieutenants*, 2:714.
2. WDP to My dear Wife, Camp Gregg, Va., Apr. 8, 1863, SHC-UNC; Hassler, *The General*, 221.
3. WDP to My dear Wife, Camp Gregg, Va., Apr. 19, 1863, SHC-UNC; Hassler, *The General*, 226.
4. WDP to My dearest Wife, Camp Gregg, Va., Apr. 17, 1863, SHC-UNC; Hassler, *The General*, 224.
5. WDP to My dear Wife, Camp Gregg, Va., May 18, 1863, SHC-UNC; Hassler, *The General*, 238.
6. Quoted in Clark, *North Carolina Regiments*, 2:690–91.
7. WDP to My dear Wife, Camp Gregg, Va., May 14, 1863, SHC-UNC; Hassler, *The General*, 237.
8. Stephen Sears noted that Brigadier General Hays got "swept up" by the 13th North Carolina, with his name appearing subsequently and prominently among the captured Union officers in a Richmond newspaper, which undoubtedly delighted Pender. *Chancellorsville*, 323.
9. WDP to My dear Wife, Camp Gregg, Va., May 23, 1863, SHC-UNC; Hassler, *The General*, 239.
10. WDP to My dear Wife, May 23, 1863; Hassler, *The General*, 239.

11. WDP to My dear Wife, Camp Gregg, Va., May 7, 1863, SHC-UNC; Hassler, *The General*, 236. Pender expressed skepticism concerning reports on Chancellorsville from the "Yankee papers" as well. See WDP to My dear Wife, May 14, 1863; Hassler, *The General*, 237.

12. WDP to My dear Wife, May 23, 1863; Hassler, *The General*, 239.

13. WDP to My dearest Wife, Camp Gregg, Va., May 27, 1863, SHC-UNC; Hassler, *The General*, 240.

14. Thomas to Dear Pa, Camp 3d N.C. Regt. near Hamilton's Crossing, Va., June 2, 1863, in Wood, *Doctor to the Front*, 87.

15. Quoted in Freeman, *Lee's Lieutenants*, 2:698 (emphasis in original).

16. A. P. Hill to Gen. R. E. Lee, Camp Gregg, Va., June 3, 1863, M331, Roll 196, NA.

17. Quoted in Hassler, *The General*, 241.

18. Taylor extract, Norfolk, Va., Jan. 31, 1907, in Young, "Reminiscences of Pender," Pender-CWC, 7.

19. Freeman, *Lee's Lieutenants* 2:699.

20. Excerpt, Hanover Junction, Va. June 4, 186, Folder 203, Box 71, Collett Leventhorpe Papers, CWC. Interestingly, the most recent authors of a biography of Leventhorpe did not discuss this matter. See Cole and Foley, *Collett Leventhorpe*.

21. Hassler, *The General*, 242.

22. Freeman, *Lee's Lieutenants* 2:700.

23. WDP to My dear Wife, Hamilton's Crossing, Va., June 7, 1863, SHC-UNC; Hassler, *The General*, 242.

24. Thomas Cotton to My Dear Sister, Near Fredericksburg, Va., June 8, 1863, in Cotton and Huntley, *The Cry Is War*, 145.

25. WDP to My dearest Wife, Hamilton's Crossing, Va., June 9, 1863, SHC-UNC; Hassler, *The General*, 243.

26. WDP to My dearest Wife, June 9, 1863, Hassler, *The General*, 244.

27. WDP to My dear wife, Hamilton's Crossing, Va., June 10, 1863, SHC-UNC; Hassler, *The General*, 244.

28. Belo, *Memoirs*, 16–17. For the full context of this unusual chapter of Longstreet's 1863 Suffolk Campaign, see Wills, *War Hits Home*.

29. WDP to My dear Wife, Hamilton's Crossing, Va., June 12, 1863, SHC-UNC; Hassler, *The General*, 246.

30. WDP to My dear Wife, Hamilton's Crossing, Va., June 15, 1863, SHC-UNC; Hassler, *The General*, 247.

31. WDP to My dear Wife, June 15, 1863; Hassler, *The General*, 247–48.

32. WDP to My dear Wife, Stephensburg, Va., June 17, 1863, SHC-UNC; Hassler, *The General*, 248–49.

33. WDP to My dear Wife, June 21, 1863, SHC-UNC; Hassler, *The General*, 249, 250.

34. WDP to My dear Wife, Camp near Berryville, Va., June 23, 1863, SHC-UNC; Hassler, *The General*, 251.

35. F. M. Parker to My dear Wife, Bivouac near Green Castle, Pa., June 23, 1863, in Parker, *To Drive the Enemy from Southern Soil*, 288.

36. G. J. Huntley to Dear Friends, Camp within 10 miles of Winchester, Va., June 23, 1863, in Cotton and Huntley, *The Cry Is War*, 114.

37. WDP to My dearest Wife, Shepherdstown, June 24, 1863, SHC-UNC; Hassler, *The General*, 252.

38. Dod to My Heart's Darling, Green Castle, Pa., June 23, 1863, Stephen Dodson Ramseur Papers, SHC-UNC.

39. G. J. Huntley to Dear Friends, June 25, 1863, in Cotton and Huntley, *The Cry Is War*, 115.
40. WDP to My dearest Wife, Fayetteville, Pa., June 28, 1863, SHC-UNC; Hassler, *The General*, 253.
41. WDP to My dear Wife, June 28, 1863; Hassler, *The General*, 254.
42. General Orders No. 72, June 21, 1863, *OR*, 27(3):912–13.
43. Lee to Davis, Opposite Williamsport, June 25, 1863, ibid., 930.
44. General Orders No. 73, Chambersburg, Pa., June 27, 1863, ibid., 942–43. The location of this directive was ironic given the town's fate as a result of a Confederate expedition under Jubal Early at the end of July 1864.
45. WDP to My dearest Wife, June 28, 1863; Hassler, *The General*, 254–55.
46. Belo, *Memoirs*, 19.
47. Steven Woodworth notes, "In one respect, however, the Confederate army in Pennsylvania was a scourge far worse than any troops who ever marched behind William Tecumseh Sherman, and that was in kidnapping free citizens and carrying them off into slavery." *Beneath a Northern Sky*, 27.
48. John McLeod Turner to Emilie, June 28, 1863, quoted in Mitchell, *Civil War Soldiers*, 237.
49. Woodworth, *Beneath a Northern Sky*, 27. Woodworth also termed Lee's order "a matter of propaganda" that has helped foster a "myth of Confederate restraint in Pennsylvania that lives on to this day."
50. Robert K. Krick, "Three Confederate Disasters on Oak Ridge: Failures of Brigade Leadership on the First Day at Gettysburg," in Gallagher, *First Day at Gettysburg*, 98.
51. Sword, "Personal Battle Weapons," 10.
52. Wert, *Brotherhood of Valor*, 100–101, 262–63.
53. Quoted in Miller, "Perrin's Brigade," 27.
54. Robertson, *General A. P. Hill*, 212–13.
55. Quoted in Miller, "Perrin's Brigade," 31.
56. Ibid.; Sword, "Personal Battle Weapons," 12.
57. Miller, "Perrin's Brigade," 31; Caldwell, *Brigade of South Carolinians*, 140.
58. Sears, *Gettysburg*, 217–21, 222–23.
59. Clark, *North Carolina Regiments*, 2:692.
60. Tucker, *High Tide at Gettysburg*, 283; Sears, *Gettysburg*, 333.
61. W. H. Lucas to J. B. Neathery, Middleton, N.C., Dec. 9, 1887, John B. Neathery Papers, Private Collections, NCSA.
62. Hassler, *The General*, 259–60.
63. W. G. Thompson to Dear Mother and Sister, Bunkershill, Va., July 20, 1863, Robert L. Brake Collection, Box 8, U.S. Army History Institute, Carlisle, Pa.
64. Ibid.
65. Brown, *Retreat from Gettysburg*, 51.
66. E. Ruffin, *Diary*, 3:86.
67. Montgomery, *Life and Character of Pender*, 27.
68. Purifoy, "Night of Horror," 96.
69. Quoted in Fox, *Red Clay to Richmond*, 191.
70. Hassler, *The General*, 260–61.
71. Lee, *Civil War Journal*, 259.
72. "In Memorium," *Tarboro (N.C.) Southerner*, Sept. 19, 1863. The author of the this piece, who was present with Pender during this period, suggested that after Dorsey offered his assurances for the fate of his soul and his love of his family, another "ten days of his life" transpired before his death. A question has remained as to the sequence and timing of Pender's last expressions.

73. S. T. Pender, "Life of General Pender," William Dorsey Pender Papers, SHC-UNC; Hassler, *The General*, 261–62.

Epilogue

1. *Richmond Daily Dispatch*, July 20, 1863; *Daily Richmond Enquirer*, July 20, 1863.
2. *Richmond Daily Dispatch*, July 20, 1863.
3. J. E. B. Stuart to My Darling, Hd. Qrs. near Culpeper, July 25, 1863, J. E. B. Stuart Letters, VHS.
4. J. E. B. Stuart to My Dearest wife, Near Hagerstown, Md., July 13, 1863, ibid.
5. Quoted in Fox, *Red Clay to Richmond*, 192.
6. W. G. Thompson to Dear Mother and Sister, Bunkershill, Va., July 20, 1863, Robert L. Brake Collection, Box 8, U.S. Army History Institute, Carlisle, Pa.
7. S. D. Ramseur to [Ellen], In Camp near Orange C.H., Aug. 3, 1863, Stephen Dodson Ramseur Papers, SHC-UNC.
8. Spencer Welch to Wife, Camp near Orange Court House, Va., Aug. 2, 1863, in Welch, *Confederate Surgeon's Letters*, 72.
9. B. T. Cotton to Dear Bro., Near Orange C.H., Va., Aug. 8, 1863, in Cotton and Huntley, *The Cry Is War*, 152.
10. "Proceedings of a Meeting of the Officers of Major Gen. W. D. Pender's Light Division, Held at the Head Quarters of Brig. Gen. A. M. Scales, 15th August, 1863," *Tarboro (N.C.) Southerner*, Aug. 28, 1863.
11. R. E. Lee to S. Cooper, Headquarters Army of Northern Virginia, July 31, 1863, *OR*, 27(2):310.
12. R. E. Lee to S. Cooper, Headquarters Army of Northern Virginia, Jan. [?], 1864, ibid., 325.
13. A. P. Hill report, Nov. [?], 1863, ibid., 608.
14. Comment in "Gen. Lee's Tribute to Gen. Pender," 137.
15. Joseph A. Englehard report, Nov. 3, 1863, *OR*, 27(2):658.
16. McCrady, "Address before the Virginia Division," 211.
17. Logan, *"Rising Star of Promise,"* 146–47.
18. Stephen Lee Pender was born in 1863. Hassler, *The General*, 262.
19. Treasury Department receipt, Jan. 30, 1864, Compiled Service Record, William Dorsey Pender, M331, Roll 196, NA.
20. Payment receipt, Treasury Department, Second Auditor's Office, Feb. 11, 1864, Controller's Office, Feb. 18, 1864, ibid.
21. Hassler, "Religious Conversion of General W. Dorsey Pender," 177–78.
22. Hassler, *The General*, 261–62.
23. Shepherd, "Gallant Sons of North Carolina," 413.
24. U.D.C. Notes, 232.
25. Historical Notes, *North Carolina Historical Review* 21 (Jan. 1944): 88.
26. Historical Notes, *North Carolina Historical Review* 37 (Jan. 1960): 132. The text on the marker reads: "(20) F-34 in Wilson County for the birthplace of General W. D. Pender, Confederate Major-General who was mortally wounded at the Battle of Gettysburg in 1863."
27. Gallagher, *Stephen Dodson Ramseur*, 170–71.
28. Ibid., 12.

BIBLIOGRAPHY

Primary Sources

Manuscripts

Eleanor S. Brockenbrough Library, Museum of the Confederacy, Richmond, Va.
　Religious Works Collection.
　Robert H. Gray Letter.

Hargrett Library, University of Georgia, Athens.
　Goggans, W. C. Letters.
　Lane, James H. Letter.

Library of Congress, Washington, D.C.
　Hartz, Edward L. Papers.

National Archives, Washington, D.C.
　M270, Compiled Service Records of Confederate Volunteers Who Served during the Civil War, North Carolina.
　M331, Correspondence, Reports, Etc., General Staff Officers, CSA.
　M567, Correspondence, Letters Received, Office of the Adjutant General, 1822–60.
　M617, Returns from U.S. Military Posts, 1800–1916.
　M619, Correspondence, Letters Received, Office of the Adjutant General, 1861–70.
　M688, Cadet Files, USMA.
　RG393, Correspondence, Reports, Etc., Letters Received, Department of the Pacific, 1854–58.

North Carolina State Archives, Division of Archives and History, Raleigh.
　Civil War Collection
　　Ashe, S. A. Reminiscences. [Second Manassas]. Folder 6, Box 70.
　　———. Reminiscences. "Wm. Dorsey Pender." Folder 45, Box 71.
　　Brown, Capt. Gary L. Papers. Folder 19, Box 70.
　　Leventhorpe, Collett. Papers. Folder 20, Box 71.

Neagle, F. N. Papers. Folder 35, Box 71.
Pender, Maj. Gen. William Dorsey. Papers. Folder 45, Box 71.
Private Collections
    Clark, Henry Toole. Scrapbook.
    Hambrick and Paylor Papers.
    Neathery, John B. Papers.
    Pender, William Dorsey. Papers.
    Phillips, James J. Papers.
    Scales, Alfred M. Papers.

Robert W. Woodruff Library, Emory University, Atlanta, Ga.
    Gourdin, Robert. Papers.

Southern Historical Collection, University of North Carolina, Chapel Hill.
    Hairston, Peter W. Papers.
    Hamilton, Eli Spanks. Papers.
    Lewis, William Gaston. Papers.
    Pender, William Dorsey. Papers.
    Profitt Family Papers.
    Ramseur, Stephen Dodson. Papers.

Special Collections, Alderman Library, University of Virginia, Charlottesville.
    Blackford Family Papers, 1847–72. Accession No. 5927.

U.S. Army History Institute, Carlisle Barracks, Pa.
    Brake, Robert L. Collection. Box 8.

U.S. Military Academy Library, West Point, N.Y.
    Circulation Records, 1852–55.
    Entry of Books Issued to Cadets on Saturday Afternoons from March 10th 1849 to April 5th 1851.
    Entry of Books Issued to Cadets by special permission of the Superintendent from May 23rd 1850 to Aug. 28th 1852.
    Entry of Books Issued to Cadets on Saturday Afternoons, 1851–53.
    Entry of Books Issued to Cadets on Saturday Afternoons, 1853–55.
    Official Register of the Officers and Cadets of the U.S. Military Academy, West Point, New York. 1851–54.
    Register of Delinquencies, 1853–54.
        Pender, William D. (N.C.).
        Shepperd, Samuel T. (N.C.).
    Stuart Files, #1643.

BIBLIOGRAPHY

Virginia Historical Society, Richmond
  Moore, L. Robert. Letters.
  Stuart, J. E. B. Letters.
  Talcott Family Papers.

William R. Perkins Library, Duke University, Durham, N.C.
  Branch Family Papers.
  Hinsdale, John W. Diary.
  Holmes, Theophilus Hunter. Papers.

Government

The War of the Rebellion: The Official Records of the Union and Confederate Armies. 70 vols. in 127 serials and index. Washington, D.C.: Government Printing Office, 1880–95.

Newspapers

North Carolina Standard.
Olympia (Wash. Terr.) Pioneer and Democrat.
Raleigh Register.
Raleigh Daily Progress.
Richmond Daily Dispatch.
Richmond Examiner.
Santa Barbara (Calif.) Gazette.
Staunton (Va.) Vindicator.
Tarboro (N.C.) Southerner.

Books

Alexander, Edward Porter. *Fighting for the Confederacy: The Personal Recollections of General Edward Porter Alexander.* Edited by Gary W. Gallagher. Chapel Hill: University of North Carolina Press, 1989.
Belo, Alfred Horatio. *Memoirs of Alfred Horatio Belo: Reminiscences of a North Carolina Volunteer.* Edited by Stuart Wright. Gaithersburg, Md.: Old Soldier Books, n.d.
Blackford, Charles Minor. *Letters from Lee's Army or Memoirs of Life in and out of the Army of Virginia in the War between the States.* Edited by Charles Minor Blackford III. New York: Charles Scribner's Sons, 1947. Abridged edition of *Memoirs of Life in and out of the Army of Virginia in the War between the States.* Edited by Susan Leigh Colston Blackford. 2 vols. Lynchburg, Va.: J. P. Bell, 1894–96.

Brunson, Joseph W. *Pee Dee Light Artillery of Maxcy Gregg's (Later Samuel McGowan's) Brigade First South Carolina Volunteers (Infantry) C.S.A.* Introduced and edited by William Stanley Hoole. Dayton, Ohio: Morningside, 1983.

Caldwell, J. F. J. *The History of a Brigade of South Carolinians First Known as "Gregg's" and Subsequently as "McGowan's Brigade."* Reprint, Dayton, Ohio: Morningside, 1992.

Clark, Walter. *Histories of the Several Regiments and Battalions from North Carolina in the Great War 1861–'65.* 5 vols. Raleigh: E. M. Uzell, 1901. Reprint, Wendell, N.C.: Broadfoot, 1982.

Cotton, Burwell Thomas, and George Job Huntley. *The Cry Is War, War, War: The Civil War Correspondence of Lts. Burwell Thomas Cotton and George Job Huntley, 34th Regiment North Carolina Troops, Pender-Scales Brigade of the Light Division, Stonewall Jackson's and A. P. Hill's Corps, Army of Northern Virginia, C.S.A.* Edited by Michael W. Taylor. Dayton, Ohio: Morningside, 1994.

Davidson, Greenlee. *Captain Greenlee Davidson, C.S.A.: Diary and Letters, 1851–1863.* Edited by Charles W. Turner. Verona, Va.: McClure, 1975.

Davis, Jefferson. *The Papers of Jefferson Davis.* Edited by Lynda Lasswell Crist. 8 vols. Baton Rouge: Louisiana State University Press, 1971–.

Ellis, John Willis. *The Papers of John Willis Ellis.* Edited by Noble J. Tolbert. 2 vols. Raleigh: State Department of Archives and History, 1964.

Evans, Clement A. *Confederate Military History: A Library of Confederate States History, in Twelve Volumes, Written by Distinguished Men of the South, and Edited by Clement A. Evans of Georgia.* Atlanta: Confederate Publishing, 1899.

Green, Wharton J. *Recollections and Reflections: An Auto[biography] of Half a Century and More.* Raleigh, N.C.: Edwards and Broughton, 1906.

Heth, Henry. *The Memoirs of Henry Heth.* Edited by James L. Morrison Jr. Westport, Conn.: Greenwood, 1974.

Hill, Daniel Harvey. *Bethel to Sharpsburg.* 2 vols. Raleigh, N.C.: Edwards and Broughton, 1926.

Howard, Oliver Otis. *Autobiography of Oliver Otis Howard, Major General United States Army.* 2 vols. New York: Baker and Taylor, 1908.

Kean, Robert Garlick Hill. *Inside the Confederate Government: The Diary of Robert Garlick Hill Kean.* Edited by Edward Younger. New York: Oxford University Press, 1957.

Keyes, E. D. *Fifty Years' Observation of Men and Events Civil and Military.* New York: Charles Scribner's Sons, 1884.

Kip, Lawrence. *Army Life on the Pacific; a Journal of the Expedition against the Northern Indians, the Tribes of the Coeur D'Alenes, Spokans, and Pelouzes, in the Summer of 1858.* New York: Redfield, 1859. Reprinted as *Indian War in the Pacific Northwest: The Journal of Lieutenant Lawrence Kip.* Introduction by Clifford E. Trafzer. Lincoln: University of Nebraska Press, 1999.

Lee, Mary Greenhow. *The Civil War Journal of Mary Greenhow Lee (Mrs. Hugh Holmes*

Lee) *of Winchester, Virginia*. Edited by Eloise C. Strader. Winchester, Va.: Winchester-Frederick County Historical Society, 2011.

Logan, David Jackson. *"A Rising Star of Promise": The Civil War Odyssey of David Jackson Logan.* Edited by Samuel N. Thomas Jr. and Jason H. Silverman. Campbell, Calif.: Savas, 1998.

Mansfield, Joseph King Fenno. *Mansfield on the Condition of the Western Forts, 1853–54.* Edited by Robert W. Frazer. Norman: University of Oklahoma Press, 1963.

Owen, William Miller. *In Camp and Battle with the Washington Artillery of New Orleans: A Narrative of Events in the Late Civil War from Bull Run to Appomattox and Spanish Fort.* Boston: Ticknor, 1885.

Parker, Francis Marion. *To Drive the Enemy from Southern Soil: The Letters of Colonel Francis Marion Parker and the History of the 30th Regiment North Carolina Troops.* Edited by Michael W. Taylor. Dayton, Ohio: Morningside, 1998.

Pender, William Dorsey. *The General to His Lady: The Civil War Letters of William Dorsey Pender to Fanny Pender.* Edited by William W. Hassler. Chapel Hill: University of North Carolina Press, 1965. Reprinted as *One of Lee's Best Men: The Civil War Letters of General William Dorsey Pender.* Chapel Hill: University of North Carolina Press, 1999.

Ruffin, Edmund. *The Diary of Edmund Ruffin.* Edited by William Kauffman Scarborough. 3 vols. Baton Rouge: Louisiana State University Press, 1989.

Ruffin, Thomas. *The Papers of Thomas Ruffin.* Edited by Hamilton J. G. de Roulhac. Raleigh: Edmunds and Broughton 1920.

Smith, W. A. *The Anson Guards: Company C, Fourteenth Regiment North Carolina Volunteers 1861–1865.* Charlotte, N.C.: Stone, 1914.

Trout, Robert J. *With Pen & Saber: The Letters and Diaries of J. E. B. Stuart's Staff Officers.* Mechanicsburg, Pa.: Stackpole, 1995.

Welch, Spencer Glasgow. *A Confederate Surgeon's Letters to his Wife.* New York: Neale, 1911. Reprinted by Marietta, Ga.: Centennial Book, 1954.

Wood, Thomas Fanning. *Doctor to the Front: The Recollections of Confederate Surgeon Thomas Fanning Wood, 1861–1865.* Edited by Donald B. Koonce. Knoxville: University of Tennessee Press, 2000.

Articles

"Brig. Gen. James T. Archer." *Confederate Veteran* 8 (February 1900): 65–66.

"Gen. Lee's Tribute to Gen. Pender." *Our Living and Our Dead* 1 (October 1874): 137.

Howard, Oliver Otis. "The Campaigns and Battles of Gettysburg." In *Battles and Leaders of the Civil War. Volume 5.* Edited by Peter Cozzens, 314–48. Urbana: University of Illinois Press, 2002.

"The James J. Archer Letters: A Marylander in the Civil War, Part I." Edited by C. A. Porter Hopkins. *Maryland Historical Magazine* 56 (March 1961): 72–93, 125–49.

Lyon, Hylan B. "Memoirs of Hylan B. Lyon, Brigadier General, C.S.A." Edited by Edward M. Coffman. *Tennessee Historical Quarterly* 18 (March 1959): 35–51.

[Mangum], A. W. M. "The Basis of True Courage: A Lesson from the Life of Gen. W. D. Pender." *University [of North Carolina] Magazine* 18 (April 1886): 216–18.

McCrady, Edward, Jr. "Address before the Virginia Division of the Army of Northern Virginia." *Southern Historical Society Papers* 14 (January–December 1886): 181–222.

Pender, Samuel Turner. "General Pender." *South-Atlantic* 1 (1877): 228–35. Copy in William D. Pender Papers, SHC-UNC, as S. T. Pender, "Life of General Pender."

Purifoy, John. "A Night of Horrors." *Confederate Veteran* 33 (March 1925): 95–97.

Robertson, Frank S. "Reminiscences of the Years, 1861–1865." *Historical Society of Washington County, Va., Bulletin*, 2nd ser., 23 (1986): 6–39.

Scales, Alfred M. "Battle of Fredericksburg," *Southern Historical Society Papers* 40 (September 1915): 195–223.

Shepherd, Henry E. "Gallant Sons of North Carolina." *Confederate Veteran* 27 (November 1919): 413–14.

U.D.C. Notes. *Confederate Veteran* 31 (June 1923): 232.

Secondary Sources

Books

Adams, George Rollie. *General William S. Harney: Prince of Dragoons*. Lincoln: University of Nebraska Press, 2001.

Ambrose, Stephen E. *Duty, Honor, Country: A History of West Point*. Baltimore: The Johns Hopkins Press, 1966.

Barefoot, Daniel W. *General Robert F. Hoke: Lee's Modest Warrior*. Winston-Salem, N.C.: John F. Blair, 1996.

Barrett, John G. *The Civil War in North Carolina*. Chapel Hill: University of North Carolina Press, 1963.

Barton, Michael. *Goodmen: The Character of Civil War Soldiers*. University Park: Pennsylvania State University Press, 1981.

Berry, Stephen W., II. *All That Makes a Man: Love and Ambition in the Civil War South*. Oxford: Oxford University Press, 2003.

Brinsfield, John W., William C. Davis, Benedict Maryniak, and James I. Robertson Jr. *Faith in the Fight: Civil War Chaplains*. Mechanicsburg, Pa.: Stackpole, 2003.

Brown, Kent Masterson. *Retreat from Gettysburg: Lee, Logistics, and the Pennsylvania Campaign*. Chapel Hill: University of North Carolina Press, 2005.

Burns, Robert Ignatius. *The Jesuits and the Indian Wars of the Northwest.* New Haven, Conn.: Yale University Press, 1966.

Burton, Brian K. *Extraordinary Circumstances: The Seven Days Battles.* Bloomington: Indiana University Press, 2001.

Carmichael, Peter S. *The Last Generation: Young Virginians in Peace, War, and Reunion.* Chapel Hill: University of North Carolina Press, 2005.

———. *Lee's Young Artillerist: William R. J. Pegram.* Charlottesville: University Press of Virginia, 1995.

Carpenter, John A. *Sword and Olive Branch: Oliver Otis Howard.* Pittsburgh: University of Pittsburgh Press, 1964.

Coffman, Edward M. *The Old Army: A Portrait of the American Army in Peacetime, 1784–1898.* New York: Oxford University Press, 1986.

Cole, Timothy J., and Bradley R. Foley. *Collett Leventhorpe, the English Confederate: The Life of a Civil War General, 1815–1889.* Jefferson, N.C.: McFarland, 2007.

Converse, George L. *A Military History of the Columbia Valley, 1848–1865.* Walla Walla, Wash.: Pioneer, 1989.

Cormier, Steven A. *The Siege of Suffolk: The Forgotten Campaign, April 11–May 4, 1863.* Lynchburg: H. E. Howard, 1989.

Coulter, E. Merton. *The Confederate States of America.* Baton Rouge: Louisiana State University Press, 1950.

Cullen, Joseph P. *The Peninsula Campaign 1862: McClellan and Lee Struggle for Richmond.* New York: Bonanza Books, 1973.

Cullum, George W. *Biographical Register of the Officers and Graduates of the U.S. Military Academy at West Point, N.Y., from its Establishment, in 1802 and 1890, with the Early History of the United States Military Academy.* 2 vols. Boston, 1891.

Dabney, R. L. *Life and Campaigns of Lieut.-Gen. Thomas J. Jackson.* New York: Blelock, 1866.

Davis, William C. *Jefferson Davis: The Man and His Hour.* New York: HarperCollins, 1991.

Diket, A. L. *wha hae wi' [Pender] . . . bled.* New York: Vantage, 1979.

Dougherty, James J. *Stone's Brigade and the Fight for the McPherson Farm: Battle of Gettysburg, July 1, 1863.* 2001.

Dunn, J. P., Jr. *Massacres of the Mountains: A History of the Indian Wars of the Far West, 1815–1875.* New York: Archer House, 1958.

Eliot, Ellsworth, Jr. *West Point in the Confederacy.* New York: G. A. Baker, 1941.

Foote, Shelby. *The Civil War: A Narrative.* 3 vols. New York: Random House, 1958–74.

Fox, John J., III. *Red Clay to Richmond: Trail of the 35th Georgia Infantry Regiment, C.S.A.* Winchester, Va.: Angle Valley, 2004.

Fraser, Robert W. *Forts of the West: Forts and Presidios and Posts Commonly Called Forts West of the Mississippi River to 1898.* Norman: University of Oklahoma Press, 1965.

Freeman, Douglas Southall. *Lee's Lieutenants: A Study in Command.* 3 vols. New York: Charles Scribner's Sons, 1942–44.

———. *R. E. Lee: A Biography*. 4 vols. New York: Charles Scribner's Sons, 1934–35.
Furgurson, Ernest D. *Chancellorsville, 1863: The Souls of the Brave*. New York: Alfred Knopf, 1992.
Gallagher, Gary W., ed. *Antietam: Essays on the 1862 Maryland Campaign*. Kent, Ohio: Kent State University Press, 1989.
———. *The Confederate War*. Cambridge, Mass.: Harvard University Press, 1997.
———, ed. *The First Day at Gettysburg*. Kent, Ohio: Kent State University Press, 1992.
———. *Lee: The Soldier*. Lincoln: University of Nebraska Press, 1996.
———. *Stephen Dodson Ramseur: Lee's Gallant General*. Chapel Hill: University of North Carolina Press, 1985.
Glassley, Ray Hoard. *Pacific Northwest Indian Wars*. Portland, Ore.: Binfords and Mort, 1953.
Glatthaar, Joseph T. *General Lee's Army: From Victory to Collapse*. New York: Free Press, 2008.
Grimsley, Mark. *The Hard Hand of War: Union Military Policy toward Southern Civilians 1861–1865*. New York: Cambridge University Press, 1995.
Hardy, Michael C. *The Thirty-Seventh North Carolina Troops: Tar Heels in the Army of Northern Virginia*. Jefferson, N.C.: McFarland, 2003.
Harris, William C. *William Woods Holden: Firebrand of North Carolina Politics*. Baton Rouge: Louisiana State University Press, 1987.
Harsh, Joseph L. *Sounding the Shallows: A Confederate Companion for the Maryland Campaign of 1862*. Kent, Ohio: Kent State University Press, 2000.
———. *Taken at the Flood: Robert E. Lee and Confederate Strategy in the Maryland Campaign of 1862*. Kent, Ohio: Kent State University Press, 1999.
Hattaway, Herman, and Richard E. Beringer. *Jefferson Davis, Confederate President*. Lawrence: University Press of Kansas, 2002.
Hennessy, John J. *Return to Bull Run: The Campaign and Battle of Second Manassas*. New York: Simon and Schuster, 1993.
Hess, Earl J. *Field Armies & Fortifications in the Civil War: The Eastern Campaigns, 1861–1864*. Chapel Hill: University of North Carolina Press, 2005.
Hilderman, Walter C., III. *They Went into the Fight Cheering!: Confederate Conscription in North Carolina*. Boone, N.C.: Parkway Publishers, 2005.
Hunt, Garrett B. *Indian Wars of the Inland Empire*. 1908. Reprint, Spokane, Wash.: Spokane Community College Library, n.d.
Iobst, Richard W. *The Bloody Sixth North Carolina Regiment Confederate States of America*. Raleigh: North Carolina Division of Archives and History, 1965.
Johannsen, Robert W. *Frontier Politics and the Sectional Conflict: The Pacific Northwest on the Eve of the Civil War*. Seattle: University of Washington Press, 1955.
Kennedy, Frances H., ed. *The Civil War Battlefield Guide*. 2nd ed. Boston: Houghton Mifflin, 1998.
Krick, Robert E. L. *Staff Officers in Gray: A Biographical Register of the Staff Officers in the Army of Northern Virginia*. Chapel Hill: University of North Carolina Press, 2003.

Krick, Robert K. *The Smoothbore Volley That Doomed the Confederacy: The Death of Stonewall Jackson and Other Chapters on the Army of Northern Virginia.* Baton Rouge: Louisiana State University Press, 2002.

———. *Stonewall Jackson at Cedar Mountain.* Chapel Hill: University of North Carolina Press, 1990.

Long, E. B. *The Civil War Day by Day: An Almanac, 1861–1865.* Garden City, N.Y.: Doubleday, 1971.

Longacre, Edward G. *General William Dorsey Pender: A Military Biography.* Conshohocken, Pa.: Combined Publishing, 2001.

Lonn, Ella. *Desertion during the Civil War.* New York: Century, 1928.

Manarin, Louis H., and Weymouth T. Jordan, eds. *North Carolina Troops, 1861–1865.* Raleigh: North Carolina Archives and History Division, 1966–).

Manring, B. F. *The Conquest of the Coeur D'Alenes, Spokanes, and Palouses: The Expeditions of Colonels E. J. Steptoe and George Wright against the "Northern Indians" in 1858.* Spokane, Wash.: John W. Graham, 1912.

Martin, David G. *Gettysburg, July 1.* Conshohocken, Pa.: Combined Books, 1995.

Massey, Mary Elizabeth. *Bonnet Brigades.* New York: Alfred A. Knopf, 1966.

Matloff, Maurice. *American Military History.* Washington, D.C.: Office of the Chief of Military History, U.S. Army, 1969.

McCormick, John Gilchrist. *Personnel of the Convention of 1861.* Chapel Hill: University of North Carolina Press, 1900.

McFeely, William S. *Yankee Stepfather: General O. O. Howard and the Freedmen.* New Haven, Conn.: Yale University Press, 1968.

McGrath, Thomas A. *Shepherdstown: Last Clash of the Antietam Campaign, September 19–20, 1862.* Lynchburg, Va.: Schroeder, 2007.

McMurry, Richard M. *Two Great Rebel Armies: An Essay in Confederate Military History.* Chapel Hill: University of North Carolina Press, 1989.

McPherson, James M. *Battle Cry of Freedom: The Civil War Era.* New York: Oxford University Press, 1988.

———. *Crossroads of Freedom: Antietam.* New York: Oxford University Press, 2002.

McWhiney, Grady, and Perry D. Jamison. *Attack and Die: Civil War Military Tactics and the Southern Heritage.* Tuscaloosa: University of Alabama Press, 1982.

Miller, Randall M., Harry S. Stout, and Charles Reagan Wilson, eds. *Religion and the American Civil War.* New York: Oxford University Press, 1998.

Missall, John, and Mary Lou Missall. *The Seminole Wars: America's Longest Indian Conflict.* Gainesville: University of Florida Press, 2004.

Mitchell, Reid. *Civil War Soldiers.* New York: Viking Penguin, 1988.

Montgomery, Walter A. *Life and Character of Major-General W. D. Pender: Memorial Address, May 10, 1894.* Raleigh: Edwards and Broughton, 1894.

Moore, Albert Burton. *Conscription and Conflict in the Confederacy.* New York: Macmillan, 1924.

Morrison, James L., Jr. *"The Best School in the World": West Point, the Pre-Civil War Years, 1833–1866.* Kent, Ohio: Kent State University Press, 1986.

Murfin, James V. *The Gleam of Bayonets: The Battle of Antietam and Robert E. Lee's Maryland Campaign, September 1862.* Baton Rouge: Louisiana University Press, 1982.

Mushkat, Jerome. *Fernando Wood: A Political Biography.* Kent, Ohio: Kent State University Press, 1990.

Newell, Clayton R. *Lee vs. McClellan: The First Campaign.* Washington, D.C.: Regnery, 1996.

Newton, Steven H. *The Battle of Seven Pines, May 31–June 1, 1862.* Lynchburg, Va.: H. E. Howard, 1993.

O'Reilly, Frank A. *The Fredericksburg Campaign: 'Stonewall' Jackson at Fredericksburg. The Battle of Prospect Hill, Dec. 13, 1862.* Lynchburg, Va.: H. E. Howard, 1993.

———. *The Fredericksburg Campaign: Winter War on the Rappahannock.* Baton Rouge: Louisiana University Press, 2002.

Patterson, Gerard A. *From Blue to Gray: The Life of Confederate General Cadmus M. Wilcox.* Mechanicsburg, Pa.: Stackpole Books, 2001.

Powell, William S. *North Carolina: A Bicentennial History.* New York: W. W. Norton, 1977.

Prucha, Francis Paul. *A Guide to the Military Posts of the United States, 1789–1895.* Madison: State Historical Society of Wisconsin, 1964.

Rable, George C. *Civil Wars: Women and the Crisis of Southern Nationalism.* Urbana: University of Illinois Press, 1989.

———. *Fredericksburg! Fredericksburg!* Chapel Hill: University of North Carolina Press, 2002.

Robertson, James I., Jr. *General A. P. Hill: The Story of a Confederate Warrior.* New York: Random House, 1987.

———. *Stonewall Jackson: The Man, the Soldier, the Legend.* New York: Macmillan, 1997.

Robertson, R. G. *Competitive Struggle: America's Fur Trading Posts, 1764–1865.* Boise, Id.: Tamarack, 1999.

Rodenbough, Theophilus F., and William L. Haskins, eds. *The Army of the United States: Historical Sketches of Staff and Line.* New York: Merrill, 1896.

Ruby, Robert H., and John A. Brown. *Indians of the Pacific Northwest.* Norman: University of Oklahoma Press, 1981.

Schenck, Martin. *Up Came Hill: The Story of the Light Division and Its Leaders.* Harrisburg, Pa.: Stackpole, 1958.

Schlicke, Carl P. *General George Wright: Guardian of the Pacific Coast.* Norman: University of Oklahoma Press, 1988.

Sears, Stephen W. *Chancellorsville.* Boston: Houghton-Mifflin, 1996.

———. *Gettysburg.* Boston: Houghton Mifflin, 2003.

———. *Landscape Turned Red: The Battle of Antietam.* New Haven, Conn.: Ticknor and Fields, 1983.

———. *To the Gates of Richmond: The Peninsula Campaign.* New York: Ticknor and Fields, 1992.

Sheehan-Dean, Aaron. *Why Confederates Fought: Family and Nation in Civil War Virginia.* Chapel Hill: University of North Carolina Press, 2007.
Skelton, William B. *An American Profession of Arms: The Army Officer Corps, 1784–1861.* Lawrence: University Press of Kansas, 1992.
Slotkin, Richard. *The Long Road to Antietam: How the Civil War Became a Revolution.* New York: Liveright, 2012.
Stackpole, Edward J. *Chancellorsville: Lee's Greatest Battle.* Harrisburg, Pa.: Stackpole, 1958.
Sutherland, Daniel E. *Fredericksburg & Chancellorsville: The Dare Mark Campaign.* Lincoln: University of Nebraska Press, 1998.
Symonds, Craig L. *Joseph E. Johnston: A Civil War Biography.* New York: W. W. Norton, 1992.
Tatum, Georgia Lee. *Disloyalty in the Confederacy.* Chapel Hill: University of North Carolina Press, 1934.
Thomas, Emory M. *Bold Dragoon: The Life of J. E. B. Stuart.* New York: Harper and Row, 1986.
———. *The Confederacy as a Revolutionary Experience.* Englewood Cliffs, N.J.: Prentice-Hall, 1971.
———. *The Confederate Nation: 1861–1865.* New York: Harper and Row, 1979.
———. *Robert E. Lee: A Biography.* New York: W. W. Norton, 1995.
Tucker, Glenn. *Front Rank.* Raleigh.: North Carolina Confederate Centennial Commission, 1962.
———. *High Tide at Gettysburg: The Campaign in Pennsylvania.* Dayton, Ohio: Morningside, 1973.
Turner, J. Kelly, and John L. Bridgers Jr. *History of Edgecombe County, North Carolina.* Raleigh: Edwards and Broughton, 1920.
Utley, Robert M. *Fort Union National Monument, New Mexico.* Washington, D.C.: National Park Service, 1962.
———. *Frontiersmen in Blue: The United States Army and the Indian, 1848–1865.* New York: Macmillan, 1967.
Vandiver, Frank E. *Mighty Stonewall.* New York: McGraw-Hill, 1957.
Walsh. George. *"Damage Them All You Can": Robert E. Lee's Army of Northern Virginia.* New York: Tom Doherty Associates, 2002.
Warner, Ezra J. *Generals in Blue: Lives of the Union Commanders.* Baton Rouge: Louisiana State University Press, 1964.
———. *Generals in Gray: Lives of the Confederate Commanders.* Baton Rouge: Louisiana State University Press, 1959.
Watson, Alan D. *Edgecombe County: A Brief History.* Raleigh: North Carolina Department of Cultural Resources, Division of Archives and History, 1979.
Weitz, Mark A. *More Damning than Slaughter: Desertion in the Confederate Army.* Lincoln: University of Nebraska Press, 2005.

Wert, Jeffry D. *A Brotherhood of Valor: The Common Soldiers of the Stonewall Brigade, C.S.A., and the Iron Brigade, U.S.A.* New York: Simon and Schuster, 1999.

———. *General James Longstreet: The Confederacy's Most Controversial Soldier—A Biography.* New York: Simon and Schuster, 1993.

———. *The Sword of Lincoln: The Army of the Potomac.* New York: Simon and Schuster, 2005.

Wiley, Bell Irvin. *The Road to Appomattox.* Memphis: Memphis State University Press, 1956.

Williams, Ruth Smith, and Margarette Glenn Griffin. *Bible Records of Early Edgecombe County.* Rocky Mount, N.C.: Dixie Letter Service, 1958.

———. *Tombstone and Census Records of Early Edgecombe County.* Rocky Mount, N.C.: Dixie Letter Service, 1959.

Wills, Brian Steel. *George Henry Thomas: As True as Steel.* Lawrence: University Press of Kansas, 2012.

———. *The War Hits Home: The Civil War in Southeastern Virginia.* Charlottesville: University Press of Virginia, 2001.

Woodworth, Steven E. *Beneath a Northern Sky: A Short History of the Gettysburg Campaign.* Wilmington, Del.: Scholarly Resources, 2003.

———. *Davis and Lee at War.* Lawrence: University Press of Kansas, 1995.

———. *This Great Struggle: America's Civil War.* New York: Rowman and Littlefield, 2011.

———. *While God Is Marching On: The Religious World of Civil War Soldiers.* Lawrence: University Press of Kansas, 2001.

Wyatt-Brown, Bertram. *Southern Honor: Ethics and Behavior in the Old South.* New York: Oxford University Press, 1982.

Yates, Richard E. *The Confederacy and Zeb Vance.* Tuscaloosa, Ala.: Confederate Publishing, 1958.

Articles and Unpublished Manuscripts

Archambault, Alan H. "Forts, Camps, and Military Posts of Early Washington." N.p., n.d.

Bardolph, Richard. "Inconstant Rebels: Desertion of North Carolina Troops in the Civil War." *North Carolina Historical Review* 41 (April 1964): 163–89.

Barrett, John G. "North Carolina." In *The Confederate Governors*, edited by W. Buck Yearns, 140–61. Athens: University of Georgia Press, 1985.

Coffman, Edward M. "Memoirs of Hylan B. Lyon, Brigadier General, C.S.A." *Tennessee Historical Quarterly* 18 (March 1959): 35–53.

Hassler, William W. "Dorsey Pender." *Civil War Times Illustrated* 1 (October 1962): 18–22.

———. "The Religious Conversion of General W. Dorsey Pender, C.S.A." *Historical Magazine of the Protestant Episcopal Church* 33 (June 1964): 171–78.

Historical Notes. *North Carolina Historical Review* 21 (January 1944): 88.

———. *North Carolina Historical Review* 37 (January 1960): 132.
Knuth, Priscilla. "'Picturesque' Frontier: The Army's Fort Dalles." *Oregon Historical Quarterly* 67 (December 1966): 293–346.
McIver, George W. "North Carolinians at West Point before the Civil War." *North Carolina Historical Review* 7 (January 1930): 15–45.
Miller, J. Michael. "Perrin's Brigade on July 1, 1863." *Gettysburg Magazine* 13 (July 1995): 22–32.
Rakes, Paul H. "The Military Career of an Ambitious Professional Confederate General William Dorsey Pender, 1834–1863." Master's thesis, Marshall University, 1994.
Reid, Richard. "A Test Case of the 'Crying Evil': Desertion among North Carolina Troops during the Civil War." *North Carolina Historical Review* 58 (July 1961): 234–62.
Samito, Christian G. "'Patriot by Nature, Christian by Faith': Major General William Dorsey Pender, C.S.A." *North Carolina Historical Review* 76 (April 1999): 163–201.
Simpson, Kenrick N. "'Patriot by Nature, Soldier by Training, Christian by Faith': The Life of William Dorsey Pender." Master's thesis, East Carolina University, 1982.
Sword, Wiley. "Personal Battle Weapons of the Civil War: Capt. James Glenn's Sword and Pvt. J. Marshall Hill's Enfield in the Fight for the Lutheran Seminary." *Gettysburg Magazine* 8 (January 1993): 9–15.
Thomas, Emory M. "The Richmond Bread Riot of 1863." *Virginia Cavalcade* 18 (Summer 1968): 41–44.
Weinert, Richard P. "The Confederate Regular Army." *Military Affairs* 26 (Autumn 1962): 97–107.

INDEX

1st North Carolina Infantry, 66, 67
1st Pennsylvania Light Artillery, 128
2nd Arkansas Infantry, 153
3rd North Carolina Volunteers, 67, 69, 71, 72, 73, 74, 84, 85, 87, 89, 106, 119, 219
6th North Carolina Infantry, 87, 88, 89, 98, 102, 122, 128, 144, 267n77
11th Mississippi Infantry, 228
13th North Carolina Infantry, 68, 69, 120, 133, 184, 186, 191, 208, 210, 214, 235, 277n8
16th North Carolina Infantry, 133, 142, 146, 148, 153, 157, 184, 188, 214
18th Virginia Cavalry, 236
22nd North Carolina Infantry, 133, 146, 149, 153, 175, 177, 184, 197, 210, 214, 275n29
22nd Virginia Infantry, 153
34th North Carolina Infantry, 133, 153, 163, 192, 214, 226, 241, 270n30
35th North Carolina Infantry, 214
38th North Carolina Infantry, 133, 141, 142, 153, 233, 272n32
55th North Carolina Infantry, 222

Abolitionists, 18, 49
Alston, Benjamin, 93, 95, 97
Amalgre Mountain, N.M., 24
Ambrose, Stephen, 11
Anderson, George Burgwyn, 2
Anderson, Joseph Reid, 133, 141
Anderson, Richard Heron, 233
Anderson, Robert, 63
Antietam Creek, Md., 173, 181; Battle of, *see* Sharpsburg, Md., Battle of,
Apostle Paul, 5, 93
Appomattox, Va., 3, 243

Archer, James Jay, 133, 141, 156, 158, 160, 163, 172, 174, 175, 180, 186, 187, 229
Arkansas, 268n25
Army of Northern Virginia (CS), 1, 2, 4, 66, 132, 133, 149, 151, 152, 153, 166, 169, 170, 171, 176, 177, 190, 195, 205, 211, 214, 216, 217, 220, 224, 225, 226, 234, 242, 243, 247n2, 267n3
Army of the Potomac (US), 107, 149, 182, 190, 205
Army of Virginia (US), 151, 152, 163
Ashe, Samuel A., 157, 160, 164, 165
Ashland, Va., 118
Avery, Isaac Erwin, 233

Baltimore, Md., 59, 60, 61, 62, 64, 248n6
Baltimore Steam Packet Company, 61
Banks, Nathaniel Prentiss, 154, 156
Barksdale, William, 182
Barr, Richard R., 208
Barrett, John G., 78
Barton, Michael, 5
"The Basis of True Courage" (Mangum), 96
Beall, B. L., 25
Beaufort, N.C., 64
Beauregard, Pierre Gustave Toutant, 60, 61, 63, 120
Beaver Dam Creek, Va., 139, 140, 141, 142, 143, 144, 146
Bell, John, 51
Belo, Alfred, 63, 228, 258n36
Berry, Hiram Gregory, 209
Berry, Stephen, 92
Berryville, Va., 224
Binney, Henry M., 172

295

INDEX

Blackford, Charles Minor, 153, 154
Blacks, 1, 103, 177, 228
Bolivar Heights, Va. (W.Va.), 170
Boyles, J. R., 187
Brady, Hugh, 249n32
Branch, Lawrence O'Bryan, 2, 101, 133, 156, 159, 160, 270n21
Brawner's Farm, 160
Breckinridge, John Cabell, 51
Brewer, Richard Henry, 164, 165, 166, 171, 172
Bridgers, Robert R., 11, 57, 131, 244
Brunson, Joseph W., 187
Buford, John, 229
Bull Run, Va. *See* Manassas, Va.
Burnside, Ambrose Everett, 113, 173, 181, 182, 190, 191
Butler, Benjamin Franklin, 113, 124

Caldwell, James Fitz James, 174, 187
California, 23, 25, 26, 28, 51
Calvary Episcopal Church (Tarboro), 6, 243, 244
Cameron, Simon, 52
Camp Barton, Va., 115
Camp Brady, N.Y., 249n32
Camp Fisher, Va., 99, 110, 111, 113, 115
Camp Gaines, N.Y., 13
Camp Gregg, Va., 191, 202, 213, 214
Camp Hill, Va., 99
Camp Jones, Va., 90
Camp Mangum, N.C., 65, 258n52
Camp Ruffin, Va., 85
Carlisle Barracks, Pa., 51, 53
Carmichael, Peter, 3
Carraway, David T., 236
Cashtown, Pa., 229

Castle Pinckney, S.C., 62
Cedar Creek, Va., Battle of, 3, 241
Cedar Mountain (Slaughter Mountain), Battle of, 156, 157, 158, 159
Cemetery Hill (Gettysburg), 233
Cemetery Ridge (Gettysburg), 235
Centreville, Va., 160
Chancellorsville, Va., Battle of, 3, 205, 206, 209, 210, 211, 212, 213, 215, 216, 217, 218, 278n11

Chantilly (Ox Hill), Va., Battle of, 163
Charleston, S.C., 60, 61, 62, 95, 98
Charleston Harbor, 62
Chickahominy River, 126
Chickamauga, Ga., Battle of, 2
Christian Sun, 74
Civil War, 1, 2, 9, 12, 83, 127, 152, 166, 205, 245, 269n61; centennial of, 245
Clark, Henry Toole, 88, 106, 261n23
Clark, Newman S., 30
Coeur d'Alene (Indians), 37
"Coeur d'Alene" (writer), 35
Cole, Christopher Columbus, 175, 177, 184, 210
"The Colonel Baptized in Presence of His Regiment" (tract), 98
Columbia River, 26, 45
Confederate States of America (Confederacy), 1, 2, 3, 4, 26, 52, 54, 55, 56, 57, 58, 59, 61, 62, 63, 102, 117, 118, 125, 199, 215, 235, 241, 243, 246, 275n34; Army of, 65; Congress of, 176; Treasury Department of, 244
Confederate soldiers, desertion of, 100, 101, 102, 116, 178, 192, 199–200, 201, 275n34
Connally, John Kerr, 222
Constitutional Unionist Party, 51
Cooper, Samuel, 22, 40, 58, 60, 61, 62, 242
Copperheads (Peace Democrats), 110, 227
Corrick's Ford, Va., Battle of, 86
Cotton, Burwell, 192, 241
Cotton, Thomas, 221
Crawford, George W., 11
Crawford, Martin, 63
Cromwell, Oliver, 17
Cullum, George Washington, 24
Culpeper, Va., 152, 225, 239
Culp's Hill (Gettysburg), 233
Cutts, Allen Sherrod, 186

Daily Progress, 214
Daniel, John R. J., 11
Daniel, Junius, 2
Davidson, Greenlee, 184
Davidson, Henry B., 31, 34
Davis, Jefferson Finis, 1, 20, 22, 58, 63, 64, 129, 130, 133, 136, 138, 144, 145, 146, 148, 166, 187, 190, 193, 201, 205, 215, 219, 220, 227, 249n32, 266n76, 267n77

INDEX

Dearing, James, 3
Democratic Party (Democrats), 51, 56, 110
Department of Oregon, 43
Department of the Pacific, 30
Dobbin, J. C., 22
Douglas, Stephen Arnold, 51
Drewry's Bluff, Va., Battle of, 123
Du Pont, Henry A., 250n33

Early, Jubal Anderson, 2, 210, 247n2, 279n44
Eastern Theater, 2
Edgecombe County, N.C., 7, 116, 203
Edwards, David, 178
Election of 1860, 51
Ellerson's Mill, 144
Ellis, John Willis, 54, 58, 63, 64, 77, 78
Eltham's Landing (Barhamsville, West Point), Va., Battle of, 122, 266n49
Emancipation Proclamation, 181
Englehard, Joseph A., 191, 234, 241, 243
Episcopal Church, 41, 94, 97, 98, 99, 262n65
Ewell, Richard Stoddert, 148, 217, 233

Fagan, Andrew, 128
Fayetteville, Pa., 226
Field, Charles William, 133, 141, 142, 172
Fisher, Charles Frederick, 87, 89, 260n17
Five Forks, Va., Battle of, 3
Florida, 22, 24, 28
Floyd, John Buchanan, 28
Foote, Shelby, 4
Forsythe, John, 62, 63
Fort Clark, N.C., 90, 113
Fort Craig, N.M., 24
Fort Dalles, Wash., 26, 29, 42
Fort Darling, Va., 123
Fort Donelson, Tenn., 113
Fort Hatteras, N.C., 90, 113
Fort Henry, Tenn., 113
Fort Leavenworth, Kan., 22, 23, 251n16
Fort Myers, Fla., 20, 21, 54
Fort Reading, Ca., 26
Fort Riley, Kan., 26
Fort Sumter, S.C., 52, 62, 63, 258n36
Fort Tejon, Ca., 25, 26, 51
Fort Thompson, Fla., 21
Fort Thorn, N.M., 23, 24

Fort Union, N.M., 24
Fort Vancouver, Wash., 26, 30, 42, 43, 44, 46, 50, 69
Fort Walla Walla, Wash., 26, 28, 29, 30, 31, 38, 42, 50
Four Lakes, Battle of, 34, 35
Fourth of July, 14, 84
Franklin, William Buel, 121, 182, 184
Frederick, Md., 169, 170
Fredericksburg, Va., 93, 95, 115, 182, 183, 186, 190, 191, 195, 210, 211, 220, 221, 222, 223, 225, 226, 229, 245; Battle of, 195
Freeman, Douglas Southall, 4, 220, 265n49
Frémont, John Charles, 109, 264n112
French, Samuel Gibbs, 220

Gaines, Edmund P., 13, 249n32
Gaines' Mill, Va., Battle of, 146, 147
Galena, USS, 123
Gamble, William, 231
Gardman, Lieutenant, 233
Garnett, Robert Seldon, 86, 91, 260n13
Garysburg, N.C., 67, 68, 69, 258n57
Gaston, William, 28, 29, 31, 36, 38
General Orders No. 38, 217
General Orders, No. 71, 133
General Orders No. 72, 227
General Orders No. 73, 227
Georgia (Georgians), 133, 240
Gettysburg, Pa., 1, 3, 4, 5, 229, 230, 231, 233, 235, 236, 237, 239, 240, 241, 243, 246; Battle of, 248n6, 281n26; Campaign of, 241, 242, 248n6
Gibbon, John, 185
Goggans, W. C., 171, 172
Goldsboro, N.C., 77
Goldsboro (N.C.) Tribune, 74
Goodmen, 5
Good Spring, N.C. (Shepperd household), 21, 40, 41, 69, 70, 71, 80, 123, 239, 246
Gordon, James Byron, 2
Gordonsville, Va., 152, 154, 159
Gray, Robert Harper, 149, 197, 275n29
Great Britain, 43
Green, Wharton, 12
Green, William J., 147
Gregg, David McMurtrie, 31, 34, 37

INDEX

Gregg, Maxcy, 133, 174, 188, 192
Grier, William N., 31, 33, 34, 35, 37
Grover, Cuvier, 160

Hairston, Peter, 14, 18, 98
Hambrick, John T., 74, 75, 76
Hamilton's Crossing, 223
Hampton Roads, Va., Battle of, 115
Hampton's Legion, 93
Hardie, James A., 254n82
Harney, William Selby, 43, 255n19
Harpers Ferry, Va., Battle of, 170, 171, 172, 173, 272n37
Harpers New Monthly Magazine, 49
Harris (servant), 103, 104, 158, 165
Harrisburg, Pa., 226, 248n6
Harrison's Landing, Va., 146
Hartz, Edward L., 18
Hassler, William Woods, 8, 21, 41, 79, 221
Hays, William, 209, 218, 277n8
Heart, Almond, 41
Heintzelman, Samuel Peter, 126
Hess, Earl, 145
Heth, Henry ("Harry"), 219, 229, 231, 235
High Bridge, Va., 3
High Point, N.C., 52
Hill, Ambrose Powell, 133, 139, 140, 141, 142, 143, 146, 147, 151, 152, 153, 154, 155, 156, 157, 159, 160, 162, 163, 171, 172, 173, 174, 175, 181, 185, 187, 190–91, 193, 196, 197, 198, 204, 205, 207, 208, 209, 210, 212, 215, 217, 219, 220, 221, 223, 226, 229, 242, 248n6, 270n18, 272n27
Hill, Daniel Harvey, 64, 129, 130, 141, 142, 193, 248n6, 266n73, 267n77
Hinsdale, John Wetmore, 138, 143, 148, 150
Hinsdale, W., 138
Hoke, William James, 141
Holden, William Woods, 65, 200, 275n40
Holmes, Theophilus Hunter, 63, 64, 138, 268n25
Hood, John Bell, 1, 2, 122, 130, 147
Hooker, Joseph ("Fighting Joe"), 190, 205, 206, 210, 211, 223, 224, 227
Houghton, A. H., 40, 255n8
Howard, Oliver Otis, 10, 11, 12, 15, 17, 18, 206
Hudson's Bay Company, 26, 43
Huger, Benjamin, 71–72

Hunt, Samuel, 84, 85
Huntley, George Job, 225, 226

Imboden, George, 236
Imboden, John Daniel, 236
Iron Brigade ("Black Hats"), 231

Jackson, Thomas Jonathan ("Stonewall"), 1, 2, 137, 138, 140, 141, 151, 152, 153, 154, 155, 156, 157, 158, 159, 160, 161, 162, 164, 170, 171, 172, 173, 175, 176, 184, 185, 193, 194, 197, 204, 205, 206, 207, 208, 209, 214, 217, 220, 272n27, 276n68
James River, 84, 85, 123, 146
Jamieson, Perry, 2
Jefferson Barracks, Mo., 23
Jim (servant), 47
Joe (servant), 103, 104, 177, 189, 228
Johns, John, 125
Johnson, Edward, 205
Johnston, Albert Sidney, 118
Johnston, Joseph Eggleston, 89, 106, 107, 115, 117, 119, 121, 122, 126, 127, 128, 132, 261n23, 266n67
Johnston, Lydia McLane, 89

Kansas ("Bleeding Kansas"), 23, 24
Kean, Robert Garlick Hill, 200
Kearny, Philip, 163, 270n32
Kentucky (Kentuckians), 2
Kern River, 25
Keyes, Erasmus Darwin, 30, 31, 34, 36, 37, 126, 253n57, 254n82
Kilby, Thomas J., 73
King, Rufus, 160
Kip, Lawrence, 30, 34, 35, 37, 38
Kirkland, S. S., 166
Krick, Robert K., 169, 205, 229

Landes, William, 193
Lane, James Henry, 185, 207, 231, 233, 241, 272n30
Lattimer, Joseph W., 184, 191
Law, Evander McIvor, 184
Leavenworth, Kan., 89, 188
Lee, George Washington Custis, 11, 15, 16, 19, 89, 111, 193
Lee, Mary Greenhow, 237

298

INDEX

Lee, Robert Edward ("Granny Lee," "King of Spades," "Bobbie Lee"), 2, 3, 5, 16, 26, 132, 133, 135, 139, 153, 154, 166, 179, 190, 191, 195, 198, 199, 200, 201, 204, 205, 214, 215, 218, 219, 220, 243, 245, 250n53, 275n46; and Chancellorsville, 205–13, 277n82; and Fredericksburg, 179–85; and Gettysburg Campaign, 1, 216–17, 221–36, 240, 242–43, 248n6, 279n49; and Maryland Campaign, 168–73, 180, 181; and Second Manassas Campaign, 159–64; and Seven Days Campaign, 139–49
Lee, Stephen Dill, 11, 15, 19, 62, 95, 97, 123, 130, 136, 180, 181, 198, 267n77
Letcher, John, 201
Leventhorpe, Collett, 220
Lewis, William Gaston, 41
Liberty Ship, 245
"Light Division," 152, 153, 159, 163, 166, 175, 176, 178, 217, 219, 220, 236, 241, 242
Lightfoot, Charles Edward, 89, 261n23
Lincoln, Abraham ("Abe"), 51, 52, 61, 63, 109, 110, 168, 170, 181, 203, 226, 256n51, 264n112
Lincolnton, N.C., 246
Little Sorrel, 156, 207
Logan, David, 244
Longacre, Edward, 55, 64, 129
Longstreet, James ("Lee's War Horse"), 121, 141, 148, 152, 153, 158, 162, 163, 201, 205
Lord Charles Cornwallis, 121
Los Angeles, Ca., 25
Los Angeles Star, Ca., 26
Loudon Heights, Va. (W.Va.), 170
Lutheran Seminary (Gettysburg), 231, 233
Lyon, Hylan Benton, 254n82

Mackall, William Whann, 29
Maine, 10, 17
Mallory, Stephen Russell, 137, 138
Malvern Hill, Va., Battle of, 3, 150
Manassas, Va., 89, 90, 159, 160, 161, 165; First Battle of, 87, 140; Second Battle/Campaign of, 159–66, 177, 178, 272n37
Mangum, Adolphus W., 93, 94, 95, 96, 97, 99, 262n57
Mansfield, Joseph King Fenno, 252n39
Marye's Heights, 182, 210
Maryland, 60, 157–58, 165, 168, 170, 171, 177, 187, 216, 223, 226, 227, 235, 240, 248n6; 1862 Campaign of, 165, 168–76, 177, 178, 179, 195, 216, 225, 228, 271n1
Maryland Heights, Md., 170
Mason-Dixon Line, 110
Mayo, Joseph, 201
McCall, George Archibald, 149, 269n61
McClellan, George Brinton ("Young Napoleon"), 14, 119, 121, 122, 124, 126, 132, 139, 144, 145, 147, 151, 169, 170, 171, 269n2
McDowell, Irvin, 126
McGowan, Samuel, 191
McGuire, Hunter Holmes, 156, 208
McIntire, D. M., 211, 213
McLaws, Lafayette, 170
McMurry, Richard, 64
McPherson's Ridge (Gettysburg), 231
McWhiney, Grady, 2
Meade, George Gordon, 182, 184, 185
Mechanicsville (Beaver Dam Creek), Va., Battle of, 139, 140, 141, 144, 146, 176, 220, 229
Methodist Church, 93, 97, 99, 259n77
Mexican-American War, 13, 17, 249n32, 270n30
Mexico, 17
Miles, Dixon S., 170, 173
Mill Springs (Logan's Crossroads), Ky., Battle of, 113
Mississippi (Mississippians), 182
Mississippi River, 49, 51, 227
Missouri, 109
Mitchell, Reid, 148
Mobile, Ala., 79
Mogollon Apaches, 24, 251n23
Mogollon Mountains, 24
Monitor, USS, 115, 123
Montgomery, Ala., 52, 54, 58, 59, 60, 63
Montgomery, D. A., 68
Montgomery, William A., 248n6
Monumental Episcopal Church, Richmond, Va., 125
Morgan, Michael, 254n82
Morrison, James L., Jr., 11, 19
"Mud March," 190
Mullan, John, 253n58

Napoleon Bonaparte, 17, 169
Napoleon III (Louis Napoleon), 192, 194

INDEX

Native Americans (Indians), 24, 29, 30, 31, 33, 35, 36, 37, 39, 46, 47, 50
New Bern, N.C., 214
New Kent Court House, Va., 122
New Mexico, 22, 23, 24, 25, 28
New Orleans, La., 42, 124
Newport News, Va., 85
Newton, Steve, 128
New York, 110
New York City, N.Y., 40, 63, 110, 264n113
New York Herald, 136
Nez Perce, 30, 31, 33
Norfolk, Va., 72, 85, 119, 258n36
North Carolina ("Old North State") (North Carolinians), 2, 4, 7, 8, 10, 12, 13, 14, 17, 18, 22, 38, 40, 41, 43, 51, 52, 55, 56, 57, 62, 63, 66, 68, 69, 77, 78, 80, 90, 101, 110, 112, 113, 114, 116, 151, 180, 181, 190, 191, 193, 199, 200, 202, 204, 205, 211, 217, 219, 221, 227, 234, 243, 245, 246
North Carolina Standard, 65, 74, 275n40

Old Capital Prison, D.C., 164, 165
Oregon, 28, 29, 43
Oregon Trail, 26
Owen, William, 173

Pacific Northwest, 4, 27, 40, 57, 66, 194
Pagan Creek, 84
Parker, Francis Marion, 203, 224
Peace Democrats. *See* Copperheads
Pearson, Richmond Mumford, 200
Peck, Guy, 12
Pee Dee Light Artillery, 187
Pegram, John, 11, 86
Pegram, William Ransom Johnson, 3
Peirce, Lizzie, 23
Pelham, John, 182
Pemberton, John Clifford, 85
Pender, David (brother), 7, 9, 10, 55, 56, 103, 104, 108, 111, 124, 134, 135, 238, 248n2, 257n7
Pender, Emeralda James (wife of Robert), 9, 10, 249n12
Pender, James (father), 7, 8, 9, 11, 108
Pender, Julie (daughter of Robert), 10
Pender, Mary (wife of David), 108, 109

Pender, Mary Frances Shepperd ("Fanny") (wife), 21, 28, 41, 71, 84, 86, 87, 91–92, 96–97, 110, 111, 112, 118, 144, 180, 181, 190, 221, 236, 237, 238, 240, 241, 246, 251n4; childrearing of, 70, 80, 108, 120; as a Christian, 8, 41, 49, 69, 92, 95, 98; correspondence with WDP, 5, 7–10, 12, 39, 42, 44–50, 53–26, 130–32, 134–39, 147–49, 153–55, 158, 163–70, 175–81, 187–89, 191–205, 209–18, 221–8, 262n58; death of, 244; domestic activities of, 48, 59, 80, 103; health of, 39, 70, 75, 112, 114–15, 125, 194, 195–96; and marriage, 40–41, 43, 114, 194, 255n8; pregnancies and childbirths of, 42, 45, 70, 71, 112, 114, 195–96; and relationship with WDP, 12, 23, 28, 39, 44–46, 47–50, 59, 65, 69, 74, 83–84, 86, 94, 106, 107, 120–21, 123, 192–93, 196–97, 202, 203, 212, 237, 246, 261n37, 274–75n27; and servants/slaves, 41–42, 59, 103; as WDP's confidant/example, 5, 53, 68, 72, 89–90, 92–100, 104, 148, 158; and WDP's family, 7, 8–10, 108–9, 135–36, 248n2; and WDP's flirtations, 75–76, 79–83, 260n3; and separation from WDP, 221; visits with WDP, 87, 110–12, 113, 151, 153, 180, 190, 218, 221
Pender, Patience (sister), 7, 8, 10
Pender, Robert (brother), 7, 9, 11, 41, 104, 105, 109
Pender, Samuel Turner (son), 5, 8, 10, 40, 42, 45, 50, 52, 53, 59, 70, 71, 80, 100, 108, 120
Pender, Sarah Routh (mother), 7, 8
Pender, Stephen Lee (son), 5, 244, 280n18
Pender, William Dorsey
  administrative duties/skills of, 29, 51, 60–61, 65, 67, 143, 222
  aggressiveness of, noted, 288n44
  ambition of, 3, 4, 8, 66, 70, 107
  ancestry of, 7
  appearance/physical description of, 17, 66, 157, 246
  assessment of contemporaries regarding, 135, 157, 187, 202
  association with West Point classmates, 23, 28, 42, 91, 123, 139, 179, 188, 206, 209, 236, 239, 244
  attitude toward leaves and furloughs, 179–80, 191, 196, 197, 218

INDEX

attitude toward parents, 8, 108, 109
attitude toward political interference in military affairs, 64, 77, 78, 109
attitude toward secession, 51, 55–56, 118
attitude toward straggling, stealing, 169, 170, 176, 178, 195, 224, 228
attitude toward waging war, 124, 182, 203–4
baptism of, 93, 95, 97, 98, 112, 132, 158, 262n57
birth/birthplace of, 7, 245, 281n26
calmness/coolness under fire, 5, 20, 34, 35, 38, 48, 141, 157, 173
childhood of, 8
child raising of, 71, 100
civilian life after service, views on, 56, 95, 138
command style of, 65, 72–73, 77–78, 88–89, 90, 107, 116, 128, 141, 144, 145, 157, 210
as a conversationalist, 12–13, 41, 49, 79, 93, 95, 96, 97, 128, 203
courage of, 3, 96, 122, 157, 187, 208, 219, 241, 242
and court-martials, 100, 101, 102, 198
curiosity of, 145, 192
death of, 1, 3, 239, 242, 244, 280n72
and desertion, 116, 178, 192, 199–200, 201
and drill, 13, 14, 17, 30, 57, 64, 66, 67, 68, 71, 74, 76, 81, 84, 88, 89, 105, 106, 112, 113, 115, 117, 128, 129, 149, 150, 199, 202, 210, 219, 246
and duty, 5, 13, 23, 34, 44, 46, 47, 52, 59, 64, 95, 96, 98, 99, 100–101, 105, 141, 143, 197, 215, 218, 237, 238
early education, 11
exposure to enemy fire, 2, 3, 121, 147, 148, 160, 242
and family, 5, 8, 9, 41, 48, 50, 55–56, 63, 70, 80, 90, 95, 108, 111, 112, 113, 135–36, 137, 153, 168, 194, 196, 203, 218, 235, 237, 238, 246, 280n72; separation from, 40, 45, 48, 83, 87, 91, 92, 95, 100, 111, 117, 191, 202, 218, 221, 237
as a father, 4, 44, 70, 71, 79, 100, 110, 114, 120, 196, 244
generosity of, 90–91, 178
health of, 46, 116, 130, 179, 217, 225
and honor, 16, 47, 65, 73, 84, 93, 104, 159, 170

and human nature, 105, 114
humor of, 134, 181
inadequacy/insecurity of, 8, 38, 68, 71, 72, 86, 91, 93, 94, 95, 100, 106, 117, 144, 145, 158
introspection of, 4, 38, 82, 91, 93, 145
Lee's opinion regarding, 1, 3, 211–12, 220, 242
and Lincoln, 52, 110, 181, 203
marriage of, 28, 40–41, 43, 45, 81, 83, 92, 100, 114, 194, 196–97, 221, 255n8
nationalism/patriotism, 56, 66, 86, 200
nomination and appointment to West Point, 11
order and discipline, emphasis on, 16, 19, 65, 66, 70, 101, 102, 103, 106, 112, 128, 129, 167, 169, 176, 180, 191, 192, 200, 202, 210, 219, 228
paternalism of, 42, 48, 59, 103
perfectionism of, 4, 93, 145, 197, 245, 246
personal habits of, 17, 46, 49, 52, 57, 65, 66, 74, 91, 93, 120, 144, 157, 177, 194, 201
and personal servants/slaves, 42, 47, 59, 103–4, 158, 165, 177, 189, 228
personality/characteristics of, 3, 4, 242
political ambitions of, 109
popularity of, 12, 73, 75, 112, 150, 186, 187
promotions of, attitudes concerning, 28, 54, 65, 66–67, 68, 70, 106, 107, 115, 116, 117, 118, 120, 179, 181, 193–94, 204–5, 213, 215, 219, 221; to First Lieutenant, 28, 40, 42, 53, 57, 65; to Brevet Second Lieutenant, 19, 250n1; to Second Lieutenant, 20, 22, 28; to Captain, 54, 58, 64, 65, 66, 67; to Lieutenant Colonel, 64, 65; to Colonel, 69, 106, 138, 187; to Brigadier General, 133, 134, 187; to Major General, 181, 198, 205, 220, 221
race, views on, 59, 103
religious views/expressions of, 4, 5, 6, 8–9, 13, 48, 49, 86, 91, 92, 93, 94, 95, 96, 98, 99, 101, 102, 107, 108, 112, 114, 119, 121, 124, 125, 132, 134, 148, 155, 158, 168, 169, 178, 180, 189, 191, 193, 194, 195, 196, 204, 213, 223, 227, 237, 238, 239, 241, 242, 244, 245, 246, 261n37
reputation of, 15, 16, 48, 65, 66, 69, 72, 75, 104, 117, 176, 187, 201, 202, 208, 217

301

Pender, William Dorsey *(continued)*
  sensitivity of, 52, 106, 145, 187, 202, 212
  secession, views of, 55, 56, 118
  and slavery, 18, 41–42, 177, 263n81
  and sons, 100, 110, 111, 112, 121, 189, 192, 194, 218
  staff of, 87, 129, 135, 137–38, 145, 147–48, 157–58, 164–66, 168, 188
  and states' (state's) (Southern) rights, 55–56, 199
  temper of, 102, 104, 107, 111, 116, 158, 194, 203, 233
  troops of : attitudes/expectations of WDP concerning, 4, 66, 166, 195, 200, 213, 226; reflection of WDP's leadership, 65, 72, 73, 76–77, 106, 112, 117, 118, 120, 200–201; relationship with, 4, 90–91, 112, 119–20, 122, 181; reviews and inspections of, 76, 81, 84, 117, 149, 150
  vanity of, 4, 65, 67–68, 74, 81, 82, 83, 100, 107, 134
  at West Point: as "Plebe" and Cadet, 4, 10–19, 31, 40, 54, 66, 177, 210; class standing, 14, 15 19; graduate of, 57, 58, 131, 239; graduation from, 19, 20, 21; training from, 24, 51, 63, 64, 105, 117
  worthiness of, 3, 28, 44, 48, 58, 64, 74, 76, 77, 84, 92, 93, 94, 95, 105, 106, 112, 118, 121, 124, 158, 218
  wounded, 3, 146, 147, 160, 164, 166, 185, 186, 211, 212, 217, 219, 220, 233–34, 236–37, 242, 245, 281n26
Pender, William Dorsey, Jr. (son) 5, 71, 75, 79, 80, 100, 120
Pender and Bridgers, 10
Pennsylvania, 4, 51, 187, 216, 223, 224, 225, 227, 228, 229, 232, 235, 240, 248n6, 279n47
Pensacola, Fla., 58
Perrin, Abner Monroe, 231, 232
Peru, 17
Petersburg, Va., 75, 164, 243
Pettigrew, James Johnston, 115, 130, 133, 138, 229, 235, 238
Philadelphia, Pa., 226
Pickett, George Edward, 43, 235
Pierce, Franklin, 20
Pioneer and Democrat (Olympia, Wash.), 35

Pope, John, 151, 152, 158, 159, 160, 162, 166, 269n2
Porter, A. Loomes, 95, 97, 98, 158, 262n57, 262n58
Porter, Fitz John, 139, 141, 142, 145, 146, 269n2
Portsmouth, Va., 119
Potomac River, 175, 176, 223, 225, 226, 235, 238, 240

Qualchin, 37, 254n82

Rable, George, 83
Raleigh, N.C., 54, 65, 69, 75, 77, 78, 87, 214, 218, 258n52, 260n17
Ramseur, Stephen Dodson, 2, 3, 193, 213, 225, 241, 245, 246
Ransom, Robert, Jr., 99, 220
Rappahannock River, 115, 181, 182, 188, 190
Republican Party (Republicans), 49, 51, 61, 109, 110
Revolutionary War, 3, 75, 118, 121, 134
Reynolds, John Fulton, 229
Richmond, Fredericksburg, and Potomac Railroad, 182
Richmond, Va., 41, 65, 66, 72, 73, 89, 99, 115, 118, 119, 122, 123, 124, 126, 129, 130, 132, 134, 135, 137, 139, 141, 144, 147, 148, 149, 151, 152, 158, 166, 176, 178, 179, 180, 186, 194, 196, 198, 201, 205, 215, 218, 239, 240, 277n8
Richmond and York River Railroad, 126
Richmond *Daily Dispatch*, 72, 178, 239
Richmond *Examiner*, 152
Richmond *Sentinel*, 65, 66
Richmond Whig, 237
Rich Mountain, Va., Battle of, 86
Riddick, Richard Henry, 160, 163, 270n30
Rio Grande River, 23
Ripley, Roswell Sabine, 139, 143
Roanoke Island, N.C., Battle of, 113, 264n5
Robertson, James I., Jr., 133, 154
Rockbridge Rangers, 68
"Rock of Ages" (song), 245
Rodes, Robert Emmett, 194, 233
Roman, Andre, 63
Ruffin, Edmund, 235

INDEX

Ruffin, Thomas, 22, 57, 68–69, 71, 249n16, 251n10
Ruffin, Thomas, Jr., 77, 87, 88

Sacra Privata (Wilson), 97
Salem, N.C., 21, 58, 59
Salem Church, Va., Battle of, 211
San Fernando Pass, 26
San Francisco, Ca., 29, 51
San Juan Island, 43
Santa Fe, N.M., 23, 24
Santa Fe Trail, 24
Scales, Alfred Moore, 68, 77, 87, 180, 186, 191, 205, 231, 232, 233, 236, 241, 276n74
School House Ridge, Va. (W.Va.), 170
Secession, 51, 56, 110, 118, 263n113, 264n113
Second World War, 245
Seddon, James Alexander, 199, 200
Sedgwick, John, 210, 211
Seminary Ridge, 231, 233
Seminole Indians, 251n15; Wars (Second), 13 (Third), 22
Seven Days Campaign, Va., 149, 152, 153, 164, 166, 205
Seven Pines (Fair Oaks), Va., Battle of, 126, 127, 132, 133, 144, 166, 245
Sharpsburg (Antietam), Md., 173, 174; Battle of, 173–75, 270n21, 272n27, 272n37. *See also* Maryland, 1862 Campaign
Shenandoah River, 171
Shenandoah Valley, 137, 140, 154
Shepherdstown, Va. (W.Va.), Battle of, 174, 175, 272n27, 272n37
Shepperd, Augustine Henry, 21, 26, 57, 71, 106, 117, 118, 125, 130, 255n8
Shepperd, Francis Edgar ("Frank"), 21, 137, 138, 251n4
Shepperd, Hamilton ("Ham"), 21, 39, 90, 137, 179, 251n4
Shepperd, Jacob ("Jake"), 21, 88–89, 113, 118, 130, 135, 136, 137, 188, 251n4
Shepperd, Mary, 21
Shepperd, Pamela ("Pam"), 21, 49, 78, 86, 125, 136, 177, 181, 189, 251n4
Shepperd, Samuel Turner, 11, 12, 14, 15, 16, 17, 19, 21, 22, 23, 31, 188, 249n19, 251n4, 251n16
Shepperd, William Henry ("Willie"), 21, 251n4

Sherman, William Tecumseh, 279n47
Shiloh (Pittsburg Landing), Tenn., Battle of, 118, 120, 265n31
Sierra Amalgre, 24
Simpson, Kenrick N., 12
Slavery, 7, 17, 18, 177
Smith, Andrew Jackson, 40, 42, 44, 47, 48, 50, 254n3, 255n24
Smith, Gustavus Woodson, 127, 132
Smith, Laura, 41, 42, 59, 103, 255n12
Smithfield, Va., 83, 84
Snake River, 31, 32, 43, 44
South (Southerners), 3, 51, 52, 55, 56
South Atlantic Magazine, 10
South Carolina (South Carolinians), 51, 133
South Carolina Tract Society, 98
Southern civilians, 114, 228, 264n9
Special Order No. 191, 170
Spokane Plains, Wash., Battle of, 35–36
Spotsylvania, Va., Battle of, 3
State's rights, 55, 56
Staunton, Va., 237, 239
Staunton Vindicator, 237
Steptoe, Edward J., 26, 29, 30, 31, 32, 33, 36, 37, 254n82
Steuart, George Hume ("Maryland"), 262n68
Stevens, Isaac Ingalls, 163
Stewart, Kensey Johns, 121, 262n65, 266n62
Stonewall Brigade, 156
Stowe, Harriet Beecher, 177, 263n81
Stuart, Flora Cooke, 28, 239
Stuart, James Ewell Brown ("Jeb," "Beauty"), 11, 12, 14, 15, 16, 17, 18, 21, 23, 26, 28, 86, 98, 139, 159, 179, 207, 209, 211, 215, 229, 239, 240, 241, 260n3, 262n68, 277n97
Suffolk, Va., 72, 73, 74, 75, 76, 78, 81, 83, 84, 119, 145, 179, 201, 202, 218, 222, 259n77
Sumner, Edwin Vose, 127, 129
Symonds, Craig, 126

Talcott, Thomas Mann Randolph, 84, 85
Tampa, Fla., 21
Tarboro, N.C., 6, 7, 8, 9, 16, 40, 41, 57, 108, 109, 113, 131, 221, 243–44, 245, 246
Taylor, Oliver Hazard Perry, 29, 31, 38, 252n50
Taylor, Walter, 220
Tennessee (Tennesseans), 118, 120

INDEX

Tennessee River, 118
Tew's Military Academy, Hillsboro, N.C., 261n24
Texas (Texans), 2, 26, 59
Thomas, Edward Lloyd, 174, 231, 233
Thomas, Emory, 201
Thomas, Lorenzo, 52
Thompson, W. G., 240
Town Creek, N.C., 7, 8, 20, 108
Trimble, Isaac Ridgeway, 159, 235
Tucker, Glenn, 4
Tulare Lake, 25

Uncle Tom's Cabin (Stowe), 177, 263n81
Unionists, 56
United Daughters of the Confederacy, 245
United States (Union), 11, 37, 51–52, 53, 54, 55, 57, 60, 61, 63, 110, 113–14, 169, 197, 203, 204, 228
United States Maritime Commission, 245
United States Military Academy, N.Y. *See*, West Point, N.Y.,
United States Regular Army ("Old Army"), 4, 19, 26, 27, 29, 43, 52, 53, 57, 58, 61, 64, 90, 99, 126, 155, 171, 236; Second Artillery, 20, 22; Third Artillery, 30, 31; First Dragoons, 22, 23, 25, 26, 28, 29, 31, 37, 51, 65, 129, 165, 255–56n24; Second Dragoons, 22; Ninth Infantry, 26, 31
University of North Carolina, 96
Utley, Robert, 19, 24, 38

Vance, Zebulon Baird, 199, 218, 222, 275n40
Vicksburg, Miss., Siege of, 227
Virginia (Virginians), 1–2, 7, 17, 67, 69, 71, 73, 75, 77, 78, 86, 87, 90, 114, 118, 133, 151, 152, 175, 178, 179, 191, 201, 205, 210, 219, 234, 236, 237, 240, 243, 248n4; Central, 153, 173, 205; Peninsula of, 119, 122, 133, 151, 173; Southeastern, 77, 89, 201, 205; Western, 86, 139, 173
Virginia, CSS (Merrimac), 115, 123
Virginia Military Institute, Lexington, Va., 147

Walker, John George, 170
Walker, Leroy Pope, 54, 57, 60, 63

War of 1812, 43, 249n32
Washington, D.C., 42, 60, 62, 63, 87, 89, 90, 163, 165, 216, 223, 248n6
Washington, George, 17, 121
Washington Artillery, 173
Washington Territory, 26, 28, 29, 59, 64, 178, 223
Welch, Spencer, 195, 241
Weldon, N.C., 67, 258n57
Wellons, William B., 73, 259n77
Western Theater, 120, 151, 152, 180
West Point, N.Y., 146, 212, 269n61. *See also*, Pender, as cadet at,
Wharton, Gabriel Colvin, 248n6
White, Benjamin, 102, 112, 130
White, Julius, 172
White, Lieutenant, 37
White Oak Swamp (Glendale, Frayser's Farm), Va., Battle of, 148, 269n61
Whiting, William Henry Chase, 107, 117, 122, 127, 128, 136, 180, 205, 261n23
Wigfall, Louis Trezevant, 59–60, 62
Wike, A. C., 178
Wilcox, Cadmus Marcellus, 17
Williams, Alpheus Starkey, 209
Williams, R. S., 210
Williamsburg, Va., Battle of, 121, 122
Wilmington, N.C., 180, 245
Wilson, Rev. T., 97
Wilson County, N.C., 258n57, 281n26
Winchester, Va., 180, 223, 237
Winder, Charles Sidney, 62
Wood, Fernando, 110, 264n113
Wood, Thomas Fanning, 219
Woodworth, Steven, 94, 228, 279n47, 279n49
Wright, George, 30–43, 253n58, 253n68, 254n81, 254n82

Yakima (Indians), 37
Yellow Tavern, Va., Battle of, 240
Young, John, 148
Young, Louis (Lewis) G., 128, 145, 164
York River, 122, 146
Yorktown, Va., 119, 121

Zuni Station, Va., 84

www.ingramcontent.com/pod-product-compliance
Lightning Source LLC
Chambersburg PA
CBHW051208300426
44116CB00006B/480